Neoliberal Hegemony

Neoliberalism is fast becoming the dominant ideology of our age, yet politicians, businessmen and academics rarely identify themselves with it, and even political forces critical of it continue to carry out neoliberal policies around the globe. How can we make sense of this paradox? Who actually are 'the neoliberals'?

This book provides a comprehensive account of the creation and reproduction of the current neoliberal hegemony; focusing on both the strategies for and opposition to the production and distribution of neoliberal ideas in a diverse range of contexts. The authors survey the global network of think tanks, policy institutes, corporate planning groups, intellectuals, political and corporate leaders which have underpinned the ideological and political dominance of neoliberalism, and consequently, neoliberal forms of globalization. This volume also analyses the following:

- Specific neoliberal projects, regional contexts and structures of knowledge.
- The effects of neoliberalism on international institutions – from the World Bank to the UN.
- The growing corporate and political connections.
- The impact of neoliberalism on popular culture, education and other ideologies.
- The various forms of opposition to neoliberalism.

Broadening our collective understanding of neoliberalism, this book will be of great interest to students and scholars of international political economy and globalization.

Dieter Plehwe is Research Fellow at the Social Science Research Center Berlin Department "Internationalization and Organization", Germany.

Bernhard Walpen is Social Scientist and Economist at the Research Department of the Bethlehem Mission Immensee at the RomeroHaus, Luzern.

Gisela Neunhöffer is a coordinator for trade union networks in transnational companies in Eastern and Southeastern Europe for the International Union of Food and Allied Workers, Moscow.

RIPE series in global political economy

Series Editors:

Louise Amoore	University of Newcastle, UK
Randall Germain	Carleton University, Canada
Rorden Wilkinson	University of Manchester, UK and Wellesley College, USA

Formerly edited by Otto Holman (*University of Amsterdam*), Marianne Marchand (*Universidad de las Américas-Puebla*), Henk Overbeek (*Free University, Amsterdam*) and Marianne Franklin (*University of Amsterdam*)

The RIPE series editorial board are:

Mathias Albert	Bielefeld University, Germany
Mark Beeson	University of Queensland, Australia
A. Claire Cutler	University of Victoria, Canada
Marianne Franklin	University of Amsterdam, the Netherlands
Stephen Gill	York University, Canada
Jeffrey Hart	Indiana University, USA
Eric Helleiner	Trent University, Canada
Otto Holman	University of Amsterdam, the Netherlands
Marianne H. Marchand	Universidad de las Américas-Puebla, Mexico
Craig N. Murphy	Wellesley College, USA
Robert O'Brien	McMaster University, Canada
Henk Overbeek	Vrije Universiteit, the Netherlands
Anthony Payne	University of Sheffield, UK
Spike Peterson	University of Arizona, USA

This series, published in association with the *Review of International Political Economy*, provides a forum for current debates in international political economy. The series aims to cover all the central topics in IPE and to present innovative analyses of emerging topics. The titles in the series seek to transcend a state-centred discourse and focus on three broad themes:

- the nature of the forces driving globalisation forward
- resistance to globalisation
- the transformation of the world order.

The series comprises two strands:

The *RIPE Series in Global Political Economy* aims to address the needs of students and teachers, and the titles will be published in hardback and paperback. Titles include:

Transnational Classes and International Relations
Kees van der Pijl

Gender and Global Restructuring
Sightings, Sites and Resistances
Edited by Marianne H. Marchand and Anne Sisson Runyan

Global Political Economy
Contemporary Theories
Edited by Ronen Palan

Ideologies of Globalization
Contending Visions of a New World Order
Mark Rupert

The Clash within Civilisations
Coming to Terms with Cultural Conflicts
Dieter Senghaas

Global Unions?
Theory and Strategies of Organized Labour in the Global Political Economy
Edited by Jeffrey Harrod and Robert O'Brien

Political Economy of a Plural World
Critical Reflections on Power, Morals and Civilizations
Robert Cox with Michael Schechter

A Critical Rewriting of Global Political Economy
Integrating Reproductive, Productive and Virtual Economies
V. Spike Peterson

Contesting Globalization
Space and Place in the World Economy
André C. Drainville

Global Institutions and Development
Framing the World?
Edited by Morten Bøås and Desmond McNeill

Global Institutions, Marginalization, and Development
Craig N. Murphy

Critical Theories, International Relations and 'the Anti-Globalisation Movement'
The Politics of Global Resistance
Edited by Catherine Eschle and Bice Maiguashca

Globalization, Governmentality, and Global Politics
Regulation for the Rest of Us?
Ronnie D. Lipschutz, with James K. Rowe

Routledge/RIPE Studies in Global Political Economy is a forum for innovative new research intended for a high-level specialist readership, and the titles will be available in hardback only. Titles include:

1. Globalization and Governance *
Edited by Aseem Prakash and Jeffrey A. Hart

2. Nation-States and Money
The Past, Present and Future of National Currencies
Edited by Emily Gilbert and Eric Helleiner

3. The Global Political Economy of Intellectual Property Rights
The New Enclosures?
Christopher May

4. Integrating Central Europe
EU Expansion and Poland, Hungary and the Czech Republic
Otto Holman

5. Capitalist Restructuring, Globalisation and the Third Way
Lessons from the Swedish Model
J. Magnus Ryner

6. Transnational Capitalism and the Struggle over European Integration
Bastiaan van Apeldoorn

7. World Financial Orders
An Historical International Political Economy
Paul Langley

8. The Changing Politics of Finance in Korea and Thailand
From Deregulation to Debacle
Xiaoke Zhang

9. Anti-Immigrantism in Western Democracies
Statecraft, Desire and the Politics of Exclusion
Roxanne Lynn Doty

10. The Political Economy of European Employment
European Integration and the Transnationalization of the (Un)Employment Question
Edited by Henk Overbeek

11. Rethinking Global Political Economy
Emerging Issues, Unfolding Odysseys
Edited by Mary Ann Tétreault, Robert A. Denemark, Kenneth P. Thomas and Kurt Burch

12. Rediscovering International Relations Theory
Matthew Davies and Michael Niemann

13. International Trade and Developing Countries
Bargaining Coalitions in the GATT and WTO
Amrita Narlikar

14. The Southern Cone Model
The Political Economy of Regional Capitalist Development in Latin America
Nicola Phillips

15. The Idea of Global Civil Society
Politics and Ethics of a Globalizing Era
Edited by Randall D. Germain and Michael Kenny

16. Governing Financial Globalization
International Political Economy and Multi-Level Governance
Edited by Andrew Baker, David Hudson and Richard Woodward

17. Resisting Intellectual Property
Debora J. Halbert

18. Neoliberal Hegemony
A Global Critique
Edited by Dieter Plehwe, Bernhard Walpen and Gisela Neunhöffer

* *Also available in paperback*

Neoliberal Hegemony
A Global Critique

Edited by Dieter Plehwe, Bernhard Walpen and Gisela Neunhöffer

LONDON AND NEW YORK

First published 2006
by Routledge
2 Park Square, Milton Park, Abingdon, Oxon, OX14 4RN

Simultaneously published in the USA and Canada
by Routledge
270 Madison Ave, New York NY 10016

Routledge is an imprint of the Taylor & Francis Group

Transferred to Digital Printing 2007

© 2006 Dieter Plehwe, Bernhard Walpen and Gisela Neunhöffer for selection and editorial matter; individual contributors, their contributions.

Typeset in Baskerville by
Taylor & Francis Books

All rights reserved. No part of this book may be reprinted or reproduced or utilised in any form or by any electronic, mechanical, or other means, now known or hereafter invented, including photocopying and recording, or in any information storage or retrieval system, without permission in writing from the publishers.

British Library Cataloguing in Publication Data
A catalogue record for this book is available from the British Library

Library of Congress Cataloging in Publication Data
Neoliberal hegemony : a global critique / edited by Dieter Plehwe, Bernhard Walpen, and Gisela Neunhöffer.
    p. cm. – (RIPE series in global political economy ; 18)
  Includes bibliographical references and index.
    ISBN 0-415-37327-1 (hardback : alk. paper) 1. Liberalism. 2. Free enterprise. 3. Free trade. 4. Globalization. 5. International economic relations. I. Plehwe, Dieter. II. Walpen, Bernhard. III. Neunhöffer, Gisela, 1972- IV. Series: Routledge/RIPE series in global political economy. Routledge/RIPE studies in global political economy ; 18.
  JC574.N453 2005
  320.51'3–dc22

    2005008208

ISBN10: 0-415-37327-1 (hbk)
ISBN10: 0-415-46003-4 (pbk)

ISBN13: 978-0-415-37327-2 (hbk)
ISBN13: 978-0-415-46003-3 (pbk)

Taylor & Francis Group is the Academic Division of T&F Informa plc.

Contents

List of illustrations x
Notes on contributors xii
Series preface xiv
Acknowledgements xvi
List of abbreviations xvii

Introduction: Reconsidering neoliberal hegemony 1
DIETER PLEHWE, BERNHARD WALPEN AND GISELA NEUNHÖFFER

PART I
Global neoliberal projects 25

1 Between network and complex organization: the making of neoliberal knowledge and hegemony 27
DIETER PLEHWE AND BERNHARD WALPEN

2 Neoliberalism, capitalist class formation and the global network of corporations and policy groups 51
WILLIAM K. CARROLL AND COLIN CARSON

3 Peddling reform: the role of think tanks in shaping the neoliberal policy agenda for the World Bank and International Monetary Fund 70
CHRISTIAN E. WELLER AND LAURA SINGLETON

PART II
Neoliberal hegemonic constellations in the (semi)periphery: transnational and domestic roots 87

viii *Contents*

4 Why is there no third way? The role of neoliberal ideology, networks and think tanks in combating market socialism and shaping transformation in Poland 89
DOROTHEE BOHLE AND GISELA NEUNHÖFFER

5 The neoliberal ascendancy and East Asia: geo-politics, development theory and the end of the authoritarian developmental state in South Korea 105
MARK T. BERGER

6 The Mexican economy since NAFTA: socioeconomic integration or disintegration? 120
ENRIQUE DUSSEL PETERS

PART III
Neoliberal discourse relations: dissemination, diffusion, and adaptation 139

7 The great lie: markets, freedom and knowledge 141
RICHARD HULL

8 Frontiers and dystopias: libertarian ideology in science fiction 156
PETER JOSEF MÜHLBAUER

9 The education of neoliberalism 171
OLIVER SCHÖLLER AND OLAF GROH-SAMBERG

10 Gender mainstreaming: integrating women into a neoliberal Europe? 188
SUSANNE SCHUNTER-KLEEMANN AND DIETER PLEHWE

PART IV
Major hegemonic battle lines 205

11 Neoliberalism and communitarianism: social conditions, discourses and politics 207
HANS-JÜRGEN BIELING

12 Neoliberalism and cultural nationalism: a *danse macabre* 222
RADHIKA DESAI

13 The world wide web of anti-neoliberalism: emerging
   forms of post-Fordist protest and the impossibility of
   global Keynesianism   236
   ULRICH BRAND

References   252
Index   284

Illustrations

Annex

1.1	Advocacy think tanks with direct relations to MPS members	48

Figures

2.1	Number of interlocks among five global policy groups, 1996	62
2.2	Mean inter-national distances among 271 corporations, based on corporate interlocks only	64
2.3	Mean inter-national distances among 271 corporations, including paths mediated by five global policy groups	65
6.1	Real exchange rate (1990–2002)	131
6.2	Mexico: export structure (1993–2002)	132
6.3	Trade balance/GDP (1980–2002)	133
6.4	Real minimum wages and in manufacturing (1980–2001)	135
6.5	Income distribution by deciles (1984–98)	136

Tables

1.1	MPS membership by country	35
1.2	MPS membership in world regions	35
1.3	MPS members' major fields of occupations	37
1.4	Clustered subjects at 32 MPS meetings 1947–98	38
1.5	Advocacy think tanks with primary links to MPS by world region and country	42
1.6	Subject areas of neoliberal advocacy think tanks	43
2.1	Classification of five leading transnational policy groups	56
2.2	The nucleus of six corporate directors and their organizational affiliations	61
2.3	Eleven additional members of the core group and their organizational affiliations	61
2.4	Numbers of corporate directors on five global policy boards	63
4.1	Major neoliberal think tanks in postcommunist Poland	102

6.1 Mexico: general employment and unemployment tendencies
    (1990–2002) 134
9.1 Chronology of education reform activities: a new perspective
    of competition 185

Contributors

Mark T. Berger is Visiting Professor of International History in the History Department at the University of British Columbia, Canada.

Hans-Jürgen Bieling is Junior Professor in the Department of Political Science at Philipps-University, Marburg, Germany. His research interests are in Political Theory and European Integration.

Dorothee Bohle is Assistant Professor in the Political Sciences Department at the Central European University, Budapest, Hungary. Her research interests are in the areas of Central and Eastern European transformation and European Integration.

Ulrich Brand is currently Visiting Professor of Political Science at Rutgers University. He teaches Political Science at the University of Kassel, Germany. His research interests are in the areas of Globalization and Politics.

William K. Carroll is full Professor in the Department of Sociology at the University of Victoria, Canada. He is currently conducting a cross-national study of Globalization and the Recomposition of Corporate Capital and a Vancouver-based study of social-movement activism.

Colin Carson is completing his M.A. research in the Department of Sociology at the University of Victoria, Canada. His research interests are in transnational policy groups and global corporate governance.

Radhika Desai is Associate Professor in the Department of Political Science at the University of Victoria, Canada. Her research interests are in the areas of Comparative Politics and Theory.

Enrique Dussel Peters is Associate Professor at the Graduate School of Economics, Universidad Nacional Autónoma de México (UNAM). His research interests are in development economics.

Olaf Groh-Samberg is conducting his Ph.D. research and teaching Sociology at the University of Münster, Germany. His research interests are in higher education and neoliberalism.

Richard Hull is Senior Lecturer in the Business School at the University of Newcastle Upon Tyne, UK. His research interests are in the history of economics.

Peter Josef Mühlbauer is currently completing his Ph.D. on libertarian ideology and technology at Ludwig-Maximilians-University, Munich, Germany.

Gisela Neunhöffer recently held a position as associated fellow at the Social Science Research Institute in Berlin. She is currently working as Coordinator for trade union networks in Transnational Companies in Eastern and Southeastern Europe for the International Union of Food and Allied Workers (Moscow office). Her research interests are in the transformation of socialism to capitalism and industrial relations in Russia.

Dieter Plehwe has recently been a fellow at the International Center for Advanced Studies at NYU. He has a permanent position at the Social Science Research Center, Berlin (WZB, department 'internationalization and organization'). His research concentrates on the study of transnational varieties of capitalism, transnational civil society formation processes, and neoliberal hegemony.

Oliver Schöller is a Research Fellow of the Research Unit 'Innovation and Organization' at the Social Science Research Centre, Berlin, Germany. His research interests include urban governance, higher education, and mobility.

Susanne Schunter-Kleemann, Professor of Political Science, currently teaches at the Hochschule Bremen, Germany. Her research interests are in gender relations, feminism, and European Integration.

Laura Singleton is currently persuing a joint Ph.D. in Political Science and J.D. at the University of Wisconsin. She recently worked on retirement-policy and international finance issues at the Economic Policy Institute, Washington DC, USA.

Bernhard Walpen holds a permanent position as social scientist and economist at Bethlehem Mission Immensee and RomeroHaus, Luzern. His research interests are in the history of neoliberalism, economic history and theory.

Christian E. Weller is senior economist at the Center for American Progress, where he specializes in retirement income security, labor markets and international finance. He is also a research associate at the Economic Policy Institute, Washington DC, USA.

Series preface

Those familiar with the task of organizing, coordinating and editing a diverse group of authors know that such work can involve much effort and frustration. Fortunately the payoff can also be rewarding, with such collections often exploring a richer vein of conceptual and empirical material than any single author could achieve, whatever their own personal accomplishments. *Neoliberal Hegemony: A Global Critique* neatly fits this equation: four years in the making, it has put its editors through a long and exhaustive process, but the result pays scholarly dividends that we hope expunges their many debts. It takes a term that is in some danger of replicating the history of that other late-twentieth-century word – *globalization* – and subjects it to an exacting set of scholarly critiques. But these critiques do not simply engage in a facile excoriation of what passes for neoliberalism today; rather they offer a sophisticated and multi-pronged sociological, praxiological and above all political-economy dissection of neoliberalism's investiture in the key deliberative networks of the modern capitalist global economy. As the editors declare in their wide-ranging and state-of-the-art introductory chapter, neoliberalism's death has been greatly exaggerated, and they have assembled a sterling group of authors to tell us how and why.

There are many ways in which we can evaluate the continuing strength of neoliberalism as a political project. This volume largely but not exclusively adopts a neo-Gramscian lens to look closely at the making and evolution of neoliberalism across a range of social terrains. Among the subjects of the various chapters are the international connections of the *Mont Pèlerin Society*, the forging of neoliberal political and economic policies in transitional and developing countries, the impact of think tanks and policy networks in core and periphery capitalist economies, the influence of neoliberal ideas in culture and education, and of course a careful evaluation of the ways in which neoliberalism has engaged with and used resistance to its project for its own evolutionary ends. What emerges from this rich volume is a much deeper appreciation of the strength of neoliberalism, and a clearer assessment of how far it has penetrated into the arteries and capillaries of deliberative life. It is precisely through such an exhaustive and critical reading of neoliberalism that our understanding of its many strengths and concomitant weaknesses must be based.

The Routledge/RIPE Series in Global Political Economy seeks to publish innovative and cutting-edge scholarship that pushes forward our understanding of how the world is organized, why it is developing in particular directions, and how globalizing tendencies across a range of social relations are reinforcing or undermining these changes. This volume fits in with this mandate precisely because it subjects a key ideological and praxiological element of our world to sustained critical analysis. And it does this by situating its analysis within and between the leading analytical frameworks currently on offer, namely those which privilege in different ways state power, the emergent transnational capitalist class, and private authority in all its manifestations. As such the editors – Dieter Plehwe, Bernhard Walpen and Gisela Neunhöffer – have made a significant and timely scholarly contribution to how we understand the dynamics and contours of the contemporary world order. They have discharged their debts, and we are the beneficiaries.

Louise Amoore
Randall Germain
Rorden Wilkinson

Acknowledgements

'The World Wide Web of Neoliberalism' conference (Berlin, 29 November–2 December 2001) was sponsored by the German Rosa-Luxemburg-Foundation and by the Social Science Research Center Berlin (WZB). We are deeply grateful for the institutional support and the personal encouragement from Rainer Rilling, Sabine Reiner (Rosa-Luxemburg-Foundation), and from Prof. Dr Hedwig Rudolph (WZB department Organization and Internationalization). The conference grew out of a workshop series under the title 'buena vista neoliberal?' developed by us and our colleague Jürgen Nordmann. He and again Sabine Reiner and Rainer Rilling need to be thanked for their enthusiasm in helping to develop a project over the course of three years (see www.buena-vista-neoliberal.de). Most of the chapters collected in this volume have been presented and discussed at the world wide web of neoliberalism conference organized by the editors. Special thanks for helping to organize the conference go to Radhika Desai and Jennifer Bair. Radhika Desai also helped to write the original proposal for this book, and provided the translation of Ulrich Brand's chapter. Special thanks go to Emily Richards who has done an excellent editing job on most chapters, and to Teresa Lynch and Jennifer Bair, who contributed to the editing process on several chapters. Dorothee Bohle and once again Jennifer Bair as well as two anonymous reviewers need to be thanked for their detailed comments on the introduction that helped us very much to organize our thoughts. Several other chapters also profited from the feedback provided by the two reviewers. We are grateful to VSA-Verlag, Hamburg, permitting the reprint of tables in the chapter of Dieter Plehwe and Bernhard Walpen from Bernhard Walpen's recent publication 'Die offenen Feinde und ihre Gesellschaft' (2004), a critical history of the Mont Pèlerin Society. Likewise we are grateful to Blackwell Publishers, Oxford, permitting to reprint a shortened and modified version of the chapter by William Carroll and Colin Carson that was previously published in *Global Networks*. We owe special thanks to Werner Kraemer who helped us to prepare the final manuscript. Finally, we are deeply indebted to Randall Germain who did an excellent job as series editor, and encouraged and helped us very much indeed to navigate the difficult waters of publishing this book.

Abbreviations

AEI	American Enterprise Institute
BAIR	Bureaucratic-Authoritarian Industrializing Regime
BIS	Bank for International Settlements
CASE	Center for Social and Economic Research
CCF	Congress for Cultural Freedom
CHE	Centre for the Development of Higher Education
CNE	Centre for a New Europe
CPG	Conservative Philosophy Group
CRS	Centre for Regional Strategies
CSR	Corporate Social Responsibility
EAGFL	European Agrarian Funds
EAP	Economically Active Population
ECJ	European Court of Justice
EEA	European Economic Area
EFRE	European Regional Funds
EMU	Economic and Monetary Union
EOI	Export-Oriented Industrialization
ESF	European Social Funds
EUC	European Union Commission
EZLN	Ejército Zapatista de Liberación Nacional
FAZ	Frankfurter Allgemeine Zeitung
FDI	Foreign Direct Investments
FTAA	Free Trade Area of the Americas
GATT	General Agreement on Tariffs and Trade
GDP	Gross Domestic Product
GM	General Motors
HIPC	Highly Indebted Poor Countries
HPAE	High-Performing Asian Economies
HRK	Hochschulrektorenkonferenz
ICC	International Chamber of Commerce
IEA	Institute of Economic Affairs
IFI	International Financial Institutions
ILO	International Labour Organization

IMF	International Monetary Fund
IMSS	Instituto Mexicano del Seguro Social
INGO	International Non-Governmental Organizations
IPE	International Political Economy
ISI	Import-Substituting Industrialization
IUHEI	Institut Universitaire des Hautes Études Internationales
LDP	Liberal Democratic Party
LSE	London School of Economics and Political Science
MAI	Multilateral Agreement on Investment
MCA	Millennium Challenge Account
MPS	Mont Pèlerin Society
NAFTA	North American Free Trade Agreement
NBER	National Bureau of Economic Research
NDA	National Democratic Alliance
NELP	Network European Learning Processes
NGO	Non-Governmental Organizations
NIC	Newly Industrializing Countries
NOW	New Opportunities for Women
NPM	New Public Management
NRR	New Radical Right
NRW	North-Rhine Westphalia
OECD	Organisation for Economic Co-operation and Development
PEF	Poder Ejecutivo Federal
PPP	Public-Private Partnership
PRI	Partido Nacional Revolucionario
SLD	Sojusz Lewicy Demokratycznej (Democratic Left Alliance)
TC	The Trilateral Commission
TCC	Transnational Capitalist Class
TINA	There Is No Alternative
TNC	Trans-National Companies (or Corporations)
TU	Technische Universität (Technical University)
TRIPS	Trade Related Intellectual Property Rights
UNCED	UN Conference on Environment and Development
UNCTAD	UN Conference on Trade and Development
UNEP	UN Environmental Programme
UPA	United Progressive Alliance
WBCSD	World Business Council for Sustainable Development
WCF	World Chambers Federation
WEF	World Economic Forum
WTO	World Trade Organization
YMCA	Young Men's Christian Association

Introduction
Reconsidering neoliberal hegemony

Dieter Plehwe, Bernhard Walpen and Gisela Neunhöffer

> It's true that many people do not know where certain ideas come from, but the important thing is that they agree with them.
> *Michael Joyce, Bradley Foundation* (http://exile.ru/118/finktanks.php)

Current world politics are marked by a manifest paradox: The triumphal procession of global neoliberalism seems to have come to an end in the new millennium. Utopian neoliberalism's pain-free, non-cyclical 'new economy' has long been transformed into real existing 'slow growth' Enron-style crony capitalism. Neoliberalism has been under constant attacks from the left (new social movements, communitarian social democracy) and right (cultural nationalists), from activists and academics, unwilling to continuously affirm prevailing neoliberal consent. At the same time, the post-9/11 *Realpolitik* of US security measures and anti-terror unilateralism are widely regarded to contradict the 'new constitutionalism' of the disciplinary neoliberal global order (Gill 1993: 11). But in spite of these challenges, a wide variety of neoliberal policies and projects, at both the national, regional and global levels, remain on the political agenda. Examples of the former include Agenda 2010 – a program designed to reform the 'sclerotic' German welfare state, courtesy of the country's Social Democratic and Green Party leadership. At the regional level, negotiations for a Free Trade Area of the Americas (FTAA) continue, as the primary thrust in the effort to institutionalize a free trade regime stretching from Alaska to Argentina. Europe's increasingly neoliberal Union does count 25 members since the first wave of accession of mainly Eastern European countries of the former socialist camp. Efforts continue to bring a wide range of services within the WTO framework and attest to the ongoing persistence of core aspects of neoliberal hegemony at the global level. Margaret Thatcher's TINA (There Is No Alternative) thus has not lost much influence in economic and social policy making even in countries openly rebelling against Neoliberalism such as Brazil.

Most of the contributions to this book argue that a range of stabilizing factors attest to the profound transformation of the social agenda that these various projects represent. Our central argument is that neoliberal hegemony must be understood not as a fait accompli, but rather as an ongoing process of struggle and compromise through which the meaning of neoliberalism is both re-examined and reaffirmed. In particular, the various analyses gathered here suggest that we need to take seriously the social practices and discourses of neoliberalism, and the way in which these have become deeply entrenched in *civil society*, if we are to understand the consolidation of neoliberal hegemony. We contend that various social and political struggles which might be read as *contestations* of neoliberalism so far should rather be seen as part of its *evolution*. Accordingly, these challenges have contributed to the simultaneous reproduction and transformation of neoliberal hegemony, rather than to its imminent demise. In short, it is our belief that the death of neoliberalism has been greatly exaggerated.

To better understand why neoliberal projects and practices do not vanish in spite of the growing challenges they face, we need to revise our understanding of two concepts central to this debate: neoliberalism and hegemony.

- With regard to *neoliberalism*, we understand neoliberal philosophy itself as a 'plural' set of ideas rather than as a singular 'pensée unique' (Ignacio Ramonet). Much like social liberalism and 'Keynesianism' (Hall 1989), we argue that neoliberalism cannot be understood as a *singular* set of ideas and policy prescriptions, emanating from one source (Kjær and Pedersen 2001). Neoliberalism is frequently equated with market radicalism and anti-statism, but a number of core principles developed by *self-conscious* neoliberals not only express their belief in the superiority of market-driven competition as the best mechanism of economic allocation, or in the privileging of property rights (above, say, democratic rights) as a foundational condition of liberty. Social minimum standards, for instance, are held to be compatible with neoliberalism if welfare schemes are designed in ways 'not inimical to initiative and the functioning of the market' (Statement of Aims, Mont Pèlerin Society 1947, reprinted in Hartwell 1995: 41–2). More fundamentally, the architects of post World War-II neoliberalism distanced themselves from the laissez-faire liberalism of their intellectual ancestors by maintaining that some degree of governmental oversight was a sine qua non of contemporary capitalism. Thus, the challenge for them was not to eliminate the state, but rather to reduce its scope and redefine its role *vis-à-vis* the market (see Plehwe and Walpen in this volume).
- Efforts to offer a comprehensive definition of neoliberalism are frustrated by the plurality of views that exists within this philosophical and political camp. Based on a range of common principles that form no more than a smallest common denominator, a diverse group of academics and intellectuals have succeeded in establishing and developing a family of neoliberalisms, including the Austrian and Chicago Schools, Ordoliberalismus as well as Libertarianism, some of which have been accommodated in quite diverse political systems and by now inform the positions of both advocates and critics of neoliberalism to a greater or lesser extent (Walpen 2000). In addition, influential contemporary paradigms that claim to be critical of neoliberalism (e.g. communitarianism) display a certain amount of overlap and compatibility with neoliberal philosophies.

- With regard to *hegemony*, we need to deconstruct a global (in the sense of universal) and overly harmonious understanding thereof, in favour of an approach that seeks to identify what we call hegemonic constellations. According to Antonio Gramsci (1975), hegemony cannot be exercised exclusively by force and repression, even though these aspects of power have to be at the disposal of the ruling classes in case of need. Hegemony requires the active consent and participation of the ruled and thus finds expression in coalitions and compromises designed to integrate diverse social forces into (asymmetrical) historical power blocs. Instead of a global, homogeneous neoliberal hegemony, we thus need to think of potentially quite distinct *neoliberal hegemonic constellations*, which may be constructed at national, transnational, world-regional and global levels. Neoliberal historical power blocs inevitably feature distinct characteristics and constituencies, although intensified 'globalization' insures some important overlap. Over time, new historical power blocs may be formed through political struggle and these can alter the orientation and content of earlier hegemonic paradigms, but this process of change will be circumscribed by the achievements and institutional legacies of the previous social forces who were successful in establishing patterns of order and disorder that circumscribe tensions and social conflict leading to new dynamics. We thus propose to study the rise, maintenance and transformation of neoliberal hegemony by way of distinguishing different neoliberal hegemonic constellations in comparative perspective with the aim of identifying both commonalities and differences across space and time.

The contributions in this book aim to shed light on a wide range of actors, networks, organizations, social forces, discourses and processes which are crucial to understand neoliberal political practices in various countries and supranational polities, in institutions, organizations and associations, and in policy arenas and discourse fields. We maintain in particular that larger political and economic structures, institutions and interests need to be better connected to social relations in the realm of knowledge, discourse, ideas and interpretation (Guzzini 2000; see Germain 2000 on 'globalization'). Peter Haas's (1992) concept of 'epistemic communities' informs our analysis of the ideational aspects of neoliberal hegemony, although the scope of our project demands the more inclusive (i.e. beyond agenda setting capacities) notion of a *comprehensive* 'transnational discourse community' (see Bislev *et al.* 2002 introducing 'transnational *issue area* discourse communities' involved both in agenda setting and implementation strategies).

We believe that far too little attention has been paid to the *political* dimensions of discourse communities imagining, nurturing, promoting and sustaining Neoliberalism – both in mainstream and heterodox contributions (see literature review below for detail). While neo-Gramscian scholars in particular have skilfully examined the capacity of and intellectual effort in elite forums such as the Congress for Cultural Freedom, the Trilateral Commission or the World Economic Forum to forge 'compromises' and 'consensus' expressive of 'historical blocs' of social forces, little attention has been paid so far to the relatively independent role of 'traditional' intellectuals (i.e. 'universalistic' rather than organically tied to social classes) in attacking and transforming an existing consensus, to the issue of intellectual politics that cannot be reduced to the role of 'organic intellectuals' closely allied with dominant forces in the social relations of production. While neo-Gramscian scholars are thoroughly critical of simplistic ideas of structural determination, students of hegemony frequently pay little attention to intellectuals as agents of change, more often than not limit themselves to ideology critique of individual intellectuals, rarely examine in closer detail competing organized intellectual forces of the centre and right, tend to emphasize the role of intellectuals as technocratic 'legislators' and 'legitimators', and frequently associate neoliberal ideas and knowledge politics closely with the work of 'organic' intellectuals of the business class (compare Cafruny and Ryner 2003 and Bieler 2000 for example).[1] Organized efforts of neoliberal intellectuals who successfully challenged the prevailing social liberal consensus and subsequently developed and promoted a hegemonic intellectual agenda, therefore, are still not well understood.

Thus to further promote the neo-Gramscian research project, we aim to narrow this gap by way of indeed taking serious one of the crucial insights of Antonio Gramsci: 'the relationship between the intellectuals and the world of production is not as direct as it is with the fundamental social groups but is, in varying degrees, "mediated" by the whole fabric of society' (Gramsci 1971: 12). Under contemporary conditions of globalizing social relations of capitalist production engendering certain forms of state internationalization and concomitant transnational processes of civil society formation (see Gill's 1993 argument and a corresponding outline of a research agenda), it is our contention that this 'mediation' process 'by the whole fabric of society' differs dramatically from the way it worked before the Second World War. These transformations require a careful effort to both further explore the historical work of Gramsci with regard to the status of the transnational sphere in the analysis of capitalism[2] and to address contemporary hegemonic constellations with an *approach* similar to Gramsci's efforts to further develop a critical theory and social practice, an unorthodox approach driven as much by historical experience as by a commitment to independent thinking (see Morton 2001a responding to challenges posed, among others, by Germain and Kenny 1998). Specific forms of translating rather than simply applying Gramsci's approach to the study of hegemony are required to confront the historically unprecedented rise of think tanks and other civil society organizations involved in contemporary struggles for hegemony within and across borders since this new layer of 'hegemony apparatuses' complementing and competing with traditional knowledge organizations constitute one of the key aspects of a transformed 'global knowledge power structure' (Strange 1988). The conscious build up of vast infrastructures in support of both national and transnational neoliberal knowledge politics in particular must be explored as a crucial aspect of contemporary mediation processes affecting the role of intellectuals (see Fischer 1996 on a similar argument of *political* technocracy in the US).

Consequently, one of our primary goals is to offer a more detailed comparative assessment of the different roles of intellectuals in the creation and dissemination of neoliberal ideas and practices, while also underscoring – and here we share the disagreement of neo-Gramscian scholarship with idealistic approaches that want to single out ideas as causes – the way in which these intellectual social forces are themselves socially structured, thence partake in the social relations of production and connect to other collective actors, networks, channels of communication and organizations that occupy crucial positions in various important political arenas of society beyond the narrow sphere of the state.[3] While originally there was a distance of neoliberal intellectuals in many places around the world to the power centres in the social relations of production that should not be underestimated, the transformations occurring with the crisis of Fordism led to a far-reaching realignment and helped to forge closer links, indeed transformed many 'traditional' neoliberal intellectuals into 'organic' intellectuals of the new ruling classes.[4] However, even under conditions of neoliberal hegemony, a relative independence from business forces is carefully guarded by highly self-conscious intellectual leaders such as Edwin Feulner of the Heritage Foundation (Feulner 2000). While a lot of common ground can be detected between the family of neoliberalisms and business elites, neoliberal and organic intellectuals cannot be simply identified because each side maintains a selective approach to the other based on partly diverting agendas and interests. A societal approach (Strange 1996) to contemporary problems of neoliberal hegemony in effect emphasizes the need to improve understanding of the diverse whole of the political, economic, social and cultural spheres which together account for an 'ensemble of social relations' (Marx) marked by complexity and many aspects of conflict, co- and cross-determination.

By drawing a distinction between neoliberalism and hegemonic constellations we thus stress the need to analyse the world of ideas beyond traditional intellectual history, especially their modes of production and distribution, in order to better understand the materiality of ideas, i.e. their social aspect.[5] The analysis of the interrelation of conceptual and social aspects within today's capitalism is important to better understand neoliberal hegemonic constellations.[6] A critical assessment of the contemporary state of neoliberal hegemony must account for flexible combinations of both ideational and material elements across time and space within a common neoliberal matrix taking precedence over preceding frames of social liberalism. We argue that neoliberal discourse communities are crucial with regard to establishing the contemporary pluralism that exists today within neoliberal confines. They were indeed extraordinarily influential and instrumental in the original effort to forge neoliberal power blocs that eventually replaced or helped to reorient previous social liberal coalitions and alliances, but the structural power position of neoliberal discourse communities was strengthened subsequently when many of the erstwhile right-wing outsider positions entered a widely accepted mainstream. Such mainstreaming eventually helped to obscure the very influence of former heretics. At the same time a neoliberal hegemonic constellation can persist even if a particular group of originally key neoliberal actors or a particular neoliberal school of thought is pushed to a marginal position of the public discourse at a later point in time, depending on what type of policies are actually pursued.

Furthermore, even if *elements* of neoliberal hegemonic constellations and historical power blocs weaken due to the electoral defeat of a neoliberal government or due to an economic (or financial) crisis, we argue that a range of internal and external stabilizing factors beyond political and economic power complexes can serve to defend, to maintain and to adapt neoliberal hegemony to new circumstances. Challenges to a neoliberal hegemonic constellation can and almost certainly will be reinterpreted by neoliberal forces who aim to deflect opposition and do indeed not fully trust in government or business to accomplish the task. Insofar as these efforts are by and large successful, a major realignment of social forces is considered unlikely. Most of the contributions to this book argue that this is the case, at least at present. Our purpose is not, however, to assert the immutability of the current world order. Rather we argue that social forces attempting to challenge neoliberal hegemonic constellations still need to develop a better grasp of the core features of these constellations, and in particular the way in which they adapt and respond to changing circumstances and criticism.

We will proceed considering three bodies of literature that offer different perspectives on the problem of global hegemony – namely, the state power, transnational class, and more recent 'private authority' approaches. We will stress the relevance and contribution of these approaches to our project, while also underscoring their limitations. In the penultimate section of this introduction, we outline our (the editors', not necessarily the contributors') neo-Gramscian perspective (Morton 2001b) to the study of emerging transnational civil society as an arena critical to the formation and articulation of hegemonic constellations. We conclude with a brief overview of the chapters and summary of the key findings that emerge from these contributions.

Three approaches to studying (neoliberal) hegemonic constellations

State power relations, transnational capitalist class and 'private authorities'

State power relations

Neo-realists posit the determining role of state power relations in world politics (Gilpin 1987: 25–6), and thus express concern about the re-emergence of imperialism and conflict due to the decline of US hegemony. Their efforts to explain both the maintenance and shortcomings of hegemony in the current world order focus on the role of the United States as the sole superpower. While the US enjoys an unprecedented military superiority *vis-à-vis* the rest of the world (see Easterbrook 2003), the risks of military overstretch (Kennedy 1987) threaten a future deterioration of America's global dominance. To put it simply, the US may be able to wage wars, but can it pay for them? New imperialism pundits also maintain that the transatlantic partnership between the US and Europe has been transformed into a new rivalry, with Europe vying for the hegemonic power position that the US can no longer maintain (Kupchan 2002; Kagan 2003). European emphasis on multilateral negotiation and problem solving, combined with a somewhat greater willingness to commit resources to environmental and social problems, are either interpreted as evidence of the coming battle for global supremacy, or as part of the effort of constructing a European identity in the wake of the United States' decline (Habermas and Derrida 2003; cf. the critique voiced by Dahrendorf and Ash 2003).

However, despite the fact that disagreements over the Iraq question before and during the US-led war in spring 2003 arguably constituted the most serious rift in the transatlantic alliance since the Second World War, all the parties involved sought to defuse tensions shortly after the war began, appearing rather keen to rebuild a transatlantic consensus. At any rate, reading the debate over Iraq as a transatlantic battle is inaccurate, since the US's closest allies in North America – Canada and Mexico – supported the French-led effort against the war, whereas the UK, Italy, Spain, the Netherlands and the Eastern part of 'new' Europe backed the US position.

While in times of crisis, the increased use of state force (both in the form of war and domestic repression) enables the dominant countries and classes to secure their position, this iron law of power does not suffice to explain hegemony. Hegemony, as proposed by Gramsci, relies to a large degree on the consent of the ruled rather than on sheer force. In his famous and concise definition of civil society, Gramsci writes: 'the notion of civil society (in the sense that one might say that State = political society + civil Society, in other words hegemony protected by the armour of coercion)' (Gramsci 1971: 263).[7] If consent is waning and force needs to be used, hegemony must be endangered. At the same time, the ability to successfully use coercion may enable the dominant power to support rebuilding a consensus.

In any case it turns out that the central explanatory variable of state power relation theories do not tell us much about what Joseph Nye (2002) calls 'soft power'. Worse still, neo-realists try to explain variations in global orders and the existence or absence of hegemonic stability across history with the same indicators of economic and ultimately military strength, without regard to the changing social and material content of such orders. Ruggie (1983) argued instead that international consensus regarding the content of international regimes allows for the construction of relatively stable institutions, even in a multi-polar world such as the one that has emerged in the wake of the relative decline of US hegemony following the crisis of Fordism (see Murphy 1994 on the historical transformation of international regimes). In fact, neoliberal hegemony was on the ascendance right at the time when many indicators pointed to the relative decline of the US hegemonic position, and 'Thatcherism' preceded 'Reaganism'. The US decline in fact coincided with the expansion and strengthening of the GATT turned WTO regime, and international cooperation on many issue areas has reached unprecedented levels due to the collapse of the Soviet Union (e.g. in the field of nuclear safety). While the reluctance of the US to embrace the Kyoto protocol and the International Criminal Court indicates hegemonic struggles typical of a multi-polar order, the US has recently rejoined several United Nations programs, following the neoliberal turn of a United Nations which is now featuring corporate partnership programs in virtually every issue area (see Paul 2001 on the UN 'global compact'). In short, neo-realist hegemonic stability theory has a lot to say about the rise and decline of a superpower. It has little to say about the rise and decline of neoliberal hegemony. The rise of neoliberalism, and its subsequent reproduction, cannot be explained by the role of the United States in the world-system.

Still, even if neo-realist theories cannot fully explain hegemonic (in)stability and are not interested in neoliberal content, their emphasis on state power, and particularly the importance of military force, nevertheless highlights factors which clearly remain important in the international political economy, as recent developments around the war on terrorism have made apparent. Even if force is not enough to secure hegemony, Gramsci certainly understood that consent alone (without the military threat securing compliance) only suffices in a global *regulated society* (as he called communism). As for now, state and military power relations clearly are an important factor in world order, but they cannot be singled out as the only or even primary explanatory variable in the study of neoliberal hegemony (compare the alternative account for American imperialism and Eurocapitalism by Panitch and Gindin 2003).

Transnational capitalist class analysis

Transnational capitalist class approaches have recently attracted attention from authors looking to challenge the dominance of the neo-realist paradigm in the field of international political economy. Different versions of transnational capitalism and class analysis, such as those represented by members of the Amsterdam School (e.g Kees van der Pijl, Otto Holman and Henk Overbeek), and Leslie Sklair's more sociological effort to investigate the contemporary formation of a transnational capitalist class, predominantly stress the structural power of transnational capital, with an eye to allies in politics, the professions and the media-culture complexes. While Overbeek (1993) and van der Pijl (1998) as well as a series of recent neo-Gramscian contributions on European Integration and Enlargement (Bieler 2000; Bieler and Morton 2001; Cafruny and Ryner 2003) emphasize the regrouping of dominant transnational capital factions in their analyses of neoliberal hegemony, Leslie Sklair (2001) focuses on the formation of a historically unprecedented transnational capitalist class centring around transnational corporations, which according to him only now are increasingly detached from their countries of origin (see Robinson 2004 for a comprehensive theoretical statement on global capitalism and the chapter by Carroll and Carson in this volume for a further discussion of the transnational capitalist class debate).

Van der Pijl understands neoliberal hegemony as a comprehensive concept of control, which has successively replaced the preceding paradigm of corporate liberal control (1998: 4). In his reading, during the Fordist era, transnational industrial capital constituted the most powerful transnational bloc supporting the US-led global system, which Ruggie has described as 'embedded liberalism' (Ruggie 1983). The crisis of Fordism led to the rise of financial and speculative business interests in the 1970s – politically enabled by measures to liberalize financial markets (Helleiner 1994) – that in turn resulted in a realignment of the dominant capitalist class faction. Compared with the corporate liberal comprehensive concept of control, neoliberalism is characterized by an open hostility to trade unions, corporatist style decision-making, state interventionism, progressive taxation and other efforts to redistribute income in favour of the working classes. However, class and power relations in the different industrialized countries require and result in specific compromises (Overbeek 1993).

While van der Pijl's research provides rich historical detail of the alliances between business factions and political forces that cooperate closely in corporate planning groups (such as the Bilderberg Group and the Trilateral Commission), factors other than dominant business interests are not given much independent weight. The definition of the control concept eventually reveals a fair amount of functionalism.[8] The insistence on comprehensiveness leaves little room for variations likely to result from specific power relations in (and between) countries, and for ambiguous, even contradictory aspects of control and participation characteristic of rather stable hegemonic constellations (e.g. many elements of continuity during the social liberal and neoliberal age of capitalism).

Leslie Sklair (2001) instead constructs his argument around what he regards as historically new structural features of transnational operating capital, and specifically changes in foreign direct investment practices. In so doing, he combines a structural analysis with attention to the dynamics of identity formation among members of the emerging transnational capitalist class. He distinguishes four class fractions, namely corporate, state, technical and consumerist parts. Although analytically separate, the different constituting groups are understood to closely cooperate on the basis of institutionalized relations. Although Sklair does not operate with a narrow understanding of class formation, the corporate fraction (heads of transnational corporations and their subsidiaries) receives much greater attention than the globalizing bureaucrats and politicians, professionals (e.g. lawyers and accountants) and merchant and media leaders making up the other three fractions. His analysis of the formation of a 'class for itself' is based on the development of global corporate concepts such as best practice, benchmarking, and corporate citizenship. The proposal of neoliberal solutions to global problems such as global warming, for instance, is predominantly tied to corporate planning groups acknowledging the 'sustainability' discourse that has emerged as one response to the environmental pressures of global capitalism. The business nexus of the culture-ideology of consumerism, finally, may be considered the most important pillar of transnational class power. According to Sklair it provides the single dominant lifestyle concept characterizing the contemporary world-system, with the only possible challenge coming from some versions of religious fundamentalism (see Jameson 1998: 64).

While Sklair thus presents a straightforward and systematic analysis, some manifest contradictions of a *single* transnational class concept are easily detectable. For instance, Sklair emphasizes that the Business Council for Sustainable Development has successfully replaced obstructionist business strategies in the ecological battlefield. Thus, the business forces behind the US efforts to block the Kyoto protocol (the Global Climate Coalition, for example) would have to be identified as members of a national capitalist class faction in Sklair's framework, regardless of the size and investment patterns of such companies and regardless of their countries of origin. But many a big business leader representing giant capital interests which clearly fall in Sklair's category of transnational enterprises both outside and inside the US supports the US position rather than the arguably more enlightened position of the Business Council. A concept of transnational (capitalist) class *formation*, which allows for a less universalizing perspective and is more aware of the tensions between competing factions, might also better illuminate the link between political and economic power, as suggested by the relationship between various capitalist factions and regionalization projects such as the European Union and NAFTA (Gamble and Payne 1996). Such a *relational* class formation perspective with an eye on competing forces would also help to make better sense of contradictions within Europe that led Cafruny (2003) to suggest that 'Neoliberalism does not provide an adequate economic or ethico-political basis for the further development of the monetary union or of a transnational European capitalist class'. 'Neoliberalism' may indeed not provide for a basis of further development of a class, but it is unlikely to not influence further class formation processes more likely than not to contribute to patterns of (dis)-order. Finally, a more nuanced understanding of parallel and possibly *competing* transnational class formation processes and projects might help to avoid what appears as a form of economic determinism in Sklair's argument, despite the strong emphasis he places on cultural and ideological aspects of class formation in his theoretical framework.

Still, transnational capitalist class approaches must be considered indispensable to the study of global neoliberal hegemony. Unlike state power relations theories, these insist on historically specific explanations, and they provide a way to make sense of the link between structural economic power and the neoliberal content of present hegemonic constellations. As much as state power approaches remind students of the importance of military power, transnational capitalist class approaches remind us of the importance of economic power structures (of industry and finance, in particular) and resources that must figure prominently in the study of hegemonic struggles.

'Private authorities'

A third and fast growing literature addresses questions related to what can be considered 'privately' exercised authority in the international political economy, involving a wide variety of actor groups, and rapidly rising channels of transnational influence. There is an overlap with transnational capitalist class approaches since arguably the most significant group discussed with regard to international 'private authority' is constituted by multinational companies and organized business interests (Cutler *et al.* 1999; Greenwood and Jacek 2000). Private authority approaches and transnational capitalist class approaches share an interest in understanding the sources and structures of power in international politics beyond the state, but the former has given greater attention to a wider range of private actors beyond corporations, including social movements, trade unions, churches, NGOs and think tanks. Many of the actors discussed in the private authority literature are at least relatively independent from private business (Keck and Sikkink 1998; Higgott *et al.* 2000; Brühl *et al.* 2001; Josselin and Wallace 2001). In spite of the structural power of capital, business forces are also frequently found to *react* to challenges arising in the wide labyrinths of civil society (see for example Paul 2001 on battles in and around the UN system).

One of the most stimulating contributions to this literature documents the rise of 'transnational advocacy networks'. According to Keck and Sikkink, these networks in various issue areas (e.g. human rights, environment, feminist, development, peace, etc.) build 'new links among actors in civil societies, states, and international organizations' and thereby 'multiply channels of access to the international system' (1998: 1). Keck and Sikkink argue that non-governmental organizations have succeeded in gaining influence due to their ability to gather and report reliable information (*information politics*), to dramatize facts (*symbolic politics*), to effectively exert material pressure by linking the issues to money, trade or prestige (*leverage politics*), and to exert moral pressure by publicly scrutinizing the extent to which institutions and organizations meet principles they have endorsed (*accountability politics*). Successes and failures of transnational advocacy networks are duly compared and (mainly) explained with reference to the particular characteristics of networks and issues, as well as leverage opportunities and 'target vulnerabilities' (e.g. Mexico being sensitive to human rights accusations due to NAFTA negotiations, the Nestlé corporation being sensitive to a consumer boycott due to the fact that many of the Nestlé products bear the company name). Due to the undeniable direct or intermediate influence of civic organizations, the authors suggest, 'that scholars of international relations should pay more attention to [transnational] network forms of organization – characterized by voluntary, reciprocal, and horizontal exchanges of information and services' (200).

While their empirical findings lead them to reject the notion of an emerging global civil society (compare Anheimer and Themudo 2002), Keck and Sikkink opt for an understanding of civil society 'as an arena of struggle, a fragmented and contested area' (Keck and Sikkink 1998: 33). In elaborating their concept of civil society, they cite Hurrell and Woods, who argue, 'the politics of transnational civil society is centrally about the way in which certain groups emerge and are legitimized (by governments, institutions, and other groups)' (1995: 468).

Although Keck and Sikkink appear to recognize that there are top-down and side influences on (transnational) civil society actors, their own research emphasis on bottom-up organized networks fails to adequately consider the weight of other transnational actors and the extent to which transnational advocacy networks are indeed shaped by institutionalized political and economic power relations. By drawing too sharp a line between business and business-related actor groups and civil society actors (which are effectively identified with non-profit or third sector groups), Keck and Sikkink fail to recognize the extent to which a broader range of 'private' actors and neoliberal forces in particular have contributed to the transformation of transnational civil society.

Dezalay and Garth (2002), for example, have described in great detail how the internationalization of organizations promoting human right and public interest law lags behind the internationalization of organizations promoting professional economics and corporate law in Latin America. This uneven development suggests not only the still relatively marginal position of global social movements at present (Rucht 2003), but also indicates structural imbalances accounting for differences in the internationalization process across issue areas. Furthermore, the extent to which the transplantation of norms and practices in the field of human rights has to be considered an element of what Dezalay and Garth call 'top-down participatory development', designed to secure legitimacy for neoliberal capitalism, suggests that a more critical reflection on transnational advocacy networks in particular, and global social movements in general, is in order.[9]

Due to their emphasis on the transnational network form of organization, Keck and Sikkink only marginally consider important transnational private actors such as foundations, think tanks and research organizations, media, trade unions and churches as possible participants in issue networks. An arguably even more important blind spot in a (transnational) civil society concept that reserves this terrain to non- or even anti-business forces is the lack of attention paid to authority exercised by private firms and corporate-related or corporate-sponsored organizations outside the sphere of business proper. This, however, is easily balanced by a great number of recent volumes, which are almost exclusively devoted to the issue of private business authority (see Cutler et al. 1999 for a typology of various forms of business authority) and their contribution to the (in)stability of the global international economy (see Sinclair 1999 on rating agencies and the financial crisis in South East Asia).

For example, the pivotal role of business associations in the shaping of economic as well as political dimensions of free trade agreements and regional integration projects such as NAFTA (Jacek 2000) and the EU (Apeldoorn 2000; Greenwood 2000) is well documented. Matthews and Pickering (2000) have provided a detailed comparison of the relation between sectoral business strategies and evolving rules in the European single market. The proliferation of regional integration projects (Gamble and Payne 1996) in turn can be considered the institutional pull factor with regard to the proliferation of business (and other) interest groups (Plehwe and Vescovi 2003).

Globalization processes in general and regionalization processes in particular have contributed to a far-reaching restructuring of firms, which in turn has helped to supplement, if not undermine, traditional, nation-state centred business associations and 'private interest governments' (Streeck and Schmitter 1985).

More recently formed *transnational* alliances of firms and associations tend to sideline traditional (national and multi-national) associations and account for some of the strongest forces with regard to the pressure to continue neoliberal projects at global and world regional levels (see Sell 1999 and 2000 on the field of intellectual property rights and Plehwe and Vescovi 2003 on transport and postal services). Transnational business alliances and associations thus play a pivotal role in the 'new regionalism' (Spindler 2002), which is crucial to understand the transnational transformation of economic, political, and civic dimensions of neoliberal capitalism. New regionalism is characterized by a systematic pattern of intensified interaction between private (predominantly transnational business) and public authority predominantly designed to strengthen microeconomic competitiveness.

The 'private authority' literature can thus be divided into a not for profit/ third sector and a private business research interest with certain amounts of overlap. Grouped around the highly significant issue of knowledge, which is frequently emphasized as a crucial surplus value generated by diverse private groups and thus constituting a core factor enabling (or restraining) the exercise of some sort of private authority, a third research interest centres around actor groups, networks and organizations that are more explicitly involved in the task of knowledge production. Both with regard to Eastern Europe's transformation processes (Bockman and Eyal 2002) and the transition of import substitution development towards export orientation (Babb 2001) scholars have examined the background of professional economists and their roles with regard to the discursive and ideological dimensions of neoliberal hegemony, its transformation, and reproduction. Diane Stone (2000b) provided us with a detailed empirical overview of the proliferation of think tanks around the globe (see also McGann and Weaver 2000). These organizations occupy a crucial position in the information and knowledge processing business. Think tanks frequently are private, not for profit organizations and can be considered among the most interesting organizations to understand the interconnections between the corporate and 'third' sector. Stone however fails to examine critical links between think tanks and other social, economic, political, and intellectual networks, as well as *between* these think tanks. The resulting impression of a pluralistic landscape of all sorts of think tanks does not help us to see in which ways neoliberal partisan think tanks in particular play an increasingly important role in the ideological class struggle, which is being waged in national and transnational civil society. An impression of think tank pluralism also fails to account for the enormous financial and more general power gaps among think tanks, for instance between neoliberal and progressive organizations. Looking at the extent to which many think tank and other civil society projects are financed and guided by US philanthropic foundations of corporations in particular, Roelofs (2003) quite convincingly speaks about a 'Mask of Pluralism'. Due to her predominant focus on US foundations, however, Roelofs tends to overrate this aspect of 'Americanization'.

'Private authority' research nevertheless has come a long way in establishing a wide range of cooperating and competing 'private actors' in civil society as subjects to be more fully considered in the contemporary transformation of the international political economy, and the creation and transformation of neo-liberal hegemonic constellations. Private groups are shown to contribute to (global, regional, sectoral, etc.) order in their own right and, more frequently than not, in close interaction and even institutionalized interrelation with public authority. The literature has shed light on the many conflicts and struggles that accompany such processes of the transformation of governance patterns. Crucial aspects of hegemonic struggles with regard to 'global governance' can be clarified by way of distinguishing ideal types of 'old' and 'new' multilateralism. 'Old multilateralism' is characterized by efforts to reinforce the prevailing state and economic system dominance in international relations by way of extending the influence of inter-governmental organizations which seek to co-opt oppositional forces 'thus securing their socialisation into the dominant market liberal ideological mode' (Higgott et al. 2000: 4). 'New multilateralism' in contrast is considered a contending philosophy, which 'attempts to "reconstitute civil societies and political authorities on a global scale, building a system of global governance from the bottom up"' (4, citing Cox 1997). Civil society in the latter framework again carries a strongly normative, positive, participatory and positively pluralist connotation. A critical political analysis of the reality of transnational civil society, however, has to carefully navigate between the effort to understand what (transnational) civil society (in formation) truly is, as well as what kind of private and public authority it helps generating, and the desire to contribute to a new understanding of what civil society ought to be. The binary opposition of 'top down' and 'bottom up' may turn out to be less convincing a guide for progressive politics once due consideration is given to other than progressive organization efforts in the realm of civil society. In particular, a more complete understanding of the formation of transnational civil society urgently requires a recognition that bottom up organizing activities are not the exclusive prerogative of progressive and anti-business forces and advocacy networks.

Towards a more comprehensive understanding of transnational civil society

Neo-Gramscian approaches to International Political Economy and the 'private authority' research community that emphasizes corporate actors and business related forces as key constituencies of civil society (Cutler et al. 1999; Higgott et al. 2000) take issue with a substantial distinction between public and private authority since 'the state' (the traditional notion of authority) cannot be confined to the public sphere. The theoretical perspective of an *expanded state* (Gramsci) regards politics as the combination of political (the state in the narrow sense) *and* civil society with the latter sphere being considered critical for the exercise of hegemony rather than merely rule, for the organization of consent rather than simple control. Both political and civil society is thus understood as a 'complex, contradictory and discordant ensemble of the superstructures' which reflects 'the ensemble of the social relations of production' (Gramsci 1971: 366). Hegemony

Introduction   15

can only be achieved if a relatively stable historical bloc is formed which constitutes the underlying source of power (though not merely in the economic or material sense) for the specific ensemble of superstructures. A sharp dichotomy between public and private, or a sharp distinction between state, market, and civil society, consequently misses the point, and a narrow and predominantly normative approach to civil society actors (i.e. NGOs) must be considered inadequate.

> In order to assess the internal relationship between the two, states and markets have to be understood as two different expressions of the same configuration of social forces. States and markets are integrated ensembles of governance involving firms, the NGOs of 'civil society', and traditional INGOs [international non-governmental organizations]. A neo-Gramscian concept of an 'historic bloc' throws light on this communality. Various social forces may attempt to form an historic bloc in order to establish an order preferable to them.
> (Higgott et al. 2000: 6)[10]

Instead of continuing the debate of public *versus* private *authority*, research directed at the issue of neoliberal *hegemony* has to focus on diverse, albeit interrelated social forces which constitute historical blocs. Because we are interested in exploring neoliberal hegemonic constellations instead of offering a definition of *a* universal neoliberal hegemony, we want to examine the way in which those constellations are formed through various combinations of public and private, with state, business and other civil society forces as key actors. Higgott *et al.* have gone further than others in clarifying the reformist character of the observed transformation of state authority:

> The fact that state authority is passed on to firms, INGOs and NGOs does not mean that states lose and non-state actors gain authority. Rather, it signifies a new way of sustaining capitalist accumulation in an era of global structural change. What appears at first sight as a competition for authority turns out to be a strategy for the continuation of the same system of economic production, only under new conditions.
> (Higgott et al. 2000: 6)

What is missing in this literature so far is a clear focus on the neoliberal content of shifting forms of governance and a more comprehensive focus on actor groups and organizations, which may be considered producers, visionaries and guardians of such neoliberal content. While many contributions to the 'private authority' literature emphasize aspects of the importance of 'knowledge' to the social construction of reality, the changing composition and configuration of transnational discourse communities, and the rise of neoliberal discourse communities in particular, has not been subject to systematic scrutiny. Neoliberal forces are starkly misrepresented and underestimated if they are equated with 'systemic forces' of the ruling elites or classes, or if the bottom up reproduction of neoliberalism on the terrain of civil society escapes attention. It is this gap in the literature that the present volume seeks to help fill.

A wide range of neoliberal associations, organizations, networks, social and cultural forces and even movements as well as their corresponding transnational civil society forces *currently* 'in defense of global capitalism' (Norberg 2001) has not received the attention they warrant in studies of neoliberal hegemony. Our efforts to do so are inspired by Susan Strange's (1988) work, which identified the global knowledge system as the fourth and final *primary* power structure determining the International Political Economy. We regard her outline of the global power structure of knowledge as complementary to and congenial with neo-Gramscian conceptualizations of knowledge and power. Whereas Robert Cox (1996) argues against postmodern relativism to explore conditions for specific ways of post-hegemonic knowledge and communication (based on a knowledge ontology of a workable set of hypotheses rather than absolute truth), Susan Strange emphasizes organizational structures and processes crucial not only with regard to what is and can be known, but also to what will be obscured in more or less systematic ways (applied postmodernism one might say and think of the extremely skilled art in deflecting what cannot be denied by a contemporary superpower administration). While both state power relations and transnational capitalist class approaches are indispensable to account for the uneven distribution of power and wealth within the contemporary world system, the hierarchy of knowledge and ideology characterizing neoliberal hegemonic constellations, as well as the ongoing ideological class struggles and the transformation of common sense belief systems which are predominantly formed in civil society spheres, need to be subject to comparative research in an effort to better understand both the reach and the limits of neoliberal hegemony.

The private authority literature has helped to establish a transnational civil society dimension and perspective in the field of international political economy and comparative capitalism. It already provides us with crucial insights into the contribution of a wide range of civil society forces in the transformation of order and hegemonic constellations, and can therefore be deepened by way of focusing on a range of hitherto neglected organized actors and processes, namely the straightforward and self-conscious production of neoliberal knowledge and ideology which we consider crucial to understand a wide range of discourses prevalent in society. We seek to establish firstly to what extent the class of self-conscious neoliberal intellectuals, knowledge entrepreneurs, and partisan organizations such as think tanks that have developed into sophisticated hegemony apparatuses serve at the core of prevailing historical blocs, and how they express themselves in different socio-geographic spaces, policy and discourse fields.[11] Since hegemony in a neo-Gramscian understanding inevitably incorporates compromises which will be reflected in the prevailing order of ideas,[12] second, we seek to establish the relations between self-conscious neoliberal and other interpretations, be they neoliberal if not self-conscious, quite distinct from neoliberalism but compatible, or more fundamentally diverse.

Our working hypothesis can be described as follows: with reference to the global power system of knowledge, the ensemble of neoliberal (or *right wing* liberal if you wish, see Bobbio 1994 and Anderson 1996) orientations has strongly influenced the mainstream, and thus by and large replaced preceding social-liberal orientations characteristic of the Fordist era. While we readily observe certain centrifugal processes with regard to the overall consensus of the ruling classes and historical power blocs in recent times, and a resurgent ideological class struggle in which new global social movements in particular challenge neoliberal paradigms, contemporary good and global governance debates, the revitalization of communitarianism, traditional social liberal and other belief systems are held to contribute to the reform of contemporary neoliberal hegemonic constellations rather than to their demise. Furthermore, the radical, self-conscious neoliberal forces and networks should not be prematurely dismissed, since they are better positioned than ever before in their history to engage in these debates.[13] That this is the case should not be surprising, as a wide range of economic, political and cultural transformations characterizing the neoliberal era are well embedded in contemporary social configurations. Even if radical neoliberal voices appear to be more marginal now compared to say the 1980s and early 1990s, it is thus crucial to shed more light on neoliberal actors, networks and discourses in order to better understand the next stage of neoliberal hegemonic struggles around the globe.

The outline of the book

The present volume aims to contribute to a deepened understanding and sharpened critique of neoliberalism, first by way of improving knowledge about neoliberal discourse, corporate planning, and neoliberal policymakers, academics and writers, and second, through comparisons of 'real existing neoliberalism' in different socio-geographic spaces, policy debates, and discourse arenas. While authors were free with regard to their individual contributions, we asked each participant to consider the role of what we consider a core agency of *self-conscious* neoliberalism, namely neoliberal intellectuals (organized since 1947 in the Mont Pèlerin Society) and think tanks closely associated with members of said global network of intellectuals. All of the authors have made an effort to weave this common thread, but the thickness is different in each chapter depending on available sources and empirical relevance. In some chapters the discussion of this neoliberal actor group is thence more marginal compared to other (neoliberal) forces than in others. However, with this source of neoliberal power hitherto almost systematically neglected, the book sheds considerable light on neoliberal laboratories, which are in turn indispensable for understanding neoliberal hegemonic constellations.

Global neoliberal projects

Two contributions to the first part of the book introduce and analyse hitherto much neglected neoliberal networks of intellectuals and think tank organizations (Plehwe and Walpen), and shed new light on some of the arguably most influential corporate planning groups (Carroll and Carson). Both contributions emphasize that neoliberal doctrines cannot be reduced to a single idea, but have to be regarded as different members (some more radical, others more pragmatic) of neoliberalism's discursive family. Central to the understanding of neoliberal hegemonic constellations is the shift of the dominant debates from social liberalism and socialism versus (neo)liberalism to a pluralistic mainstream within neoliberal confines, which is strongly influenced by transnational neoliberal discourse communities.

Plehwe and Walpen provide a systematic overview over the origins and the development of organized neoliberals from the humble beginnings in the Colloque Walter Lippmann organized in Paris in 1938 (where the term 'neoliberalism' was adopted) to the more successful launch of the Mont Pèlerin Society in 1947 to the present day. Close attention is paid to the global composition of the Mont Pèlerin Society and its close links to more than 100 partisan think tanks and foundations supplementing the primarily academic forum with a more direct opportunity to intervene in public policy and general debates.

Carroll and Carson engage in the transnational class debate with their corporate network analysis of five corporate planning groups, the International Chamber of Commerce, the Bilderberg Conferences, the Trilateral Commission, the World Economic Forum and the Business Council on Sustainable Development. While the different transnational policy planning groups can be sorted into three varieties of neoliberal orientations – free market conservative, neoliberal structuralist and neoliberal regulationist – the analysis of corporate-policy group interlocks reveals that a few dozen 'cosmopolitan' leaders primarily from Europe and North America knit the network together: Neoliberal pluralism practiced in the academic networks must be regarded as an important feature of the corporate family as well.

The chapter by Weller and Singleton complements the focus on global neoliberal projects with an analysis of the nexus between the US administration and neoliberal civil society with regard to reform proposals for the international financial institutions, the IMF and World Bank. While radical neoliberal reform proposals originating from within the networks of organized neoliberals have not been implemented by the Clinton administration, the widespread mobilization of neoliberal discourse communities successfully influenced the terms of the debate, and much of the advice of the Meltzer Commission has been heeded in the formulation of President Bush's 'millennium challenge account', which is deliberately designed to sideline the global financial institutions. While organized neoliberal agents certainly attempt to gain maximum influence, the contemporary power of neoliberal discourse communities may be better grasped by understanding their role in influencing the terms of the debate and as guardians of what has been termed 'new constitutionalism' and 'disciplinary neoliberalism' (Gill 1998).

Neoliberal hegemonic constellations in the (semi)periphery: transnational and domestic roots

While the domestic roots of neoliberalism in capitalist core countries have been the subject of previous comparative research (see Overbeek 1993), international financial institutions and other external forces are usually credited with the rise of neoliberal hegemonic constellations in the developing world. Adopting neoliberal agendas of export orientation reversed a century-old pattern of developing country strategies and developmental (to a certain extent protectionist) ideologies vis-à-vis leading industrial producers. Did developing countries indeed succumb to purely external powers and ideologies? In chapters on Poland (Bohle and Neunhöffer), South Korea (Berger) and Mexico (Dussel Peters), the authors explore the domestic and transnational roots of neoliberal hegemonic constellations in countries close to the capitalist core. Their analyses suggest that these are deserving of greater attention than they have received, even if external institutions and constraints can hardly be overestimated (see Hay 2000 for a useful distinction between internally generated and externally institutionalized (monetary) constraints).

The former socialist bloc is clearly a crucial example of a seemingly paradoxical situation: the establishment and persistence of neoliberal hegemony despite numerous critiques and questionable results. Still, there is little analysis of an important feature of this 'success' – namely, transnational networks as crucial agents. Bohle and Neunhöffer forcefully argue the importance of East/West relations for the development of neoliberalism on both sides of the iron curtain in the course of the crisis and breakdown of state socialism in their study of Poland. There exists a specific Polish twist on the question, why neoliberal hegemony? Why and how could the neoliberal transformation succeed despite Poland's long market-socialist tradition and a strong, rather socialist-democratic movement, namely Solidarity? Bohle and Neunhöffer carefully trace the parallel development of Solidarity and initially informal neoliberal networks and show that the two were only partially aligned against a common enemy, namely the Polish Communist Party. Brought to ministerial power on the back of Solidarity's mass movement, neoliberal economists successfully utilized the historical opportunity to administer shock therapy, which not only locked the country into a neoliberal reform trajectory, but also tore the erstwhile alliance between the trade union movement and neoliberal intellectuals apart. The influence of organized neoliberals did not wane under conditions of frequent government crisis, however, since neoliberal think tanks in Poland provided neoliberals a sheltered space and continuous public access.

While South Korea was celebrated throughout the 1980s and early 1990s for its stellar economic performance and sound development strategy, this country also seemed to be a likely stronghold against a more complete implementation of neoliberal economic policy doctrines. Mark Berger explains that this situation changed when, in the aftermath of the East Asian financial crisis, South Korea lost the preferential status that allowed it to combine an export orientation with a considerable degree of state intervention in its domestic economy. Although Berger shows the nexus of external and internal neoliberal forces, his analysis underscores the external influence of neoliberal development experts such as MPS member Peter Bauer, and structural aspects extending neoliberal hegemony to a newly-industrialized country that had been hailed as one of the four 'Asian tigers' just a decade earlier.

Enrique Dussel Peters traces the story of transnational networks of economists promoting export orientation in explaining Mexico's decision to embrace a far-reaching program of economic reform and restructuring. His chapter provides a detailed analysis of Mexico's liberalization strategy and the implications of the North American Free Trade Agreement (NAFTA) in particular. The major finding is a sharp polarization in the Mexican economy and rising inequality. While he insists on a narrow concept of neoliberalism in the Latin American context – defining the term as the odd mix of authoritarianism and radical free market economics prevalent in Chile under General Pinochet – his findings nevertheless resonate with the Polish and South Korean stories that round out this part of the book. Continentalism and the legal framework of NAFTA must be regarded as crucial aspects of North American hegemonic constellations, developed and shaped to a certain extent by (transnational) intellectual agency. Peter Bauer again deserves mentioning here since his principled neoliberal opposition against development aid finds literal expression in the preamble of the NAFTA treaty stressing 'trade, not aid', as the means to development.

Neoliberal discourse relations: dissemination, diffusion, and adaptation

Neoliberal intellectuals fought their battle for hegemony not only by spreading their world views geographically, but also by disseminating them across various discursive fields. To analyse the influence of neoliberal ideas and the impact of neoliberal intellectual networks is the aim of the third part of the book. It opens with a chapter by Richard Hull tracing the emergence of the notion of 'knowledge as a unit of analysis' in the economic discipline, which emerged in the intellectual battles of Marxist and (future) neoliberal intellectuals in the 1920s through the 1950s in Budapest, Vienna, London and Manchester. Apart from Karl Mannheim's development of a sociology of knowledge and his notion of the true intellectual as a free floating individual in response to Georg Lukács turn towards scientific socialism, key members of the Mont Pèlerin Society such as Friedrich August von Hayek, Ludwig von Mises, Michael Polanyi and Karl Popper laboured untiringly to attack academic efforts to ground socialist calculation and economic planning on scientific grounds. Concepts such as 'tacit knowledge' and a general scepticism towards positivism not only succeeded in establishing a general neoliberal theory of knowledge, but helped pave the way for other versions of post-positivism as well.

While Hull's chapter shows how the intellectual debates between Marxist and neoliberal thinkers of the first half of the twentieth century influence the philosophical, economic and political debates of our time, the next chapter traces the rarely considered ways in which neoliberal ideas are diffused to broader publics. Peter Mühlbauer's pioneering chapter focuses on popular science fiction literature which has been strongly inspired by libertarian and 'objectivist' thought (in particular the work of Ayn Rand). Major features akin to core elements of neoliberal doctrines include 'frontier thinking', narratives of adventure capitalists

Introduction 21

and merchant heroes, anti-bureaucratic and anti-statist tales, which are shown in turn to inspire many neoliberal thinkers such as Milton Friedman. Mühlbauer's chapter helps to better understand otherwise 'invisible' dimensions of popularization and dissemination of neoliberal ideology to mass audiences.

Turning to more recent developments, Oliver Schöller and Olaf Groh-Samberg's chapter bridges the worlds of intellectuals and corporations with their study of how corporate think tanks facilitate neoliberal problem solving in a single policy field. The role of the Bertelsmann Foundation, one of the most important think tanks in Germany, in forging a neoliberal alliance to reform higher education in Germany provides an excellent example of the manufacturing of neoliberal consent. The Bertelsmann Foundation managed to stimulate a new higher education agenda by way of forging alliances that include radical neoliberal networks of intellectuals and think tanks as well as traditional constituencies of social liberalism. As a result, the recent debate about how to reform the German system of higher education has been dominated by a set of ideas which can be considered pragmatically neoliberal, a compromise between radical neoliberal and traditional social liberal concepts on neoliberal terms, that was originally developed by a private corporate think tank connected to one of the world's largest media conglomerates.

Susanne Schunter-Kleemann and Dieter Plehwe's chapter is another case study on the reconfiguration of debates and policy approaches in a particular issue area. The emergence and application of the new concept of 'gender mainstreaming' is scrutinized to ask if gender mainstreaming provides an effective policy tool to overcome gender-based inequality. Locating the origins of the concept in the human resource literature on 'managing diversity', the authors argue that 'gender mainstreaming' was pushed by European elites in an attempt to shore up women's support for the European Integration project, which many women were viewing with increasing scepticism due to its neoliberal policy orientation. The analysis documents that gender mainstreaming is a highly ambiguous concept. While gender mainstreaming is at odds with more radical neoliberal concepts such as 'individualist feminism' which are more outrightly hostile to any sort of state intervention to improve the position of women *vis-à-vis* men, policies developed under the umbrella of gender mainstreaming have not yielded the promised impact and may in fact undermine institutional positions won by more autonomous feminist movements of the past.

Major hegemonic battle lines

In the concluding part we focus on contemporary ideologies that claim to challenge neoliberalism and present themselves as alternatives. First, Hans-Jürgen Bieling explores the relationship between neoliberal and communitarian forces and discourses. While communitarians clearly diverge from neoliberalism in perceiving unfettered market relations as one cause of the weakening and dissolution of social community structures, they share with neoliberals the rejection of a centralized and bureaucratic state, which is regarded as an impediment to both free markets and self-organized community structures. If the discourses converge on the issue of anti-statism, third way concepts inspired by communitarianism attempt to synthesize neoliberal and communitarian thought. In conclusion Bieling stresses the power of neoliberalism to absorb and neutralize potentially counter-hegemonic forces and ideas, like some strands of communitarianism.

Cultural nationalism is often presented (and presents itself) as a countervailing force to neoliberalism. Cultural nationalist forces on the one hand draw support from this apparent opposition, and proponents of neoliberalism gather support from people who are suspicious of the fundamentalist tendencies of various cultural nationalisms. Opposed to this view, Radhika Desai argues in her chapter that there are important and systematic ideological, socio-economic and political linkages between neoliberalism and cultural nationalism. She identifies the characteristics of the New Right, which make it distinct from previous political formations on the right, and, in that context, explores the relationship between cultural nationalism and neoliberalism to tease out connections between them that have hitherto been neglected in the study of the right.

Finally, Ulrich Brand focuses on the movement that arguably most forcefully challenged neoliberalism in the last decade – the so-called anti-globalization movement. His chapter starts by reviewing some controversial interpretations in the movement itself about its forms and contents. He then examines why the heterogeneous movement constituted itself and under which conditions it acts, using the insights of regulation and Gramscian hegemony theory to highlight some key ambivalences of the movement(s). Pointing to the inherent dangers of a movement that is threatened to share the fate of global NGOs that were integrated into, and swallowed up by, neoliberal discourse and policy procedures, the chapter aims to support a more principled stance against both neoliberal thinking and policy formulation.

At the end, Brand stresses not only the need for critical self-reflection of social movement intellectuals, but the importance of critical intellectuals reflecting on and being part of social movements as well. Our goal for this book, and for the conference from which it emerged, was to gather critical intellectuals to contribute to a better understanding of the rise of neoliberalism in various hegemonic constellations, as well as its contestation, transformation, and, we argue, largely successful adaptation and stabilization which requires a heightened awareness of the continuing need for principled opposition in what amounts to an ongoing war of position in a neoliberal and transnational civil society. We understand this analysis as a contribution to the larger goal of clarifying perspectives with regard to neoliberal hegemonic constellations and, on this basis, of searching for ways to more comprehensively challenge neoliberal hegemony in the medium and long run.

Notes

1 See Scott-Smith (2002) for an excellent introduction to Gramscian perspectives on intellectuals and hegemony. While Scott-Smith underlines the importance of the

'perception of the technocrat-intellectual as part of a vanguard, having the potential to play a vital role in the transformation of society' (26) his emphasis on the 'consensus' building effort fails to more fully account for the tension between social liberal and neoliberal activists in the Congress for Cultural Freedom. While the success of the Congress during the post-war era expressed the hegemony of social liberalism, it included right-wing neoliberal activists such as MPS members Hayek, Michael Polanyi and Raymond Aron among others, who did not subscribe to the 'end of ideology consensus'. The neoliberals in fact re-conceptualized technocracy as a problem to henceforward politicize technocracy. Their work in the important intellectual-cultural arenas of social liberalism in fact is most interesting with regard to their subsequently rising fortunes as key intellectuals of neoliberal hegemonic constellations.

2 While Gramsci certainly emphasized and focused on the relation of '*national*' political and civil society, already an eclectic reading of the *Prison Notebooks* reveals the extent to which Gramsci was aware of the importance of transnational aspects of the analysis of capitalism in general and of transnational aspects of civil society in particular. He took note of the need to examine transnational links in a prospective examination of conservative catholic forces (azzione catholica) in the first notebook and certainly inspired van der Pijl's (1998) detailed historical analysis of early transnational class formation processes centring on the freemasons with his notes on the role of organizations such as the Freemasons, the Rotary Club, or the YMCA. He emphasizes their educational activities designed to establish and promote new cultural norms and moral values as well as economic practices within specific countries as well as across borders. Gramsci also provides a historic account of freemasonry to show how it became one of the most effective forces *of the state in civil society* (Gramsci 1975: NB 19, ° 53). At the same time we agree with Bieler and Morton (2001: 12) on the need to clarify 'shortcomings involved in the task of theoretically and practically translating Gramsci's work as a framework for contemporary analysis'.

3 See Campbell's (2001, 2004: Ch. 4) useful distinction between cognitive and normative, foreground and background levels of the knowledge/idea complex and his correlation of the different levels with specific actors.

4 Gramsci already at this time took notice of conscious efforts of intellectuals to separate from the ruling class 'in order to more intimately unite, to become a true superstructure rather than an unorganic and non-differentiated element of the structure-corporation' (Gramsci 1975: NB 5, ° 105, 659; our translation).

5 To avoid misunderstanding it is necessary to explain the differences between the English and the German concerning the term 'material'. The English 'material' designates the German 'materiell' as well as 'stofflich'. The latter captures the physical aspect of an 'object'. Since the *Theses on Feuerbach* (1845/46) Marx distinguished between 'materiell', which designates the 'social' part or the 'form', and 'stofflich' (physical). His concept of capital in *Capital* represents a social relation and therefore cannot be reduced to 'stofflich' even if capital is invested in production centres. In Marx's approach capital is always 'materiell' however, and he thus would be at odds with today's talking of 'immaterial capital'. Financial capital or capital in the service sectors likewise are social relations and therefore 'materiell'. Capital is not a 'thing' which one perceives with the senses. A materialistic analysis of the 'role of ideas' is beyond the western dualisms of consciousness versus being/existence (Sein vs. Bewusstsein), idea versus materiality, etc. (see Walpen 2004: 354, note 55). In this perspective ideas matter because they are an inseparable part of the social.

6 The frequently close association of ideational or 'material' aspects with the whole story has been the cause of many debates and misunderstandings of neoliberalism. If scholars primarily look at neoliberal rhetoric, they tend to emphasize the departure from previous social liberalism, and speak about neoliberalism in revolutionary terms. When students of neoliberalism mainly look at institutional change and larger patterns of societal transformation, the emphasis tends to highlight continuities

with regard to the preceding social liberal era and incremental change at best (see Hay 2001).

7 See especially in this context the state theories developed by Nicos Poulantzas 1978 and 2001; Leo Panitch 1998; Joachim Hirsch 2001; Bob Jessop 2001a and 2001b; and Mario Candeias 2004: 42–55.

8 Concepts of control, then, are the projects of rival political alliances which on account of their appropriateness to deal with current contradictions in the labour, intersectoral/competition, and profit distribution processes, as well as with broader social and political issues, at some point become *comprehensive*, crowding out the others by their greater adequacy to a historically specific situation – until they themselves unravel in the course of further development and struggle (van der Pijl 1998: 4).

9 Despite the great achievements of human rights organizations in the north and the south in mobilizing new legal rights and institutions against the dictatorships of the 1970s and 1980s, the organizations – in contrast to many of those who had been active in them – did not succeed in becoming important actors once the state was transformed. Business law firms, in contrast, have taken root and have started to thrive in the new economic and political environments (Dezalay and Garth 2002: 248).

10 C. Wright Mills (1956: 288f.) certainly contributed a lot to such an understanding with his introduction of the categories of 'in-betweens' and 'go-betweens' designed to capture individuals who belong to and express different parts of (military, political and economic) power elites simultaneously and consecutively, respectively.

11 In his analysis of the role of intellectuals in the emerging Fordist constellation, Gramsci underlined that a new type of intellectual was separating from the ruling class in the United States (unlike in Europe) in order to better unite with it, namely to be able to provide the necessary analysis and develop appropriate strategies (see Note 4). We observe a similar, albeit better-organized, separation and eventual re-unification of neoliberal intellectuals in the post-war period, this time not confined to the United States (see Plehwe and Walpen in this volume).

12 'The philosophy of an epoch cannot be any systematic tendency or individual system. It is the ensemble of all individual philosophies and philosophical tendencies, plus scientific opinions, religion and common sense' (Gramsci 1971: 455). The unifying moment is the distinctiveness of such an articulation of varieties of belief systems compared to previous or subsequent epochs (Jacobitz 1991: 18).

13 It is indeed characteristic of the common-sense utopianism and zeal of self-conscious neoliberals that they think along lines analogous to Trotsky's permanent revolution: 'Our fight will never end' (Martino 2001: 84).

Part I
Global neoliberal projects

1 Between network and complex organization

The making of neoliberal knowledge and hegemony

Dieter Plehwe and Bernhard Walpen

Neoliberal hegemony: is it all over now, or only contested?

The hegemony of neoliberal discourse and practice – the claim of the superiority of the market mechanism and competition-driven processes of capitalist development over state-driven pathways of social and economic organization, the limitation of government to the protection of individual rights, especially property rights, privatization of state enterprises and the liberalization of formerly strictly regulated and government administered markets – has been challenged in different national and international arenas around the globe. Failures of 'shock therapies' in Eastern European transition economies, the Asian financial crisis of 1997, and the collapse of the dot.com market certainly have not aided arguments in favor of self-regulation and private enrichment as beneficial to all. Some observers have – somewhat prematurely, to be sure, considering recent successes of the neoliberal right in Italy and France, for example – suggested that the rise of new social democratic parties to power in various European countries constituted the end of neoliberalism (equated with Thatcher/Reagan government policies). Nobel Prizes in economics in recent years – previously awarded to hard-core neoliberal thinkers such as Hayek, Friedman, Buchanan, and Becker – have gone to the likes of development economist Amartya Sen and World Bank insider-turned-critic Joseph E. Stiglitz. These developments, along with others, have been interpreted by some as indications that a 'post-Washington consensus' is emerging, reinserting an ethical dimension into the holy triad of global 'liberalization, privatization and deregulation' (Higgott 2000). Last but not least, the Enron collapse linked to the bursting of the bubble economy and the protectionist moves of the US government of George W. Bush after the September 11 attacks[1] certainly helped to undermine the legitimacy of global neoliberal agendas.

The recent rise of myriad social movements protesting what is denounced as corporate-led globalization may have to be regarded as the most successful challenge to neoliberalism thus far. Flexible networks of protest movements have followed the call from Chiapas in 1994 to engage in a global battle against neoliberalism and capitalist globalization (see Klein 2002). Critical analysis of a variety of issues has been undertaken by these new left social movements and to some extent bundled to popular demands (such as the so-called Tobin tax). Albeit far from a coherent program for a global alternative to neoliberalism, social protests at about every meeting of the World Bank, IMF, G-7, World Economic Forum, WTO, and European Union conferences have attracted much media attention, leading to speculation that neoliberal hegemony is in decline (see Brand in this volume).[2]

Still, we will argue in this chapter that an end to neoliberal hegemony[3] is not yet in sight. Though neoliberal paradigms and policies are increasingly contested due to structural transformations of neoliberal capitalism and challenged by new social actors opposing neoliberal globalization, core aspects of neoliberal hegemony remain in place and are likely to grow stronger in the near future in various arenas, such as the European Union. We attribute the continuing strength of neoliberal paradigms in particular (though by no means exclusively, see Carroll and Carson on global corporations and corporate elite policy groups in this volume) to well-developed and deeply entrenched networks of neoliberal knowledge production and diffusion, intellectuals and think tanks.

These networks of intellectuals and think tanks constitute a salient feature in the analysis of agents and structures of neoliberal globalization, as well as the globalization of neoliberalism.[4] While Kees van der Pijl and Leslie Sklair, for example, have theorized transnational processes of elite integration and class formation in recent works, a transnational class concept that focuses mainly on corporate and political elites is both too broad and too narrow to shed light on other crucial factors sustaining neoliberal hegemony, namely well-organized networks of neoliberal knowledge production and dissemination operating in relative autonomy from corporate and political centers of power. A predominantly corporate transnational class concept is too broad because conflicts between different forces and orientations within the ruling classes and global elites are underestimated, and too narrow because the important contribution of radical neoliberal intellectuals, scientists and 'second-hand dealers in ideas' (Hayek 1949b: 221) has not yet been adequately taken into account. Leslie Sklair (2001: 24) recognizes the role of intellectuals like Hayek and others of the Mont Pèlerin Society (MPS) in orchestrating the neoliberal counter-revolution against social-liberal and Keynesian welfare state thinking, but his subsequent analysis of transnational class formation processes is hampered by his predominant focus on corporate actors. While his emphasis on the role of culture in class formation processes avoids narrow class definitions relying on material interest, his focus on 'consumerism' as a central integrating factor should be considered but one of a set of cultural expressions of neoliberalism.

Kees van der Pijl (1995, 1998) has intensively discussed global elite planning groups, such as the Trilateral Commission and the Bilderberg Group on the one hand, and the organized network of neoliberalism constituted by the Mont Pèlerin Society on the other. In his more recent contribution, van der Pijl (1998: 129–30) moved beyond a sometimes rather too homogeneous representation of global planning groups by way of highlighting a number of important aspects that set the MPS network of organized neoliberals apart. First, unlike Bilderberg, the MPS did not restrict itself to serving as a forum for the articulation of still nascent ideas, but instead offered coherent principles for a foundational ideology (*Weltanschauung*). Second, unlike other 'planning groups', MPS relied on the mass dissemination of knowledge and ideas. Alas, while van der Pijl correctly observes the integration of influential members in think tanks around the globe and the coordination of think tank efforts under the umbrella of the Atlas Foundation, he dismisses this effort as transparently ideological. His assessment that the MPS network depends 'on the dissemination of a largely preconceived gospel' (van der Pijl 1998: 130) underestimates the ability of MPS intellectuals to engage in serious research, scientific projects and knowledge production, as well as the strategic and tactical capacities of neoliberal networks. The correctly observed 'militant intellectual function' – different from the 'adaptive/directive role in the background' (van der Pijl 1998: 130) of other planning groups – does not only or even mainly stem from firm ideological principles, but from the ability of the neoliberal MPS network to engage in pluralistic (albeit neoliberal pluralistic) debate in order to provide a frame for a whole family of neoliberal approaches (such as ordo-liberalism, libertarianism, anarcho-capitalism, etc.), and its innovative approach to generating and disseminating new knowledge. In the latter regard, the rise of the new type of 'advocacy think tank' as an organizational form distinct from traditional supply systems of scientific, technocratic and partisan knowledge (e.g. academic and state-planning-related knowledge centres and political parties) is critical for processes of knowledge production, distribution and circulation (see Smith 1991; Ricci 1993; Stone 1996). The strength of these neoliberal networks results from their ability to articulate the core principles of neoliberalism in a trans-disciplinary fashion not only in the arenas of 'political society', but also in the wider power arenas of 'civil society' as well (Gramsci).

This chapter proceeds as follows. First, we will provide a descriptive analysis of the development of the Mont Pèlerin Society network of organized neoliberals itself. From its humble origins, the group which contained 38 intellectuals at its founding in 1947 has developed into a truly global network with over 1,000 members so far. Second, we will introduce the origins and the concomitant rise of neoliberal advocacy think tanks closely connected to individuals or groups of MPS members. This discussion allows us to examine and assess both the strength and the limits of organized neoliberals in the contemporary phase of contested neoliberal hegemony.

The creation and institutionalization of neoliberal knowledge: experts and 'second-hand dealers' in ideas

Despite socialist revolutions, the Great Depression and other clear indicators of capitalist development's failures in the 1930s, neoliberal intellectuals insisted that the 'free market' was a superior mechanism for interactions, exchange and production, and promoted the extension of market mechanisms through the valorization and commercialization of many aspects of public and even private life. At the core of the neoliberal agenda remained a deep scepticism about the scope and reach of the state, particularly with regard to welfare and redistributive policies, though the 'neo' of 'neoliberalism' indicates an acknowledgment of the state's appropriate and necessary function in safeguarding capitalism (Walpen 2004: 62–83). Wilhelm Röpke, for instance, explicated two meanings of liberalism:

(a) a movement away from feudal institutions and toward greater social mobility and personal freedom; and
(b) the advocacy of laissez-faire capitalism and a radically individualist view of the social order.

He embraced the former and rejected the latter. Hence, Röpke and his allies came to adopt terms such as 'neoliberal', 'social market', 'humane economy', and 'Third Way', to describe their programs (Zmirak 2001: 13). Thus the neoliberals learned from the experiences of earlier right-wing liberal traditions, and wanted to overcome the previous dualist 'state/economy' perspective that dominated liberal thinking in the pre- Second World War era. Much like Hayek and other right-wing liberals, Röpke also understood that 'economics had been irreversibly politicized':

> The growth of mass democracy, the mobilization of millions of men of every social class during the First World War, rising nationalist sentiment and class mistrust – all these currents had joined to overwhelm the levee behind which classical liberals had hoped to protect economic life from the turbulence of politics. No longer would it be enough to convince the economics professors, the King's ministers, and the responsible classes of the virtues of the free market.
>
> (Zmirak 2001: 11)

Therefore, paradoxically, the neoliberals recognized the growing need 'to organize individualism'. Unlike previous power elites, neoliberal intellectuals and businessmen were not at the center of political and economic power in the postwar 'Lockean heartland' to use Kees van der Pijl's (1995) language for the capitalist center (which was under heavy influence of Keynesianism and social liberal conceptions of welfare state capitalism except Germany; compare Hall 1989). Neoliberals exercised even less influence in the 'Hobbesian contendor states' formed after the Second World War in the more or less peripheral areas of the second and third world experimenting with anti-colonialist disintegration from the world market and socialist trajectories. A small group of concerned liberals met in 1938 in Paris invited by the French philosopher Louis Rougier to discuss Walter Lippmann's book *The Good Society* (compare the important work by Denord 2001 and 2003). A total of 26 intellectuals participated in this early effort to create a framework for the innovation of liberalism. Fifteen of the 26 intellectuals (among others Raymond Aron, Louis Baudin, Friedrich August von Hayek, Ludwig von Mises, Michael Polanyi, Wilhelm Röpke, and Alexander Rüstow) would participate in the founding of the Mont Pèlerin Society nine years later in 1947.

Lippmann's core message was a principled statement of the superiority of the market economy over state intervention, which anticipated Hayek's much wider recognized argument in his 1944 book *The Road to Serfdom*. Unlike later theories of totalitarianism emphasizing the absence of pluralist/democratic principles (e.g. the approach by Hannah Arendt and her successors), the binary opposition of 'market' versus 'planned' economy was introduced to warn against a society under total control no matter whether organized according to Marxist–Leninist or Keynesian principles. To invoke the re-institutionalization of market mechanisms, Lippmann also anticipated Hayek's long-term strategy. Only steadfast, patient and rigorous scientific work and a revision of liberal theory were regarded as a promising strategy to eventually beat 'totalitarianism'. At the 1938 meeting, participants discussed names for the new philosophy in need of development and suggested a variety of terms, such as 'positive liberalism'. At the end, the group agreed on the term 'neoliberalism', giving the term both a birthday and an address. Another concrete result of the deliberations was the founding of the Centre International d'Études pour la Rénovation du Libéralisme, an early think tank effort of neoliberal intellectuals which would not survive the turmoil of the Second World War (Denord 2001 and 2003).

By 1947, the time was ripe to renew the 1938 effort. Under the leadership of the Swiss businessman Albert Hunold and Friedrich August von Hayek, a number of hitherto more loosely connected neoliberal intellectuals in Europe and the United States assembled in Mont Pèlerin, a small village close to Lake Geneva. The immediate internationalist outlook and organization effort was possible due to some corporate/institutional support. The Foundation for Economic Education in Irvington-on-Hudson (which dated from 1946 and employed Ludwig von Mises among others) and the William Volker Fund founded in 1944 and based in Kansas City provided for such bases, as did the London School of Economics (where Lionel Robbins and Hayek taught) and the University of Chicago (where Milton Friedman and other relevant figures held posts). The Volker Fund was headed by later MPS member Harold Luhnow and provided travel funds for the US participants in the meeting. Travel money for the British participants of the second meeting in Seelisberg, Switzerland, was secured from the Bank of England.[5]

What was the rationale for the founding of the Mont Pèlerin Society? The key paper for understanding this effort had been written by Hayek himself. He presented his article 'The Intellectuals and Socialism', which would be published in 1949, at the second meeting of the Society. In this paper, Hayek refines the general analysis of the threat to freedom and democracy resulting from 'the revolt of the masses' (Ortega y Gasset) and of the threat to elite control and capitalism as a whole resulting from the 'politicisation of economics', by focusing on education and knowledge. He specifically underlines the role of intellectuals, institutions, and ideas for the rise of socialism. In classical Fabian tradition, the policy turn towards socialist principles is explained by the influence of socialist intellectuals on decision makers. The time preceding socialist politics is described as a phase 'during which socialist ideals governed the thinking of the more active individuals' (Hayek 1949b: 221). Once the intellectuals turn to socialism, it is only

> a question of time until the views now held by the intellectuals become the governing force of politics. ... What to the contemporary observer appears as the battle of conflicting interests has indeed often been decided long before in a clash of ideas to narrow circles.
> (Hayek 1949b: 222)[6]

Hayek did not, however, propose a purely idealistic conception relying on great intellectuals as the driving force of history. Instead, he underlines the role of institutions, networks and organizations. Rejecting the conventional wisdom that intellectuals wield only limited influence, he explains that the traditional role of scientists and experts has been replaced by an

> all-pervasive influence of the intellectuals in contemporary society [which] is still further strengthened by the growing importance of 'organization'. It is a common but probably mistaken belief that the increase of organization increases the influence of the expert or specialist. This may be true of the expert administrator or organizer, if there are such people, but hardly of the expert in any particular field of knowledge. It is rather the person whose general knowledge is supposed to qualify him to appreciate expert testimony, and to judge between the experts from different fields, whose power is enhanced.
> (Hayek 1949b: 224)

Hayek observes the rapid spread of such institutions breeding intellectuals (and not experts) such as universities, foundations, institutes, editors and other knowledge spreading organizations such as journals, etc. 'Almost all the "experts" in the mere technique of getting knowledge over are, with respect to the subject matter which they handle, intellectuals and not experts' (224). The role of intellectuals as knowledge filters and disseminators is according to him a 'fairly new phenomenon of history' and a by-product of the mass education of the non-propertied classes. Due to their social status and experiences, such intellectuals or 'second-hand dealers in ideas' (221) are leaning towards socialism. Hayek particularly elaborates on the influence of journalists who, he contends, counteract the controlling power of the non-socialist owners of the media.

Hayek emphasizes the strength of liberal values in Germany unlike Great Britain (in the immediate post-war era), which he attributes to the former country's experience with fascist dictatorship. As part of his effort to de-legitimize socialist ideas and principles, he proceeds by way of equating fascism and socialism:

> Does this mean that freedom is valued only when it is lost, that the world must everywhere go through a dark phase of socialist totalitarianism before the forces of freedom can gather strength anew? It may be so, but I hope it

need not be. Yet so long as the people who over longer periods determine public opinion continue to be attracted by the ideals of socialism, the trend will continue. If we are to avoid such a development we must be able to offer a new liberal program, which appeals to the imagination. We must make the building of a free society once more an intellectual adventure, a deed of courage. What we lack is liberal Utopia, a program which seems neither a mere defence of things as they are nor a diluted kind of socialism, but truly liberal radicalism which does not spare the susceptibilities of the mighty (including the trade unions), which is not too severely practical and which does not confine itself to what appears today as politically possible. ... The practical compromises they must leave to the politicians.

(Hayek 1949b: 237)

Hayek draws two conclusions from his analysis, which can be regarded as the guiding principles of the neoliberal organizing, networking and institutionalization effort. First, the 'right' lacks capable scientists and experts able to match the rising stars of social liberal and socialist orientation (such as Lord Keynes and Harold Laski in England). This problem can only be overcome if a strong effort is made to rebuild anti-socialist science and expertise in order to develop anti-socialist intellectuals. Second, the socialist filter in the knowledge-disseminating institutions of society, universities, institutes, foundations, journals, and the media has to be attacked by the establishment of anti-socialist knowledge centers capable of effectively filtering, processing, and disseminating neoliberal knowledge.

The first task was taken on by the Mont Pèlerin Society, which assembled 'intellectuals', mostly scientists but also 'practical men', including businessmen, editors, professional journalists and politicians. The second task was tackled primarily for a long time by way of helping to found and run 'independent' institutes, foundations, journals, etc., promoting neoliberal knowledge: The core institution in this realm represents a deliberate effort to breed a fairly new type of civil society knowledge apparatus: the advocacy think tank.

Expert networking: an introduction to the Mont Pèlerin Society

The MPS did not establish a full-fledged academic or even political program. Instead, its membership of neoliberal intellectuals agreed on a set of core principles recorded as a statement of aims. The six core principles were:

1 The analysis and explanation of the nature of the present crisis so as to bring home to others its essential moral and economic origins.
2 The *redefinition of the functions of the state* so as to distinguish more clearly between the totalitarian and the liberal order.
3 Methods of re-establishing the rule of law and of assuring its development in such a manner that individuals and groups are not in a position to encroach upon the freedom of others and private rights are not allowed to become a basis of predatory power.

34 *Dieter Plehwe and Bernhard Walpen*

4   The possibility of establishing minimum standards by means not inimical to initiative and the functioning of the market.
5   Methods of combating the misuse of history for the furtherance of creeds hostile to liberty.
6   The problem of the creation of an international order conducive to the safeguarding of peace and liberty and permitting the establishment of harmonious international economic relations.

(Hartwell 1995: 41–2, emphasis added)

Notably absent are a number of traditional liberal core principles relating to basic human and democratic rights (e.g. 'collective organization', equality in political participation, etc.). From 1947 on, the society organized yearly conferences either of 'global' or 'regional' scale. Aspiring members required the support of two existing members in order to join MPS. Attempts of some members (notably Hunold and German economist Röpke) to have the MPS speak out politically in the public were blocked by an alliance led by Hayek in the 1950s. Thus the principle to engage only in scientific debate has been preserved through to the present. The only publicity for the Society itself was and is launched by members who work in major newspapers, such as the *Frankfurter Allgemeine Zeitung*, *Le Monde*, *Neue Zürcher Zeitung* and *Financial Times*. While clearly not a secret (or even conspirational) society, the members decided to preserve as much privacy as possible to enable an open discussion and to promote rigorous internal debate. A side effect, though probably not an unwelcome one, is that public attention is directed at the individual contributions of neoliberal scientists as opposed to the collaborative and institutionalized efforts of the neoliberal scientific and discourse community.[7]

Based on member lists available at the Liberaal Archief in Ghent (Belgium) and other MPS internal documents available at the Hoover Institute in Stanford (USA), as well as Internet-based research (many members proudly announce their membership in the MPS), we have assembled a profile that introduces the scope and content of the MPS network of neoliberal intellectuals.

Total membership comprises 1,025 individuals, 933 members are male and 48 are female (for 44 names no gender could be identified). Thus approximately 91 per cent of MPS members are male. The distribution of members according to countries is illustrated in Table 1.1.

As Table 1.1 makes clear, the network is global in scope, though a strong concentration of membership can be observed in the United States (437 members amount to 39.4 per cent of the total), followed by Germany, UK, France, Japan and Switzerland. A significant and rising number of members live outside the heartland of developed capitalism. Most recently, new members have been recruited in the post-socialist countries of the former Soviet bloc. Table 1.2 provides an overview according to world regions and shows that the MPS is clearly most strongly represented in Western Europe and North America, though a quite impressive presence can be observed in Latin America as well. In 1951, four

Table 1.1 MPS membership by country

USA	437	Columbia	3
Germany	95	Costa Rica	3
Great Britain	93	El Salvador	3
France	69	India	3
Japan	41	Ireland	3
Switzerland	37	Norway	3
Italy	26	Portugal	3
Spain	23	Poland	3
Argentina	22	Uruguay	3
South Africa	19	Russia	3
Austria	17	Luxemburg	2
Sweden	17	Finland	2
The Netherlands	16	Turkey	2
Australia	15	Bahamas	1
Guatemala	15	Ecuador	1
Venezuela	15	Egypt	1
Belgium	14	Greece	1
Canada	11	Hungary	1
Chile	11	Israel	1
Brazil	10	Island	1
Mexico	10	South Korea	1
Taiwan	10	Thailand	1
New Zealand	7		
Cuba	4		
Czech Republic	4		
Denmark	4		
Peru	4		
China	4	N/A	12

Source: Compiled by authors from Membership lists of the MPS available in the Liberaal Archief, Ghent.
The total number (1,107) exceeds the number of MPS members (1,025) due to relocations.

Table 1.2 MPS membership in world regions

North America	458
Europe	438
EU	383
Eastern (former socialist) Europe	11
Latin America	105
South America	69
Central America	21
and the Caribbean*	22 (26)
Asia	60
Australia	24
Africa	20

Source: see Table 1.1.
* with/out Cuba (1959)

years after the organization's founding, the MPS had members on all continents, with a strong concentration in the US and in Europe. Argentina and Mexico were the first countries in Latin America with MPS members. Guatemala's participation dates from 1966; by 1991, it was second only to Argentina as the Latin American country with the most members. From the 1970s onwards the development of membership in Venezuela, Brazil, Chile and Costa Rica is remarkable. In Africa the MPS has – with the exception of a single member at the end of the 1950s in Egypt – its exclusive anchoring in South Africa. Japan is the MPS center in Asia. Starting in 1957 with a single member Asian membership reached 24 by 1991. Besides Japan the MPS's representation in Asia is notable in Taiwan, where the number of members grew from two in 1966 to 10 in 1991 (see Walpen 2002). In the meantime, India's importance is growing. In the 1980s members from Australia and New Zealand were added. The importance of the Australasia region is reflected by the creation of the 'Special Asian Regional Meetings'. The first meeting was held in Bali, Indonesia in 1999 and the second, in Goa, India, took place at the beginning of 2002. In Europe we observe the increase of members especially in Spain and Eastern Europe.

In addition to its progress in terms of an expanding membership (both in terms of numbers and global reach), the MPS network has also managed to initiate both short- and long-term research projects on an individual as well as on a collective level (such as in the meantime competing versions of an *Index of Economic Freedom* coordinated and published yearly by the Fraser Institute and the Heritage Foundation). Normally, the impetus for such research projects comes from MPS, whereas think tanks implement them either alone or in collaboration (the Fraser Institute-led effort is a joint product of many think tanks around the globe; see Walpen 2004: ch. 4–6).

Table 1.3 provides data on the major fields of occupations of MPS members. We can distinguish the academic field, advocacy think tanks, business, government/politics, media, international organizations and associations as important clusters. Not surprisingly, most members are employed at universities, many in economics departments.[8] Only the members involved in academia outnumber the members who are employed in advocacy think tanks founded and/or promoted by MPS members holding leadership functions (serving on boards, etc.). A sizeable group is employed in corporations or business associations, followed by government employees and media people. An interesting aspect is the cross-field aspect of members employed in the management of money, be it in business (commercial banks), government (central banks) or international organizations such as the World Bank and the IMF. Certainly the core contribution of MPS members Milton Friedman (USA) and Sir Alan Walters (UK) in monetary theory and politics ('monetarism') attracted quite a number of 'practical men' to an international society which remains quite selective in its efforts to include corporate and political leaders.

Apart from the numerous ties of MPS members to more than 100 think tanks, foundations and neoliberal societies organized on a national basis (e.g. the US Philadelphia Society or the German F. A. von Hayek Gesellschaft), MPS members participate in other global elite groups such as the World Economic Forum (WEF) with eleven members participating so far. Despite a shift of elite planning groups such as Bilderberg and the Trilateral Commission towards their own varieties of neoliberalism, no significant overlap can be reported with regard to these groups.[9] The MPS members seem to prefer the maintenance of a separate global 'network of networks' (Pasche and Peters 1997) committed to more original, pure and radical version of neoliberalism. However, links do exist to corporate elites in the International Chamber of Commerce, which can be described as a core group of 'conservative neoliberalism' (see Carroll and Carson in this volume).

The neoliberal insight that the influence of socialism is not restricted to economic doctrines finds a clear expression in the wide field of discourses and sciences covered by the Mont Pèlerin Society. Indeed, there is hardly a subject of general scientific, philosophical or practical political that the MPS has not covered in its meetings, activities, and member publications. An index of 32

Table 1.3 MPS members' major fields of occupations

University	438
Economics*	299
Law	32
History	10
Business schools	3
Colleges	12
Think tanks, foundations	132
Business	96
Banking	20
Business associations	17
Government/politics	43
Central banks	6
Presidents	4
Judges	4
Ambassadors	2
Media	38
Newspapers, Weeklies	26
Publisher	3
Radio	2
TV	1
International organizations**	11
IMF	6
World Bank	7
Other associations	5
N/A of 1,025	4

Source: See Table 1.1, additional research on individuals.
* 19 can be directly recognized as 'public choice' economists.
** Some members served both at the IMF and the World Bank.

Table 1.4 Clustered subjects at 32 MPS meetings 1947–98

Economic topics
    Monetary order
    Gold standard
    Central banks
    Fiscal policy and taxation
    Methodological questions
    Teaching economics

State and welfare state
    Education
    Health care
    Pension system
    Privatization

Philosophy of Liberalism
    Liberal tradition
    Free society
    Moral questions
    Christianity/religions
    The image of entrepreneurs

Politics
    Agriculture
    Europe, European Integration and EU Germany
    Migration
    Under-developed countries

Law
    Rule of law
    Law and economics
    Liberal order

Neoliberal knowledge production, policy and agenda setting
    Strategies and tactics
    Deliberate discussion of influence, policy and work of think tanks

Socialism
    Planned economy
    Calculation
    Political development and influence of communism

Labour and Trade Unions

Keynesianism

Enemies of the market
    Environmentalism
    Feminism
    Interventionism
    Theology of liberation

Source: Own clustering of topics discussed at MPS meetings, compiled by Liberaal Archief, Ghent.

major MPS meetings between 1947 and 1998 (the last being the 50 year 'golden anniversary' meeting) yields the list of topics discussed at one or various sessions (Table 1.4).

Of course one can also highlight some individual MPS members who are well-known public officials such as Vaclav Klaus, Czech president and former head of the government, or Antonio Martino, the current minister of defense of Italy in the Forza Italia government of Silvio Berlusconi; Germany's ex-chancellor Ludwig Erhard or Italy's former president Luigi Einaudi; the EU Commission's single market official Frits Bolkestein. One could also highlight the total of eight Nobel Prize-winning economists who are or were members of the Mont Pèlerin Society,[10] much like Eric Lundberg, an official of the Central Bank of Sweden who was instrumental in creating the separate Prize based on funding from the Swedish Central Bank – The Bank of Sweden Prize in Economic Sciences in Memory of Alfred Nobel – which benefits from the renommée of the Nobel Prize (Lebaron 2002). It is more important, however, to understand that the strength of this transnational neoliberal discourse community derives not from the highly visible and publicly acknowledged experts in politics or science and scholarship; rather, neoliberal hegemony is produced and reproduced through an expansive network that ranges across diverse institutional arenas, including academia, business, politics, and media. A viable ideology or '*Weltanschauung*' cannot be generated by purely academic work; neither can it result from purely practical fields. It is the interrelation of the different areas important to hegemony, which can generate a crucial influence if the members of the network can agree on core principles and a common ground (as expressed in the MPS's *Statement of Aims*), and then work towards their 'liberal utopia' through a clearly defined division of intellectual and practical labor. Members actively share information, educate each other on a wide range of issues and discuss critical matters in pursuit of neoliberal 'solutions' to troubling questions to be promoted in appropriate channels (via service of individual members in policy and corporate advisory functions, through think tanks and media channels, etc.). What we hold as the MPS's core principle of pluralism in principled neoliberal confines can be regarded an important aspect with regard to internal as well as wider public(ized) discussions. While attempts are made to resolve conflicts on critical issues, conflicting views can also prevail as long as they are not in contradiction to the overall principles.

The decision of the MPS *as an organization* to not become directly involved in the political sphere additionally has helped to keep the society integrated by avoiding potential conflicts among members who might disagree on any specific issue, while agreeing on the MPS's general guiding principles. No matter which party is in power in any particular country at any given time, the society remains dedicated to its mission of articulating the neoliberal position on any question, which becomes a critical issue of public importance. Sometimes more than others, neoliberal experts are closer to the government in power, but even then the immediate exercise of power is not the concern of the network. This 'weakness' compared to other global elite groups can be regarded as the main difference as well as the core strength of the MPS's effort to reproduce and constantly mobilize neoliberal knowledge, and to develop neoliberal futures and planning capacities.[11] This relative 'political absenteeism' should not be misunderstood, however. It was clear for Hayek and his colleagues from the beginning that the task of translating neoliberal expertise into usable knowledge (such as policy proposals) should be well organized. For this purpose, the 132 MPS members working in think tanks and the links of many more MPS members to a total of more than 100 think tanks and foundations, not to mention media organizations, etc., are crucial. It was not a strategy of 'infiltration' of existing institutions, which yielded this sizeable group of neoliberal 'second-hand dealers in ideas' (Hayek 1949b: 221) and knowledge filters, but rather a self-conscious effort to build up 'independent' capacities. Many members of MPS found financial support from practical people to organize a still growing army of neoliberal advocacy think tanks.

Think tank networks and the strategic placement of neoliberal intellectuals and knowledge filters

We have already mentioned the first neoliberal think tank, the Centre International d'Études pour la Rénovation du Libéralisme which was organized in the late 1930s and failed to survive the Second World War.[12] This effort was renewed in the 1950s when British businessman Antony Fisher approached Hayek, offering his help to promote neoliberalism. Fisher supplied the seed money to set up the Institute of Economic Affairs in London, the prototype of the many neoliberal advocacy think tanks that followed throughout the world.

Think tanks[13] have been recognized in the comparative study of political systems in a number of pioneering contributions from several scholars (see Stone *et al.* 1998). Studies have explained the fundamental contribution of think tanks to the transformation of politics for example in the US (Ricci 1993); in-depth studies have shown the 'new ideological divide' (Smith 1991) as well as the extent of neoliberal/neoconservative[14] control capacities of elite networks during the Reagan and Bush administrations in the United States (Diamond 1995; Burch 1997a, 1997b and 1997c). Scholars have scrutinized the role of neoliberal think tanks in the policy process in general (Cockett 1994; Desai 1994) and with regard to individual policy issues such as privatization (Stone 1996) and deregulation (Plehwe 2000). Compared to early studies, which documented the 'social movement' character of neoliberalism as an organized endeavor to build up a 'counter establishment' against the Keynesian welfare state (Blumenthal 1986; Cockett 1994), much of the more recent work by and large fails to grasp the importance of the institutionalization of advocacy think tanks in securing neoliberal hegemony. Emphasis is placed instead on innovative capacities generated by think tanks, the wide range of opinions available from and thence an alleged pluralism with regard to advocacy think tanks (Gellner 1995; McGann and Weaver 2000; Stone 2000b).

Certainly a number of relatively new institutes of the left, e.g. the Center for Policy Alternatives founded in Canada in the 1980s or the – much more modest in scale and scope – recently established foundation WISSENTransfer (knowledge transfer) in Germany as well as quite impressive think tanks and networks operating in the realm of the 'new social democracies' (e.g. the 'Stockholm Progressive Summit', the 'Progressive Policy Institute' of the New Democrats in the US, the self proclaimed 'leading' social science publisher *Polity* and the foundation *Italianieuropei*) have learned from the success of the neoliberal advocacy tanks.[15] In particular the 'new social democratic' networks have to some extent successfully challenged neoliberal hegemony in the 1990s. However, it is not all that easy to clearly distinguish utopian neoliberalism from the communitarian versions of neoliberalism promoted by Tony Blair, Gerhard Schröder, and the New Democrats in the US. A more serious challenge to neoliberal hegemony may arise from the global networking activities of the new left 'anti (neoliberal) capitalism' movement, though it is too early to fully assess the knowledge-creation and distribution capacities of this diverse group, let alone their weight relative to existing neoliberal networks. In any case, comparative research is needed to examine the role of anti-globalization networks in resisting and potentially transforming neoliberal hegemony. Our hypothesis is that to date no force has emerged that can match the neoliberal networks in terms of organizational capacities, knowledge production and dissemination on a wide range of policy issues.[16]

The evidence we present in Annex 1.1 gives some indication of the scope and organization of these networks.[17] It catalogues the list of neoliberal advocacy think tanks defined as specialized or diversified ideology and knowledge organizations set up to establish and/or defend neoliberal hegemony in diverse social arenas such as the academic system, political consulting, mass media, and general public opinion and discursive and policy fields (e.g. economic theory, affirmative action, etc.) *with direct links* to MPS members (as founders, board members and/or senior officials) in alphabetic order. The work of some of the institutes such as the Fraser Institute in Canada, Heritage Foundation in Washington, the Institute of Economic Affairs and the Adam Smith Institute in the United Kingdom or Germany's Frankfurter Institut – Marktwirtschaft und Politik are very well known at the national level, while some of them even earned an international reputation. However, the *collective* efforts in many of the better- and lesser-known institutes have so far escaped attention. One example is the collaboration of several of these think tanks in the production of the Freedom of the World Report, which is used by neoliberal intellectuals (e.g. Norberg 2001) to provide counter information to some of the findings of the development index (known as the Human Development Report) published yearly by the United Nations.

While a large concentration of MPS-related think tanks can be found in the US and in the UK, it is important to underscore that neoliberal advocacy think tanks have proliferated in all world regions as the breakdown of think tanks by world regions and countries in Table 1.5 shows.

Another interesting aspect with regard to the rise of organized neoliberal knowledge networks and hegemony relates to the timing of institutionalization processes related to advocacy think tanks. Founding and networking activities begin in earnest after the Second World War, despite the earlier founding of a few institutes which can be regarded as important to 'neoliberalism avant la lettre'.[18] The growth of neoliberal institutes has been steady, though relatively slow until the 1970s with 18 new advocacy think tanks compared to five during the 1960s. Still, the crisis of Fordism in the 1970s was preceded by the setting up of a number of advocacy think tanks that early on interpreted the failures of Keynesianism and welfare statism. The largest number of neoliberal advocacy tanks has nevertheless been established in the 1980s and 1990s (30 and 23, respectively; Walpen 2004: 405). The demise of demand side policies and the sharp contraction of the welfare state did not lead to a self-satisfied withdrawal of the neoliberal movements. Rather, the organizational capacities of neoliberal networks have been steadily increased since neoliberalism became the dominant discourse in the early 1980s. No less than 45 new institutes have been added to the phalanx of neoliberal centers of knowledge production and dissemination and the number continue to grow, particularly in areas that have become integrated into the global capitalist economy more recently.

Due to the scale and scope of neoliberal advocacy think tanks it is virtually impossible to briefly summarize the subject areas covered by their research, publication and campaign activities. The Washington-based Heritage Foundation single handed offers comprehensive advice in many if not all US public policy matters, for example by way of publishing its government program, the 'Mandate for Leadership'. Publishing government programs has become an effort

Table 1.5 Advocacy think tanks with primary links to MPS by world region and country

North America	41	Asia	7
USA	35	Hongkong	1
Canada	2	India	2
Mexico	4	Japan	1
		Taiwan	2
Europe	36	Israel	1
Great Britain	7		
Germany	5	Africa	2
France	5	South Africa	2
Belgium	2		
Switzerland	3	Australasia	3
Poland	3	Australia	2
Austria	2	New Zealand	1
Turkey	1		
Sweden	2	South America	15
Slovac Republic	1	Peru	3
Ireland	1	Chile	3
Iceland	1	Brazil	3
Italy	1	Guatemala	2
Czech Republic	1	El Salvador	1
Spain	1	Uruguay	1
		Argentina	1
		Venezuela	1

Source: Internet and various other sources provided by think tanks with specified links to MPS (see Annex 1.1 on the method).

shared by sister institutes in Europe. Scrutinizing the web sites of the MPS-related think tanks yields a list of subject categories presented in Table 1.6 which might nevertheless be useful to assess the breadth and depth of neoliberal research and policy advisory activities carried out by individual organizations and in cooperation between think tanks.

Table 1.6 Subject areas of neoliberal advocacy think tanks

Economics
    Economic policy/support/growth
    Economic education/propagating the market economy
    Privatization
    Regulation/deregulation
    Labor market/wages/employment
    International trade/free trade/globalization
    Europe/European Union/European Monetary System
    Consumer protection/risk
    Development/politics of transition (from socialism to capitalism)

Law and society
    Legal protection/institutional protection of private economic activity
    Rule of law/order of market economy
    Criminal law/crime

Government and social/economic infrastructures
    Efficiency/limitation of government
    Taxes/state budget
    Social minimum security/welfare/philanthropy
    Family/moral values
    Gender/feminism
    Migration/racism
    Pensions
    Health politics
    Postal service/transport/infrastructure
    Telecommunications/Internet
    Energy politics
    Ecology/environmental protection
    Regions/federalism

Education and media
    Higher education
    Schools/pedagogics
    Science/technology
    Media/public discourse/culture
    Philosophy/ideological fundamentals
    Theoretical Fundament/theory history
    Monitoring (of left wing activities)

Foreign policy/military

Networking/cooperation of think tanks

Source: web sites of 104 MPS-related think tanks (see Annex 1.1; compare www.buena-vista-neoliberal.de. We gratefully acknowledge the research assistance of Werner Kraemer on the coverage of policy issues and clustering of subject areas).

Obviously not all think tanks work on all of these or even a majority of these subjects. But many issue areas are now covered not only by individual think tanks but also by groups of think tanks. Apart from the general coordination activities for many of the think tanks listed in Annex 1.1 by the Atlas Foundation in the United States, many issue-specific networks of neoliberal think tanks have been created in recent years, such as the 'Economic Freedom Network' (collaborating around the globe on the yearly Freedom of the World Reports), the 'Stockholm Network' of think tanks across Western Europe (concerned with neoliberal advice for the direction of European integration politics), the 'Balkan Network' and the expanded '3E Network' (including think tanks from all over Eastern Europe) providing neoliberal guidance for the transition from Socialism to Capitalism or the US State Policy Network covering neoliberal think tanks in each state in the US. Due to the close links between and the increasingly intensive cooperation of many of these neoliberal advocacy think tanks, it is very easy to spread work across countries, to effectively divide labor, and to create 'knowledge, policy and discourse campaigns' if need is perceived.[19]

In assessing the role of think tank networks in the production and reproduction of neoliberal hegemony, what is critical is the collective capacity of the network to resist challenges to this hegemony, not the activities of any individual organization. Those who predict neoliberalism's demise in light of the rising critique against it and 'corporate-led' or 'capitalist globalization' may not be aware of or seriously underestimate the entrenched power of neoliberal networks of knowledge production to meet this challenge, as they have many others before. The networks that have mobilized quite effectively in recent years to challenge neoliberal hegemony may yet have to learn from the 'technology'[20] of neoliberal masters in the art of creating and running advocacy think tanks, and may have to strengthen certain characteristics more typically to be found in 'complex organizations' (Perrow) and intelligently coupled interorganizational networks (i.e. comprehensive coordination) to gain an effectiveness and comprehensiveness with regard to the everyday and multi-issue struggles influencing public opinion similar to the extremely well-organized neoliberal networks of knowledge production and dissemination (compare George 1997).

Process dynamics and relations of forces: concluding remarks

We can thus observe both a widening and deepening of neoliberal networks of intellectuals and advocacy think tanks, a considerable increase in reach and scope around the globe as well as specific national and supranational arenas and discourse areas.[21] Neoliberal knowledge production and dissemination certainly has not declined in the most recent period, rather the opposite: a very solid intellectual force and constitutive part of historical power blocs that defend and maintain neoliberal hegemonic constellations is strongly entrenched in many (civil and political) societies around the globe, capable of working on almost any subject of concern, and able to strategically develop capacities and competencies if needed. Reliable and tested channels of communication can be used to eventually disseminate the result of the work, and the neoliberal networks are capable to rapidly change tactics.

Underscoring this reality is particularly important given the recent attention afforded to the supposed emergence of a post-Washington Consensus, representing a kinder, gentler version of globalization. The World Bank's discovery that 'institutions matter' and ubiquitous references to the importance of good or global governance, which pervade the international financial institution's discourse today, should not be interpreted as evidence for neoliberalism's defeat. In fact, many of the recent critiques of neoliberalism and the proposed reforms, which arise from them, turn out to be consistent with a pluralist neoliberal agenda. Many neoliberals agree that the state should be strengthened in order to secure the institutional foundation of a market economy. A close look at the statement of aims of the Mont Pèlerin Society reminds us that neoliberalism's core tenets cannot be reduced to vulgar market radicalism, but rather include reflection on the appropriate role of a limited state. Thus, neoliberalism's opponents do themselves a disservice in defining their opposition against this straw man.

Indeed, part of the reason why it is not easy to distinguish anti-neoliberals and neoliberals is because the left lacks a coherent statement of an alternative that makes it clear what it is for, as opposed to what it is against. Nevertheless a principled effort to overcome neoliberal hegemony must entail a statement of aims similar in scope to those that have guided the MPS, and it must include a consideration of the kind of transnational organizational capacities needed to cope with and counteract the scope and achievements of neoliberal networks of intellectuals and think tanks. Bidding neoliberalism a premature adieu fails to understand that neoliberal hegemony does not find expression in the achievement of a defined end state of 'neoliberalism'; rather, neoliberal hegemony is better understood as the capacity to permanently influence political and economic developments along neoliberal lines, both by setting the agenda for what constitutes appropriate and good government, and criticizing any deviations from the neoliberal course as wrong-headed, misguided, or dangerous. The working principle and hegemonic strategy of radical neoliberalism in any case is not concerned with specific details and political compromises; neoliberal networks of intellectuals and advocacy think tanks predominantly aim to influence the terms of the debate in order to safeguard neoliberal trajectories. Our analysis of the Mont Pèlerin Society and the neoliberal networks that are its descendants suggest that a core aspect of this endeavor, and one of the keys of its success, is the ongoing process of knowledge production and dissemination, as well as the relative absenteeism from power.

Notes

1 The Bush administration's protection of the US steel and agricultural sector (in the form of subsidies and increased tariffs on imports) triggered similar moves on the part of the European Union and generated considerable hostility in many countries, e.g. in Mexico, where large demonstrations of Mexican farmers denounced the hypocrisy

of the US's free trade rhetoric and demanded similar subsidies from their government.
2 The 2003 World Economic Forum is paralleled for the third time by the Porto Alegre Global Social Forum. Whereas the social movements in Porto Alegre are certain to celebrate the win of the Brazilian presidency of labor activist and PT leader Lula, the WEF crowd is contemplating how to regain trust lost for the globalization project (*New York Times*, 24 January 2003).
3 We employ the term 'hegemony' in Gramsci's sense suggesting a system of rule based on a high degree of consent of the ruled (rather than based on force).
4 Susan Strange correctly observed that the 'power derived from the knowledge structure is the one that has been most overlooked and underrated. It is no less important than the other three sources of structural power [military, production, finance] in the international political economy but is much less well understood. This is partly because it comprehends what is believed (and the moral conclusions and principles derived from those beliefs); what is known and perceived as understood; and the channels by which beliefs, ideas and knowledge are communicated – including some people and excluding others' (Strange 1988: 115).
5 Letter from Alfred Suenson-Taylor to William E. Rappard (16 March 1949, in: Swiss Federal Archive, Berne, J.I.149, 1977/135, Box 48; see Walpen 2004: 107).
6 Hayek cited Keynes' analogous insight from the *General Theory* (1936: 383) at the MPS founding conference: '[T]he ideas of economists and political philosophers, both when they are right and when they are wrong, are more powerful than is commonly understood. Indeed the world is ruled by little else. Practical men, who believe themselves to be quite exempt from any intellectual influences, are usually the slaves of some defunct economist.'
7 An argument made in the 1960s and 1970s about the rise of the scientific power elite was rejected as a chimera by Peter Weingart (1982). According to Weingart, the scientification of politics immediately led to the de-institutionalization and politicization of Science and thus potentially resulted in a loss of expert influence. Although his point (notably similar to Hayek's argument) is well taken, Weingart fails to account for the rise of specific discursive communities such as the one organized by the Mont Pèlerin Society.
8 Apart from the predominant group of economists among the MPS members, considerable numbers are found in law and philosophy departments. Further disciplines include History, Sociology, Theology, Agronomy, Biology, Chemistry, Engineering, Mathematics, Physics, Political Science, Psychology, other Social Sciences and Zoology. The academic training and involvement of about two-thirds of MPS members remains to be researched.
9 Germany's Alfred Müller-Armack, one of the early members of MPS, appears to be one of the few who attended Bilderberg conferences.
10 The Prize winners are Hayek (1974), Friedman (1976), George J. Stigler (1982), Buchanan (1986), Maurice Allais (1988), Ronald H. Coase (1991), Becker (1992) and Vernon L. Smith (2002).
11 While many left-wing social movements did not escape the integrative powers of 'parliamentarization', the neoliberal right seems to have learned the lesson with regard to the necessity of autonomy to avoid disintegration by way of absorption.
12 The 'prototype' of a think tank-like organization is the Fabian Society. Neoliberals like Hayek learned a lot from the Fabians (Cockett 1995: 111–12).
13 Compare about the term 'think tank', a very long 'definition' of think tanks and different types (Stone 1996, ch. 1). Attempts to universally define the term 'think tank' in a concise way are bound to fail due to substantial differences between scientific, technocratic and partisan varieties.
14 Edwin J. Feulner, head of the Heritage Foundation and long-time secretary treasurer as well as president of the MPS, vividly describes the problem of the term neo*liberal* in

the US context. 'The Mont Pèlerin Society was founded ... to uphold the principles of what Europeans call "liberalism" (as opposed to "statism") and what we Americans call "conservatism" (as opposed to "liberalism"): free markets, limited governments, and personal liberty under the rule of law' (Feulner 1999: 2).
15 John Gray can be regarded as an outstanding example of a new right renegade with intimate knowledge of neoliberal think tanks. After supporting the Thatcherite movement in various intellectual functions, Gray defected to join the new labor movement of Tony Blair. In the high times of neoliberalism he was a member of the MPS, but as he recognized the 'False Dawn' (Gray 1998) he did quit the Society in 1996 (Walpen 2004: 379).
16 See Krugman (2001) for an excellent example of the effectiveness of a think tank campaign against a proposed inheritance tax (labeled death tax by the Heritage Foundation).
17 A larger effort is under way to establish a database of more complete networks of neoliberal advocacy think tanks and can be accessed at the web page of the study group *Buena Vista Neoliberal?* (www-buena-vista-neoliberal.de). We wish here to acknowledge the able research assistance of our colleague Werner Krämer in compiling this database.
18 These include the US Hoover Institution (1919) and Rappards Institut Universitaire des Hautes Études Internationales (IUHEI) in Geneva (1927).
19 Two recent campaigns concentrate on arguments against Jeremy Rifkin's analysis of 'the end of work' and globalization critiques advanced by the new social protest movements.
20 The technology school or contingency theory in organization studies 'focuses on something more or less analytically independent of structure and goals – the tasks or techniques utilized in organizations' ('technology' is used here in its generic sense of the study of techniques or tasks; Perrow 1986: 141). The neo-Weberian approach as described by Perrow also has to offer interesting insights with regard to advocacy think tank research. It starts out from a specific understanding of 'communication': '...communication strategies center around checkpoints in the channels, the specialization of channels, the widening and deepening of favored channels that may bypass key stations inadvertently, the development of organizational vocabularies that screen out some parts of reality and magnify other parts, and the attention-directing, cue-establishing nature of communication techniques' (125).
21 A closer analysis of a range of more specific discourse and power *relations* in which the neoliberal networks of intellectuals and think tanks are a key force is beyond the scope of this chapter. We have discussed the case of European integration elsewhere (Plehwe and Walpen 2004) as a good example of the relative influence of organized neoliberals. While long-term MPS member and one-time president Herbert Giersch (1985) successfully introduced the 'Eurosclerosis' analysis underpinning the single market program in the 1980s, organized neoliberals found themselves fighting an uphill battle in the 1990s with regard to new efforts to further develop the *political* union of Europe, namely to draft a European constitution. Within a very short period of time, however, the 1992-founded European Constitutional Group (www.european-constitutional-group.org) was mobilized to draft a neoliberal constitution. Seven of the ten original members (from six different countries) share the commonality of MPS membership and access to domestic think tank channels used to disseminate their collective work. In a parallel effort, new supra- and transnational think tank capacities have been developed by the neoliberal camp. In 1993, German and British members of the MPS network introduced the *Centre for a New Europe (CNE)* – the first neoliberal think tank designed to play a role at the supranational level. In addition to the CNE, the *Stockholm Network* has been created in 1997. The British think tank Civitas, a year 2000 spin off from the Institute of Economic Affairs, has been given the task to coordinate the work of associated neoliberal advocacy think tanks in

England, France, Belgium and Germany as well as corresponding partners in other member states of the European Union (and the US Galen Institute). Compare Bohle and Neunhöffer in this volume on the role of organized neoliberals in the socialist transformation discourse, and Weller and Singleton in this volume on the development discourse, particularly the reform debate on International Financial Institutions.

Annex 1.1 Advocacy think tanks with direct relations to MPS members

Name	Country	Year
Acton Institute for the Study of Religion and Liberty	USA	1990
The Adam Smith Institute (ASI)	GB	1977
Agencia Interamericana de Prensa Económica (AIPE)	USA	1991
American Enterprise Institute (AEI)	USA	1943
Aktionsgemeinschaft Soziale Marktwirtschaft (ASM)	D	1953
Association for Liberal Thinking (ALT)	TR	1994
Association pour les Libertés Economiques et le Progrès Social (ALEPS)	F	1968
Atlantic Institute for Market Studies (AIMS)	CDN	1995
Atlas Economic Research Foundation	USA	1981
Carl Menger Institut	A	1980s
Cato Institute	USA	1977
Center for Private Conservation (CPC ? CEI)	USA	2000
Center for Social and Economic Research (CASE)	PL	1991
Centre for Civil Society	IND	1997
Centre for the New Europe (CNE)	B	1993
Centre International d'Études pour la Rénovation du Libéralisme	F	1938–1939
Centre Jouffroy Pour la Réflexion Monétaire	F	1974
Centre d'Etudes du Développement International et des Mouvements Economiques et Sociaux (CEDIMES)	F	1972
Centre for the Independent Studies (CIS)	AUS	1976
Centre of Policy Studies (CoPS)	AUS	1982
Centre for Research into [Post-]Communist Economies (CRCE)	GB	1983
The Centre for the Study of Economics and Religion	ZA	N/A
Centro de Divulgación del Conocimiento Económico (CEDICE)	YV	1984
Centro de Estudio Sobre la Libertad (CESL)	RA	1957
Centro de Estudios Economico Sociales (CEES)	GCA	1959
Centro de Estudios Públicos	RCH	1980
Centro de Estudios de la Realidad Económica y Social (CERES)	ROU	N/A
Centro de Investigaciones Sobre la Libre Empresa (CISLE)	MEX	1984
Centro Einaudi	I	1963
Centro Mises	MEX	1950s
Centrum im. Adama Smitha (CAS)	PL	1989
Chung-hua Institution for Economic Research (CIER)	RC	1981
Civitas, the Institute for the Study of Civil Society	GB	2000
The Claremont Institute	USA	1979
Competitive Enterprise Institute (CEI)	USA	1984
David Hume Institute (DHI)	GB	1985

(continued on next page)

Annex 1.1   (continued)

Name	Country	Year
Foundation for Economic Education (FEE)	USA	1946
Foundation Francisco Marroquin (FFM)	GCA	1980
Foundation for International Studies	USA	N/A
Frankfurter Institut – Stiftung für Marktwirtschaft und Politik (Kronberger Kreis)	D	1982
Fraser Institute	CDN	1974
Free Market Foundation (FMF)	ZA	1975
Friedrich A. von Hayek-Gesellschaft	D	1998
Friedrich Naumann Stiftung (FNS)	D	1958
The Heartland Institute	USA	1984
Heritage Foundation	USA	1973
The Hong Kong Centre for Economic Research (HKCER)	HKG (TJ)	1987
Hoover Institution on War, Revolution and Peace	USA	1919
The Howard Center for Family, Religion, and Society	USA	1997
The Independent Institute	USA	1985
Independent Women's Forum (IWF)	USA	1991
Institut Economique de Paris	F	1970s
Institut Universitaire des Hautes Études Internationales (IUHEI)	CH	1927
Institute for Contemporary Studies	USA	1974
Institute of Economic Affairs (IEA)	GB	1955
Institute for Humane Affairs	USA	N/A
Institute for Human Studies	USA	1961
Instituto Cultural Ludwig von Mises (ICUMI)	MEX	1983
Instituto de Economía Política	RCH	1970s
Instituto de Estudos Empresariais	BR	1984
Instituto de Investigaciones Economicas y Sociales	ES	N/A
Instituto de Investigaciones Economicas y Sociales (IIES)	MEX	1955
Instituto de Libre Empresa (ILE)	PE	N/A
Instituto de Economia de Libre Mercado (IELM)	PE	N/A
Instituto Libertad y Democracia	PE	1980
Instituto de Pesquizas Economicas e Sociais	BR	N/A
Instytut Badañ nad Gospodark[1] Rynkow[1] (IBnGR) Institute for Researches in Market Economy)	PL	1989
Intercollegiate Studies Institute (ISI)	USA	1953
International Institute of Austrian Economics (IIAE)	A	1993
International Policy Network (IPN)	GB	1971
Israel Center for Social & Economic Progress (ICSEP)	IL	1984
James Madison Institute (JMI)	USA	1987
John Locke Institute	USA	1990
Jon Thorlaksson Institute	IS	1983
Liberal Institute	BR	1983
Liberales Institute	CH	1979
Liberální Institut	CZ	1990
Libertad y Desarrollo (LyD)	RCH	1990
Liberty Fund, Inc.	USA	1960

(continued on next page)

Annex 1.1 (continued)

Name	Country	Year
Liberty Institute	IND	1990s
Ludwig von Mises Institute (LVMI)	USA	1982
Ludwig von Mises Institute Europe	B	1984
Mackinac Center for Public Policy	USA	1987
Manhattan Institute	USA	1978
Nadácia F. A. Hayeka (NFAH)	SK	1991
Nomura Research Institute	J	1965
Pacific Research Institute for Public Policy Research (PRI)	USA	1979
Pioneer Institute for Public Policy Research	USA	1988
Political Economy Research Center – The Center for Free Market Environmentalism (PERC)	USA	1980
Ratio Institute	S	2002
Reason Foundation	USA	1978
Reason Public Policy Institute (RPPI)	USA	1997
Rockford Institute	USA	1976
Ronald Coase Institute (USA)	USA	1996
Sociedad para el Estudio de la Acción Humana (SEAH)	E	1991
Schweizerisches Institut für Auslandforschung (SIAF)	CH	1943
Skrabanek Foundation (SF)	IRL	1994
The Smith Center for Private Enterprise Studies	USA	1991
The Social Affairs Unit (SAU)	GB	1980
State Policy Network (SPN)	USA	1992
Taiwan Institute of Economic Research (TIER)	RC	1976
Tasman Institute	NZ	1990
Timbro Free Market Institute (S)	S	1978
Walter-Eucken-Institut (D)	D	1954

Source: Internet and literature-based search for think tanks which have either been founded by MPS members or which include MPS members in senior positions. MPS membership data was compiled from member lists available at the Liberaal Archief, Ghent, Belgium (see Walpen 2004: 399–408). The international country abbreviations are taken from: www.iol.ie/~taeger/tables/tab9.htm (accessed 21 January 2005).

2 Neoliberalism, capitalist class formation and the global network of corporations and policy groups

William K. Carroll and Colin Carson

In recent decades the development of a transnational phase of capitalism, said to include the global integration of national economies, the mobility of capital and global reach of accumulation circuits, and the growing role of organizations like the World Economic Forum (WEF) and the World Trade Organization (WTO), has claimed the attention of legions of social scientists. With this interest has come a concern to theorize the segment of the world bourgeoisie purported to represent transnational capital and the ideology, neoliberalism, which seems to underwrite its expansion. These issues have gained additional salience as scholars such as Robinson and Harris (2000) and Sklair (2001) have discerned the formation of a fully transnational capitalist class (TCC). In this chapter we focus on the contribution that neoliberal policy groups have made, through elite-level directorship interlocks, to transnational capitalist class formation.

A range of theoretical perspectives relevant to this issue now exists. In the early 1970s, dramatic increases in direct foreign investment through multinational corporations led Hymer (1979) to observe that 'an international capitalist class is emerging whose interests lie in the world economy as a whole system of international private property which allows free movement of capital between countries' (262). In the 1980s, the Gramscian turn in IPE, advocating a 'historically grounded conception of the dialectic totality of structure and agency' in processes of class formation and world order (Overbeek 2000), demonstrated that while the mechanisms of international trade and investment furnished structural conditions for global capitalist expansion, they could not provide the long-term vision needed for capitalist class formation. Van der Pijl (1998) and Overbeek and van der Pijl (1993) situate transnational class formation in the context of restructuring and stabilizing capitalist fractions (bank, commercial, industrial capital) under the global economic hegemony of neoliberalism. Of specific interest is the development of strategic vision in the social networks of the directors of corporations, banks and planning groups of various sorts (van der Pijl 1998: 5). Cox (1987), Gill (1990, 1992) and Robinson and Harris (2000), describing similar practices in relation to transnational state apparatuses, view the TCC as both an embodiment of transnational capital and an expression of political power manifest by transnational (or interstate) institutions such as the International Monetary Fund (IMF) and the WTO. 'World hegemony', as such, 'is describable as a social structure, an economic structure, and a political structure; and it cannot be simply one of these things but must be all three' (Cox 1983, in Overbeek 2000: 176). In a somewhat separate vein, Sklair (2001) places significant emphasis on the ideological awareness of transnational executives and views the dissemination of a culture – ideology of consumerism as integral to transnational capitalist class formation.

Robinson and Harris (2000) draw on many of these perspectives to announce the emergence of a fully transnational capitalist class whose 'organic composition, objective position and subjective constitution ... [is] no longer tied to the nation state' (14). As might be expected, the claim of such an epochal shift has forced a closer assessment of how the TCC is identified. Indeed, the collection of critiques that followed the article's publication brings to light several unresolved issues and questions, including the extent of the TCC's geopolitical scale – particular emphasis is placed on the recalcitrance of a North/South divide – and its alleged autonomy from national contexts.[1] From all sides of the current debate it is agreed that more direct evidence is needed.

In fact, precious little systematic empirical data have been marshaled to date. However, a recent longitudinal study of the social structure of the international business community by Carroll and Fennema (2002) does speak to several of the key issues raised in the aftermath of Robinson and Harris's (2000) intervention. While network analysis has long contributed to an empirical understanding of elite integration (and, by extension, class formation) at the national level (Useem 1984; Domhoff 1998), it was only with Fennema's (1982) study of international networks of banks and industry that this analysis took transnational scale. Carroll and Fennema's research builds from Fennema's earlier work to examine changes in the network of interlocking directorates between 1976 and 1996, a period associated with the most recent surge in economic globalization. Among their key findings were, on the one hand, moderate increases in transnational integration via weak ties that transect national borders, but on the other, recalcitrant national patterns of organization – thus their characterization of the transnational network as 'a kind of superstructure that rests on rather resilient national bases' (2002: 414). Carroll and Fennema conclude that while corporate interlocks within countries are often associated with the strategic control of capital, 'transnational corporate interlocking is less about intercorporate control than it is about the construction of an international business community' (2002: 415).

Such a community would be a rather pallid affair if it were confined to the corporate boardrooms. In fact, given the persistence of national corporate networks, we might say that *the articulation of a transnational capitalist interest requires sites beyond the boardrooms* – places where business leaders can come together to discuss issues of shared concern, to find common ground and to devise strategies for action. Business activism of this sort would seem an integral aspect of community development at the higher reaches of corporate power. The significance of such arrangements is only enhanced by processes of globalization and the search for new forms of governance. In recent years these conditions have indeed prompted a range of scholarly attention on institutions of private authority and their self-regulatory potential (Ronit 2001: 562; Keck and Sikkink 1998).

Building on the concept of an international business community, and asserting the basic premise that those who direct the largest corporations are the leading edge of a capitalist class, this chapter situates five global organizations of elite consensus-building within a larger structure of corporate power that is constituted through interlocking directorates. The elite policy-planning groups operate within an incipient 'global civil society' (Shaw 2000) that is distinct from both state power and economic power yet intimately linked to both. It is from these sites that the strategic and moral visions and policy frameworks informing a transnational capitalist interest have been forged. By mapping the corporate-policy network we hope to shed light on the role that global policy groups are playing in the formation of a transnational capitalist class.

Policy groups as sites for constructing transnational neoliberal hegemony

In the years since the Second World War we can trace the development of a neoliberal tendency within a differentiating global field of elite consensus formation. Set in motion with Friedrich Hayek's convening of the Mont Pèlerin Society in 1947 (see Walpen 2004; Plehwe and Walpen in this volume), its austere market-monetarist orientation gained a distinct, yet still marginal, voice in an organizational ecology dominated by corporate liberal tendencies – a regulatory strategy upheld at the time by the first truly North Atlantic planning body, the Bilderberg Conferences (est. 1952). Rising to dominance decades later under the regimes of Reagan and Thatcher, undiluted neoliberal doctrine responded to structural shifts that beleaguered the post-war Keynesian-Fordist state and accelerated the spread of transnational corporations, the expansion of foreign direct investment and the interpenetration of capital. Lending sanction to the distinctly global regime of accumulation that was taking shape were the policy imperatives of privatization, trade liberalization, deregulation, tax reform, and the introduction of market proxies and benchmarking into the public sector – a grouping of corrosive neoliberal initiatives that John Williamson (1990), World Bank Chief Economist for South Asia (1996–9), termed the 'Washington consensus' (see Weller and Singleton in this volume).

Integral to the political and cultural reproduction of this new order has been a synthesis of public and private elements from the states and civil societies of the capitalist world in several new private international policy groups, most notably the World Economic Forum (est. 1971), the Trilateral Commission (est. 1973), and the World Business Council for Sustainable Development (est. 1995). While such groups make distinct strategic contributions to the field of transnational neoliberal policy, they share three critical attributes. Each inhabits a space within civil society as 'embedded elements of a social network, within which neoliberal business activism [takes] shape and form' (Carroll and Shaw 2001: 196). They also act as vehicles of international elite integration, linking capitalists to a political-cultural community where class extremes are mediated and a 'collective will' thrashed out (van der Pijl 1998). Finally, all, to varying degrees, endeavor to 'translate class interests into state action by defining and promoting lines of policy that ensure the stability and reproduction of a system shaped by capitalist social relations' (Peschek 1987: 216). In these ways, neoliberal policy groups can be said to function as 'collective intellectuals' – 'deputies' or agents of the capitalist class 'entrusted with the activity of organizing the general system of relationships external to ... business itself,' as Gramsci described (1971: 6).

Still, the struggle to spread the neoliberal economic project on a global scale has been far from straightforward, and has experienced several major setbacks over the course of the past decade, including global recession and crises,[2] and the emergence of new forms of civil resistance crystallized around opposition to the legal incursions of capitalist globalization, including the MAI, the WTO, and World Bank and IMF initiatives. In turn has come 'increasing concern with how best to co-ordinate actions to promote and consolidate it on different scales, with its social and environmental costs and their adverse political repercussions, and with identifying and pursuing flanking measures that would help to re-embed the recently liberated market forces into a well-functioning market society' (Jessop 2000). Indeed, by the mid-1990s neoliberal order was increasingly fragmented around the question of how best to assure long-term stability and reproduction of transnational capital.

For Robinson and Harris it is precisely this new regulatory positioning within the neoliberal paradigm, and the tensions this creates among globalizing elites, that have given rise to a transnational capitalist class defined by both economic structure and strategic-political rule – a class both in-itself, and for-itself (21).[3] Their analysis very usefully divides the globalist policy field into three neoliberal factions, which we will employ to help frame our discussion of the projects of transnational policy groups. The first faction is *free-market conservative*. Influenced by economist Milton Friedman, this faction calls for a complete global *laissez-faire*, drawing on fundamental neoliberal tenets of monetarism, state deregulation, 'spontaneous order' of market relations, and possessive individualism. Reigning as neoliberalism's singular voice under the so-called Washington consensus, the project would be splintered and somewhat marginalized amidst the global economic crises of the 1990s. Stemming from these actualities, the fraction that according to Robinson and Harris (2000) is now dominant, *neoliberal structuralism*, advocates a 'global superstructure that could provide a modicum of stability to the volatile world financial system ... without interfering with the global economy' (43). Following progenitors Bill Clinton and Tony Blair, its politics are distinctly 'Third Way' – 'finding a synergy between private and public sectors' as Giddens put it (1998: 99–100). Gill (1995), notably, has discerned a very similar policy shift in the 'new constitutionalist' discourse, launched during the G7 Summit in Halifax, Nova Scotia, in June 1995 (413). Responding to the Mexican crisis of 1994–5, G7 members opted to 'strengthen [economic] surveillance mechanisms under the aegis of the IMF, World Bank, and the BIS' (413). Contrasting with the position of free-market conservatives the new perspective held that 'ideology and market power are not enough to ensure the adequacy of neoliberal restructuring ... [and must be] institutionalized at the macro-level of power in the quasi-legal restructuring of the state and international political forms' (Gill 1995: 421). The third, and/or emergent, faction is *neoliberal regulationist*. This current calls for a 'broader global regulatory apparatus that could stabilize the financial system as well as attenuate some of the sharpest social contradictions of global capitalism' (Robinson and Harris 2000: 43). World Bank senior vice president Joseph Stiglitz's vision of a 'post-Washington consensus' – an international capitalist system which better contemplates the world's struggles over health and education, environmental preservation and equitable development – exemplifies this perspective (Stiglitz 1998). Although each globalist faction is divided on the amount of structural interference that should occur in the new 'global economy', all three are neoliberal in that 'none question the essential premises of world market liberalization and the freedom of transnational capital' (Robinson and Harris 2000: 43).

The five international policy groups

In this section we focus on five organizations that have come to comprise a field of transnational policy formation, two with longstanding histories, and three whose origins lie within the contemporary wave of economic globalization. That field has taken a historically stratified and pluralistic shape as the groups have developed around specific visions, issues and networks (see Table 2.1).

The Paris-based *International Chamber of Commerce* (ICC), founded in 1919, is the oldest of the business policy groups discussed here and the only one to maintain a primarily free-market conservative strategic vision. It is also the largest, grouping some 7,000 member companies and associations from over 130 countries. As a forum for transnational capitalist consultation launched by investment bankers in the shadow of the First World War, the ICC has historically functioned as the most comprehensive business forum committed to liberalization, and has 'long been a triumphant lobbyist for global economic deregulation in fora such as the WTO, the G8 and the OECD' (Balanyá *et al.* 2000: 166).

The ICC's primary function is to institutionalize an international business perspective by providing a forum where capitalists and related professionals (e.g., law firms and consultancies, national professional and sectoral associations) can assemble to forge a common international policy framework in arenas ranging from investment to specific technical and sectoral subjects. Since the mid-1990s its efforts to institutionalize an agenda of corporate self-regulation have fostered close working relationships with international institutions such as the WTO, UN Conference on Trade and Development (UNCTD), and the UN General Secretariat (Balanyá *et al.* 2000: 166–74). The ICC's secondary function is to knit national chambers throughout the world into a single global network through its World Chambers Federation (WCF). The WCF also provides a vertical organizational link between the network of transnational capitalist interests carried by the ICC membership and the untold numbers of small- and medium-sized

Table 2.1 Classification of five leading transnational policy groups

	Neoliberal variant	Agenda priorities	Organizational form	Core membership	Geopolitical reach
International Chamber of Commerce Est. 1919 Paris headquarters	Free-market conservative	Corporate self-regulated, global *laissez faire*	International business organization; government lobbyist; linking to locals	7,000 corporations from 130 countries	Global: corporations & regional committees worldwide, including the Americas, Europe, the Middle East, Africa, and the Asia Pacific
Bilderberg Conference Est. 1952 Netherlands origin	Neoliberal structuralist	Economic order amongst 'Heartland' states	Secretive policy-planning and elite consensus-seeking forum	115 national and international corporate, govt, military and academic elite; no set membership	North Atlantic 'Heartland': draws elite representation from Western Europe, North America
Trilateral Commission Est. 1973 Washington, Paris, & Tokyo headquarters	Neoliberal structuralist	Economic order amongst 'Triad' states	Policy-planning and elite consensus-seeking forum; research task forces; discourse producer	350 national and international corporate, media, academia, public service, and NGO elite	'The Triad': draws elite representation from North Atlantic, Japan, ASEAN
World Economic Forum Est. 1971 Geneva headquarters	Neoliberal structuralist	'Global' economic order	Combined elite transnational business organization, and policy-planning and consensus-seeking forum; research task forces; discourse producer	1,000 top transnational corporations	Global: draws elite representation from Western Europe, Central and Eastern Europe, Africa, North America, Latin America, Asia and Oceania
World Business Council for Sustainable Development Est. 1995 Geneva headquarters	Neoliberal regulationist	'Global' environmental and economic reform	Combined elite transnational business organization, and policy-planning and consensus-seeking forum; research task forces; discourse producer	123 top transnational corporations	Global: draws elite representation from Western Europe, Central and Eastern Europe, Africa, North America, Latin America, Asia and Oceania

businesses which comprise the ranks of local national chambers of commerce. It is, however, a combination of the group's free-market conservative vision, its institutionalization of transnational business practices, and its incorporation of local-level business into a global capitalist perspective, that gives the ICC a unique niche within the organizational ecology of global policy groups.[4]

Offering a counterpoint to the austere, free-market conservative vision of the ICC, the Bilderberg Conferences have provided a context for more comprehensive international capitalist coordination and planning. Founded in 1952, the Bilderberg, named for the Hotel de Bilderberg of Oosterbeek, Holland, 'assembled, in the spirit of corporate liberalism, representatives of Right and Left, capital and organized labor' (van der Pijl 1998: 121). Activities have typically revolved around issues of long-term planning and international order, and to this end Bilderberg Conferences have furnished a confidential platform for corporate, political, intellectual, military, and even trade union elites from the North-Atlantic heartland to reach mutual understanding. The group is run by a chairman, and a small, permanent steering committee, which invites approximately 115 participants to the yearly Conference.

Compared to the ICC, Bilderberg's lack of guaranteed membership, the breadth of its elite constituency and its historically less doctrinaire political agenda have made it a more flexible vehicle for transnational class formation. A good indication of this is the group's migration from a predominantly corporate-liberal strategy, to one that in recent years appears more aligned with neoliberal structuralism. Indeed, by the mid-1990s organized labor was all but excluded – the single invited delegate being John Monks, General Secretary of the British-based Trades Union Congress. While labor was effectively shut out, neoliberal intellectuals – including Timothy Garton Ash of the Hoover Institute, Michael H. Armacost of the Brookings Institution, and William W. Lewis of the McKinsey Global Institute – have attended in numbers.[5]

Emerging at the watershed of recent economic globalization in 1973, The Trilateral Commission (TC) was launched from within the Bilderberg meetings by David Rockefeller as a forum to foster effective collaborative leadership in the international system and closer cooperation among the core capitalist regions of northern Europe, North America and Japan – the 'triad'. It maintains a consultative ruling class tradition, bringing together transnationalized factions of the business, political, and intellectual elite during several yearly meetings, which it convenes at the national, regional, and plenary levels. Unlike the secretive Bilderberg, however, the TC 'sought to develop a profile with greater transparency, public activities and sophisticated publications, responding to the greater sensitivity towards public relations' (van der Pijl 1998: 124). Consistent with this strategy, its magazine, *Trialogue* (first published in October 1973), pioneered what has become a mainstay in the cultural arsenals of transnational business policy groups: the widespread dissemination of neoliberal opinion and analysis, as in the World Economic Forum's *World Link* magazine. A director, three regional chairmen, and three regional executive committees guide the TC; its 350 members are chosen on a national basis.

In marked contrast to the ICC, the TC's attempts to enshrine the discipline of capital have generally favored elements of regulation. In this regard, its influential 1975 report, *The Crisis of Democracy*, called for stronger economic planning measures, including job training and active intervention in the area of work, all in the service of 'sustained expansion of the economy' (quoted in Wolfe 1980: 298). Deeply motivated by the 1970s energy crisis, the TC has also lobbied for integrating capitalism's (semi)periphery into contexts of international regulation, including 'allowing the neocolonies a symbolically greater voice in organizations like the IMF, [and] tying neocolonial economies even closer to Western finance' (see Frieden 1980: 72). An influential series of 'Task Force Reports' (or *Triangle Papers*) on this issue have been delivered over its three-decade history (e.g. Watanabe et al. 1983). Overall, the TC's project is to institutionalize elite economic, political, and intellectual/cultural bonds between the North-Atlantic heartland and the Asia-Pacific and to expand the regulatory sphere of capitalist discipline to incorporate metropolitan labor and (more recently) peripheral states. These aims draw it in line with Robinson and Harris' (2000) neoliberal structuralist formulation.

Founded two years earlier, The World Economic Forum (WEF) convened Europe's CEOs to an informal gathering in Davos, Switzerland to discuss European strategy in an international marketplace. Organized by renowned business policy expert, Klaus Schwab, the meetings were intended to secure the patronage of the Commission of the European Communities, as well as the encouragement of Europe's industry associations. By 1982 the first informal gathering of 'World Economic Leaders' took place on the occasion of the Annual Meeting in Davos, bringing cabinet members of major countries and heads of international organizations (including The World Bank, IMF, GATT) together with a burgeoning core membership of top international capitalists.

The WEF moved beyond the TC to establish 'global initiatives' that distinguish it as the most paradigmatic example of neoliberal structuralism. Initially, the Forum promoted a free-market conservative agenda, but by the mid-1990s persistent capitalist crisis forced it to adopt a more regulatory tack (van der Pijl 1998: 134). By early 1997 the new mood was expressed in a project on 'human social responsibility', followed by a litany of 'social issue' task forces culminating with the Global Health Initiative (2001) and the Global Governance Initiative (2001). These initiatives crosscut with the widespread practices of Corporate Social Responsibility (CSR) among TNCs and the rise of a culture of 'global corporate citizenship' Sklair (2001) considers integral to transnational capitalist class formation.

Unlike the ICC, Bilderberg, and TC, the WEF is organized around a highly elite core of transnational capitalists (the 'Foundation Membership')[6] – which it currently limits to '1,000 of the foremost global enterprises'. Invited 'constituents', however, represent a variegated range of globalist elites, including members of the scientific community, academics, media leaders, public figures, and various NGOs. Constituents populate a hodgepodge of policy work groups and forums, including the InterAcademy Council, the Business Consultative

Group and the Global Leaders of Tomorrow. Like the ICC, however, the WEF actively extends its geopolitical reach and influence. It has done so primarily through yearly meetings apart from Davos and beyond the triad, as in the 1996 meetings in Turkey, China, and India (*Annual Report* 1995–6), and recently established a distinct operating body called the Centre for Regional Strategies (CRS) to 'advance regional development and cooperation in the global economy'.

The last group to have taken up a niche within the field of global elite policy-planning is the World Business Council for Sustainable Development (WBCSD), founded in 1995. It is also the only group that can be characterized within Robinson and Harris' (2000) typology as neoliberal regulationist. Formed in a merger of the Geneva-based Business Council for Sustainable Development and the Paris-based World Industry Council for the Environment (a branch of the ICC), it instantly became the pre-eminent business voice on the environment. By 1997, WBCSD membership comprised 123 top-TNC chief executives.

A child of the UN's Conference on Environment and Development (UNCED) 1992 Rio Earth Summit, the WBCSD reflects a maturing elite awareness that entrenchment and expansion of transnational enterprise must be coupled with consensus over environmental regulation. Drawing primarily on the expertise and prestige of senior transnational executives, it articulated a critical connection between neoliberalism and regulatory struggles over the environment, especially those associated with the UN Environmental Programme (UNEP) and the UN Conference on Trade and Development (UNCTAD). What makes the WBCSD unique in the global policy field are its efforts to surpass the prevailing dualism of 'business versus the environment' by forwarding a more comprehensive vision of capitalist social and moral progress – anchored by its central axiom of 'eco-efficiency'.[7] Within this retooled version of sustainable development business, governments and environmental activists make concessions around a general interest in sustaining both the health of the natural world and the 'health' of the global economy.

The discourses and strategies of the WBCSD work to advance a global regulatory perspective (Robinson and Harris 2000) which moves beyond neoliberal structuralism. The WBCSD's reflexive discursive and organizational frameworks endeavor to draw realms free-market conservatives call 'externalities' – from employee relations to the health and safety of consumers – into an inclusive regulatory regime. The practices and discourses of corporate environmentalism – now employed by TNCs from Proctor & Gamble and Mitsubishi to Monsanto and Broken Hill Proprietary – are vital in this regard, and have in their own right contributed to a persuasive globalizing capitalist ideology (Sklair 2001). What the WBCSD furnishes is a reflexive orchestration of these corporate initiatives into a class-wide hegemonic project.

With these five policy groups we can see how variants of transnational neoliberalism have found organizational bases in the policy-formation field. Only the International Chamber of Commerce functions from the perspective of free-market conservatism and speaks for and to a strictly business-centered constituency. The Bilderberg group, Trilateral Commission, and World Economic

Forum in their own ways incorporate broadly neoliberal structuralist perspectives. The most recent addition to the field, the World Business Council for Sustainable Development, orients itself primarily in terms of neoliberal regulationism. Taken as a whole, these global policy groups can be regarded as agencies of transnational capitalist class formation. They provide intellectual leadership that is indispensable in the ongoing effort to transform transnational capital from an economically dominant class to a class whose interests take on a sense of universalism. The empirical questions to which we turn now concern the social relations that embed these groups within a structure of global corporate power.

The global corporate-policy network[8]

Our empirical analysis maps the social structure of the global corporate elite, the collection of leading corporate directors who participate in the network of major corporations and transnational policy groups. Our analysis is restricted to what we consider *the global corporate elite* – those directing at least one of the top 350 global corporations and one other organization in our sample (whether corporation or policy group). These 622 individuals are a globally-connected subset of the 6,751 directors of the world's major corporations.

Our first research question directs attention to the individuals who carry the transnational network: who are they and how do they create social structure through their group-affiliations? We find that the network's *inner circle of cosmopolitan linkers* – 105 corporate directors whose affiliations span national borders, or link global policy boards to each other.[9] Through their networking, these 105 individuals make the most immediate structural contributions to transnational class formation. Indeed, the six most well-connected people create through their directorships a tightly-knit nucleus of 18 corporations and four policy groups (see Table 2.2). Most of the six directors sit together on multiple policy boards. Bertrand Collomb (president of Lafarge and 1997 'manager of the year' according to *Le Nouvel Economiste*) sits on all four policy boards and thus meets Minoru Murofushi, Chair of Itochu Corporation, on three of them. Within this nucleus the integrative function of the policy boards is clear: without them these transnational linkers would be for the most part detached from each other; with them they comprise a tightly-knit social unit, with representation from the US, Britain, Japan and continental Europe.

When we extend the analysis to all corporate directors with two or more policy-group affiliations, we add to the nucleus 11 individuals, 14 corporations and the remaining policy group (the ICC) (see Table 2.3). This core group of 17 individuals provides all the direct linkages among the five global policy boards. Within it the integrative role of the four policy groups stands out. For instance, all three Japanese directors in the core group sit on both the TC and WBCSD. Not only do these policy boards serve as transnational meeting points for the Japanese directors, equally, these individuals serve as ambassadors between the fields of global policy work and of Japanese corporate governance, while also linking the TC with the WBCSD. As a group, the core group shows an obvious

Table 2.2 The nucleus of six corporate directors and their organizational affiliations

Name	Policy boards	Corp. boards	Corp. statuses
Paul Allaire	TC	Xerox	President
	Bilderberg	Sara Lee	Director
	WBCSD	Lucent	Director
		SmithKline	Director
Percy Barnevik	Bilderberg	ABB	President
	WBCSD	Dupont	Director
	WEF	GM	Director
Bertrand Collomb	Bilderberg	Aquitaine	Director
	WBCSD	Unilever	Director
	WEF	CIBC	Director
Etienne Davignon	Bilderberg	Fortis	Dep. Chair
	TC	Generale Bank	Director
		Fina	Director
		BASF	Director
Minoru Murofushi	TC	Itochu	Chair
	WBCSD	HSBC	Director
	WEF		
Peter Sutherland	Bilderberg	BP	Vice-Chair
	WEF	ABB	Director
		Ericsson	Director

Table 2.3 Eleven additional members of the core group and their organizational affiliations

Name	Policy boards	Corp. boards	Corp. status
Conrad M. Black	TC	CIBC	Director
	Bilderberg		
John H. Bryan	Bilderberg	Sara Lee	President
	WEF		
Livio D. Desimone	ICC	3M	President
	WBCSD		
George M. Fisher	TC	Eastman Kodak	President
	WBCSD		
Rokuro Ishikawa	TC	Kajima	Chair
	WBCSD		
Donald R. Keough	TC	Home	Depot Director
	WEF		
Henry Kissinger	Bilderberg	Amex	Director
	TC		
Helmut O. Maucher	ICC	Nestlé	Chair
	WEF		
Kosuka Morita	TC	Hitachi	Man. Director
	WBCSD	Bank of Yokohama	Man. Director
J.B. Prescott	WBCSD	BHP	CEO
	WEF		
Robert N. Wilson	TC	Johnson & Johnson	Vice-Chair
	WBCSD		

Note: To simplify the presentation only the main corporate affiliations are shown.

Euro-North American bias. Corporations sited on the semi-periphery are entirely absent from it, and only five Asia-Pacific companies (four of them Japanese) are represented.

The network as an inter-organizational field

We now move to a representation of the corporate-policy network as a set of inter-organizational relations. In Figure 2.1 the Trilateral Commission emerges as a central meeting point for the transnational corporate elite, but the WBCSD also plays a highly integrative role. In contrast to the other groups, the ICC's distinctive contribution to transnational class formation is to integrate global capitalism's center with its margins; hence the ICC board blends a smattering of the global corporate elite with various representatives of national and local capital.[10]

If direct interlocks among policy boards provide some basis for elite consensus-formation, another source of elite integration can be found in the extent to which the *social circles* of the policy groups intersect. A social circle is the set of organizations with which a given organization is directly linked. An overlap between social circles means that the same corporate boards that interlock with one policy group also interlock with the other. Table 2.4 lists the 27 corporations maintaining at least three directorship interlocks with the policy groups. Heading the list is Zurich-based industrial conglomerate ABB, whose directors serve on all

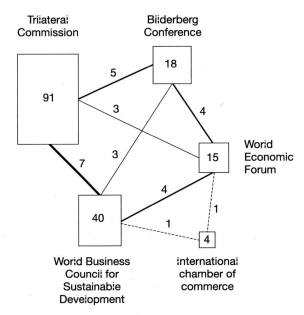

Figure 2.1 Number of interlocks among five global policy groups, 1996
Note: Boxes are proportionate in size to the number of corporate-elite members affiliated with each group (indicated in each box). Line thicknesses reflect the number of shared elite members.

five policy boards. Although there is no one 'nationality' that predominates in the policy-board social circles, the North Atlantic presence is striking. Extensive interlocking with policy boards is the prerogative of the corporations listed in Table 2.4, all but two of which interlock with multiple policy groups. The 27 corporations, barely 8 per cent of our sample, account for 128 of the 305 directorship interlocks between all corporations and the five global policy groups. Moreover, corporations whose boards overlap with the policy groups also tend to be central in the network of corporate interlocks.[11] However, 198 of our 350 corporations, including nearly all companies domiciled in the semi-periphery, share no directors with the policy groups. The only really salient regional fracture in the network is the massive divide between the world system's center and its (semi)periphery.

The integrative contribution of elite policy groups

To test the integrative impact of policy-board affiliations we calculated the extent to which corporate ties to the policy groups *reduce the distance between corporations* in

Table 2.4 Numbers of corporate directors on five global policy boards

Corporation	Domicile	TC	WBCDS	BLD	WEF	ICC	Total
ABB	Switzerland	2	2	2	3	1	10
CIBC	Canada	4	1	2	1	0	8
GM	USA	1	3	2	2	0	8
Unilever	Dutch/UK	3	2	1	1	0	7
Sara Lee	USA	2	1	3	1	0	7
Xerox	USA	2	3	2	0	0	7
BP	UK	1	2	1	1	0	5
Aquitaine	France	1	1	2	1	0	5
Nestlé	Swiss	1	2	0	1	1	5
Hong Kong Saving Bank	UK	2	1	0	1	0	4
Fina (Total)	Belgium	3	0	1	0	0	4
Generale Bank (Fortis Bank)	Belgium	3	0	1	0	0	4
Ericsson	Sweden	1	0	2	1	0	4
Kansai Energy	Japan	4	0	0	0	0	4
3M	USA	2	1	0	0	1	4
American International	USA	3	0	1	0	0	4
Chase Manhattan	USA	4	0	0	0	0	4
Dayton Hudson	USA	2	1	0	0	1	4
Lucent	USA	2	1	1	0	0	4
SmithKline Beecham	UK	1	1	1	0	0	3
Deutsche Bank	Germany	1	0	1	1	0	3
Siemens	Germany	1	0	1	1	0	3
VW	Germany	2	0	0	1	0	3
Itochu	Japan	1	1	0	1	0	3
American Express	USA	1	0	2	0	0	3
DuPont	USA	0	1	1	1	0	3
Prudential	USA	3	0	0	0	0	3

the global network. To calculate this reduction we examined the distances between points in the inter-corporate network, with and without the mediating ties provided by policy-group affiliations.[12] At this systemic level, the contribution of the policy groups to overall network integration is quite striking. Overall, the mean distance between corporations falls from 4.91 to 3.09 when we take into account directors' affiliations with policy boards. At the outer reaches of the network, the diameter (the largest distance between two points) drops from 15 to 9.

A key issue is whether the broad pattern of participation in the policy groups draws corporate capital sited in particular locations in world system into the international business community. To assess this we calculated the mean distance among corporations based in different countries, with and without corporate-policy board ties in the analysis. When only corporate interlocks are considered it is north-west continental Europe that is most transnationally integrated (see Figure 2.2).[13] Mean distances among the German, Dutch, Swiss, Swedish and Belgian networks are typically less than 3.0. We find Spanish- and Italian-based firms and companies based in Australia and Hong Kong in somewhat peripheral locations, and Mexican and Japanese corporations in very peripheral locations. The largest mean distances in the international network occur between Italian and Japanese firms (9.88) and between Mexican and Japanese firms (9.33).

In the second step (Figure 2.3), when we included the corporate-policy interlocks as indirect, mediating ties, mean transnational distances decreased sharply.

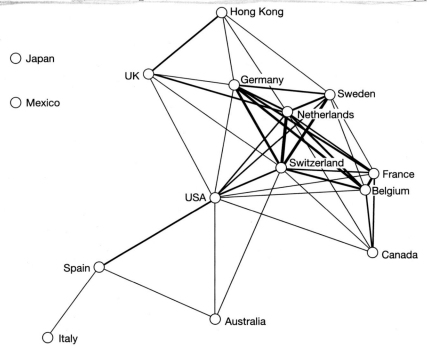

Figure 2.2 Mean inter-national distances among 271 corporations, based on corporate interlocks only

Companies sited in the three Anglo-American countries – heavy participants on the policy boards – become fully integrated with the continental European bloc, whose own transnational distances fall further. Once the policy-board ties are taken into account, the mean distances between corporate Japan and firms domiciled in the North Atlantic plummet from a range of 6.15 to 8.00 to a range of 3.33 to 3.64, showing that for corporate Japan the policy groups play an important bridging role into global management. However, firms domiciled outside the North-Atlantic heartland remain relatively peripheral. Thus, the pattern of differential regional participation in the network is maintained, even as the absolute distances drop.

Discussion

In conclusion, let us first revisit our three research questions and take stock of what we have learned. The first question we posed concerned the role of key individuals at the centre of the network. We have found that a few dozen cosmopolitans – primarily men based in Europe and North America and actively engaged in corporate management – knit the corporate-policy network together

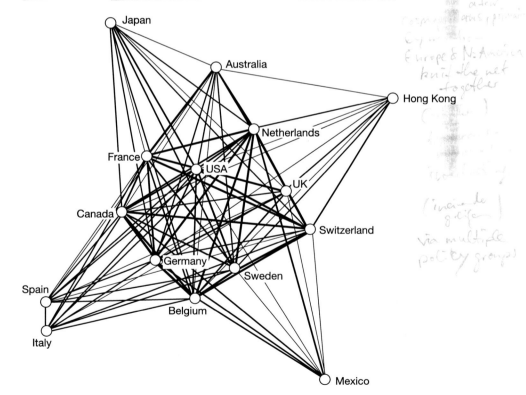

Figure 2.3 Mean inter-national distances among 271 corporations, including paths mediated by five global policy groups

by participating in transnational interlocking and/or multiple global policy groups. This inner circle creates the interlocks that make the network a transnational formation. A mere 17 corporate directors, some of whom serve on as many as four policy boards, create a plethora of relations among the policy groups. As a structure supporting transnational capitalist class formation, the network is highly centralized in the individuals and organizations that participate in it. Yet from its core it extends unevenly to corporations and individuals positioned on its fringes.

Our second question focused on the organizational level, at which we found that the neoliberal policy groups differ markedly in the extent to which the directors of the world's leading corporations participate on their boards. The International Chamber of Commerce (ICC), whose contribution to transnational capitalist class formation is focused around the integration of the center with its margins within a discourse of free-market conservatism, is least involved at the core of the network. In contrast, the other four groups, which advocate more structuralist or regulationist variants of neoliberalism, are deeply enmeshed within the global corporate elite. They are substantially interlocked with each other as well as with common corporate boards, a small number of which account for two-fifths of all the corporate-policy links. Most significantly, while the North Atlantic is especially well represented in the contingent of interlocked corporations, corporate capital domiciled outside the world system's core states is almost entirely detached, suggesting that van der Pijl's (1984) image of a North Atlantic ruling class retained its cogency to the close of the twentieth century. Compared to this dominant pattern, other elements of possible fractionation – as in the elective affinities that appear to attract financial capital to the Trilateral Commission (TC) and industrial capital to the World Business Council for Sustainable Development (WBCSD) – barely register.

Finally, although the practice of interlocking corporate directorates already links most of the world's leading corporations into a single network, the neoliberal policy boards make a dramatic contribution to global corporate-elite integration. This additional layer of social structure, within which leading corporate capitalists step beyond their immediate economic interests to take up matters of global concern, pulls the directorates of the world's major corporations much closer together, and collaterally integrates the lifeworld of the global corporate elite. But if the policy groups mediate and thereby strengthen inter-corporate relations they do so selectively, in a way that reproduces regional differences in participation. Thus, even as the presence of 27 Japanese corporate directors, distributed among three of the five policy boards, pulls corporate Japan closer to the network's North Atlantic center-of-gravity, that center becomes even more tightly bound through the heavy participation of North Americans and Europeans on the policy boards.

These findings support the claim that a well-integrated global corporate elite or business community has formed, and that neoliberal policy groups, themselves vehicles of globalization, have been instrumental in its formation. Whether this elite confirms the arrival of a transnational capitalist class is partly a matter of semantics and partly a matter of substance. From one perspective, it is striking how selective participation in the corporate-policy network is, and how centralized its structure is. Within an already elite group of leading corporations and corporate directors, those who actually constitute the network comprise a small core of cosmopolitan individuals and corporations, with a strongly Euro–North American bias. In contrast, most individuals who participate in the global network do not hold elite positions beyond their home nation. As a mode of business activism the network, centralized as it is around a compact inner circle, evokes the image of a vanguard more than a mass movement. Yet as we have seen, it comprises a single connected formation, with considerable reach, and the policy boards effectively draw the national sub-networks into an integrated transnational structure. Moreover, claims about the formation of a transnational capitalist class do *not* depend exclusively on the structure of elite networks. Sklair (2001), for example, points to cultural practices – the worldly assumption of social responsibility, the shared ideology of consumerism – as integral aspects of transnational capitalist class formation. As Gramsci understood, class formation involves both structure and culture, and although network analysis gives some purchase on the former we have done no more than telegraph some of the discursive elements of neoliberal globalization as a hegemonic project.

However one might assess the thesis of transnational class formation, conspicuously absent from the corporate-policy network are corporations and capitalists based on the periphery and semi-periphery of the world system, and in this sense the network seems to present one facet of a collective imperialism, organized so as to help manage global capitalism from the center (see Steven 1994). In the blending of persuasion and coercion that such management entails, the policy groups clearly seek to persuade. They operate at one remove from the structural adjustment programs, 'poverty reduction strategies' and other enforcement mechanisms, including military intervention, that are the province of statist bodies, whether national or international. They foster discussion of global issues among members of the corporate elite, often in combination with other influential political and professional elites. They facilitate the formation of a moving elite consensus that is framed within one or another variant of neoliberal discourse. They educate publics and states on the virtues of the neoliberal paradigm. In short, they are agencies of political and cultural leadership, whose activities are integral to the formation of a transnational capitalist class.

The network of interlocks between neoliberal policy boards and the world's major corporations forms an important communication structure in this process. All five of the policy groups are embedded in the global network, and with extensive interlocking among four of them and a key elite-level connection between the most 'regulationist' and most 'free-market' group,[14] there is no evidence of political fracture along the lines of Robinson and Harris's (2000) typology. By the same token, each group has its own history and modus operandi, occupies a unique niche in the organizational ecology of transnational neoliberalism, and finds a distinctive location in the network. We have seen that the ICC is comparatively marginal to the life of the global corporate elite as we have defined it, yet its policy work sustains a very broad network that links local capital from sites throughout the world system into the center, in a hard-line project of free-market conservatism. In contrast, the Bilderberg Conference is exclusively Euro-North American and well ensconced in the corporate network, and its gatherings bring business leaders together with political leaders in informal discussions that have tended to promote a neoliberalism that retains a managerial role for the state. The World Economic Forum (WEF) and Trilateral Commission (TC), both strongly integrated with the corporate network, champion a similar project, but they render it more tangible in the activities of various working groups and the issuance of extensive policy documents and other texts. Both groups bring together agents and interests beyond the Euro-North American core and beyond the corporate elite *per se*, in explicit attempts to articulate a global political-economic interest. Finally, the WBCSD extends the general interest to the peaceful coexistence of capitalism and nature, and like the WEF and TC, draws Japanese business leaders into the network. Instead of political fracture, we submit that neoliberalism's own pluralism, as enunciated by the different groups, ensures that the consensus is a loose and variegated one, not a monolithic doctrine.

Although our systematic data refer to 1996/7, subsequent developments suggest that the policy groups have continued their efforts to articulate a general transnational interest within a broadly neoliberal paradigm, but not without significant contestation, beginning with the 'Battle in Seattle' that raged around the World Trade Organization's 1999 Ministerial meeting and continuing through the mass protests that have greeted meetings of the IMF and World Bank in Washington (April 2000) and in Prague (September 2000), and the World Economic Forum in Davos (2000) and New York (2002). Against these de-legitimating moves from below, we can note that in July 1999 the UN Secretary-General and the President of the ICC announced a 'global compact' between the UN and the private sector 'to spread the benefits of globalization'; that as of 2000 the Trilateral Commission was restructured to include representation of the Asia-Pacific semi-periphery (People's Republic of China, Taiwan, Thailand); and that in 2000–1 the World Economic Forum began to include NGOs representing 'civil society' in its annual deliberations and designated a Non-Governmental Organizations Council. For its part the World Business Council for Sustainable Development continued to expand its project of corporate environmental hegemony, forging a crucial regulatory alliance of transnational capitalist development. The structural analysis we have presented here provides only a glimpse of a contentious formation that is very much under construction.

Notes

1 'The Transnational Ruling Class Formation Thesis: A Symposium', in *Science & Society*, 2001–2, 65(4): 464–508.
2 These include Mexico in 1995, Asia in 1997, and Russia and Brazil in 1998.
3 Sklair (2001), quite similarly, sees 'proactive global corporate citizenship' as a cornerstone of contemporary processes of transnational capitalist class formation.

4 For instance, see the *Building Cooperation in Africa Report* (December 2001) and the *ICC Business Charter for Sustainable Development* (April 1991).
5 *The Spotlight* – Special Bilderberg Issue, 1995–6.
6 https://members.weforum.org/site/homepublic.nsf/Content/Our+Organization%5CForum+Centres.
7 'Eco-efficiency' was first coined by the WBCSD in 1992. In its *1997 Annual Review*, the WBCSD defined eco-efficiency as 'a management approach ... that allows companies to improve their environmental performance while meeting the demands of the market ... [by increasing] economic and ecological efficiency' (8).
8 The following is an abridged account of our method, network analysis and findings. For full details see Carroll and Carson (2003).
9 These directors are cosmopolitans much in the sense originally employed by Gouldner (1957): they are oriented not toward particular national firms and networks but toward a wider field of action.
10 Specifically, its 1996 executive board of 27 members and international officers included 12 corporate directors based on the semi-periphery, 11 based in Europe, three in the USA or Canada, and one in Japan.
11 Among our 350 corporations, the Pearson correlation between n of interlocks with policy groups and n of interlocks with other corporations is 0.434.
12 The distance between two points in a network is the 'shortest path' between them: the minimum number of steps one must take to reach one point from the other. Corporate boards that are directly interlocked are connected at a distance of 1; corporate boards that are not interlocked but that both share directors with a third board are connected at distance 2, and so on.
13 Note that the thickest lines represent the shortest mean distances. Mean distances greater than 4 are represented as absent ties, although in fact all corporations in the component are, by definition, ultimately connected. The full matrices of mean distances are available from the first author.
14 Note that the Chair of the regulationist WBCSD is also an *ex officio* director of the ICC, owing to the ICC's founding sponsorship of the WBCSD.

3 Peddling reform: the role of think tanks in shaping the neoliberal policy agenda for the World Bank and International Monetary Fund

Christian E. Weller and Laura Singleton

Neoliberals have established an influential network of think tanks, foundations, media and policymakers to further their agenda. In the US, this network has helped to advocate publicly for neoliberal policies, even when conservatives' grip on power was loose. One example was the Meltzer Commission that was charged with reviewing the international financial institutions (IFIs) in the wake of the Asian financial crisis.

Following the Asian and Russian crises in 1998, US policymakers began to vigorously debate the future of the IFIs, especially the World Bank and International Monetary Fund (IMF). Central to the discussion were the questions why these international institutions had been unable to prevent, or at least anticipate, the impending financial disasters, and what actions could be taken to remedy these institutional failures.

Two options emerged for the IFIs: reform or abolition. To explore potential reform options and to recommend future US policy toward the seven IFIs,[1] Congress established, in connection with the authorization of $18 billion in additional US funding for the IMF, the International Financial Institution Advisory Commission in November 1998, also known as the Meltzer Commission.

The Republican-controlled Congress appointed six of the commission's eleven members,[2] while the Democrats appointed the remaining five commissioners.[3] The Commission's final report received a lot of attention and gained notoriety for its thinly veiled attempts to eliminate the IFIs. Perhaps most decisive in ensuring the Commission's infamy was the appointment of Allan Meltzer as its chairman. An unyielding advocate of free markets and a well-known critic of the World Bank and the IMF, there was little doubt that the tenor of the Commission's findings would fall squarely in the abolitionist camp, although with a market-based twist.

The importance of the Meltzer Commission is twofold. First, it reflects the neoliberal agenda that in addition to furthering free market principles is also a thinly veiled attempt to undermine the IFIs, thereby ensuring their eventual demise. Second, it represents the canonization of the anti-IFI sentiments of the political right,[4] and thus gave strength to the neoliberal reform efforts. Although the Commission's proposals were not enacted, many of the ideas continued to inform the debate with respect to international development finance in subsequent US Congresses and presidential administrations.

This chapter examines not only the Meltzer Commission and its recommendations, but we also trace its neoliberal ideological development and movement from academia and think tanks to the political realm, and analyze the neoliberal support structure in which it operated.

Neoliberalism and the Mont Pèlerin Society

During the political and social changes that ensued following the Second World War, many western intellectuals feared that (European) liberalism was threatened. A small group of these intellectuals decided to form an association, the Mont Pèlerin Society (MPS, see Plehwe and Walpen in this volume) that would work to promote and to preserve small, decentralized governments worldwide.

The Society's 'Statement of Aims,' issued in 1947, simultaneously outlined the perceived problem and proposed corresponding action. The MPS asserted that the rise of totalitarian and authoritarian regimes had been 'fostered by the growth of a view of history which denies all absolute moral standards and by the growth of theories which question the desirability of the rule of law' and 'by a decline of belief in private property and the competitive market'. The latter, it was argued, is imperative, 'for without the diffused power and initiative associated with these institutions it is difficult to imagine a society in which freedom may be effectively preserved' (MPS 2002).

The MPS identified and developed many venues of academic research to defend and to promote a world order based upon open markets and small governments. It was established to facilitate the intellectual exchange between neoliberal researchers and scholars, which would in turn assist the spread of free market practices and policies around the globe.

Policy influence through a network of think tanks, media, foundations and policymakers

A partial list of MPS membership illustrates the ideological links between various US research institutes, universities, government and media. The four most frequent think tank associations of MPS members in the US are AEI, Cato, Heritage, and the Hoover Institution on War, Revolution and Peace. Affiliated with Stanford University, the Hoover Institution occupies a privileged intellectual position in scholarly and policy debates. Started by Herbert Hoover in 1919, the Institution seeks 'to secure and safeguard peace, improve the human condition, and limit government intrusion into the lives of individuals' through recognizing 'the principles of individual, economic, and political freedom; private enterprise; and representative government' (Hoover Institution 2002).

The Hoover Institution has strong ties to the MPS as well as to the other think tanks. For example, Edwin Feulner, president of the Heritage Foundation, was a Hoover fellow, as was Gary Becker, MPS president from 1990–2, Milton Friedman, MPS president from 1970–2, James Buchanan, MPS president from 1984–6 and a Cato fellow, and Michael Boskin, chairman of Bush Sr.'s Council of Economic Advisors and a fellow at the AEI.

Moreover, the Hoover Institution not only reflects the academic and political influence of MPS members, but also their close ties to the media. Appropriately entitled Hoover Media Fellows, the program enables print and broadcast journalists to spend time in residence at Hoover to exchange information and perspectives with Hoover fellows through seminars, informal meetings, and public lectures. Additionally, the Institution makes all of its research resources available to the Media Fellows. As testament to the program's success, many US-based MPS members maintain close ties to both Hoover and a media group, most frequently the *Wall Street Journal*.

A more academic research network that has aided the neoliberal cause to some degree, in particular with respect to international economic issues, is the National Bureau of Economic Research (NBER). The NBER was founded in 1920 to promote economic research. Theoretically, 'the NBER is committed to undertaking and disseminating unbiased economic research among public policymakers, business professionals, and the academic community'. The NBER publishes research faster than academic journals do, thereby largely determining what research will receive wide attention. Although the NBER is nominally independent, it has received almost $10 million from staunchly conservative foundations over the years (Media Transparency 2002).[5]

Moreover, the NBER has played an important role in promoting neoliberal policies with respect to international economic issues due to its president since 1977, Professor Martin Feldstein, an MPS member who served as chairman of President Reagan's Council of Economic Advisors. His writings include strong criticisms of the World Bank and the IMF (for example: Feldstein 1999, 2002). As if to eliminate any notions of impartiality, one of Feldstein's protégés, Richard Clarida, reported that '[n]obody gets very involved in the Bureau without Marty wanting it to happen' (Media Transparency 2002). Moreover, Feldstein's influence extends easily into the political realm. Much of President George W. Bush's economic team studied under, or was recommended by, Professor Feldstein. Among these are Lawrence Lindsey, R. Glen Hubbard, Richard Clarida, Assistant Secretary of the Treasury for Economic Policy, and Paul O'Neill, former Secretary of the Treasury. Indeed, Feldstein is generally credited as the father of 'supply-side' economics and helped to create President George W. Bush's 2001 tax cut plan (Leonhardt 2002).

Aside from the use of think tanks and the media to advance the neoliberal policy agenda, several well-endowed foundations enabled these institutions to conduct and promote their research. One of the reasons the neoliberal network has been so successful is that it understands government policy is based upon, and has subsequently developed, 'a conveyer belt of thinkers, academics, and activists' (People for the American Way 2002: 4) to promote their agenda. Thus, foundations give money to a variety of sources to promote its neoliberal philosophies. Among the various recipients of conservative foundation funds are think tanks, which serve to package and repackage conservative policy ideas, academics, who push the intellectual boundaries on various issues, and graduate students, who form the next generation of conservative researchers. An analysis of conservative foundations and American politics done by the People for the American Way (2002) – a progressive advocacy and research group – emphasized the role of think tanks, funded by conservative foundations, in conservative policy formation. One journalist noted that '[W]ith increasing frequency, legislation, proposed and enacted, can be traced directly to think-tank position papers on such conservative agenda items as welfare cuts, privatization of public services, private options and parental choice in schools, deregulation of workplace safety, tax limitations and other reductions in government, even selling of the national parks' (People for the American Way 2002).

Most notable among the conservative foundations are the Bradley, Olin, Scaife and Smith Foundations. The Bradley Foundation provides substantial aid to academia, specifically toward research, program development, and graduate student studies, as well as to controversial and conservative publications. The Olin Foundation provides financing for AEI, Heritage and Hoover, as well as supporting academics and university programs that embrace ultraconservative economic and social policies. The Scaife Foundation provides generous funding to AEI, Heritage, Cato, and Hoover. Finally, the Smith Foundation, frequently referred to as one of the 'four sisters', generally funds in conjunction with the Bradley, Olin and Scaife Foundations. As a result, the AEI received $2.2 million from these four foundations in 2001, the Heritage Foundation $2.5 million and the Cato Institute $0.9 million (Media Transparency 2002).

The funding from the conservative foundations alone was almost half as large as the total funding of four leading left-leaning think tanks. The Center for Policy Alternatives, the Institute for Policy Studies, the Center for Budget and Policy Priorities and the Economic Policy Institute had a combined budget of $10.2 million (PFAW 2002).

The Meltzer Commission's Report and its recommendation

The Meltzer Commission exemplifies both the neoliberal policy orientation with respect to international economic development and the intricate workings of the MPS.

In its final report, the majority of the Meltzer Commission proposed a reorganization of the global financial architecture. To reform the IFIs, it advocated the restructuring of programs to alter incentives for both the donor institutions and the recipients as well as the delineation of donor institutions' responsibilities to prevent an overlapping of activities. The proposed reforms would have dramatically altered the current financial landscape, if they had been enacted.

The Meltzer Commission addressed the future role of the IMF at length in its final report. While the majority of the Commission conceded that the IMF should remain the global financial crisis manager, it outlined a new set of procedures to guide IMF intervention in the case of financial crises. First, the majority agreed that 'the IMF should serve as quasi lender of last resort to emerging economies' (Meltzer 2000). Such lending should be limited to the provision of short-term funds to solvent member governments at a penalty rate and should be guaranteed by a priority claim on the borrowing country's assets.

Additionally, the IMF could act as a stand-by lender to prevent financial panics or crises. To qualify for short-term loans, countries would have to meet four conditions. First, the countries would have to allow free entry of foreign financial institutions. Second, borrowers would have to publish the maturity structure of their debts. Third, commercial banks would have to be adequately capitalized. Finally, 'a proper fiscal requirement', as defined by the IMF, would have to be realized 'to assure that IMF resources would not be used to sustain irresponsible budget priorities' (Meltzer 2000).

The Commission's majority also agreed that long-term lending for development assistance, poverty reduction, and structural transformation would remain the purview of the World Bank and the regional development banks. To achieve this goal, the majority argued that the banks must be transformed from capital-intensive lending institutions 'to sources of technical assistance, providers of regional and global public goods, and facilitators of an increased flow of private sector resources to the emerging countries' (Meltzer 2000). Central to this paradigm shift would be the gradual elimination of all resource transfers to countries with capital market access or an annual per capita income greater than $4,000 over the subsequent five years. In addition, the banks would limit assistance to countries with an annual per capita income greater than $2,500.

Development assistance would instead be provided through performance-based grants. Instead of giving governments money to either subsidize or fully fund health care, education and physical infrastructure, the banks would pay these fees directly to the service provider. Service providers could be either private entities or public agencies, and contracts would be awarded to the most competitive bidder.

Also, institutional reform loans would be granted based upon the merits of government reform programs. In the poorest nations, lending 'should be conditional upon implementation of specific institutional and policy changes and supported by financial incentives to promote continuing implementation' (Meltzer 2000).

A counter-productive development framework

Four issues raised by the Commission's report – debt forgiveness, capital controls, development policies, and loss of national sovereignty – warrant further consideration as they raise concerns for sustainable development in emerging economies. For instance, the Commission agreed that debt forgiveness for highly indebted poor countries (HIPCs) should be one of the first steps in reforming global finance. While this goal is certainly laudable, the Commission's majority would have attached unacceptable conditions to debt forgiveness. The second issue is capital controls. The Commission did not recognize these as useful public policy tools. Furthermore, its recommendations regarding the usage and appropriateness of capital controls are contradictory.

And moreover, the Commission's report raised concern about the possible adverse effects from the proposed mix of economic policies for emerging economies. Generally, the Commission defined the parameters of the development debate too narrowly. More specifically, the Commission encouraged fiscal and monetary restraint and financial deregulation – all of which have been shown to be harmful to the majority of people by reducing employment and wage growth – and ignored the widespread criticism that increased labor market flexibility has also hurt the world's workers. Moreover, its recommendations for the World Bank were bound by a similar narrow-mindedness. While the Commission advocated a shift in emphasis at the World Bank from lending to grant giving, it would have required the World Bank to attach conditions to these grants that, in reality, would have been untenable. As a result of the proposed economic policies, the loss of national sovereignty for many industrializing economies would be accelerated.

Although there may be a number of examples for inefficient governments, development economists have increasingly recognized that successful development policies have to be tailored to each country's institutional context. For instance, Aidt and Tzannatos (2002) conclude that well-functioning labor market institutions, embedded in each country's economic and political institutions, can help to promote stable and sustainable growth. The loss of national sovereignty, which would in essence result in a persistent policy framework of 'one-size-fits-all' development policies, would undermine such country specific and promising development strategies.

Debt forgiveness

The Commission unanimously agreed that the HIPCs' debt should be forgiven. Under what conditions the debt should be forgiven, however, was a point of contention among the commissioners. The Commission's majority recommended that debt forgiveness be conditional upon the adoption of fiscal restraint, capital account liberalization and flexible exchange-rate arrangements or currency boards. These conditions would also logically require monetary restraint and financial market deregulation and would generally accompany labor market deregulation. Although there is a history of strong criticism of the IMF and World Bank's labor market policies, reiterated in Democratic commissioner Levinson's separate dissenting statement (Levinson 2000), the Commission's majority failed to meaningfully address them. This obvious omission would seem to indicate that the majority implicitly endorsed increased labor market flexibility as part of an effective development policy.

Unfortunately, the majority's policies are harmful to the poorest countries. Pro-cyclical macro policies, such as tight fiscal and monetary policy in the middle of an economic downturn, hamper growth and aggravate the burden of business cycles. Similarly, several researchers have identified financial market liberalization as one of the root causes of the increased frequency of currency crises (Arestis and Demetriades 1999; Kaminsky and Reinhart 1999; Weller 2001). As much as the Commission did to push the envelope on debt forgiveness, attaching it to harmful policies made the recommendation a damaging policy proposal. Indeed, the Commission's majority's strict conditions would effectively have offset and undermined the value of debt forgiveness to poor countries. In contrast to the majority, the minority did not attach a lengthy set of conditions to debt forgiveness and merely advocated the complete elimination of debt.

Capital controls

Capital controls are useful public policy tools. Even the IMF, which still champions capital account liberalization as witnessed in its September 2002 World Economic Outlook (IMF 2002), has acknowledged the importance of capital controls – albeit under certain circumstances – in its own recent study on 14 developing economies (Ariyoshi et al. 2000). Given the present financial climate, which is characterized by more frequent and bigger financial crises, it seems understandable that some countries may want to use capital controls to maintain control over their own economic policies and to protect themselves from the vagaries of global financial markets.

Financial liberalization limits a country's ability to use capital controls as a policy tool for long-term projects or for socially desirable outcomes. The limitations of financial liberalization were illustrated in France where the government, under pressures from international capital markets, abandoned its attempts to use expansionary fiscal and monetary policies to fight unemployment in 1982.

Furthermore, short-term capital flows, better known as 'hot money,' have been identified as one of the major causes of economic instability in developing economies. The quick resumption of short-term lending following economic crises, as was illustrated in the mid- to late 1990s, is testament to the need for capital controls on 'hot money'. For example, following years of capital outflows in Mexico, international investors loaned it $1.3 billion in short-term loans in the fourth quarter of 1995, less than a year after its crisis. These short-term loans continued to increase through the third quarter of 1996, totaling a stunning $8.3 billion in that quarter alone. Similarly, short-term loans to Korea resumed about a year after its crisis, with $1.3 billion in the third quarter of 1998 and $2.8 billion in the first quarter of 1999, thus reaching almost pre-crisis heights.

By slowing capital inflows with the help of capital controls, countries can reduce the pool of funds that can be removed from the economy at the first sign of trouble, the rapid removal of which could precipitate a crisis. Thus, the Commission should have given more consideration to the role of capital controls, especially since its own thinking on capital controls seems internally contradictory. Evidence of these incompatible policy proposals can be found in its recommendations for the IMF and the World Bank, as the Commission's proposal for each institution implicitly requires different approaches to capital controls.

The Commission's proposals for the IMF would require a reduction in use of capital controls. To pre-qualify for IMF stand-by facilities, countries would have to allow for the free entry and operation of foreign banks. Similarly, the Commission recommended that client countries establish fully flexible exchange rates or currency boards. The Commission calls for these extreme choices – either entirely fixed or fully flexible exchange rates – because they are immune or respond instantaneously to large swings in capital flows. However, in economies with capital controls in place, capital flows have less impact on exchange rates and the choice of a regime is less of an issue. Thus, the recommendation for an exchange rate regime only makes sense if capital controls are expected to be reduced.

The need for the IMF as lender-of-last-resort would actually decline if capital markets were more regulated and capital controls were used more effectively. The report, however, seemed to accept the view that markets, especially capital markets, are efficient, and that capital flows will take capital to where it is most productive. Hence, the majority accepted the notion that opening borders and letting private investors decide what projects are the most efficient would enhance global competitiveness and make everybody better off. According to this rationale, labor and environmental standards are seen as barriers to capital efficiency and thus counter to economic efficiency.

In reality, however, investors may not invest in the most efficient projects. They may disregard productive investments if speculation is more profitable. The disruptive effects of speculative investments were felt by Turkey in 1994, by Thailand, Malaysia, Indonesia, and Korea in 1997 and 1998, and by Russia in 1998. These are not isolated events. An IMF study in 1996 reported that two-thirds of IMF member countries experienced serious banking-sector problems between 1980 and 1996 when capital markets became more liberalized (Lindgren *et al.* 1996). In a summary of studies on capital mobility, Blecker (1999) found that, at least for developing economies, there was strong evidence that increased capital mobility raises the likelihood of crises. Weller (2001) also found that countries became systematically more susceptible to crises after financial market deregulation. Thus, the IMF recommendations for fewer capital controls were partly responsible for the increased frequency of financial crisis. Therefore, more capital controls – at least on short-term capital – would actually increase financial stability and reduce the need for the IMF to serve as international lender-of-last-resort.

On the other hand, the Commission's proposal for the World Bank implicitly required some capital controls in order for it to work properly. Openness to international capital flows constrains a nation's sovereignty in designing economic policies,[6] making it difficult for countries to make the massive, long-term public expenditures necessary to pursue the worthwhile development programs that the Commission recommended, such as vaccines, public health, AIDS research, education or infrastructure improvements. In the current design of open global financial markets, financial investors are likely to interpret the resulting budget deficits as bad signs and force governments to scale back these efforts. Ultimately, for the Commission's recommendations for the World Bank to be effective, capital controls are needed (although the Commission never explicitly acknowledged this fact).

If the Commission was able to accept the idea that capital controls could be used to promote sustainable economic development policies, the debate could move forward. The focus of the debate could turn toward identifying those capital flows that are the most beneficial for the aid recipients, and how capital controls can be designed to allow necessary capital to flow into these economies while keeping harmful 'hot money' from disrupting them.

Development policies

One of the benefits of capital controls is that they provide countries with more leeway in designing their own policies. Once short-term capital flows are under control, developing countries can then focus more on internal development.

To wean domestic borrowers off international capital, domestic financial institutions should be strengthened. Part of Japan's success during its high-growth era was based upon its ability to channel deposits into large development projects via its postal savings system. The Meltzer Commission, though, relied on foreign banks as the main mechanism for domestic financial market development. Research, however, has shown that increased international competition actually results in a reduction of the credit supply in developing economies (Weller 2000a, 2000b and 2002). Small- and medium-sized enterprises, start-ups, rural producers, and low- and middle-income households will experience more financial constraints than others if international competition in domestic financial markets is increased.

More importantly, if foreign direct investment is given priority over domestic development in creating viable financial markets, the need for international capital will continue, as large sectors of the economy will remain underserved by financial institutions.[7] Thus, developing economies will have to continue to borrow on international capital markets, which will likely result in export-led growth strategies to repay international debts. These strategies, in turn, will encourage environmentally harmful and unsustainable economic policies. Developing economies should instead focus on strengthening their own financial institutions, which would reduce the need for more international capital.

A framework for sustainable development should also include strong labor market institutions. To the detriment of workers worldwide, the Commission's report implicitly accepted the IMF's patent recommendation of greater labor market flexibility. Yet, even the World Bank (1995c) reported that countries that allow for more worker involvement have higher growth rates. Similarly, in his January 2000 speech, then-World Bank chief economist Joseph Stiglitz recommended improvements in labor relations and the promotion of core labor standards as the basis for democratic economic development. And Aidt and Tzannatos (2002) argued that unions and collective bargaining can be important institutions to promote strong and sustainable growth within a well-functioning institutional setting.

Loss of national sovereignty

There is an important subtext to the Commission's proposed development strategies, which principally rely on the private sector to ameliorate the situation of the world's poor. In particular, the proposed development framework would lead to the further erosion of the national sovereignty of poorer countries, a profound lack of confidence in the ability of a government to efficiently provide basic goods and services for its people, and the subsidization of privatization of national goods and services.

Though the loss of sovereignty has been briefly touched upon above, it warrants closer analysis, as the Commission purports to be attempting to reestablish national sovereignty. Indeed, in their analysis of the IMF, the Commission claims that the

> [t]ransformation of the IMF into a source of long-term conditional loans has made poorer nations increasingly dependent on the IMF and has given the IMF a degree of influence over member countries' policymaking that is unprecedented for a multilateral institution. Some agreements between the IMF and its members specify scores of required policies as conditions for continued funding. These programs have not ensured economic progress. They have undermined national sovereignty and often hindered the development of responsible, democratic institutions that correct their own mistakes and respond to changes in external conditions.
> (Meltzer 2000: Chapter 2)

Despite the fact that the Commission's first of six guiding principles of IMF reform is 'sovereignty – the desire to ensure that democratic processes and sovereign authority are respected in both borrowing and lending countries' (Meltzer 2000), the Commission did not explain how its policy recommendations would improve the status quo. In lieu of eliminating the source of the loss of national sovereignty – the forced implementation of predetermined neoliberal policies, regardless of the country or situation – it appeared that the Commission had merely masked it by requiring countries to pre-qualify for loans, in lieu of the current practice of conditioning loans on specific criteria. Indeed, this policy change could potentially exacerbate the loss of national sovereignty as countries would be forced to implement policies *before* they could qualify for loans, rather than merely agree to implement policies as a condition of the loan.

The Commission's recommendations for the development banks would undermine national sovereignty by forcing countries to open their markets to procure much needed funds for basic services. However, the Commission would further undermine governments by paying service providers directly, rather than providing governments with the necessary funds to pay for a project. Nominally done to minimize the siphoning off of development funds by corrupt officials, the policy would simultaneously remove government from its role as administrator and service provider.

The aforementioned recommendations that functionally abrade national sovereignty are probably the by-product of policy recommendations driven by a fervent belief that private enterprise and unbridled competition are the most effective and efficient means of delivering goods and services, despite a dearth of evidence to support this position. Under the Commission's restructuring plan, the development banks would award project grants on competitive bid. Thus, all development projects, including improvements made to primary education, health care, and physical infrastructure, would seemingly be allotted to the lowest bidder. As a result, a developing country's basic services, including primary education, water, and electricity, could be provided by foreign private entities and paid for by the World Bank. Thus, under the Commission's recommendations, the government would have absolutely no say in the provider of services to its citizenry and no role in the provision of even the most basic services, except for the token amount for which they would be required to pay.

In addition, the Commission's World Bank restructuring program would facilitate, and functionally subsidize, the privatization of public goods and services in developing economies by two principal means, thereby effectively overriding national development policies. First, the Commission would have required countries with capital market access to seek funding for development projects from these private sources rather than from a multinational entity, such as the World Bank or IMF. Thus, countries would be forced to either borrow large sums of capital at high interest rates, or to allow private corporations to enter the country and assume responsibility for various functions previously under the government's purview. Second, for countries that are both poor enough and lack access to international capital markets, the World Bank would essentially auction off the rights to certain goods and services to the lowest bidder – guaranteeing payment by directly delivering the funds to the service provider. Furthermore, user fees would be subsidized for the poorest countries, thereby assuring multinational corporations a certain return on their investments, as long as the country remains poor.

The loss of national sovereignty that would follow from the implementation of the Commission's policy recommendations runs counter to recent insights of what may constitute promising development strategies. As mentioned before, Aidt and Tzannatos (2002) argue that unions and collective bargaining can play an important role in promoting strong and sustainable growth as long as they are embedded in efficient institutions. According to Aidt and Tzannatos, these institutions will have to vary from country to country to account for each country's historical, political and economic development so far. Similarly, Ariyoshi *et al.* (2000) suggested that countries may have a use for capital controls on a case-by-case basis. In contrast, the Commission's policy recommendations would have promoted a 'one-size-fits-all' policy approach that would have negated the importance of national institutions and the relevance of national sovereignty.

The Meltzer Commission's reach

The recommendations of the Meltzer Commission were never implemented, largely because the report was released during the administration of Democratic President Clinton, who supported the reform of the IFIs, rather than their abolition. Also, high-ranking officials of the Clinton Administration, especially Lawrence Summers and Joseph Stiglitz, had served within the IFIs. Lawrence

Summers, former chief economist at the World Bank, was Secretary of the Treasury when the Commission's report was released. The Treasury's influence ensured a certain amount of security for the IFIs (Lobe 2000). In particular, Treasury Secretary Summers preempted the Meltzer Report by releasing a more modest reform proposal in December 1999. The proposal, while addressing many similar issues, still advocated an influential role for the IFIs in the global economy, arguing that the Commission's recommendations would leave the IFIs unable to promote policies in the US's interest (AFX 2000; Lobe 2000).

Nevertheless, Congressional Republicans tried to implement the recommendations of the Meltzer Commission's majority by tying their implementation to debt relief for Highly Indebted Poor Countries (Harrison 2000).

Although the initial attempt at implementing some or all of the Commission's recommendations by political allies failed, the recommendations showed some staying power in the policy debates. Republican George W. Bush's debt relief initiative, the so-called Millennium Challenge Account, reflects the neoliberal policy agenda with respect to global finance.

On 14 March 2002 during an address at the Inter-American Development Bank, President Bush announced plans for a new development program. This program, the Millennium Challenge Account (MCA), would create 'a new compact for global development, defined by new accountability for both rich and poor nations alike' (White House 2002). As testament to the US's commitment, it would increase its development aid by 50 per cent over the next three years, at which point annual donations would total at least $5 billion.

Instead of additional funding for the IFIs, the MCA would be managed by a US government corporation, to be headed by a presidential appointee. Similar to the Meltzer Commission's recommendation, only countries with per capita incomes below a certain threshold will be considered for aid. In addition, potential recipients will be rated on 16 indicators in three categories – governance, social investment, and economic rights – to determine whether they are eligible for aid. Again similar to the Commission's recommendations, successful countries need to meet certain conditions to receive aid. Specifically, countries should score above the median ranking on half the indicators in every category. In particular, the economic rights category reflects the neoliberal policy agenda. Its six indicators include trade policy (rankings will be taken from Heritage's annual trade survey), inflation, regulatory quality, country credit rating, three-year budget deficit, and the number of days required to start a business. US aid will in effect become an overt policy tool to further the spread of free market policies (White House 2002).

A positive reform agenda

The failures of the Meltzer Commission to promote effective development policies become especially apparent in comparison to a more positive reform agenda.

The IMF and World Bank have been rightfully criticized for both their mishandling of financial crises and the ineffective design and implementation of development projects, providing an impetus to reform these and others. Fortunately, the issue is no longer whether, but how, these institutions should be reformed. New and improved IFIs are needed, requiring both a reconsideration of the IMF and the World Bank's policies and operations, as well as increased transparency.

To make funding more relevant to fulfilling the IFIs' principal goal, namely to improve the living standards of working people worldwide, certain policy reforms should occur. These policy changes should include, but are not limited to:

- providing more grants and fewer loans, which would give recipient countries fewer incentives to raid their environment and exploit their workers to repay international loans;
- encouraging internal development over dependence on external capital flows;
- encouraging and providing assistance in the design and implementation of effective capital controls; and
- requiring adherence to labor and environmental standards by international borrowers or grant recipients. International Labor Organization certification of labor standards, for instance, could become a condition for receiving IFI grants or loans.[8]

Transparency is the second component to IFI restructuring. The external accountability of the IFIs could be increased by making policy decisions more public. Greater transparency of IFI operations will be useful once appropriate policies have been identified and regulatory authority of the IFIs has been established. Thus, the IFIs should create or improve mechanisms for consultation with and accountability to all member countries and civil society. Labor unions and NGOs would seem to be natural partners in increasing the external accountability and transparency of the IFIs. Simply changing IFI policies without increasing these institutions' accountability to a broader share of the population will do little to improve the living standards of the world's poor and disenfranchised. Once external accountability of the IFIs is increased, a new policy orientation is likely to benefit everybody and not only international financial investors.

The political infrastructure supporting the Meltzer Commission

The pursuit of a neoliberal development agenda, as manifested by the final report of the majority of the Meltzer Commission, makes a more promising development agenda less likely. The recommendations for the IFIs could be detrimental not only to developing nations and their economies, but also to the global financial structure, as the recommendations, if implemented, would actually increase the likelihood of financial crises. Furthermore, not only would the recommendations not help to eliminate poverty, they would actually make life significantly more difficult for the world's citizenry, as the recommendations would impede the implementation of worker and environmental protections, in addition to jeopardizing access to basic services. The Meltzer Commission's recommendations by themselves, though, are not the only concern, but rather the fact they reflect the political influence of neoliberal academics, think tank researchers and policy makers, which has grown over the decades.

The Meltzer Commission presents a good example for the vast reach of the MPS since it had very strong ties to not only the MPS, but also to its expansive network. For instance, Allan Meltzer, the Commission's chairman, is a member of the MPS. Professor Meltzer was a vocal opponent of the World Bank and IMF before he was chosen to lead the Commission in late 1998. One month before the Commission's creation he presented a paper in which he outlined the same recommendations the Commission's majority would endorse nearly two years later (Meltzer 1998).

Professor Allan Meltzer's influence spanned beyond his role as academic at Carnegie Mellon University since he has also close ties to one of Washington's oldest think tanks, the American Enterprise Institute. Founded in 1943, AEI is a well-known and respected conservative think tank that 'is dedicated to preserving and strengthening the foundations of freedom – limited government, private enterprise, vital cultural and political institutions, and a strong foreign policy and national defense' (AEI 2002). Among AEI scholars, a number have had close ties with Republican presidential administrations and the Republican part of the US Congress, which allows them to inject their policy ideas most directly into the political debate. For instance, AEI's scholars include Lynne Cheney, wife of Vice President Dick Cheney and chairman of the National Endowment for the Humanities under Presidents Reagan and George Bush, Jeane Kirkpatrick, the US Representative to the United Nations under President Reagan, Lawrence Lindsey, former economic advisor to President George W. Bush and to President Reagan, R. Glen Hubbard, chairman of President George W. Bush's Council of Economic Advisors, Michael Boskin, chairman of President George Bush's Council of Economic Advisors, and Newt Gingrich, former Republican speaker of the US House of Representatives.

In addition to Professor Meltzer, another AEI scholar, Charles Calomiris, was also a member of the Commission. Charles Calomiris is a co-director of the financial deregulation project at AEI and a member of its Shadow Financial Regulatory Committee, as well as a professor of finance and economics at Columbia University. In February 1998, he argued that IMF bailouts were counterproductive and resulted in distorted markets that prohibit the realization of liberalization's benefits. Calomiris further argued that the IMF did not require additional capital and that the US should try to limit the IMF to its pre-1994 goals of advising countries on macroeconomic policies, serving as an international monitor, and providing global financial information. In addition, Calomiris argued the World Bank should be prevented from providing bailout support during financial crises, and be permitted to subsidize the privatization of national banks. Finally, Calomiris argued that the IMF's lack of transparency was fundamental to its ineffectiveness, and that all IMF decisions and rationale should be publicized.

With Calomiris as a commissioner, another conservative think tank, the Cato Institute, gained influence on the Commission. The Cato Institute provided Professor Calomiris with frequent opportunities to publish his ideas on the IMF and World Bank (Calomiris 1998). Cato's goal is to inject 'the traditional American principles of limited government, individual liberty, free markets and peace' into public policy debates (Cato Institute 2002). Named after the libertarian letters published in the 1700s under the name Cato, the Institute was founded in 1977 by Edward Crane, a MPS member.

Publications by the Cato Institute are an important medium for the dissemination of conservative research and have comprised numerous pieces critical of the IFIs. For example, W. Lee Hoskins, another member of the Meltzer Commission, argued in a co-authored Cato Analysis that Congress should 'withdraw its support for the IMF and the World Bank' (Hoskins and Coons 1995). Following the Mexican crisis, Hoskins and Coons (1995) argued that the solution to the crisis was a 'full embrace of free market principles'. Financial crises, they asserted, are the result of unsound policies, and the offending countries must be allowed to 'suffer the consequences of investor wrath'.

The Heritage Foundation, another conservative think tank, was also represented on the Commission. Led by Edwin Feulner, MPS member, its treasurer, one of its trustees, and a former MPS president, Heritage strives 'to formulate and promote conservative public policies based on the principles of free enterprise, limited government, individual freedom, traditional American values, and a strong national defense' (Heritage Foundation 2002). Heritage has a long history of opposing the IMF and additional funding for it (Johnson and Schaefer 1998, 1997a, 1997b; Schaefer 1998). In April 1998, Feulner detailed his opposition to increased funding for the IMF, and urged Congress to withhold funds to force institutional reform (Feulner 1998).

Earlier that same month, in Heritage Foundation *Backgrounder* No. 1167, the author argued that although Congress should ideally eliminate the IMF altogether, the next best option was to enact legislation akin to the IMF Transparency and Efficiency Act of 1998 (HR 3331), sponsored by Representatives Jim Saxton (R-NJ), Richard K. Armey (R-TX), and Tom Campbell (R-CA). Incidentally, Tom Campbell, a member of the House Banking and International Relations Committees and a law professor at Stanford University, was also a member of the Meltzer Commission. HR 3331 proposed to increase IMF transparency, mitigate current market distortion caused by the IMF, and establish an independent advisory board to 'review the research, operations, and loan programs of the [IMF]' (Schaefer 1998). The sponsoring legislators acted based upon a firm belief that by acting as the de facto lender of last resort without adherence to strict market principles, the IMF disrupted global markets, thereby impeding market efficiency.

Conclusion

An intricate network of academics, think tanks, foundations and the media helps to promote neoliberal policies with respect to international economic development. A clear case of this influence was the so-called Meltzer Commission, charged by the US Congress to study the international financial institutions, such as the IMF and the World Bank, in the wake of the Asian and Russian financial crises. The recommendations of the Commission, if implemented, would have been largely counter productive to the achieving the goal of strong and sustainable growth for emerging economies. Instead, the proposed policies would have most likely resulted in a greater chance of financial and economic crises and increasingly unequal income distribution globally and in a lack of progress in poverty reduction for many industrializing economies.

Although the Meltzer Commission's recommendations were not implemented, two facts reflect its influence. For one, the majority of the Commission supported the recommendations, reflecting the broad Congressional and intellectual support that the neoliberal policy agenda had gained over the years. And second, some of the recommendations made their way into other proposals, such as President George W. Bush's Millennium Challenge Account. To a large degree, the successful development and promotion of the Meltzer Commission's recommendations beyond its initial release was due to the fact that the neoliberal policy agenda is supported by a vast network of conservative think tanks, which are well funded by conservative foundations and supported by conservative academics with close connections to conservative politicians.

The lessons from the example of the Meltzer Commission are threefold. First, the free exchange of ideas is not quite as free as one may think. The connection of influential academics, well-funded think tanks and conservative politicians gives the neoliberal agenda a greater platform than other policy ideas. Second, money and access to the right public institutions and decision-makers matter for the development, promotion and implementation of ideas. And third, conservative institutions in the US appear to have mastered, after decades, the use of a vast conservative network to their advantage. Even in adverse political situations, such as a Democratic President, those interested in promoting a neoliberal agenda can successfully engage in the political debate at the highest level. Moreover, the neoliberal network provides a support structure for specific ideas that allows policy proposals to gain staying power in public debates.

Notes

1 The seven IFIs are: the International Monetary Fund (IMF), the World Bank Group, the Inter-American Development Bank, the Asian Development Bank, the African Development Bank, the Bank for International Settlements and the World Trade Organization.
2 The Republican appointees were Allan H. Meltzer, Charles W. Calomiris, Tom Campbell, Edwin J. Feulner, W. Lee Hoskins and Manuel H. Johnson. All supported Meltzer's final report.
3 Democratic appointees were C. Fred Bergsten, Richard L. Huber, Jerome I. Levinson, Jeffery D. Sachs and Esteban Edward Torres. Only Professor Sachs supported Meltzer's final report.
4 There is also an anti-IMF, anti-World Bank movement of the political far left. In contrast to the political right's complaints that the IFIs are market distorters, the

political left generally argues that the IFIs undermine national governments' sovereignty and force harmful policies on individual countries.
5 The funding came from the Bradley, Olin, Scaife and Smith Foundations, who also fund conservative think tanks as discussed further below.
6 For a discussion of factors that constrain interest rate and to a lesser extent fiscal policy under capital mobility see Blecker (1999: 20–31).
7 This is especially true if IFIs oppose the development and public support of small indigenous financial institutions, such as credit unions or publicly owned savings banks (Weller 2002).
8 Levinson (1999) proposes using the ILO labor rights certification process when the United States considers giving countries trade preferences.

Part II
Neoliberal hegemonic constellations in the (semi)periphery

Transnational and domestic roots

4 Why is there no third way?
The role of neoliberal ideology, networks and think tanks in combating market socialism and shaping transformation in Poland

Dorothee Bohle and Gisela Neunhöffer

> Democratic socialism and 'corporativism' alike were delusions: their mounting problems leave as the only alternatives a return to competition or an extension of state control which if it is to be made effective, must become progressively more complete and detailed.
>
> (Hayek 1991[1944]: 41)

Introduction

Nowhere in the world could neoliberal ideology and practice win so radically and quickly against competing paradigms as in the former state socialist countries of Eastern Europe. Poland was the starting point with its implementation of the 'shock-therapy' reform package, the Balcerowicz Plan, on 1 January 1990. Other countries in the region quickly followed, and, no matter whether their reforms were located on the more radical or more gradual end of the reform spectrum, altogether the East European transformation constituted the most dramatic period of liberalization in economic history (Murrell 1996).

One of the biggest puzzles of Poland's, the front-runner's, transformation is why its reformers at the beginning of the 1990s rejected all possibilities of a third way and implemented neoliberal reforms.[1] Polish reformers could have built on a strong market socialist tradition in reform thinking, which was almost unique in the region. Market socialism also inspired earlier reforms of the socialist system, as the result of which Poland had one of the most liberal economies in the region before 1990 (Corricelli 1998). Moreover, the first post-communist Polish government originated from a social movement 'so clearly governed by the principles of workers' self-government, self-management and the "self-liberation of civil society"' (Shields 2003: 225), that the shock therapeutic program had to be implemented against much of its own social base and intellectual tradition.

How then to explain that, against the background of a democratic market socialist orientation of most of the reform circles in Poland, and of the experimentation with (non-democratic) market socialist reforms during the 1980s, the Polish reformers at the beginning of the 1990s rejected this tradition and implemented neoliberal reforms? What are the sources of the relative continuity and strength of neoliberalism in Poland throughout the 1990s?

Existing mainstream analyses of the Polish transformation fail to address these questions convincingly due to two shortcomings. First, they tend to take for granted that neoliberalism is superior to any other competing reform paradigm in the transition from a planned to a market economy, and thus pay little attention to how the superiority of neoliberalism is constructed. Thus, it has quickly become common sense that the economic crisis of the late 1980s, which hit Poland harder than most of the other countries in the region, was a clear sign that market socialist reforms had failed. Rather than leading to economic recovery, these reforms seemed to have reinforced the distortions of the socialist system. In order to break out of the economic crisis, a stronger (i.e. market-radical) medicine was required (Balcerowicz 1995). However, why was it that virtually nobody asked whether it was the *undemocratic* nature of market socialist reforms, imposed by a government that completely lacked legitimacy, which can explain their inefficacy? And consequently, why did nobody propose the implementation of a deepened and more democratic version of market socialism once a government that did enjoy broad legitimacy was in power? In order to understand the almost complete absence of a market socialist reform discourse at such a decisive turning point in Poland's recent history, we investigate the significance of the outcome of a long-lasting 'battle of ideas' which has helped to limit the range of reform options available for the Polish reformers. Specifically, we are interested in the role of neoliberal ideology, networks and think tanks in combating market socialism and in shaping and limiting current alternatives to neoliberalism.

Second, the existing analyses of the (Polish) reforms tend to share an understanding of transformation as a *national* process. Seemingly untouched by the growing literature on globalization and transnationalization, transformation studies still tend to reinstate the analytical prejudice of comparative politics by focusing on categories like the state, national economies, and national varieties of transformation (see e.g. Stark and Bruszt 1998). Little attention has been devoted to the question of how transnational structures, institutions, actors and ideas frame the range of options available for local reformers. By demonstrating the international embeddedness of Polish reform ideas, networks and think tanks, we also seek to locate the Polish transformation in the broader global context of neoliberal restructuring, and thus promote an understanding of *neoliberalism as a transnational configuration of state–society relations*.[2]

Underlying our analysis is a Gramscian concept of hegemony, i.e. an understanding of bourgeois rule as based to a large extent on the consent of the ruled, rather than based on force (Gramsci 1971). A full-fledged Gramscian analysis of the emergence and reproduction of neoliberal hegemony in Poland would obviously have to extend to the material sphere of production and class formation. We chose to restrict our analysis to the role of ideology, networks and think tanks, because in line with other chapters of this volume, we assume that these have a decisive and often underestimated impact on hegemony production (see Plehwe and Walpen in this volume). Specifically in the Polish and other East European cases one can argue that the ideological establishment of the neoliberal hegemony has actually preceded its material basis (Bohle 2002; Ost 1993 and Weinstein 2000). Gramsci's concept of a *passive revolution* seems to be helpful to analyze this specific configuration of social forces. In a case of passive revolution, the

> impetus to change does not arise out of a 'vast local economic development ... but is instead the reflection of international developments which transmit their ideological currents to the periphery'. The group which is the bearer of the new ideas, in such circumstances, is not an indigenous social group which is actively engaged in building a new economic base with a new structure of social relations. It is an intellectual stratum which picks up ideas originating from a prior foreign economic and social revolution.
> (Cox 1993: 59; compare Gramsci 1971: 58 and 105)

In the next section we will analyze the conditions under which neoliberalism has emerged as a separate opposition trend in Poland, and evaluate its relative strength and weakness *vis-à-vis* the market socialist paradigm. We will argue that during the 1980s, the democratic market socialist reform tradition came under attack from two sides. The Communist government used martial law to appropriate the economic reform program of market socialism. At the same time, Solidarity's ideas of reforming real existing socialism came under scrutiny of newly emerging neoliberal groups. Communist reformers and neoliberals at this point met on one *common* ideological ground: they sought to *depoliticize* reform thinking in Poland. Until the end of the 1980s, however, any 'anti-political' reform project failed to gain support from the majority of the opposition leaders and the population. It was only with the implosion of the political system and the defeat of the Communist Party in the first, half-free elections, that a 'window of opportunity' opened for neoliberals to seize power.

The third part of the chapter concentrates on the ideological appeal of the neoliberal reform project in this first period of the Polish transformation. We will show how the Polish neoliberals, who 'lacked everything except an idea; they had no tradition, no social base, no experience, no detailed programme of action' (Szacki 1995: 147), managed to construct their reform paradigm as *superior* to its alternative, the market socialist third way.

The years after the 'Big Bang' witnessed the emergence of a fundamental consensus in Polish society, according to which market economy was basically understood in neoliberal terms. This consensus facilitated a remarkable continuity in the reform process regardless of frequent changes of government. In the concluding part, we briefly touch upon the role of newly established advocacy think tanks in stabilizing neoliberalism in Poland.

The strange alliance of communists and neoliberals against democratic market socialism (1980s)

The evolution of neoliberalism and its ultimate breakthrough in the early 1990s has to be situated against the background of a strong democratic-market socialist tradition in Poland's reform thinking. Only Hungary and Yugoslavia had a similar or even stronger reform tradition.

The evolution of market socialism in Poland

The earliest Polish contribution to the idea of 'market socialism' can be traced in the context of the so-called 'socialist calculation debate' (see also Hull in this volume). Its starting point was an article published by Ludwig von Mises in 1920, claiming that comprehensive, rational central planning in a socialist economy was bound to fail (Mises 1935 [1920]). In response to von Mises, the Polish economist Oskar Lange, together with Frederick Taylor (1938 [1937]), argued that within an economy where the means of production are owned by the state, it is possible for the planners to *substitute* for the market and its functions. The general idea was that supply and demand could be adjusted through an incremental process, in which planners would react to an observed over- or undersupply by changing the price level accordingly. Lange and Taylor's specific contribution was to show 'how such a notional process of price adjustment could be fitted into the general equilibrium theory developed in the 1870s by the neoclassical economist Léon Walras' (Hodgson 1998: 407). Market socialism thus referred to a highly centralized and statist economy, where the market mechanism would be simulated. The importance of Lange and Taylor's (among others) contribution lay in the fact that they successfully challenged von Mises' claim about the unfeasibility of socialism on the theoretical level. As for socialist practice, Lange and Taylor's model had no significance, as no socialist government ever implemented it.[3]

It was only in the aftermath of the de-Stalinization process that market socialist ideas guided reform efforts in Poland. In 1956, as a consequence of a worker revolt, and a renewal within the Communist Party, political and economic steps toward liberalization were initiated. Under the leadership of Oskar Lange, an economic council was created which advised the government on economic reforms. The council included prominent Warsaw economists like Czesław Bobrowski, Włodzimierz Brus, Michał Kalecki and Edward Lipiński (Chavance 1994). In April 1957, it developed the 'theses on certain directions of change in the economic model'. In terms of economic regulation, the *theses* proposed the introduction of indirect financial instruments in order to achieve plan targets instead of direct administrative controls, a greater responsibility for enterprises regarding investments and performance, and a price reform. Furthermore, the *theses* argued that 'democratizing the management of the national economy calls for the active participation of employees, workers' councils, local authorities, and Parliament in the development of the plans' (Brus 1986, cited in Chavance 1994: 38).

While the reform ideas in Poland represented the 'cutting edge of reformist thought in the 1950s' (Chavance 1994: 38), their implementation was rather short-lived. They eventually proved to be more influential in Hungary and Yugoslavia. It was only in the early 1980s with the formation and recognition of

Solidarity and against the background of a deep economic crisis that market-socialist reforms re-entered the agenda in Poland. The formation of Solidarity itself was an extraordinary event in the history of the communist world, and it was an indicator, that – at least for a very short time – the Communist rulers seemed to be willing to tolerate an unprecedented form of democratized socialism (Ost 1990; Holzer 1984).

Retrospectively, 1980–1 proved to be the climax and the turning point in Poland's history of market socialist reform thinking and practice. At that time Solidarity could base its economic reform proposals on the local theoretical tradition, the experience of the (short-lived) reforms of 1956, and the reforms in Yugoslavia and Hungary. A specific stress was put on self-management proposals, which were not restricted to the workplace. The first National Solidarity Congress called for a 'self-governing and democratic reform at every management level and a new socioeconomic system combining the plan, self-government, and the market' (cited in Weinstein 2000: 52). The program could count on the support of a vast social movement, the ten-million-member Solidarity trade union. For a very short period it looked as if an alternative kind of socialism was in the making. The Polish flirt with democratic and decentralized socialism came to an abrupt end, however. As well known, on 13 December 1981, the Communist authorities under General Jaruzelski imposed martial law, banned Solidarity, and imprisoned thousands of opposition activists.

Martial law did not mean the end of reforms in Poland. But the unique *combination of economic reforms with industrial democratization,* so characteristic for Polish market socialist reform thinking, came under attack from two sides. Communist rulers used martial law to introduce purely economic reforms. On the other hand, Solidarity's ideas on reforming real existing socialism came under the scrutiny of newly emerging neoliberal groups. The Communist rulers and the newly emerging neoliberal opposition were equally opposed to Solidarity's emphasis on economic democracy. While ruling Communists and emerging neoliberals were strange bedfellows indeed, they did meet on the common ground of propagating economic reforms without political-democratic dimensions.

Reforms under and after martial law

Martial law was used by the Communist party to consolidate its political power while introducing a first phase of economic reforms in 1981–3, concentrating on changing the status of state enterprises. Its principles became known in Polish as the 'three S's'[4]: autonomy (abolition of mandatory planning targets), self-management, and self-financing (end of discretionary redistribution and the possibility of bankruptcy) (Chavance 1994: 151). However, the implementation of self-management was delayed and tightly controlled.

A second stage of reforms starting in 1987 went much further. It envisioned the equal treatment of state, cooperative, and private sector. Laws from the 1930s were reintroduced to facilitate the transformation of state enterprises into joint-stock or limited-liability companies, and to extend (albeit to a limited degree only) the market mechanism to capital and labor. A banking reform was implemented, and the branch ministries were abolished (Chavance 1994). Finally, the last Communist government in Poland encouraged privatization. This led to a first wave of *nomenklatura* privatization and the formation of an 'embryo of a bourgeois class in the making' (Ost 1993: 471).

A remarkable opening and radicalization of the reform discourse furthermore accompanied the second reform phase. In preparing the reforms, the government initiated a 'great debate'. Between 1984 and 1986 'these mainstream and pro-system forces managed to dissect and then reject virtually every pillar of what until then had been understood as the core of the socialist/statist economy' (Zubek 1994: 811). Communist rulers, commentators in official newspapers, journals, and underground publications alike started to see 'a market economy as the only reliable means of overcoming the economic crisis, and postulated the development of "socialist entrepreneurship" and "socialist competition"' (Walicki 1991: 357).

What motivated the Communist rulers to debate and implement these far-reaching economic reforms? The calculation was simple. As they were not prepared to share political power, they hoped that by loosening their grip on the economy they would simultaneously reduce some of the pressure on the regime. Economic reforms thus were seen as a means for pacifying and depoliticizing the opposition. In this particular matter of concern, communist reformers found allies in the newly emerging neoliberal opposition.

The 'new anti-politicians'[5]

Martial law also laid the foundations for the neoliberal opposition in Poland to emerge and develop into 'the most influential and dynamic intellectual group, one that was strategically located and that put other currents of thought on the defensive' (Walicki 1991: 355). This assessment was written under the impression of a visit to Poland in 1987, and might exaggerate the role of the neoliberals at the time. However, neoliberal networks did indeed acquire strategic importance and visibility in the course of the 1980s (Smolar 1991; Rupnik 1993; Szacki 1995).

Although some neoliberals had already expressed their ideas earlier, the decisive date for the formation of (neo-)liberalism as a separate opposition trend in Poland seems to be 13 December 1981. 'Only after the crushing of Solidarity was the intellectual and programmatic weakness of the Polish Left laid bare. It lost its ideological impetus and turned out to be politically hopeless, making room for other groupings' observed one of the participants of the First Gdańsk Congress of Liberals (1988) in retrospect (Przegląd Polityczny, cited in Szacki 1995: 120–1). The specificity of the neoliberal position was that for the first time, the critique of the communist system shifted from politics to economics. Liberals argued that:

(a) the political fight against the communist regime could not be won; and

(b) any form of political democratization of the communist system which left its economic base intact would only serve to replace one socialist system with another.

Instead, opposition activities should focus on economic changes alone.

Centers of informal neoliberal networks

(At least) three centers of neoliberalism emerged in Poland, organized at the time mostly in informal circles. The first one, the so called 'Cracow School of Liberalism', developed around the writings and activities of Stefan Kisielewski, Bronisław Łagowski, Janusz Korwin-Mikke and Mirosław Dzielski. The latter is considered one of the pioneers of contemporary liberalism in Poland (Szacki 1995). In 1980 he published the book *Kim są liberałowie* (Who are the liberals?), which 'may be regarded as the symbolic starting point of contemporary Polish liberalism, and perhaps even of East European liberalism as a whole' (Szacki 1995: 133). He furthermore was the publisher of the underground journal *13 grudnia* (13 December, later *13*, the date of martial law). In 1988 he co-founded the political club 'Dziekania', which started unofficially as a political 'salon', and evolved into one of the more important conservative-neoliberal think tanks in Poland.[6] Dzielski's activities were especially aiming at influencing the ecclesiastical establishment. This distinguished him from Łagowski, another very influential member of the Cracow group, who, as a member, tried to influence debates within the Communist Party (Walicki 1988). Dzielski was also one of the founders of the Industrial Association of Cracow (*Krakowskie Towarzystwo Przemysłowe*) aiming to

> teach Polish private entrepreneurs to understand themselves in a wider civilizational and moral context, and to acquaint them with the ideas of free market conservatives and libertarians. This was intended to prepare them to treat their enterprises not only as a means of private enrichment, but also as an important part of a program of national revival.
>
> (Walicki 1991: 368)

The second important center of Poland's emerging neoliberalism was Gdańsk. The Gdańsk circle constituted itself after martial law. It included Donald Tusk, a Solidarity member and editor of one of the first liberal underground journals, *Przegląd Polityczny*, Jan Szomburg, Janusz Lewandowski, who later became a member of the Mont Pèlerin Society (MPS, see Plehwe and Walpen in this volume) and Jan Krzysztof Bielecki. In the early 1980s, many of the liberals were still ardent architects of self-management reforms. Martial law and its consequences however taught them otherwise. By 1986, they were strongly committed to a neoliberal reform agenda. The Gdańsk circle of liberals had an important influence in the politics of post-Communist Poland. Janusz Lewandowski became minister of privatization in 1991. Together with Jan Szomburg, he had developed a concept of mass privatization in the 1980s that eventually served as a model in several countries of the region. Bielecki was Prime Minister between January and December 1991. Later he became Minister for European integration and the Polish representative in the European Bank for Reconstruction and Development. Donald Tusk has good prospects of winning the presidential election in 2005. In 1989, this circle created the Gdańsk Institute for Market Economics, one of the most important neoliberal think tanks in Poland. During the 1980s, however, the activities of the Gdańsk circle of liberals were more modest. Similar to their Cracow counterpart, they concentrated on studying and discussing liberal classics, issuing underground publications and organizing the first regular associations and platforms. In 1988, they organized the first national meeting of Polish liberals. They also became heavily involved in the elaboration of Solidarity's new economic program of 1987.

The third center of Polish neoliberalism was obviously Warsaw. The Warsaw activities profited especially from the fact that Poland's economic science could develop comparatively independently and in relative openness to the West (Bockman and Eyal 2002; Kowalik 2002). These networks allowed East European academics to become acquainted with neoliberal (as well as Keynesian) thought, and to critically engage with state socialism. In Poland, many of the international contacts were centered on the Warsaw School of Planning and Statistics (now the Warsaw School of Economics) (Kowalik 2002). Its graduates played an important role in developing and implementing neoliberalism in Poland: Leszek Balcerowicz, the architect of the Polish shock therapy, studied here. As early as 1978 he formed a group committed to work on economic reforms. Various members later served in his reform team (Balcerowicz 1995). One of them, Marek Dąbrowski, assumed a number of political and advisory posts in post-Communist Poland. Balcerowicz and Dąbrowski were among the founders of the Center for Social and Economic Research (CASE), yet another influential neoliberal advocacy think tank in Poland and the wider region of Eastern Europe.

The contribution of neoliberal ideology in socialist Poland

What was the contribution of the neoliberal ideology in socialist Poland? Most importantly, it 'reversed the hierarchy of problems characteristic until then of both communism and its various opponents, by pushing politics into the background' (Szacki 1995: 127–8). This *anti-political orientation* of the opposition to Communism had several consequences:

First, in comparison to other opposition groups, the neoliberals proposed an entirely different program for combating Communism. They saw the solution in a radicalization of economic reform and especially in the restoration of private property relations. Individual freedom, according to their view, was uniquely based in the freedom to pursue economic activities.

Second, this re-evaluation of the hierarchy in fighting communism went hand in hand with a more moderate view on the necessity of political change. For – at least some – Polish neoliberals, 'autocracy is not a greater threat to economic freedom than democracy, but democracy is not the *sine qua non* for economic freedom. Autocracy may even facilitate the achievement of economic freedom' (Szacki 1995: 127). Thus some neoliberals could imagine very well accommodating themselves within the existing political rule of the communists, as long as the economic foundations were altered. During the 1980s, both the Chilean and the Chinese example were discussed as possible analogies for Poland's transition toward economic liberalism and the market.

Third, the neoliberal opposition turned out to be 'a whip against the left' (Szacki 1995: 145). The main 'enemy' was the democratic opposition advocating market-socialist positions. Neoliberals argued that opposition forces that concentrate on fighting the political–authoritarian system do not touch the core of dictatorship, which was based in the economy. Indeed, liberals tended to see Solidarity as a socialist movement because of its collectivist and egalitarian values (Walicki 1991). Neoliberals were strongly opposed to the idea of mixing economic reforms with the aim of political and industrial democracy:

> It [Solidarity] is a movement aiming not so much at the separation of economics from politics, but rather at the democratization of politico-economic decision making. ... It wants to *divide* political power, but is not sufficiently aware of the desirability of *limiting the scope* of all political power, including democracy. In this sense we can even say that the political thinking of the leaders of Solidarity ... is contaminated to some extent by the spirit of socialist totalitarianism.
>
> (Walicki 1991: 354)

In a similar vein, Korwin-Mikke, when comparing the government thesis for the second stage of reforms with the 'Charter of Private Economic Enterprise'[7] and the Solidarity Program, came to the conclusion that the Solidarity Program was the weakest. In Solidarity's program he found 'misguided efforts to combine marketization with the policy of full employment, indexing of wages and governmental subsidies', and 'attempts to link economic liberalization to political democratization on the one hand and "economic democracy" (workers' management) on the other' (Walicki 1991: 358).

Summary

Thus, during the 1980s Poland's democratic-market socialist reform tradition came under pressure. The imposition of martial law served as a trigger for the radicalization of the opposition. Democratic oppositionist Jacek Kuroń 'vehemently argued from his jail cell for armed insurrection and anti-communist guerilla warfare' (Zubek 1994: 809). Facilitated through longstanding transnational networks, neoliberalism emerged as a separate opposition trend, shifting anti-communist radicalism from political to economic views, and attacking democratic market socialist ideas for their egalitarian and collectivist values. While the political situation did not yet allow for the institutionalization of neoliberal ideology in formal organizations such as institutes and think tanks, early informal groups were formed and found ways of disseminating neoliberal thought in a systematic fashion.

At the same time, the communist government effectively undermined the appeal of market socialist reforms by appropriating the economic program, but cutting off the political–democratic component. Half-hearted economics failed to facilitate an economic recovery in Poland. On purely economic terms, the neoliberal program of radical reforms remained a convincing alternative.

Until the end of the 1980s, however, this 'anti-political' economic reform project failed to gain support from the majority of the opposition leaders and population. This lack of support did not necessarily reflect an opposition to radical economic reforms, which were propagated by neoliberals and communists alike. Rather, it was the result of the lack of political legitimacy of the communist rulers and the neoliberal opposition. Neoliberals still 'swam against the stream of majority opinion and ran the risk of finding themselves in the morally ambiguous position of "straddling" the barricade' (Szacki 1995: 124). It was only with the implosion of the political system and the defeat of the Communist Party in the first, half-free elections, that a 'window of opportunity' opened for neoliberals to seize power.

The seductive force of neoliberalism: the Balcerowicz Plan

The half-free elections of September 1989 gave Solidarity a landslide victory. The new Solidarity-led government under Tadeusz Mazowiecki appointed the neoliberal economist Leszek Balcerowicz as Minister of Finance and deputy premier. With Tadeusz Syryjczyk, a close friend of Dzielski and deputy chairman of the Industrial Society in Cracow as the Minister for Industry, Aleksander Paszyński as Minister for Housing, and Marek Dąbrowski as the deputy finance minister, three other neoliberals held important positions in the Mazowiecki cabinet. At the same time, Ryszard Bugaj, a known left-wing Solidarity economist, was left without a governmental post (Walicki 1991: 381). Within a very short period of time, Balcerowicz elaborated the outline of his economic reform program, which stated that 'the government of Poland intends to transform the Polish economy into a market economy, with an ownership structure changing in the direction of that found in the advanced industrial economies' (cited in Johnson and Kowalska 1994: 196). Moreover, the memorandum stated that 'we see monetary and price stabilization as an immediate task and a precondition for structural adjustment' (ibid.). With its basic features of liberalization, stabilization, and privatization, the program strongly reflected neoliberal orthodoxy. The Balcerowicz Plan passed the Sejm (Polish Parliament) without significant problems and was implemented from 1 January 1990. That the Balcerowicz Plan was – at least initially – endorsed both within and outside of Parliament can most significantly be explained by the fact that it was the policy of a government created by Solidarity.[8]

What really has to be explained, therefore, is why the Solidarity-led government chose to back a market-radical reform project instead of coming back to its own tradition of democratic market socialism. Partly this can be explained by developments during the 1980s, which undermined democratic market socialist reform thinking in Poland. However, just some months earlier, during the round table negotiations, only a minority of the Solidarity representatives opted for radical economic reforms. The majority backed a program which looked like a version of the 'self governing republic' program of 1981 (Kowalik 1994, 2002). This makes Poland the only country in the region that indeed had an alternative program to neoliberal reforms (Kowalik 2001: 43).

Another factor was the role of the International Monetary Fund (IMF) that strongly influenced the Polish transition strategy toward an orthodox direction. This argument is especially plausible against the background of Poland's high external indebtedness. However, it has often been pointed out that the Polish–IMF relationship should not be characterized as an adversarial relationship, but rather as a transnational alliance (Modzelewski 1993; Bjork 1995; Greskovits 1998; Bockman and Eyal 2002). We therefore suggest that (at least) one important explanation can be added to those mentioned above, namely the fact that the Polish neoliberals, at this decisive moment in Poland's history, managed to construct their reform paradigm in a way that it appeared *ideologically superior* to its third way alternative. In other words, neoliberals managed to capture the imagination of people, including the social base and elites of Solidarity, in a way that no market socialist was able to. Six aspects leading to market radical success can be considered.

First, the economic crisis provided radical reformers not only with a serious problem, but it also served as a fruitful background in the ideological battleground. Balcerowicz repeatedly evoked the danger of an economy getting totally out of control when calling for immediate and radical action (Balcerowicz 1995). Evoking an *imminent danger* is, as brilliantly demonstrated by Hirschman (1991: 153), a typical rhetorical weapon of pro-reform forces who feel that 'it is not good enough to argue for [a certain policy,] on the ground that it was right; for greater rhetorical effect they urged that the policy was imperatively needed to stave off some threatening disaster'. In the Polish context it is obviously true that hyperinflation indeed called for a drastic stabilization program. However, it is less clear why, in order to fight inflation, Poland had to 'jump to the market economy' (Sachs 1993). To convince his adversaries, Balcerowicz evoked another possible danger, namely the reaction of society to reforms. Balcerowicz's argument that society is basically reform-averse and therefore has to be quickly subjected in order not to threaten reforms was not confirmed by reality. It proved, however, to be a weapon against the implementation of gradual reforms, which according to Balcerowicz exhibited the *risk of getting stuck*.[9]

Second, the proponents of neoliberalism produced *a clear vision of the future*. This vision was called 'capitalism without adjectives', or in the words of Vaclav Klaus:[10] 'We need an unconstrained, unrestricted, full-fledged, unspoiled market economy, and we need it now' (cited in Szacki 1995: 147). This clear vision of a future stood in stark contrast to the proponents of gradualism or a third way, who 'tend to focus on the initial steps and the process of reformation rather than on its final stages', because they 'lack a definite image of the future (where does the third way end?)' (Kovács 1991: 59). Although some proponents of the third way came up with their own vision of a future, namely the Swedish model of capitalism, neoliberals successfully undermined this vision. They argued that 'Sweden and Britain alike have nearly complete private ownership, private financial markets and active labor markets. Eastern Europe today has none of these institutions; for it, the alternative models of Western Europe are almost identical' (Sachs 1990: 19).

Third, neoliberals relied on a *dichotomic thinking*, which gave them an ideological advantage over market socialist ideas. Neoliberals managed to construct their vision of the future as the most radical alternative to the existing and delegitimized socialist system. In contrast to this, market socialists or gradualists appeared to be contaminated by elements and legacies of the past system.

Fourth, neoliberals successfully managed to *sell their utopia* of capitalism without adjectives *as a feasible, realistic, sober and tested project*, and instead accused gradualists of having dangerous utopian tendencies. Donald Tusk, for instance, wrote back in 1989:

> We do not propose a ready-made program. We do not have a gripping vision. We do not carry out spectacular actions. We have however our own imagination of the Polish future, an imagination based on what are for us elementary principles and values. We want to move towards a Poland where power will result out of free elections, but where at the same time power will be limited by civil rights, where the priority of persons over institutions will be recognized, where property rights are guaranteed, and where liberty stems from private property. *'This is nothing new,' somebody might say. And he may be right. But all new ideas, all those 'third ways', 'non-bourgeois civil societies', 'socialism with a human face', 'solidarities' smell of utopia and political fiction. Of these goods, we already had more than enough.*
>
> (Tusk 1989, translation D.B./G.N., emphasis added)

Fifth, *external support and influence* was crucial to reinforce the neoliberal promise 'professing views which had been successfully tried out elsewhere and were not advocating any risky experiment' (Szacki 1995: 145). The support of international experts like the Harvard economist Jeffrey Sachs or other economists like David Lipton, Wladyslaw Brzeski, Jacek Rostowski and Stanislaw Wellisz provided a 'mark of quality' for the neoliberal reforms.[11] Moreover, they were crucial in assuring external financial support. Thus, they were instrumental in Poland's adherence to the new, transnational ideological formation. Contrary to the view, however, that neoliberalism was imposed by these Western actors, the Polish example clearly shows that the foundations of the integration into the transnational neoliberal 'concept of control' (Overbeek 1993) had been laid earlier, with the intellectual defeat of Poland's democratic market-socialism reform thinking and the emigration of many of its advocates. It was at this moment, that Poland stopped producing original third-way concepts responding to its local economic and social reality and started the process of 'passive revolution', adapting and translating neoliberal agendas.

Sixth, it seems that neoliberalism also managed to capture the public imagination more thoroughly than any other project because its rhetoric and remedies were considered in line with *everyday life experiences*. In contrast to what Balcerowicz constructed as an imminent danger, society had rather patiently endured the hardship of economic reforms (Greskovits 1998). Especially in the beginning, society in general and workers and trade union leaders in particular were rather pro-radical reform, because they seriously hoped that 'the market' and private property would do away with many of the perversities of the socialist system (Weinstein 2000). After the experience of an absurd economic system in which 'the state pretends to pay while workers pretend to work' (communist era quip, cited after Ost and Weinstein 1999: 8) workers could look forward to a system based on private property that promised to reward 'honest and hard labor' (ibid.). Having experienced waste of all kinds coupled with shortages of all kinds, the promise of economic efficiency was inspiring. Entrepreneurship itself had a positive connotation, as it promised the chance for everybody to obtain material rewards and upward mobility unavailable under the socialist system. The wealth accumulated through petty entrepreneurship and semi-legal economic activities in the 1980s provided a background of experience that seemed to confirm this positive perception of a free market system.[12]

Thus, at a decisive moment in Poland's recent history, the neoliberal paradigm proved to be ideologically superior to its market socialist or third-way counterpart. Polish neoliberals, using the 'window of opportunity' at the beginning of the 1990s, managed to alter the foundations of society.

Conclusions: the sources of neoliberal continuity in Poland in the 1990s

The aim of the chapter was to show how originally quite narrowly confined neoliberal networks in Poland eventually managed to shape major aspects of the transition process. Neoliberalism emerged in the 1980s as a separate opposition trend, which shifted anti-communism from political to economic views, and attacked democratic market socialist ideas for their egalitarian and collectivist values. While the political situation did not yet allow for the outspoken institutionalization of neoliberal ideology, personal networks and paths to disseminate neoliberal thought were systematically developed and first international contacts established. Until the end of the 1980s, however, the neoliberal project failed to gain significant support either from the majority of the population or among the opposition leaders.

It was only with the defeat of the Communist Party in the first half-free elections in September 1989 that a window of opportunity opened for neoliberals to seize power. In this crucial phase of the breakdown of the old order, self-conscious neoliberals did not only capture key political positions but were also able to mobilize popular support for their reform project and occupy the ideological

Table 4.1 Major neoliberal think tanks in postcommunist Poland

Name and Location	Year established	No. of full-time employees	Budget and main financial sources	Mission/Main activities
Adam Smith Research Center (CAS), Warsaw	1989	10	240,000 USD (2001) Contract research, foundations, intergovernmental organizations	Mission: Popularization of free market ideas Current focus of research and publication: taxation
Center for Social and Economic Research (CASE), Warsaw	1991	13 (+ more than 100 experts on contract basis)	1,382,180 USD (2003) International and foreign government organizations, international corporate foundations	Mission: Provides expertise to Polish and many other former communist countries in relation to problems of economic transition, European integration, and the world economy. Activities: policy research, consultancy, research, education
Institute for Market Economics (IbnGR), Gdańsk	1989	57	1,700,000 USD (2000) Corporate donations and international organizations	Mission: Building a dynamic market economy and a stable democratic order in Poland. Activities: Policy formulation and monitoring, education, research. Current Research Areas linked to economic performance in relation to the EU accession.
Center for Political Thought (OMP), Cracow	1992	3	40,000 USD (1998) Foundations, intergovernmental organizations	Mission: Promoting individual freedom, the free market, liberal democracy, the rule of law, and the idea of a limited state. Special focus on tradition and moral values. Activities: conferences and summer schools, research, translations

Sources: Compiled on the basis of Freedom House (1999), Atlas Foundation (2002), Kowalik (2002), NIRA (2002) and the homepages of the think tanks.

field. Neoliberals managed to construct their project as the superior alternative to third-way projects by pointing to the imminent danger of economic chaos and the risk of getting stuck with half-way reforms, and by presenting the 'free market capitalism' project as a clear, tested, and feasible vision of the future. Neoliberals thereby produced a dichotomic view according to which market radicalism was the only alternative to the bankrupt state socialist system. Last but not least, Polish neoliberals successfully mobilized external support.

Popular support of neoliberal reforms however soon faded. The social hardship of economic reforms gave rise to societal discontent (Ekiert and Kubik 1998). Moreover, as a result of intense inter-elite struggles, Solidarity disintegrated. Frequent government changes led repeatedly to the neoliberals' loss of political power positions, and at the same time, the communist successor party SLD re-emerged as a major political force. It has however often been observed that neither societal discontent, nor the political fragmentation of Solidarity or the consolidation of the post-socialist SLD, altered Poland's neoliberal reform path over the 1990s significantly. A number of explanations account for the continuity of economic reforms. On the one hand, neoliberalism as an ideology continued to strongly appeal to both politicians and the general public, because it constituted the most radical alternative to the discredited socialist system. This legacy made it very difficult to construct more left-wing alternatives. Indeed, the groups that present the most visible alternative to neoliberalism in Poland tend to be right-wing currents, based on conservative Catholicism, nationalism or patriotism, some of them with open xenophobic tendencies. The force of these groups has however been constrained by Poland's transnational integration, and especially its EU accession. The latter also reinforced the structural power of the neoliberal constellation. Finally, the post-socialist political forces were politically 'tamed'. In order to regain legitimacy, they avoided all references to concepts that could be associated with the socialist system.

The chapter suggests that an additional reason for the strength of neoliberalism in Poland can most probably be found in the existence of well-entrenched networks and think tanks. Right after it became legally possible, all major neoliberal centers that emerged in the 1980s founded their own think tanks (Table 4.1).

As the table shows, think tanks can be considered important actors who popularize the neoliberal discourse, provide reform expertise, and stabilize and renew neoliberal thoughts on which policy makers can draw. Their embeddedness in transnational networks constitutes an additional important asset. It is the task of future research to establish in how far the activities of these think tanks have contributed to the continuity of neoliberalism in Poland.

Notes

1 We define the term 'third way' in its older meaning as a market socialist system which is understood as an alternative to state socialism and neoliberal capitalism. Neoliberalism refers to both an economic and a political program. As an economic program, neoliberalism aims at making the absolute priority of private property

rights in a competitive environment the leading principle of economic organization, reducing direct state intervention and 'freeing' the 'market forces'. As a political program, neoliberalism is most clearly defined by its *opposition* to state socialism (see Hayek 1991[1944]), and the Keynesian welfare state (Hayek 1990[1960]), relying on an individualized concept of freedom and responsibility.

2 There is an increasing awareness of the international dimension of transformation. Much of the literature however tends to reduce this dimension to an external aspect of the transformation, and does not see it as one of its constituent parts.
3 Bockman and Eyal (2002: 318) forcefully argue that the socialist calculation debate owes much of its significance to a struggle over the introduction of mathematical techniques in the academic field of economics in the US.
4 From the Polish terms *samodzielność, samorządność, samofinansowanie*.
5 This term for denominating the liberal opposition was coined by Smolar (1991). The concept of anti-politics was widely spread among dissidents, who stressed a vision of politics strongly opposed to the ubiquitous presence of politics (read the state) in public and private lives. 'Anti-politics' has a strong moral stance: it denotes the fight for a sphere protected from politics, in which society can regain its dignity. In most dissident accounts, anti-politics was linked to a vision of guaranteed social protection and collective societal values (see Staniszkis 1984; Konrád 1985; Ost 1990; Brannan 2003). In these two points it differs from the neoliberal 'anti-politics', which was grounded in the economic sphere and its relevance for *individual* freedom.
6 Dziekania already existed as a political salon prior to its unofficial/official foundation in 1988 (or 1987, according to different sources). The club's meetings were initiated by Stanisław Stomma, a Catholic politician, and its members came from five political groups, including the Cracow Christian Liberals from the journal *13* (Smolar 1991). It evolved into the 'Center for Political Thought' (*Osrodek Mysli Politicznej*), which was founded in 1992.
7 This was a manifesto of an economic conference organized by the Catholic University of Lublin.
8 Moreover, the strange alliance between neoliberal reformers and Communists was once more successful. Obtaining a majority for the Balcerowicz Plan in parliament was a remarkable success, because it was still a 'contract Sejm': Solidarity was allowed to contest for only a third of the seats, of which it acquired all but one. The Communists, however, 'adopted the slogan "Your government, our Program"', suggesting that the new program had been prepared by the Rakowski government and thus rationalizing its support' (Johnson and Kowalska 1994: 198).
9 Emphasizing the risk of getting stuck is another rhetorical figure identified by Hirschman, which is employed by pro-reform forces in order to get heard (Hirschman 1991: 130). See Bockman and Eyal (2002: 341) on neoliberal reformers' 'deep suspicion of the people'.
10 Vaclav Klaus is the Czech counterpart of Balcerowicz, and arguably the most prominent MPS member in Eastern Europe.
11 The most famous and influential foreign advisor was Jeffrey Sachs, who designed Bolivia's 'New Economic Policy' in 1985. In the Polish case, he supported shock therapy, and was crucial for the negotiation of debt relief (Norton 1994). Shields convincingly argues that the Balcerowicz Plan should be known as the 'Sachs–Balcerowicz Plan to indicate the degree of consistency between the two' (Shields 2003: 232).
12 Weinstein points to the significance of this everyday life experience for some of the neoliberal Solidarity elites, who were pushed into the second economy after being released from prison. It is in this private economic sphere where they experienced responsibility and dignity for the first time (Weinstein 2000: 55).

5 The neoliberal ascendancy and East Asia

Geo-politics, development theory and the end of the authoritarian developmental state in South Korea

Mark T. Berger

The end of the Cold War precipitated the deepening of the US-led globalization project and the emergence of celebratory visions of a new era of global liberalism.[1] Nevertheless, Japan, the Newly Industrializing Countries (NICs) of South Korea, Taiwan, Hong Kong and Singapore, and the growing capitalist dynamism of Thailand, Malaysia, Indonesia and coastal China, were widely perceived by the early 1990s as a serious challenge (or threat) to the post-Cold War neoliberal order centered on North America and Western Europe. Much of this concern dissipated rapidly with the onset of the Asian financial crisis (1997–8), while 9/11 has further dramatically reoriented the global political economy. Meanwhile, at the present juncture China is the pivot of wider politico-economic trends in East Asia, while the earlier East Asian Miracle, centered on Japan, and driven by the formerly authoritarian developmental states of South Korea and Taiwan, has passed into history. In fact, it is now clear that the potential challenge that even the most successful developmental states of East Asia represented for the US-led globalization project was always circumscribed. The power and resilience of US hegemony in East Asia in the 1980s and 1990s was reflected in the way in which, contrary to both a close reading of the history of capitalism generally and the growing oligopolistic character of the global political economy of the 1990s more specifically, the most influential analyses of what became known as the East Asian Miracle explained the region's capitalist transformation after 1945 primarily in terms of a commitment to the virtues of the free market and free enterprise (Aikman 1986: 116).

Of course these analyses did not go unchallenged by advocates of the developmental state, or proponents of 'Asian values' (Berger 1997 and 2003). However, despite the Asian triumphalism of the late Cold War and early post-Cold War era, the developmental states of East Asia were under growing internal and external pressure to liberalize economically and politically in the 1990s. With the Asian crisis, there was even greater assertion of US hegemony in the region, via the International Monetary Fund (IMF) in particular. In this context, neoliberal economic policies were further imposed/embraced, at the same time as they were represented more than ever as the key to universal prosperity (Wolf 1998; Woodall 1998). In the aftermath of the Asian crisis the one-time developmental states of East Asia have been increasingly accommodated, albeit unevenly, to the post-Cold War neoliberal order. In fact, the US response to the Asian financial crisis represented both an attempt to bring a definitive end to state-guided national development in one of its last redoubts, South Korea, and send a signal to a rising China where the aging leadership has been attempting for many years to emulate the erstwhile state-led national development trajectories of South Korea and Japan (Cumings 1998: 51–2; Berger 2004a).

This chapter begins with a brief discussion of the rise and decline of the idea of state-guided national development (in its capitalist and socialist forms) between the 1940s and the 1970s. This is followed by an examination of the rise of neoliberalism and the promulgation of a reading of the East Asian Miracle that meshed with the increasingly dominant neoliberal approach to capitalist development. The efforts by the Japanese government, and advocates of the developmental state, to challenge neoliberalism and the emergent US-led globalization project are then examined. These challenges were met via a process of accommodation, against the backdrop of unequal international power relations and the end of the Cold War, which ensured that much of the opposition to the neoliberal agenda was domesticated by the liberal institutions and discourses of the international political economy. By the second half of the 1990s the dominant neoliberal narratives had undergone some revision, but they continued to privilege a technocratic understanding of development grounded in ahistorical assumptions about the dynamics of capitalism. While neo-classical economics interpreted the rise of Japan and the East Asian NICs in terms of comparative advantage and free market principles, it is clear that imperfect competition and oligopoly have been central to the history of capitalism in East Asia and globally. At the same time, it is increasingly clear that developmental state theorists share many of the key assumptions on which neoliberalism rests. Like neoliberalism, theories of the developmental state naturalized the nation and produced explanations for the East Asian Miracle that were increasingly ahistorical and technocratic. Like neoliberalism they also often implicitly, if not explicitly, legitimated military dictatorship and authoritarianism.

The second part of the chapter provides a brief historically grounded analysis of the rise of state-guided national development in the Asia-Pacific in the Cold War era with a focus on South Korea. This section examines the way in which capitalist, developmental states took shape in South Korea and Taiwan (or, in the case of Japan, were re-organized) after 1945, emerging as explicit counter-models and geo-political counter-weights to the state-socialist regimes of North Korea and the People's Republic of China and beyond. This is followed by an examination of the South Korean trajectory emphasizing the complex history of the rise and eventual demise of the authoritarian developmental state. The final section looks at how, by the 1970s, the incipient US-led globalization project began to reconfigure the role of states in the global political economy and challenge the idea of state-guided national development. With the consolidation and elaboration of the globalization project in the 1980s, capitalist nation-states in East Asia were confronted by growing internal and external pressure for liberalization, deregulation and privatization. Across Asia (and beyond) the end of the

Cold War, followed by the Asian crisis and its aftermath, facilitated the continued unraveling of state-guided national development generally and the waning of the developmental states more specifically. This chapter concludes by emphasizing that in South Korea and Japan (and in other nation-states in the region) the legacy of the ideas and instrumentalities associated with state-guided national development continue to exert a significant, albeit declining, influence in the context of shifting visions of these nations and their futures. South Korea and Japan reflect both the overall pattern and the historical specificity of the sustained, but still unfinished transformation of state-mediated national development projects (of all politico-ideological types) into neoliberal states. South Korea and Japan are undergoing crises of national development and dramatic processes of national reorientation in the context of the elaboration of the US-led globalization project (Berger 2004a).

Theories of development and the historical political economy of the Cold War and post-Cold War order

The Bandung Era: the rise and decline of state-guided national development 1940s–70s

After 1945 the idea and practice of state-guided national development was consolidated and universalized in the context of the major historical trends of decolonization, the Cold War and the global spread of the nation-state system. During what has been called the Bandung Era (1950s–70s) the nation-state was increasingly represented as a universal and constitutive element of freedom, self-determination and modernization (Berger 2004b). The waning colonial empires framed the territorial boundaries and provided the foundations for the new nation-states at the same time as the Cold War became the overall context for the pursuit of a range of historically contingent, politically and ideologically diverse and formally sovereign state-guided national development projects around the world by the 1950s. In Asia and Africa, Bandung regimes such as India under Nehru (1947–64), Egypt under Nasser (1954–70), Indonesia under Sukarno (1945–65), and Ghana under Nkrumah (1957–66) anchored a wider effort to ostensibly steer national development in the Third World between the capitalism of the United States (and the First World) and the communism of the Soviet Union (and the Second World). In the late 1960s and 1970s a second generation of Bandung regimes emerged, inspired by the Cuban and/or the Chinese and Vietnamese, revolutions (Scott 1999: 197–8). They included Chile under Salvador Allende (1970–3), Tanzania under Julius Nyerere (1965–85), Jamaica under Michael Manley (1972–80) and Nicaragua under the Sandinistas (1979–90) (Robert J.C. Young 2001: 213). They attempted to radicalize the national development project in various ways in the name of socialism and national liberation. The second generation of Bandung regimes emerged as an explicit reaction to the apparent failure of less radical forms of state-guided national development, but even where state-guided national development had been relatively successful it was under increasing pressure by the 1980s and not necessarily committed to the Third Worldism of the Bandung Era. The rise of South Korea and the other NICs in East Asia (and the more short-lived enthusiasm for the Mexican and Brazilian Miracles) by the 1970s highlighted both the potential, and the limits, of state-guided national development. Mexico and Brazil were initially grouped as NICs, but the world recession and the Debt Crisis of the 1980s undermined their claim to that status (Harris 1986).

In the 1970s and even more in the 1980s East Asia emerged as the key zone of the relocation of industrial production and the geographical restructuring of the world economy precipitated by the combination of the waning of the Fordist era in North America and Western Europe (and Australia and New Zealand) and the rise of the US-led globalization project (Wallerstein 1999: 36–7). But, the developmental states of East Asia were also subjected to growing pressure for economic and political liberalization with the world recession and the Debt Crisis at the start of the 1980s, and the subsequent spread of neoliberal economic policies and practices. The International Monetary Fund and the World Bank, supported by the administration of Ronald Reagan (1981–8), the governments of Margaret Thatcher in Britain (1979–90) and Helmut Kohl in West Germany/Germany (1982–98), encouraged governments in Asia, Africa and Latin America to liberalize trade, privatize their public sectors and deregulate their financial sectors. This trend also coincided with the renewal of the Cold War. From the end of the 1970s to the late 1980s the Reagan administration presided over an unprecedented military build-up and a reinvigorated anti-communist crusade directed at the Soviet bloc and the state-socialist model that it embodied (Halliday 1986). Against this backdrop neo-classical economics and a romanticized version of *laissez-faire* capitalism increasingly meshed with the aims and assumptions of a complex array of transnational socio-economic forces linked to the US-led globalization project (Sklair 2001).

Challenging national development: the rise, promotion and revision of neoliberalism 1970s–90s

The intellectual leaders of the neoliberal ascendancy were primarily economists and politicians whose main concern, initially, was to influence the political struggle and policy debate in North America and Western Europe. In much of Asia, Africa, the Middle East and Latin America after 1945 development economics, and then, more radical, Marxist and dependency theories of development had provided a body of ideas and policies that were used by nationalist political and economic elites seeking a state-guided late-industrializing path to national development. By the end of the 1970s, however, neo-classical economics (in the context of the wider shift in international power relations) had begun to emerge from relative obscurity and extend its reach beyond its British and North American heartland. One of the more famous and long-standing exponents of the neo-classical approach to economic development in the so-called Third World was Peter T. Bauer (1981, 1984).[2] He and other neo-classical economists took the view that none of the explanations and policy prescriptions provided by development economics specifically, and post-war development theory more generally, had the answer to the problem of development in Asia, Africa and Latin America. From their perspective the whole idea of state-guided national development was misguided (Leys 1996: 17–9). For example, in his well-known critique of development economics, Deepak Lal (like Bauer a member of MPS; compare Plehwe and Walpen in this volume) argued that the case for state intervention in the economy (*dirigisme*) had been undermined by the 'experience' of a wide range of developing economies after 1945. He concluded that there were only two 'feasible alternatives' – 'a necessarily imperfect planning mechanism' and 'a necessarily imperfect market mechanism' – and 'the latter is likely to perform better in practice' (Lal 1985: 103–6; also see Lal 1998).

The work of Bauer and Lal, along with a large number of other neo-classical economists, provided the overall intellectual framework for the neoliberal reforms, increasingly promoted by the International Monetary Fund and the World Bank by the start of the 1980s (Mosley *et al.* 1991: 22–3). This shift was symbolized by the end of Robert McNamara's presidency of the World Bank. In the McNamara era, from 1968 to 1981, the World Bank's overall approach to development reflected a formal commitment to state-mediated capitalist development and anti-communism grounded in development economics. In particular the idea that poverty facilitated the spread of communism meant that 'poverty alleviation' became a major focus of the World Bank's activity (Packenham 1973: 52–3; Kapur *et al.* 1997: 215–329). By contrast, McNamara's successor, Tom Clausen (1981–6), was an ardent proponent of liberalization and deregulation whose previous position had been at the head of the Bank of America. Clausen made it clear at the outset that he had no intention of maintaining his predecessor's focus on poverty alleviation and he was adamant that 'the only constituency that mattered' was the government of the United States (Mahbub ul Haq cited in Caufield 1996: 144). Closely linked to the World Bank's dominant position as a promoter of neoliberalism in the 1980s, was its vigorous articulation of a version of the East Asian model that conformed to the main tenets of neo-classical economics (Berger and Beeson 1998). For, example, in the 1980s, Bela Balassa, a well-known neo-classical economist with strong links to the World Bank, consistently sought in his work to accommodate the East Asian trajectory to neo-classical economics (Balassa 1981, 1982, 1988).

By the second half of the 1980s, however, there was also a growing challenge to neoliberalism by the government of Japan (as well as other regional leaders, most notably Prime Minister Mahathir Mohamed of Malaysia). They sought to explicitly refute the neo-classical interpretation of East Asian success (Wade 1996: 126–7). It was against this overall backdrop that the now famous East Asian Miracle report appeared (World Bank 1993). The report, which was funded by the Japanese Ministry of Finance, reluctantly conceded that government intervention had played some role in economic development in East Asia. More broadly the 1993 Report reflected the wider renovation of neoliberalism that had been under way since the mid-1980s (Kiely 1998; Schmitz 1995). The revision of neoliberalism was even more apparent in *The State in a Changing World* (the 1997 World Development Report), which was premised on the idea that the state is not just an important factor in economic development, but that 'its capability', which was *'defined as the ability to undertake and promote collective actions efficiently'*, had to be 'increased' (World Bank 1997: 3, 6, 24, 46, 61; italics in original). However, the 1997 study defined an 'effective state' in a way that remained inoculated from historical and political concerns, while the wider social context was sidestepped and the authoritarian character of most of the developmental states in East Asia was given implicit, if not explicit, legitimacy. Ironically, the publication of the 1997 report coincided with the onset of the Asian crisis and the discrediting of the state-guided model that the World Bank had reluctantly and partially accommodated during the 1990s. Meanwhile, by the end of the 1990s, the World Bank had also engineered a shift from structural adjustment to the 'comprehensive development framework' that ostensibly again foregrounded poverty alleviation. This did not, however, represent a retreat from any of the core elements of the US-led globalization project (Pender 2001).

The revision of neoliberalism was also facilitated by the rise of rational choice theory in the 1980s (Leys 1996: 82–4). As with the approach to economic behaviour taken by neo-classical economics, rational choice theory built its explanations for political behaviour on assumptions about the rational calculations that informed the policies and actions of the individuals and groups concerned. The terminology of rational choice theory, if not the more rigorous versions of its conceptual framework, is now widely deployed.[3] The weaknesses of rational choice theory, and its key role in the process of reinventing neoliberalism in a way that accommodated the state-led development trajectory of East Asia to neo-classical economics, is apparent in *The Key to the Asian Miracle* which was published in 1996. It was written by Jose Edgardo Campos, a World Bank economist and co-author of the 1993 East Asian Miracle report, and Hilton L. Root, an economic historian based at the Hoover Institution at Stanford University. Campos and Root attempted to outline 'concrete lessons for the rest of the developing world' by examining 'the rationality of the structure and performance' of key institutions in East Asia. They argued that the governments of the high-performing Asian economies, or HPAEs (Japan, South Korea, Taiwan, Hong Kong, Singapore, Thailand, Malaysia and Indonesia), were aware that successful economic development necessitated coordinating the 'expectations' of various groups. This led to the crafting of institutional arrangements that sought to distribute 'the benefits of growth-enhancing policies widely'. They also argued that the long-standing perception of the East Asian regimes as 'authoritarian' and 'even dictatorial' is misleading and 'occurs largely because of the failure of Western observers to recognize in East Asia systems for ensuring accountability and consensus building that differ from Western-style institutions' (Campos and Root 1996: viii, 1–3, 174–7). Ultimately their analysis legitimated authoritarianism and endeavored to accommodate the developmental state and ideas about Asian democracy and Asian values to the dominant neoliberal discourse on development.

Challenging neoliberalism: the rise and limits of the theory of the developmental state 1980s–90s

The revision of neoliberalism in relation to East Asia in the 1980s and 1990s reflected the relative influence of the Japanese government at the World Bank and the growing significance of theories of the developmental state that emphasized the importance of state-directed industrial policy. The rise of developmental state theory was also connected to the wider effort in various branches of the social sciences (including political science, development economics and sociology) to 'bring the state back in' (Skocpol 1985). The 1982 study of industrial policy in Japan by Chalmers Johnson is usually seen as the foundational text of the theory of the developmental state (Johnson 1982, 1999). Other important studies, which increasingly moved away from the more explicitly historical approach outlined by Johnson, include the work of Alice Amsden (1989, 2001), Stephan Haggard (1990), Robert Wade (1990), Peter Evans (1995), Sanjaya Lall (1996) and Linda Weiss (1998). The theory of the developmental state was often embraced, in the 1980s and early 1990s, with considerable enthusiasm by progressive opponents of neoliberalism. The importance of the state in socialist and social democratic thinking resulted in the relatively uncritical acceptance of developmental state theory in many quarters (Castañeda 1994: 434). However, the developmental state was increasingly conceptualized as a policy-making body, while insufficient, or no recognition was given to the complicated and contested social relations out of which it emerged. Like earlier theories of development and modernization and like their neoliberal opponents, advocates of the developmental state were increasingly oriented toward government officials, technocrats and planners (Preston 1987: 43). Alice Amsden's overall argument captures the elite-oriented, technocratic and ahistorical perspective of proponents of the developmental state when she argues that industrialization in South Korea flowed from 'government initiatives and not the forces of the free market' and this is 'applicable to similar countries' (1989: 27). Furthermore, Amsden's identification of South Korea in the 1960s and 1970s as a more general model also provided implicit, if not explicit, justification for military dictatorship and authoritarianism (also see Weiss 1998: xii–xiii; Leftwich 2000: 15, 80–1). This approach sidesteps the authoritarian character of the South Korean state prior to the late 1980s and the way in which the relinquishing of state control over the economy was linked to wider political and social struggles, spearheaded by workers and students, against authoritarian politics and military rule.

Ultimately the state-guided national development project in South Korea was undone by its own success and by the wider historical context in which it operated. The authoritarian developmental state, or what Bruce Cumings called the bureaucratic-authoritarian industrializing regime (BAIR), in South Korea was able to pursue certain developmental objectives for many years because the state was particularly well insulated from the wider social order in the context of its particular colonial and Cold War history, especially from those classes that might have challenged or undermined its developmental goals (Cumings 1987). The economic success of the authoritarian developmental state in South Korea, however, led to a strengthening of various social classes whose growing political demands had dramatically weakened the autonomy and authoritarian character of the state by the second half of the 1980s. When this change intersected with the waning of the Cold War and the rise of the US-led globalization project, the result was the retreat of the authoritarian developmental state in South Korea. Most importantly for the argument being outlined here, globalization is not just an economic process, but an uneven, heterogeneous and multi-faceted process of political, social and cultural change that is conditioned, but not determined, by processes in which the state is increasingly oriented toward intervening in economic activity in a globalizing, rather than a national developmental, capacity (Appadurai 1996; Mittelman 2000: 15–26). The globalization project is being consolidated via the nation-state system and the US state is central to, and one of the strongest states in, the highly uneven transformation of nation-states into neoliberal states.

National development and the historical political economy of the Cold War and post-Cold War order

US hegemony, the rise of national development and the historical political economy of the Cold War order

The emergence of state-guided national development projects in East Asia after 1945 was profoundly shaped by the Cold War and centered on the interaction between the United States, Japan (which was Washington's key post-1945 client-ally in East Asia), the People's Republic of China (Washington's main concern in the region after 1949) and the Soviet Union (Beijing's ostensible patron-ally) (Cumings 1987, 1997; Berger 1999, 2002; Stubbs 1999). In the context of the Cold War the protection of private property and the interests of capital were not the only things driving US expansion after 1945, but they were central to the wider fabric of US anti-communist globalism (Cox 1987: 211–67). The US had a crucial stake in the capitalist reconstruction of as much of Europe and Asia as possible and the extension of this process to the rest of the world. In 1947 the Marshall Plan for Western Europe demonstrated US economic power and represented an important precedent for subsequent capitalist nation building initiatives in Asia, Africa, the Middle East and Latin America (Hogan 1987; van der Pijl 1994: 138–77).

Not long after the promulgation of the Marshall Plan, the US embarked on a full-scale effort to facilitate the industrial rebirth of Japan (Schonberger 1989). In fact, Japan received some funding under the Marshall Plan itself. US efforts at nation building in Japan were part of what would become a wider effort to turn as much of North East Asia (and later South East Asia) as possible into a capitalist bulwark against the USSR and then increasingly China (Forsberg 2000). With the Chinese Communist Party's victory in October 1949 and the onset of the Korean War (1950–3), the governmental and military institutions and bureaucratic structures of the US national security state were increasingly consolidated as instruments of regional and global power (McGlothlen 1993). Meanwhile, the arrangements laid down at Bretton Woods in 1944, before the coming of the Cold War, contributed to the wider framework for economic recovery and capitalist development in Western Europe and North East Asia between the late 1940s and the early 1970s (Borden 1984).

Within this framework, the Korean War provided a crucial stimulus to industrial production in Japan as a result of the dramatic increase in the purchase of military equipment and war-related products by the US after 1950. After the Korean War the sustained US economic and military aid (and capital) that went to South Korea and Taiwan in the 1950s and 1960s played a major role in strengthening the capabilities of these emergent national security and developmental states (Woo-Cumings 1997, 1998). Between 1945 and 1979 US military aid to South Korea was US$ 7 billion, while US economic aid from 1945 to 1979 was over US$ 6 billion (Kim and Roemer 1979: vi). This was more than all the US economic aid to Africa and half the figure for all of Latin America over the same period. In the 1950s more than 80 per cent of South Korean imports were financed by US economic assistance. The growing power of these states was also linked to the relative weakness of capitalist elites in South Korea and Taiwan and the undercutting of large landowners after 1945, as a result of the implementation of land reforms, under US auspices (Wiegersma and Medley 2000: 17, 20, 35–49).

In the 1950s and increasingly in the 1960s, manufacturers based in South Korea and Taiwan (and, of course, Japan) also gained privileged access to the North American market, for US geo-strategic reasons, at the same time as the US tolerated Taiwan and South Korea's protected markets and their governments' tight controls on foreign investment. Furthermore, the four NICs (South Korea and Taiwan, as well as Singapore and Hong Kong) all entered the world export markets in the 1960s when a consumer boom was under way. Meanwhile, Japan-based corporations had begun to emerge as a key element in the wider US-centered Cold War political economy of East Asia by the 1950s. And, in the 1960s and 1970s, Japanese companies avoided the rising cost of labor in Japan by relocating operations to their former colonies. At the same time, by the 1970s Japanese trading companies controlled 50–70 per cent of the international trade of South Korea and Taiwan. In this period Japanese corporations also provided a substantial portion of the machinery and the other components needed for industrialization in Taiwan and South Korea, and they were also an important source of technology licenses (Stubbs 1994: 366–8).

From authoritarian developmental state to crisis of national development in South Korea

While Japanese companies played an important role in South Korea and Taiwan in the post-1945 era, Japanese colonialism had earlier laid the foundations for authoritarian state-guided national development. In fact, the Japanese colonizers provided both a foundation and a model for post-colonial capitalist development (Cumings 1984). In particular, Park Chung Hee, who ruled South Korea from 1961 until 1979, the heyday of the developmental state, had been an officer in the Japanese Kwantung Army during the Pacific War. His approach to economic development was directly influenced by the Japanese colonial industrial pattern, most importantly the state's close links with the *zaibatsu* (Woo 1991: 7–8, 20–1, 40). Under Park, national economic development was represented as his government's 'sacred mission'. Between the 1960s and the 1980s state-guided national development in South Korea rested on a close relationship between the national security state and the country's burgeoning conglomerates, at the same time as workers and trade unions were controlled via repression and top-down corporatist arrangements (Koo and Kim 1992: 124–31). In this period important and historically specific cultural practices and nationalist narratives emerged as constitutive elements of authoritarian developmentalism in South Korea. During the Cold War, South Korea's corporate elite, and their allies in the national security state, sought to advance their economic interests by deploying selected aspects of Korean culture to mobilize employees and the population generally, while downplaying cultural traditions that might contribute to resistance to their rule (Janelli and Yim 1993: 232–4, 238–9).

Despite, or because of, these authoritarian efforts to emphasize harmony and hierarchy (in the context of a virulently anti-communist and authoritarian nationalism backed up by a coercive national security apparatus), the history of South Korea in the 1960s and 1970s was a history of ongoing social and political struggles (Hart-Landsberg 1993). The rapid economic growth and the dramatic social changes of these decades paved the way for the relative decline of the authoritarian developmental state in South Korea during the regime of General Chun Doo Hwan (1980–8). Although the US reinvigorated the security alliance with Seoul in the Reagan era, Washington also increasingly began to question South Korea's financial and trading practices. These external shifts meshed with domestic pressures for political (and economic) liberalization and resulted in an elite-negotiated transition to parliamentary democracy by the end of the 1980s. The liberalization of the political system was closely connected to the liberalization of the economy and the first civilian president of South Korea in over three decades, Kim Young Sam (1993–8), made globalization (*segyehwa*) the centerpiece of his administration (Kim 2000: 2–4).

With the Asian crisis in 1997, however, the pressure for neoliberal economic reform in South Korea increased. The IMF loan to South Korea, an unprecedented US$ 58 billion (as well as smaller but still substantial loans to Thailand and Indonesia) was conditional on the implementation of a range of austerity measures and economic reforms. IMF officials demanded the setting-up of new regulatory procedures, the shutting-down of a range of banks and financial institutions and the liberalization of capital markets. The IMF also demanded that public enterprises be privatized and cartels be broken up. In South Korea the Fund also pushed for the introduction of flexible labor markets and it initially found a willing ally in the government of Kim Dae Jung, whose political and economic goals were strengthened by the early IMF demands (Chang 1998: 1560). Kim Dae Jung was as committed as his predecessor to globalization, while the combination of the crisis and his assumption of the presidency in early 1998 was seen as opportunity to undermine key aspects of the collusion between the *chaebol* and the political elite that had been central to the authoritarian developmental state. While the crisis and Kim Dae Jung's efforts at reform undermined key aspects of the developmental state, many of its trademark arrangements and practices remain in place (Kang 2000: 97–101).

In fact, as a result of the economic downturn in the second half of 2001 and 2002, the South Korean government considered slowing down, and even reversing, some of its efforts to place restrictions on the size of the *chaebol* (Larkins 2001: 66–7). Nevertheless, in the context of the dramatic decline in the size of the South Korean economy, there has been a major, albeit uneven, opening to foreign investors and foreign manufacturers, complemented by legislative changes that have liberalized the labor market and weakened job security. This shift was symbolized by the purchase, in May 2002 after lengthy negotiations, of the bankrupt Daewoo Motor by General Motors (GM). The uneven character of this process was reflected, meanwhile, in the almost simultaneous eleventh-hour refusal by the board of the embattled South Korean firm, Hynix Semiconductor, to sell its memory-chip operation to the US-based Micron (The Economist 2002c: 79). The process of national reorientation under way in South Korea is also complicated by the fact that North and South Korean soldiers are still lined up along the 38th parallel and the US remains forward-deployed in support of its South Korean ally. South Korea's prospects remained tied up with the increasingly decrepit character of the North Korean regime and the uncertainty surrounding the continued division of the peninsula, a direct legacy of the Cold War (Hart-Landsberg 1998: 209–37; Noland 2000).

US hegemony, the decline of national development and the historical political economy of the post-Cold War order

As the South Korean trajectory makes clear, the end of the Cold War marked a new phase in an increasingly global, but highly uneven, process of economic liberalization, deregulation and privatization that had been building momentum since the 1970s. The decline of state-guided national development, and the rise of the US-led globalization project, involve the intersection and elaboration of a number of trends that can be traced to the 1970s, but were increasingly consolidated in the 1990s. To begin with, the rise of the US-led globalization project is linked to dramatic technological changes in which the information economy has emerged as the leading sector, increasingly shaping industrial and agricultural production, political activity and social and cultural life. The rise of information technology is grounded in research and development in the 1970s with important links to the military imperatives of the Cold War (Westad 2000: 559). Another crucial trend was the modifications of the overall shape of the political economy of the Cold War during the administration of US president

Richard Nixon (1969–74). In 1971 Nixon effectively signalled the demise of the formal and informal aspects of the Bretton Woods bargain when he floated the US dollar and suspended its convertibility to gold, at the same time as he introduced a new 10 per cent surcharge on all imports into the United States (Brenner 1998). The termination of the global financial protocols associated with the Bretton Woods system had at least four crucial results. First, it ensured that private banks (particularly those based in the US) began to play a much greater role in global finance. Second, it dramatically weakened government supervision of global financial organizations. Third, the currency exchange rates and financial systems of other nation-states were increasingly influenced by trends in the financial markets in the United States. Fourth, it encouraged growing competition within the banking systems of the various countries in the OECD and allowed US government to more or less determine the shape of the regulatory framework for global financial markets. Between 1975 and the end of the Cold War, subsequent US administrations built on these changes (Gowan 1999).

This shift in the 1970s signaled the end of the high-period of state-guided national development and the emergence of an increasingly global liberal economic order in which governments, ruling elites and transnational actors use the institutions of the state to advance the process of globalization and undermine or roll back national institutions erected in earlier decades. However, as is apparent in South Korea and elsewhere, elites still attempt to mobilize people using nationalist idioms and symbols. In fact the dismantling of the institutions and arrangements associated with state-guided national development is often carried out in the name of the nation. While the benefits of this process are regularly said to be widespread this has coincided with increased levels of inequality worldwide. Importantly, while this process has also been characterized as promoting competition and greater opportunities for small and medium businesses, by the 1990s a key characteristic of the globalization project was the growing concentration of economic power in the hands of a small number of large oligopolistic corporations (Nolan 2001).

The rise of the US-led globalization project and the promotion of neoliberalism have pushed 'new' and 'old' nation-states in many parts of the world to the limits of their potential (which was never great in many cases) as a vehicle for progress and prosperity (Berger 2001b). As the global market unfolds the territorial boundaries of nation-states become more porous, while national sovereignty is reconfigured and diluted (Bamyeh 2000: 1–8, 52–8). The US trajectory is both a driving force of, and a template for, this wider process. Since the 1980s the orientation of the US government has increasingly been toward the redirection of government funds away from social programs and toward the promotion of economic and geo-political initiatives overseas. This is linked to the ongoing efforts to bring down domestic wages and standards of living in support of higher profits and the pursuit of increased global market share for US-based corporations. These initiatives have been carried out over the past two decades by governments influenced by an externally oriented elite that is the primary beneficiary of a regressive tax system that effectively redistributes income upwards. The socioeconomic order in North America is one in which large numbers of people are connected to declining national institutions and national economic networks, at the same time as transnationalized elites and important sections of the middle class have benefited dramatically from the economic boom of the 1990s (Berger 2004a).

In the past twenty or thirty years US companies have globalized their supply networks, production systems, labor forces, management and financing. A significant number of Fortune 500 companies now receive over 50 per cent of their income from overseas, while 'global diversification' continues to be a key goal of most of the remaining companies in this group (Garten 2002: 46–7). Of course, Washington's orientation after 11 September 2001 has shifted to security with important implications for economic liberalization and deregulation. Meanwhile, the Bush administration's introduction of significant new tariffs on steel imports and major new subsidies for farmers in the early months of 2002 (not to mention Congressional constraints on Bush's 'trade promotion authority' legislation), are also interpreted by proponents of globalization as a setback (The Economist 2002b: 55–6). Despite these shifts, and despite the apparent increase in bilateral trade negotiations that are viewed in free-trade circles as a far less effective way to advance globalization than the multilateralism of the WTO, it should be emphasized that what has occurred in the realm of security and economics is a reorientation of, rather than a retreat from, the globalization project. The US government and US companies will continue to 'have much more interest in an open world economy than in one focused on increasing regulation' (Garten 2002: 47).

This emergent and uneven, neoliberal order, based on a new relationship between the global political economy and the nation-state system, has transformed rather than obviated the role of states. While the rise of the globalization project has dramatically reoriented the state away from national development, state intervention continues to be necessary in order to successfully realize the globalization project. Ultimately, the nation-state system itself has been transformed by and has provided the framework for the emergence of the US-led globalization project. For example, the elimination of constraints on international financial flows, the privatization of public sectors and a whole range of deregulating initiatives (which are arguably the most advanced and most important economic components of the globalization project), occurred as a result of state intervention across the nation-state system. This process demanded new, or reconfigured, state-provided legal frameworks and new relationships between national governments and/or international bodies. In practice this has meant that one of the main objectives of the US had been to promote the 'Americanization' of international and national legal frameworks for the regulation of financial activities (Panitch 2000b: 6–8, 14–15).

Despite the historical specificity of the sustained, but still uneven, transformation of particular state-mediated national development projects into globalizing states against the backdrop of the transformation of the nation-state system, two generalized national trajectories are apparent. The first involves a process of national reorientation and a crisis of national development. Apart from South Korea, the nation-states in Asia included in this category range from Japan to Thailand, Malaysia and Singapore (Goss and Burch 2001; Hilley 2001; Wee 2001). This is in contrast to some nation-states where the end of the high period of state-mediated national development has increasingly coincided not only with dramatic national reorientation, but with sometimes virulent struggles over the ethnic or religious content and/or territorial boundaries (usually, but not always, at the margins rather than the center) of the nation itself. This is the case for India and even more dramatically for Indonesia (Cohen and Ganguly 1999; Aspinall and Berger 2001). China also has the potential to follow this second path. Other countries more obviously included in the category of polities undergoing a crisis of the nation-state (or that are already 'failed states') might be Burma or Afghanistan (Smith 1999; Goodson 2001; Rubin 2002). More broadly, the present juncture represents a moment of both consolidation and incipient crisis for the US-led globalization project (Bishop 2002). Central to the incipient crisis, and symbolized by the events of 11 September 2001 in the United States, is the way that the post-Cold War instability, national crisis and state failure in parts of Asia, the former Soviet bloc, the Balkans, the Middle East and sub-Saharan Africa may well foreshadow the increasing occurrence of this kind of turmoil in North America and Western Europe (Mestrovic 1994; Job 2001).

Conclusion: the neoliberal ascendancy and East Asia

In the aftermath of the East Asian crisis and the post-9/11 world revised neoliberal economic prescriptions continue to be central to the powerful US-led globalization project. In an effort to engage critically with the significance and influence of neoliberalism and its relationship to US hegemony and other influential approaches to development, such as the theory of the developmental state, this chapter briefly examined the rise and transformation of dominant forms of development knowledge in the Cold War and post-Cold War era with particular emphasis on the Asia-Pacific. Between the mid-1940s and the mid-1970s, the dominant development discourse was grounded in the assumption that nation-states could be treated as natural units of a wider international politico-economic system, and development planning by national governments could, should, or would lead to outcomes beneficial to the majority. In the 1970s and early 1980s, however, the rise of neoliberalism and the emergent US-led globalization project increasingly reconfigured the role of the state and challenged the idea and practice of state-mediated national development. The contest between national development and an ascendant neoliberalism was nowhere more apparent than in the Asia-Pacific where the Cold War era saw the emergence of a number of developmental states that were widely represented by neoliberal commentators as free-trade models of capitalist development. Theories of the developmental state rejected the neoliberal interpretation of the rise of East Asia, but proponents of the developmental state, like their neoliberal counterparts, also often implicitly, if not explicitly, legitimated authoritarianism. In fact, like neoliberalism, theories of the developmental state naturalized the nation and increasingly produced explanations for the East Asian Miracle that were ahistorical and technocratic, despite their theoretical origins in historically grounded studies of the state in East Asia.

In this context a historically grounded approach more successfully captures the dynamics and significance of the rise of East Asia. After 1945, capitalist nation-states in East Asia were incorporated into a US-centered regional order on terms that, while they often allowed for considerable autonomy within their territorial borders, dramatically limited their actions in international terms and ensured that the developmental states waxed and waned as a result of the interaction between US hegemony and social and political changes on the ground. The rise of the US-led globalization project, the end of the Cold War, and then the Asian crisis and its aftermath, facilitated the steady but uneven decline of state-guided national development in Asia and beyond. South Korea is undergoing a crisis of national development and a dramatic process of national reorientation (as is Japan). More broadly, the deepening of the US-led globalization project in the post-Cold War era has also been characterized by an incipient crisis of neoliberalism. Post-Cold War instability and the passing and/or failure of state-guided national development are linked in part to the increasing levels of inequality facilitated by the spread of neoliberalism. The neoliberal era brings with it new political opportunities. In the shadow of the US-led globalization project, various political movements are making the global linkages and outlining and implementing the global strategies that will allow them to address and move beyond the serious limitations of nation-states, limitations that have become even more pronounced as the US-led globalization project enters a more militarized period.

Notes

1 The US-led globalization project is conceived of here as being pursued at a wide range of sites and centered on the reconfiguration of state-mediated national development projects into neoliberal states. The globalization project is linked, in particular, to the growing concentration of control over the global economy by a relatively small number of large oligopolistic transnational corporations that have emerged from the dramatic merger-driven and technology-facilitated changes to the global political economy of the past two decades (McMichael 1995: 350, 354).
2 Bauer's career as a development economist stretched back to the late colonial era and the Second World War. Bauer, who died in May 2002, was a member of the Mont Pèlerin Society (MPS). He also had close links with the Institute of Economic Affairs, a free-market think tank established in 1955, and with the Conservative Philosophy Group (CPG), which was set up in the 1970s by members of the Conservative Party and eventually provided staff and policy advice to Margaret Thatcher's government (Cockett 1994; also see Desai 1994a).
3 The US-based political scientist Robert H. Bates is widely perceived as a key figure in the rise of rational choice theory and its role in the revision of neoliberalism as is the economic historian Douglass C. North (Leys 1996: 36–7, 80–2, 86–90, 94–103; Bates 1981, 1989; North 1981, 1990).

6 The Mexican economy since NAFTA

Socioeconomic integration or disintegration?

Enrique Dussel Peters

Introduction

The North American Free Trade Agreement between Canada, Mexico and the United States (NAFTA) has become an example to follow for many countries and for most multilateral agencies, such as the World Bank and the International Monetary Fund. The conceptual and policy 'charm' of NAFTA lies not only in the dimension of the treaty and the negotiations *per se*, but also in the relevance of a long-term agreement that goes far beyond trade issues between countries that are so different socioeconomically, as well as in culture, and which have even had a highly conflictive history over previous centuries.

The chapter aims to examine the impact of NAFTA on Mexico's economy and society. The main objective, however, will be to present the principal socioeconomic effects of NAFTA in Mexico on issues such as industrial organization, trade, employment, real wages and income distribution. In some cases it will be difficult, if not impossible, to distinguish between the specific impact of NAFTA and 'other' events such as the economic crisis of Mexico's economy in 1994–5, and the uprising of the Ejército Zapatista de Liberación Nacional (EZLN), which began on 1 January 1994, the same day NAFTA was implemented. However, and as discussed in the chapter, NAFTA, the crisis of 1994–5 and other socioeconomic events since 1988 have to be understood in the context of the new socioeconomic strategy that has been followed in Mexico since then, and, with a few changes, up to 2003.

From this perspective, the chapter will be divided into three sections. The first section analyzes the conceptual and theoretical pillars of the new development strategy followed in Mexico, as well as in most of Latin America and even at the periphery, since the 1980s. As discussed, export-oriented industrialization has theoretically, historically and even politically little to do with neoliberalism. This distinction is also relevant for discussing alternatives to the current development strategy in Mexico.[1] The second section presents the specific form of implementation of the export-oriented industrialization-liberalization strategy in Mexico since 1988, as well as the structural effects of NAFTA on Mexico's economy. The third and final section concludes on the prior chapters and discusses potential alternatives to the liberalization strategy in Mexico.

Neoliberalism and export-oriented industrialization

This chapter will distinguish between the theoretical and historical genesis of neoliberalism and export-oriented industrialization (EOI), and the political consequences of each school of thought. Based on an analysis of the latter, the final part will discuss the relevance of deepening the understanding of the development model presented for most of the periphery, including Mexico. *To be clear*, it is not a matter of being for or against neoliberalism, but of defining clearly the theoretical basis, goals and implications of the policies that have been implemented. Moreover, neither is it a matter of 'names', i.e. of calling the specific policies 'neoliberal', 'EOI' or 'xyz'; on the contrary it is a matter of *understanding the socioeconomic and territorial processes in time and space* that are actually evolving in the periphery. From this perspective, a critical consensus on 'neoliberalism' would not be sufficient or complete. Proposals for alternatives to 'neoliberalism' will be even more difficult without a clear conceptualization (compare a more exhaustive discussion in Dussel Peters 2000a).

Neoliberalism

Although there has been an apparent widespread consensus against 'neoliberalism' since the 1990s, both in periphery and in core countries, there has been little discussion and definition of the concept in the 1990s (see Babb 2001, for example).[2] What does 'neoliberalism' in the 1990s mean? Clearly, it is not sufficient to argue that 'it' is a movement/line of thought that favors market policies, as authors such as Adam Smith already argued several centuries ago. Moreover, the concept and its implementation already have, concretely in Latin America, a long tradition. Neoliberalism is not a new concept in the social sciences. At least since the 1960s this concept has been related to a school of thought, and in general to the theoretical work of the Chicago Boys and the application of their work in several nations via policy, particularly in South America during the 1960s and 1970s (Foxley 1988; Valdés 1995); i.e. neoliberalism already has a certain 'tradition' on the continent. Neoliberalism, as opposed to other schools of thought such as liberalism and conservatism, emerged since the 1930s strictly in opposition to the rising of Keynesianism in OECD nations, but also in reaction to Marxism, Leninism and later Stalinism in the former Soviet Union and other nations around the world.[3] It is in this historical context that authors such as Karl Popper and later Milton Friedman, but *particularly Friedrich August von Hayek*, highlight the core of neoliberal thought (compare Hinkelammert 1984, Gómez 1995 and Gutiérrez R. 1998), which, commencing in the US and Europe, had a deep impact on other schools of thought.

What are the basic concepts of neoliberalism?[4] The concept of *science* is of critical importance for neoliberal thought. Hayek differentiates between simple and complex phenomena. Social sciences, which in general deal with 'complex phenomena', should not analyze what is, but 'what is not: a construction of hypothetical models of possible worlds that could exist, if ... All scientific knowledge (*wissenschaftliche Erkenntnis*) is knowledge, not of specific facts, but of the hypotheses which have survived in the presence of systematic efforts to refute them.' (Hayek 1981, I: 33). According to Hayek, the main scientific discrepancies in social sciences are the result of two schools of thought: *critical rationalism* and *constructive rationalism*. Constructive rationalism, which searches for a specific and determined social construction, is a reflection of socialist thought and all those 'totalitarian doctrines' which are not erroneous 'because of their values, on which they are based, but on a wrong conception of the forces that allowed for the Great Society and civilization' (18). On the other hand, critical rationalism is based on the premise that information is limited, 'the necessary ignorance of the majority of details ... is the central source of the problems of all social orders' (28). Thus, the attempt of any form of planification is irrational and non-scientific, since it attempts to determine and overcome individual and natural attitudes and behaviors. Furthermore, individuals that persist in attempting different forms of planification or construction are dangerous for Great Society and civilization, and in some cases there is an explicit reference to their elimination, since they become a threat to the existing social order.

From this perspective, social science should distance itself from history and historical experiences such as *social justice* and any form of economic and social planification (Hayek 1981, II: 188). Given the information constraint and the ignorance of reality, any pretension to plan or construct welfare state types of society are non-scientific, utopian, useless and a threat to human development.

Cultural evolution or Hayek's social Darwinism is based on the belief that 'all sustainable (*dauerhaft*) structures ... are the result of processes of selective evolution and that they can only be explained in this framework' (Hayek 1981, III: 215). From this perspective, such a process of evolution determines the development and history of human beings: *selection* among human beings and the survival of the strongest and fittest. The final motive of this is competition, since 'our current order is in first line not a result of a project, but emerged out of a process of competition, in which the most efficient establishments (*Einrichtungen*) won through' (211). *Competition* is, from this perspective, also raised to the most successful methodological approach, as 'trial and error' or as a 'method of discovery' (Hayek 1975b). Historical processes thence are processes of the survival of the fittest and strongest individuals, i.e. a process of competition beginning historically with the most primitive societies.

Neoliberalism assumes that individuals and their respective *private properties*, which are assigned by competition, generate their respective societies. Thus, freedom, and particularly economic freedom, is the main mean and end for any society. Most neoliberal authors, but especially Friedman (Friedman 1962: 7ff.), stress that economic freedom is an indispensable condition for social development, while political freedom will result from economic freedom. Most important, freedom is understood as a utopian concept: 'the need for government in these respects arises because absolute freedom is impossible' (Friedman 1962: 25). Neoliberalism adopts from liberalism the concept of freedom, and 'new' (*neo*) is its open, legitimizing intention (Gutiérrez R. 1998). On the one hand, capitalism is a necessary condition for political freedom. On the other hand, authoritarianism does not limit economic freedom, and 'it is therefore clearly possible to have economic arrangements that are fundamentally capitalist and political arrangements that are not free' (Friedman 1962: 10).

The *market* is the main theoretical and historical social, economic and political institution of neoliberal thought, which is a 'system of communication, which we call market, and that has demonstrated itself to be a more efficient mechanism for the use of dispersing information than any other that human beings have consciously created' (Hayek 1975a: 20–1). The market is an institution in which 'the price system is a system of signals and allows human beings to participate and adapt to facts, of which they know nothing; that all our modern order, all our world market and welfare are based on the possibility of an adjustment of facts which we ignore ...' (Hayek 1981, I: 66). But what are the functioning conditions for the market? It is impossible to know the specific properties regarding conditions and results of this 'spontaneous order'. From this perspective, the market constitutes an apparent autopoietic system, i.e. it self-reproduces its conditions and needs. The market, apparently, creates its own supply and demand. Where do prices – the last instance to which human beings can relate their needs and their relationship to the rest of the human beings – come from? Prices, as planification, are also utopian, and neoliberalism becomes an apparent theology: '... the *pretium mathematicum*, the mathematical price, depends on so many specific events, that it will be never known by any human being, but only by God' (Hayek 1975a).

Neoliberal thought does not only justify the status quo and does not consider time and space in the development of individuals and societies, but it also creates a polarized thought: the market or planned economies, capitalism or socialism, freedom of individuals or chaos, God or devil. This rather dogmatic and anti-utopian thought is extremely violent and a response to any attempt to plan societies and economies, from Keynesianism to Marxism and other socialist proposals formulated during the twentieth century and after World War II and, explicitly, against the 'social welfare state'. Thus, it proposes among other things a minimalist state, or even its abolishment, the installation of market mechanisms at all economic and social levels and, as a basic condition for development and evolution of modern and Great Societies, private property and free competition and trade, without any state interventions or any form of institutional barriers.

Neoliberal thought thus is a highly dogmatic and legitimizing theory of the capitalist market and *status quo*, and goes far beyond economic theory and policy. Its methodology is intolerant of different perspectives. These authors had a direct impact in the 1960s and 1970s in 'specimens' such as Pinochet and J. Kirkpatrick (Kirkpatrick 1979), who in many cases leant strongly to fascism, and have lost presence since the 1980s in Latin America, at least up to now and particularly in official circles. The dogmatic, aggressive and authoritarian form of neoliberalism, as experienced in several countries in South America during this period, has, with a few exceptions, not been seen in most of Latin America during the 1980s and 1990s.

Export-oriented industrialization and neoliberalism

The crises of ISI since the late 1960s, of Keynesianism, and of the welfare state, along with the debt crisis of the 1980s, gave a new impetus to a new version of neoclassical, industrial and trade literature. The crisis of the historic compromise that emerged as a result of the Depression of the 1930s and of World War II in most OECD nations not only weakened the respective states and its institutions, but also specifically labor (Glyn *et al.* 1989). The emergence of export-oriented industrialization (EOI) and of its particular applications varies according to the respective country. Nevertheless, it is remarkable that at least since the middle of the 1980s most of the Latin American countries have followed similar economic strategies based on stabilization and other market-friendly economic reforms to fight populism and reduce the role of the state in the name of economic efficiency. The specifics of the respective political systems, e.g. of authoritarian, federalist and/or democratic political systems among others, are significant, since they allow at least for a different pace of implementation of the new policies, as well as for modifications or even opposition to them, depending on the degree of negotiation between political sectors (Bresser Pereira *et al.* 1993).

This new school of thought focused on the need for an export-oriented industrialization and a radical departure from the ISI model of the relationship between the market and the state, i.e. EOI became a theoretical and political response and alternative to ISI. EOI also became a significant part of the so-called 'Washington Consensus' (Williamson 1992) since the 1980s.

However, EOI is not 'external' to developing countries. In addition to the crisis of ISI and of corporatist sociopolitical structures since the late 1960s, most developing nations have also undergone significant ideological changes and experienced a shift in power between capital and labor. Not only has EOI become mainstream economic theory in international trade and development theory, but also many, if not most, government officials in Latin America have been strongly influenced by this school of thought. Since the 1980s, most of the secretaries or ministers in Latin America, through undergraduate or graduate studies in top-ranking US schools of economics, have directly been inspired by EOI.

The argument in favor of EOI builds on the positive association between exports and economic growth or development. Contrary to ISI, EOI stresses that the world market, through exports, is the 'point of reference' for any economic unit (firm, region, nation, group of nations, etc.). Exports, in general, reflect efficiency; i.e. non-exporting economic units are not efficient from this perspective. EOI emphasizes neutral or export-oriented production by manufacturers to maximize the efficient allocation of factors of production and a specialization among nations according to their respective comparative cost-advantages (Balassa 1981). Moreover, it underlines the central role of manufacturing in the periphery's economies, even though the theoretical justification for doing so has not been sufficiently developed to date. Contrary to structural restrictions or 'bottlenecks' imposed by industrialization – as stressed by some ISI authors – this 'intuitive Darwinian rationale for free trade' (Bhagwati 1991: 17) argues that the degree and the structure of protection in the periphery under ISI had a significant negative impact in the allocation of resources, and subsequently on exports and overall economic structure.

Probably the strongest argument of EOI supporters against ISI's 'infant industry' protection and overall interventions is the 'rent-seeking behavior' it generates. As a result of market intervention (import licenses, tariffs, etc.) under ISI firms and countries generate perverse (or non-market-conforming) results in this environment: excess capacity to obtain rents provided by the state, over-utilization of ISI instruments for development, and, in general, an economic structure aimed at reaping the incentives provided by the state. In parallel, these mechanisms generate perverse social incentives and structures, since, in most of the cases, incentives are not taken by the initially expected groups (potential 'modern/industrial' groups), but rather by 'rent-seeking' and corrupt groups, which do not have an incentive to modernize/industrialize. The establishment of a rent-seeking bureaucracy is, from this perspective, one of the most significant obstacles for development (Krueger 1983, 1992 and 1997).

From the perspective of EOI, East Asian countries in particular provide empirical evidence to support the contention that export performance, especially of manufactured goods within a market-oriented production system, is positively associated with economic growth (Balassa 1981; Srinivasan 1985; Balassa and Williamson 1990).

Macroeconomic conditions for development – the generation of a 'market-friendly environment' – are at the center of economic policy. Free trade and complete openness of economies, the abolition of tariff and non-tariff barriers, anti-inflationary strategies, a minimalist state, and restrictive monetary and fiscal policies are the main macroeconomic goals of EOI. The private sector is conceived as the motor for future development and industrialization (Balassa 1988; Krueger 1978, 1983; World Bank 1991; cf. Dussel Peters 2000a).[5]

In the EOI view, industrial development is conceptualized as an outcome of perfect competition and the free development of market forces, i.e. macroeconomic conditions will result in changing microeconomic conditions. This is the main reason why discussions of industrial policies have 'typically been neglected' (Pack 1988: 344). Demanded are neutral policies since the industrial structure will adjust 'automatically' through comparative cost advantages according to the respective endowments. Thus, 'social profitability' (Balassa 1989: 303; World Bank 1991: 99) calls for neutral policies, which provide equal incentives to exports and to import substitution. EOI rejects the possibility of granting preferential treatment to sectors due to society's lack of information and ignorance of correctly calculating the social costs and of the potential of these sectors.

EOI accepts the case for little state intervention. Even where it is acknowledged, state interventions are 'second-best options'. These potential distortions are regarded as deviations from the general theorem and are marginal within a market-friendly environment. In spite of these considerations, the practical application of interventionist policies is beset with 'many difficulties and dangers

... and suggest strongly that common sense and wisdom should prevail in favor of free trade' (Bhagwati 1991: 33). It is essentially the economic performance of several export-oriented nations' manufacturing sectors that supports this argument (Bhagwati and Krueger 1985: 68–72; World Bank 1987, 1993).

With regard to trade policy, as with industrial policy and any other economic and social issue, macroeconomic stabilization plays a crucial role. Overall economic liberalization and export orientation should be strongly implemented on a continuous basis; the greater the reductions of market interventions and of bias toward export promotion, the higher the probability of economic success (Krueger 1978; World Bank 1991). Balassa and Williamson (1990) stress the importance of stability of policies, especially in the case of fiscal policies and real exchange rates. These measures not only create confidence and incentives within the export-oriented private sector, but are also a significant factor in stabilizing the balance of payments.

Despite the adjustment costs in the short term – balance of payment deterioration, decreasing output and subsequent unemployment – the benefits will always exceed these initial costs. Assuming that these reforms will not increase unemployment, the World Bank (1991) concludes that liberalization should not worsen the distribution of income and the conditions of the poor.

Finally, the employment issue within EOI is viewed as an exogenous variable and has been left aside in most of these studies. This is not surprising given that EOI is based on the full employment assumption of neoclassical economic theory. As a result, it is assumed that the elimination of overall market distortions and export-orientation will have a positive impact on employment.

The discussion on export-oriented industrialization versus neoliberalism is relevant from several perspectives. On the one hand, in Latin America and Mexico – as well as in most of the periphery – there are currently few authors and policy makers that would subscribe to neoliberalism. Without a doubt, this may simply reflect ignorance of the concept and/or the unwillingness to subscribe to a school of thought that has been highly criticized. In addition, however, there are historical, conceptual and political differences between neoliberalism and export-oriented industrialization. In the Mexican context, for example, a debate took place among political parties and social movements which disassociated from neoliberalism, including President Zedillo (1994–2000), Partido Acción Nacional leader and winner of the 2000 elections, Vicent Fox (2000–6), and even former President Carlos Salinas de Gortari (Salinas de Gortari 2000; Salinas de Gortari and Mangabeira Unger 1999).

Who, then, are the neoliberals? It is too easy, but also superficial, to point at neoliberalism as the cause of all economic and social 'evils'. As discussed in this chapter, the widespread criticism of neoliberalism in Latin America is questionable since neoliberalism has not been the predominant conceptual and policy-making framework in the region since the 1980s. Even though it is possible to argue that EOI is a form of neoliberalism, this still has to be analyzed in detail, theoretically, historically, and empirically. The work of Plehwe and Walpen (Plehwe 2002; Plehwe and Walpen 1999; Walpen and Plehwe 2001) argues in this direction, but this analysis needs further historical and theoretical elaboration. While it is suggestive that the Mont Pèlerin Society (MPS) has had a global structure and diffusion, even in Latin America and in Mexico, these studies are so far not conclusive regarding the effects on other socioeconomic movements, in policy and socioeconomic strategies on EOI and specific strategies in periphery.

As analyzed, neoliberalism is far more aggressive, dogmatic and authoritarian than EOI. Since the 1980s, and particularly in the 1990s, no government would argue, at least explicitly, for authoritarian governments and against totalitarian doctrines, to impose 'economic freedom' at all social, economic and military costs. Neoliberal authors are also more 'coherent' and consistent in their arguments: free trade and markets are the solution to all problems, from commodities to capital flows, drugs and labor, among many others. In Latin America, however – from Color de Melo to Menem, Fujimori, Salinas de Gortari, Zedillo and Fox, among many others – the dictate of the world market, rather, seems to be the motto. These policymakers – backed by economists, who have in most of the cases studied in US Ivy League universities and have been strongly influenced by EOI (Babb 2001) – are not fighting wars against totalitarianism and for 'national security', and are not heavily supported by security institutions and the military as in most of Latin America during the 1960s and 1970s. The new 'EOI-rationale' dictates that all economic units have to be competitive and efficient in world markets through exports. Additionally, macroeconomic stability and overall horizontal/neutral policies, based on the notion of a 'lean' State, are of critical importance for EOI-policies.

If it is argued that Pinochet's and Salinas's policies, even economic policies, are undifferentiated, such a conceptual and historical/empirical view obscures more than it clarifies. Most significantly, such a simplistic perspective does not allow for a discussion on alternatives to EOI, since it makes it impossible to analyze the newly imposed development strategy in space and time.

The impact of NAFTA on Mexico's economy

This section examines the performance of Mexico's economy for 1988–2002 and distinguishes for the period before and after NAFTA, since January 1994. The first part will briefly present the particular implementation of export-oriented industrialization in Mexico, i.e. the liberalization strategy. The second part will present, in more depth, the main socioeconomic structures that have evolved in Mexico, in several cases as a result of NAFTA. However, and as discussed in the first part, NAFTA has to be understood as a necessary condition for, at least potentially, the success of the liberalization strategy.

The liberalization strategy and NAFTA

Mexico's crisis in 1982, which initially resulted from the private and public sectors' inability to service foreign debt, did not reflect a 'solvency' or 'liquidity' crisis, but the unsustainability of ISI. Trade surplus in agriculture since the 1940s (which turned into a deficit from the late 1960s), oil revenues and massive international credits since the late 1970s, were not sufficient to finance the crisis of ISI (Ros 1991). The specific international conditions, particularly of the US, did not allow for 'recycling' old international credits for new ones since 1982. Paradoxically, it was the demand of capital of the US economy in international markets that increased interest rates and changed capital flows to the US and other OECD nations, resulting in massive international inability to service external debt after 1982. Moreover, in 1979–80 a two-fold increase in oil-prices caused exaggerated future oil revenue estimations (Gurría Treviño 1993), while prices began to fall in 1981 and eventually collapsed in 1986.

It is from this perspective – considering that the period 1982–7 could be understood as a 'transition period' to manage the socialization of economic crisis of ISI, including the failure of a gradual approach to liberalization which ended in 1987 with an inflation rate of 159 per cent and a fiscal deficit of 16.1 per cent of GDP, as well as a drastic fall in GDP, of investments and overall economic activity and in the increasing pressure of foreign debt-servicing and of multilateral agencies – that December 1987 reflected the culmination of the crisis of ISI and the beginning of a new socioeconomic development strategy.

These specific circumstances added to the charm of EOI, while the contact of most Mexican policy-makers with US academic institutions and government officials, in which context export-oriented industrialization was the conceptual mainstream, permitted the implementation of the liberalization strategy. The Salinas administration became the starting point of the liberalization strategy in 1988.

Mexico's liberalization strategy was consolidated by means of a series of *Pactos Económicos* (Economic Pacts), the first one being agreed in December 1987. The respective Pacts – which included wage ceilings and allowed for an *ex post* indexing of wages – were negotiated jointly by union officials, the government, and the private sector. These pacts became the centerpiece of the new strategy under the Salinas administration, which Zedillo has continued with few changes since 1994.

It is in this international and national economic context that the major pillars and guidelines of this strategy of liberalization, in contrast to ISI, are as follows (Aspe Armella 1993; Zedillo 1994; Dussel Peters 2000a; Gurría Treviño 1993; Salinas de Gortari 2000):

1   Macroeconomic stabilization was to 'induce' the process of microeconomic and sectoral growth and development, i.e. all sectoral subsidies and specific policies were to be abolished in favor of neutral policies.
2   As an extension of point 1, the main priority of the government was to stabilize the macroeconomy. Since 1988, the government has viewed controlling inflation rates[6] (or relative prices) and the fiscal deficit, as well as attraction of foreign investments – as the main financing source of the new strategy, since oil revenues and massive foreign credits were not available and/or sufficient. The macroeconomic priorities of the liberalization strategy were backed up by restrictive money and credit policies of Banco de México.

The Mexican economy since NAFTA 129

3   The nominal and real exchange rates are a result of the control of the inflation rate (the nominal exchange rate as an anti-inflationary anchor), i.e. since the control of the inflation rate is the macroeconomic priority of the liberalization strategy, the government will not allow for devaluation, the latter resulting in increasing inflation rates because of imported inputs.
4   Supported by the reprivatization of the banking system beginning in the mid-1980s, and the massive privatization of state-owned industries (*paraestatales*), the Mexican private sector is to lead Mexico's economy out of the 'lost decade' of the 1980s through exports. The massive import liberalization process, initiated at the end of 1985, was supposed to support the private manufacturing sector in order to orient it toward exports, as a result of cheaper international imports.
5   Finally, government policies toward labor unions were of utmost significance. As reflected in the respective *pactos*, only a few (government-friendly) labor unions were deemed acceptable to negotiate inside firms and with the government, while the rest were declared illegal. This process, which has included violent disruptions of independent labor unions, has, since 1987, made national wage-negotiations in Mexico possible within the framework of the respective economic pacts.

Up to 2002 the Mexican government has continued, with a few exceptions, consistently with the liberalization strategy. Overall abolishment of subsidies regarding goods – culminating at the beginning of 1999 with the abolition of subsidies for *tortillas* and most commodities of the 'basic food basket' – services and credits reflect this process.

What is the rationality of the liberalization strategy, i.e. the specific implementation of EOI in Mexico? In general, as EOI, it assumes that an export-orientation of the private manufacturing sector will provide for the new growth and development basis for Mexico. Following this view, imports were substantially liberalized, and most of the state-owned firms were privatized. This new strategy assumes that macroeconomic stabilization, added to export-orientation, would allow for a 'trickle-down effect' in the rest of the socio-economic variables.[7] Thus, and contrary to import-substituting industrialization, any economic unit had to prove its efficiency through its export-orientation to the world market.

NAFTA is of fundamental relevance for the liberalization strategy. In the best of the cases, and allowing for a significant structural change toward exports in the Mexican economy, the economy required a guaranteed demand for these commodities. Otherwise, let us try to imagine a successful export-orientation without a market to sell these commodities.[8]

It is in this context that the Mexican and US governments began free trade negotiations since the beginning of the 1990s. Independently of the specific agreements, which in many cases are at the 10-digit level of the Harmonized Tariff System and include thousands of items, it is possible to establish that (Hufbauer and Schott 1993; Dussel Peters 2000b; López-Córdova 2001):

1   NAFTA goes far beyond tariff-reductions and the creation of a free-trade agreement region. On the one hand, Mexican free tariff imports from the US increased from 37.66 per cent in 1990 to more than 51.08 per cent in 1998 and levels above 90 per cent by 2003. However, NAFTA also includes relevant issues such as regional content and rules of origin, investments, intellectual property rights, labor and ecological topics some of which required constitutional changes in Mexico.
2   Until 2002 specific disputes among Canada, Mexico and the US, in the context of trade flows between Mexico and the US of above $330 billion in 2002, were relatively low.
3   In spite of 1, in general NAFTA has focused on tariff, trade and investment issues. Labor and ecological side agreements have, so far, received little attention. Moreover, the main institutions created by NAFTA, such as the NAFTA-Commission and Commission for Labor Cooperation, among others, have remained understaffed and with little decision-making power. Central issues in the US–Mexican relationship, such as migration, regional and national disparities, institutions to reduce poverty, among many others, have so far not been envisioned.

However, NAFTA became a requirement for the liberalization strategy since the end of the 1980s given that the US has been, throughout the twentieth century, Mexico's main trading partner. A legal framework that allowed for massive Mexican exports was fundamental.

Macroeconomic performance since 1988

It is important to acknowledge, and with some irony, that the liberalization strategy *has been relatively successful since 1988 in its own terms*. Inflation since 1988 has been reduced significantly from levels above 150 per cent in the 1980s to levels below 20 per cent until 2002, with the exception of the period 1995–6. Similarly, the fiscal deficit, as a percentage of GDP – also as a result of drastic cuts in social and investment spending – fell from levels above 15 per cent to levels below 3 per cent during the 1990s; in several years it even reached a surplus. Foreign direct investments (FDI) reached annually levels above $9.5 billion for 1994–2002, and doubled in terms of GDP of the 1980s; Mexican exports increased from $30.7 billion in 1988 to $160.7 billion in 2002, representing less than 15 per cent and more than 25 per cent of GDP, respectively. As a result, Mexico, during the 1990s, was one of the most successful cases internationally regarding FDI-attraction and export-orientation.[9]

In spite of these issues, it is relevant to highlight several other aspects and macroeconomic results. First, GDP and GDP per capita were well below results obtained during ISI.[10] Second, since 1988 investments as a percentage of GDP fell constantly until 1994–5, and have recovered since then, but at levels still below those of the beginning of the 1980s. Third, and this will be discussed more in detail in the next section, exports have increased, but so have imports. The latter, and as a result, a structural and increasing trade deficit, have been one of the main macroeconomic challenges of Mexico's economy: the increasing uncertainty regarding the trade and current account deficit. As we shall see in what follows, this reflects one of the main outcomes of EOI and the liberalization strategy since 1988, a process that has deepened through NAFTA.

Two other macroeconomic outcomes of the liberalization strategy are relevant. On the one hand, and strictly as a result of the liberalization strategy, the continuous overvaluation of the exchange rate, since the nominal exchange rate is used as an 'anchor' against inflation. In 2000, the exchange rate is estimated to be overvalued by around 40 per cent, according to official estimations (see Figure 6.1); this process has deepened throughout 2001–2. As a result, exporters have lacked the incentive to continue with their activities, while imports have continued massively. Second, real interest rates in $US have been high since 1988, also to attract both portfolio and FDI. Additionally, the commercial banking sector has not been able to channel resources to the private sector: in 2002, in terms of GDP and normalized for 1994, it represented 20.13 per cent.[11]

Third, exports have specialized in relatively capital-intensive activities, if compared with the rest of the Mexican economy, in sectors such as automobiles, autoparts, and electronics, among others. As a result, the gap between the growth in the economically active population and the generation of employment has widened significantly during the 1990s and since NAFTA, and has become one of the main socioeconomic challenges in Mexico.

The outcomes of the liberalization strategy thus are mixed at best, and questionable. While it has been able to stabilize several macroeconomic variables, at best it has not been able to link these benefits at the meso- and micro-level. The strategy in fact has generated a profound process of socioeconomic polarization.

Manufacturing's performance since 1988

Since the beginning of the 1980s, manufacturing's GDP increased constantly its share over total GDP and reached 23 per cent in 1988. Since then, however, and also as a result of the penetration of imports, manufacturing's share decreased to

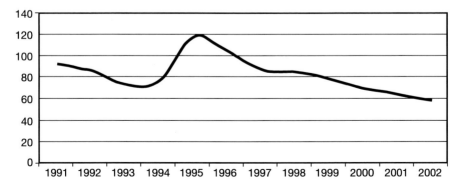

Figure 6.1 Real exchange rate (1990–2002) (1990 = 100)

levels below 17 per cent in 2002. Independent of this general trend, it is relevant to highlight the main structural changes of Mexico's manufacturing sector since 1988.

First, and considering that total economy's share of exports/GDP increased from less than 15 per cent to more than 25 per cent for 1988 and 2002, the same coefficient increased from 31.63 per cent in 1988 to levels above 65 per cent since 1995. Manufacturing as suggested by EOI has effectively become the motor of exports and growth of Mexico's economy. Only three out of 49 manufacturing branches (automobile, auto parts and electronics) generated 47.40 per cent of these exports in 2000. Figure 6.2 also reflects the increasing concentration of exports at the 2-digit level of the Harmonized Tariff System since only three sections represent more than 60 per cent of Mexican exports during the 1990s.

Second, the dynamics of manufacturing imports was no less impressive, and, as a percentage of GDP, increased from 47.04 per cent to 105.15 per cent for 1988 and 2000, respectively. As with exports, and at a branch level, only five branches (non-electrical machinery, electronics, autoparts, other manufacturing and electrical equipment) increased their share over total imports from 47.29 per cent to 51.79 per cent for the period. This net penetration of imports reflects one of the main characteristics of manufacturing since the liberalization strategy: its increasing dependency on imports, and, as a result, an increasing rupture of backward and forward linkages and value-added chains. These tendencies are also reflected in the trade balance/GDP coefficient (see Figure 6.3): since 1988 the coefficient fell significantly for total economy and manufacturing, and only recovered as a result of the crisis of 1994–5. From this perspective, manufacturing has been the main cause of this crisis, since its trade deficit/GDP, of less than 30 per cent in 1994, reflected a trade deficit of more than $30 billion. This, as we shall see, is one of the main outcomes of the liberalization strategy.

Third, it is important to analyze the processes – and in contrast to products – of transformation behind export growth of Mexican manufacturing since 1988:

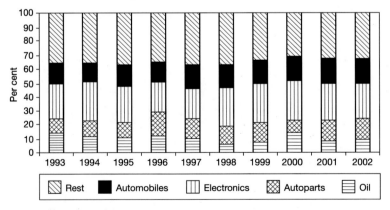

Figure 6.2 Mexico: export structure (1993–2002) (as a percentage of total exports)
Source: Own calculations based on Bancomext (SIC-M).

for 1993–2002 on average, temporary imports to be exported, including *maquiladoras*, have accounted for 78.78 per cent of total exports (more than 80 per cent since 1998). Considering that since the 1960s national inputs over total inputs have been less than 3.5 per cent of total inputs for *maquiladoras*, Mexican exports continue to be characterized by a minimal transformation process and display a high dependency on imports. More than 95 per cent of the processes involve the US. Neither tariffs nor value-added taxes or any other taxes are due. Thus, of total Mexican exports in 2002, only 18 per cent did not depend on programs for temporary imports, out of which 46.11 per cent were oil products. This product and trade specialization (more than 90 per cent of Mexican exports go to the US) has high economic and social costs for Mexican society and requires specific NAFTA compatible legal norms to secure temporary imports (Alvarez Galván and Dussel Peters 2001).

Fourth, the export growth has been concentrated in a small number of regions and firms since 1988. At the firm level, the main 300 exporting firms and around 3,500 *maquiladoras* accounted for 93.83 per cent of exports during 1993–2001, the rest of the 3.1 million firms thus accounting for less than 7 per cent. On the other hand, these exporting firms and *maquiladoras* only accounted for 5.70 per cent of Mexico's economically active population during 1993–2001. These tendencies are fundamental for understanding the export activities in Mexico. They display a high degree of intrafirm trade and capital intensity compared to the rest of the Mexican economy and have been unable to generate employment according to the requirements of Mexican society (see below).

Fifth, it is relevant to stress that intra-industry trade in Mexico has increased constantly throughout the 1990s to reach levels of 50 per cent of total trade (León González Pacheco and Dussel Peters 2001). Thus, almost half of total exports account for similar imports from similar items at the four-digit level of the Harmonized Tariff System. In many cases intra-industry trade seems to reflect intra-firm trade, although there are as yet no studies to underpin this affirmation. The share of intra-industry trade increased significantly after the implementation of NAFTA and the crisis of 1994–5.

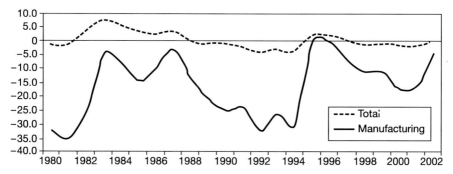

Figure 6.3 Trade balance/GDP (1980–2002) (percentage over GDP)
Source: Own elaboration based on INEGI (SCN).

Table 6.1 Mexico: general employment and unemployment tendencies (1990–2002) (thousands)

	1990	1991	1992	1993	1994	1995	1996	1997	1998	1999	2000	2001	2002 Preliminary
Total population	83.800	85.500	87.100	88.800	90.400	92.000	93.571	95.127	96.648	98.132	99.600	101.000	102.378
Economically active population	–	31.229	32.440	33.652	34.605	35.559	36.581	38.345	39.507	40.669	41.832	42.994	44.156
Officially employed population	–	30.270	31.427	32.585	33.082	33.578	35.006	37.043	38.363	38.939	38.785	39.421	–
Ensured employees Insured at Instituto Mexicano del Seguro Social (IMSS).	9.360	10.022	10.175	10.076	10.071	9.460	9.700	10.444	11.261	11.906	12.607	12.541	12.371
Official unemployment	–	817	880	1.075	1.224	2.082	1.925	1.371	1.228	973	853	946	–
Open unemployment rate	2.7	2.7	2.8	3.3	3.7	6.2	5.5	3.7	3.2	2.5	2.2	2.4	2.9
Insured employees/EAP	–	32.1	31.4	29.9	29.1	26.6	26.5	27.2	28.5	29.3	30.1	29.2	–

Source: Own calculations based on PEF (2002).

Employment, productivity, real wages and income distribution

Labor market and employment generation in Mexico are historically determined by the increase of the economically active population (EAP). EAP in Mexico increased during 1991–2001 at an average annual growth rate of 3.3 per cent, which reflects on average an annual growth of 1.2 million persons that have integrated into the labor market for the period. Table 6.1 reflects that, according to official sources, the open unemployment rate[12] in Mexico has not been above 7 per cent for 1991–2002. This, however, is strictly a result of the definition of the open unemployment rate and makes sense mainly for OECD countries. In Mexico and most of Latin America, however, this definition is useless, since there is no public social network and no unemployment insurance that allows for 'unemployment' under these terms. Thus, it is even surprising that unemployment is above 0 per cent!

Since official estimates of unemployment are very limited, the main trends to understand the challenge of employment in Mexico are related to EAP and the generation of employment. The EAP increased by 9.2 million during 1991–2001 whereas the economy generated 2.5 million jobs insured under Instituto Mexicano del Seguro Social (IMSS) only. The gap explains migration to the US and the search for a job in Mexico's informal labor market among other subsistence strategies. These tendencies express the profound and severe socioeconomic challenges not reflected in the one-digit open unemployment rate.

In addition to the lack of sufficient employment generation it is of the utmost importance to consider that real wages in Mexico in 2001 accounted for less than 30 per cent and 80 per cent of 1980 for minimum and manufacturing wages, respectively (see Figure 6.4). Thus, real wages have been far below the levels of two decades ago, and they have not recovered since the implementation of NAFTA in 1994.

What have been some of the main characteristics of the employment-generating branches since 1988 and 1994? In general, manufacturing has not created proportionally more employment than other economic sectors; the average annual growth rate (AAGR) for 1988–2000 has been 2.5 per cent, 2.4 per cent for the total

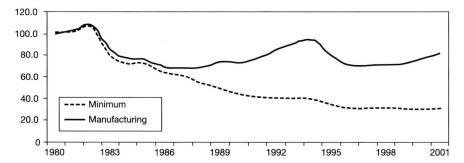

Figure 6.4 Real minimum wages and in manufacturing (1980–2001) (1980=100)
Sources: Own calculations based on CEPAL (2002).

economy, and both well below the 3.3 per cent of the EAP. Several issues stand out for the most dynamic branches of Mexico's economy in terms of employment:

1 Within manufacturing, *maquiladoras* generated 86.53 per cent of total manufacturing employment, although they only represented 1.62 per cent and 4.07 per cent of total Mexican employment in 1988 and 2000.
2 Out of 73 branches of Mexico's economy, five stand out in 1988–2000 for their average annual growth rate in employment of above 6 per cent: electronics, other manufacturing industries, autoparts, electronic appliances and construction.
3 Out of these five dynamic branches, construction alone generated 24.69 per cent of the employment of Mexico's economy and 77.06 per cent of the employment generated by these five branches for 1988–2000 (Dussel Peters 2003).

These trends are substantial for understanding the quality of the new employment generated since 1988, but also since 1994 through NAFTA: during 1988–2000 labor productivity decreased by 11.81 per cent for these five branches, the trade balance/GDP coefficient increased from 28.75 per cent in 1988 to 52.57 per cent in 2000 and real wages fell by 4.0 per cent for the period. As a result, the difference between real wages and labor productivity was positive for this group of branches, however, under the worst conditions: labor productivity fell more than did real wages, both under negative signs.

As a result of these socioeconomic trends in GDP, trade, labor productivity and real wages, income distribution has also polarized substantially. Since 1989 the poorest decile (or decile one) lost more than 0.58 per cent of total monetary income; for the period, the first seven deciles lost their share in monetary income. On the other hand, deciles eight, nine and ten increased their share. In the case of decile ten, it increased its share since 1984 by more than 7 per cent (see Figure 6.5).

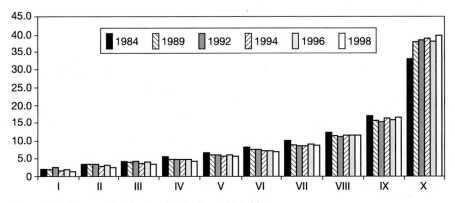

Figure 6.5 Income distribution by deciles (1984–98)
Source: Own calculations based on Dussel Peters (2000a).

Conclusions

The main arguments of this chapter were presented in two parts. The first distinguishes between neoliberalism and export-oriented industrialization (EOI). The second discusses the effects of the specific form of EOI in Mexico, the liberalization strategy, and NAFTA.

In the first part I argued that the conceptual, historical and political differences between neoliberalism and EOI are substantial. This is of particular relevance if we are to search for alternatives to the policies that are being implemented in Mexico, Latin America and most of the periphery. Moreover, more in-depth historical analysis is required in order to obtain a better understanding of the linkages between, for example, the Mont Pèlerin Society, neoliberalism, and export-oriented industrialization.

In the second part I have argued that NAFTA is functional and necessary for the EOI development strategy imposed in Mexico since 1988. Mexico's subsequent economic development *has been extremely successful in terms of EOI reasoning*. EOI, however, does have several serious flaws, including the dramatic and increasing socioeconomic and territorial polarization since the end of the 1980s. Both the liberalization strategy and NAFTA have been significant in creating a small and highly dynamic export-oriented private manufacturing sector, which is mainly integrated to the US economy, but has failed to generate a sustainable growth and development model for Mexico as a whole.

What could be an alternative to EOI and the liberalization strategy? Although this is not the place to discuss theoretical and policy alternatives (compare Dussel Peters 2000a), a few guidelines might be relevant.[13] Theoretically, and against EOI, the concept of '*territorial endogenous growth*' might be significant. One of the main challenges for countries such as Mexico in the context of NAFTA and globalization is to integrate local production in value-added chains that do allow for an increase in wages, employment, technological development and socioeconomic wealth, among other variables. Endogenous growth within a meaningful sense with regard to the social geography of the domestic territory is fundamentally different from the pattern of socioeconomic polarization. A few 'successful' households, firms, branches and regions are integrated into the world market, but they develop or maintain few linkages with the rest of the territory. This assessment should open the debate to oppose a false and simplistic causal linking of exports and development. Two discussions arise in this respect: one regarding the potential of territories to develop in a global capitalist system, and the other related to the specific regional and sectoral opportunities to link to global commodity chains. Neither of them, so far, presents definitive and 'universal' answers. However, ahistorical proposals without consideration of specific spatial and territorial context (like EOI) are neither particularly helpful to improve the understanding of the complex reality of the (semi)periphery as a whole nor do they provide a sufficient knowledge base to develop sound and comprehensive policy solutions in the concrete case of Mexico.

Notes

1 The topic will be discussed in length, also as a result of its importance for the Conference.
2 An excellent example of the absence of definition of the concept, although it is widely used, is Babb (2001).
3 Hinkelammert (1984) makes an excellent distinction between liberalism, conservatism and neoliberalism, both historically and theoretically.
4 For a historical and conceptual discussion of neoliberalism, see Hinkelammert (1984).
5 There is not sufficient space, and it is not the objective of the chapter, to develop the treatment of EOI here in depth, particularly regarding the association between exports, productivity, economic growth and overall development.
6 Aspe Armella (1993) stressed lowering the inflation rate as the crucial targeted variable since high inflation rates (caused in general by domestic demand and particularly by inertial tendencies of real wages) did not allow the reduction of the fiscal deficit during 1982–7.
7 The view of 'macroeconomy' is a further primitivization of EOI since every textbook in economics includes macroeconomic issues far beyond relative prices, fiscal deficit and foreign investment. Topics such as employment, wages, consumption and income distribution, etc., were not considered in the liberalization strategy.
8 At the end of the 1980s, this was not merely a hypothetical possibility. Politicians such as Perot and Buchanan as well as voices in the European Union presented strong criticisms of imports. Stepped up protectionism would have acted against an export orientation in Mexico and EOI in general.
9 The United States has played a substantial role in its increasing presence in FDI and trade with Mexico. More than two-thirds of FDI comes from the US, whereas 90 per cent of Mexican exports go to the US (Dussel Peters *et al.* 2003).
10 GDP and GDP per capita grew between 1940 and 1981 at an annual rate of 6.1 per cent and 3.3 per cent, respectively. Annual growth rates during the 1990s were less than half of those achieved during the 1940–81 period.
11 The main financing sources of Mexican firms are suppliers (BANXICO 2003); i.e. firms simply pay later than stipulated in contracts (or not at all).
12 The open unemployment rate refers to the percentage of persons of the EAP above 12 years that have worked for less than an hour a week and have been actively looking for a job the two previous months of the survey (PEF 2000: 43).
13 For a full discussion, see Dussel Peters (2000a).

Part III
Neoliberal discourse relations
Dissemination, diffusion, and adaptation

7 The great lie
Markets, freedom and knowledge

Richard Hull

Introduction

A central feature of neoliberal thought is the twin claim that first, markets are more efficient at resource allocation than centralised government planning, and second, that central planning leads to infringements on the freedom of individuals. The first argument is often justified through Hayek's 'problem of knowledge' – the problem of co-ordinating all the diverse knowledge required for central decision-making. This connection between markets, co-ordination and knowledge has apparently become a deeply-held belief, even on the part of some left-leaning academics (Wainwright 1994; Hodgson 1999). This chapter challenges this connection by suggesting that its history reveals the social and political context for two significant and related intellectual inventions – Hayek's 'problem of knowledge' and Michael Polanyi's 'tacit knowledge'. These inventions will both be shown as politically-motivated intellectual devices, as opposed to the reasoned advancement of thought. The story emerged during my research into the relationships between the history of computing and the parallel changes in social, economic and political theory.[1] One part of that research entailed uncovering exactly how 'knowledge' had come to be seen as an entity that could be studied and managed to such an extent that people would start talking about 'managing knowledge', and about a 'knowledge economy' or a 'knowledge society' (see Hull 2000a, b).

This chapter will suggest that the emergence of the notion of 'knowledge as a unit of analysis' can be traced through two separate 'problematisations' (Castel 1994), that were however closely connected in terms of the ideas, concepts, political critiques, and the personnel involved. In the early years, from the 1920s to the 1940s, these connections were especially evident in their political positions with respect to the Russian Revolution, the varieties of Marxism, and concerns about totalitarianism, especially couched in terms of 'freedom versus planning'.

In the first strand 'knowledge', and specifically the sociology of knowledge, emerges as a pivotal issue in debates within political and social theory about questions of science, culture, ideology and the role of intellectuals in social change.

In the second strand, new 'problems' of knowledge are mobilised in debates within economics and political economy over 'scientism' in methodology, about the relative merits of markets versus planned economies, and about the character of complex markets which rely on the distribution of data and information.

Crudely speaking, both strands have at their heart the opposition between 'knowledge and freedom' versus 'ideology and totalitarianism'. More specifically, there is a determination to develop critiques of, and alternatives to, Positivist methods in social science, philosophy and the natural sciences. In the course of this, the understanding of knowledge is transformed from the traditional Analytic and Positivist position that it is something that is only of interest in terms of whether it is true or false, into something that can take an increasingly wide range of forms and types, and can additionally be mapped and measured.

The two problematisations became more closely linked in the UK between the 1930s and late 1940s, as the ideas of four key refugee intellectuals – Michael Polanyi, Friedrich Hayek, Karl Mannheim and Karl Popper – moved closer together. We have described in detail elsewhere (Hull 2001a, b) the ways in which the ideas of Polanyi, Popper and Hayek became even further bound together as they each worked within the Mont Pèlerin Society, and we have described how the notion of 'knowledge as a unit of analysis' was helped into the public policy sphere through the (unwitting) involvement of Daniel Bell. Here, however, we are principally concerned with the earlier history.

Knowledge, the state, society and the economy

It is in the first decades of the twentieth century that we begin to see extensive debates about the 'problem' of knowledge in relation to firms, society, the economy and government. Although there has been recent interest in the early 1900s work of Thorstein Veblen, it is clear that his discussions of 'knowledge' and economics were part of an argument about the role of institutions within 'socioeconomic evolution'; it was not an argument about 'knowledge' *per se*. Later, however, Austrian economists in 1920s Vienna began to debate the possibilities for 'socialist calculation' which centred on the determination of 'value'. The debates (without explicitly citing Veblen or other institutionalists) accepted the heterodox role of institutions, and accepted Veblen's notion of 'habitual knowledge' or 'technique of thought' (Hayek 1935b: 210), but the debates problematised the use of 'knowledge' within the economic calculations made by individuals and by 'socialist planners'. However, before discussing those debates we shall sketch developments in Budapest which were essential elements of the intellectual and political background that has so far escaped scholarly attention (e.g. Murrell 1983; Wainwright 1992, 1994; Hodgson 1998, 1999), namely the debates between Lukács and Mannheim, and the close connections to both Michael and Karl Polanyi.

Budapest – Lukács and Mannheim

In Budapest the Syndicalism of George Sorel had been transposed to Hungary by Ervin Szabó, the 'leading Marxist of the time' (Nagy 1994: 85),[2] with *Syndic-*

alism and Social Democracy (1908) calling for a 'moral-cultural revolution' and for '"direct action"' against those parliamentary and party activities within which the working class movement had seemed to lose its "revolutionary spirit"' (Nagy 1994: 85). Two groups of intellectuals were inspired by Szabó's work: the Gallilei Circle, which formed in 1908 and included Karl Polanyi and Michael Polanyi, with Karl as first 'president' (Szabó was first cousin to the Polanyi brothers[3]); and The Szellemkek (The Sprites) which existed between 1916 and 1919 and included Béla Bartók, Karl Mannheim, and Georg Lukács (Jay 1994 [1974]). Whilst the Gallilei Circle was focused on the 'moral-cultural' and the Hungarian Nationalist aspects of Szabó's work, and hence became a somewhat fashionable educational circle both for 'workers' and for radical liberal literary and cultural figures, The Sprites were focused around determined intellectual opposition to what they saw as the 'mechanical materialism' of Orthodox Marxism, and advocated a distinct 'revolutionary culturalism'. An additional forum was the journal *The Twentieth Century*, which became a focus for debates about Fabianism, Marxism and Syndicalism.

In addition to the works of Szabó, The Sprites took as their 'manifesto' an essay by Mannheim titled 'Soul and Culture' which was the source for 'revolutionary culturalism'. However, when Lukács joined the Communist Party this apparently was quite a shock to The Sprites, and especially to Mannheim (see Jay 1994 [1974] and Lichtheim 1970). Up to this point Lukács had maintained an intellectual position that pointed away from such a political move. In 1910 *The Soul and the Forms* had reflected his involvement with the Heidelberg School and Dilthey's utilisation of the concept of *Geisteswissenschaft*, or 'science of the spirit'. From 1913 to 1914 Lukács moved explicitly towards Hegel intellectually, and towards Sorel politically, and this was reflected in his 1916 *Theory of the Novel*.

From 1919 to 1922 he wrote a series of essays for journals such as *The Twentieth Century* and the journal of the Gallilei Circle, then edited by Karl Polanyi, which were published together in 1923 as *History and Class Consciousness: Studies in Marxist Dialectics*. These marked his final break with the Romantic and 'aestheticist' elements of *Geisteswissenschaft*, but also his notorious break with the dialectical materialism which had become the official line of the Marxism–Leninism of the Second Internationale and its attempts to 'Bolshevise' the various national sections. The break with earlier formulations of *Geisteswissenschaft* came in the form of asserting that only the proletariat could possess the *total* vantage point required of *Geisteswissenschaft*, because only they were both the subject and object of history through their position within the labour process. The break with dialectical materialism came with the argument that Engels had misunderstood Kant and Hegel, that Marxism had no bearing on the natural sciences, and that the materialism of the Enlightenment (and the natural sciences) was 'the ideological form of the bourgeois revolution' – in other words, he repudiated the Orthodox Marxist doctrine which, in opposition to Hegel's supposed 'idealism', understood 'materialism' as meaning that 'matter' was more fundamental than 'spirit'. However, following Lukács' acceptance back into the mainstream folds of the Second Internationale, he refused to defend this position, especially from the attacks from Mannheim, until 1962, and that defence fell instead to the early proponents of Critical Theory in the Frankfurt Institute.

Jay (1994 [1974]) argues convincingly that Lukács' intellectual and political shift, especially after the 1923 publication of *History and Class Consciousness*, had a decisive effect on Mannheim's thinking and writing. Prior to 1924 Mannheim had argued in an unpublished essay 'On the Peculiarity of Cultural-sociological Knowledge', that there was no relation between the validity of values and their social origin, and that sociological analysis could neutrally judge values. In 1924, though, he argued in 'A Sociological Theory of Culture and its Knowability' that 'conjunctive' knowledge – by which he meant the moral, cultural, practical knowledge of *Geisteswissenschaft* – was indeed linked to social origin. He also argued, as did many at that time, that the rise of bourgeois society had meant the unfortunate domination of what he called 'communicative' knowledge (i.e. that arising from the natural sciences). However, *contra* Lukács, he argued that 'conjunctive' knowledge was the preserve of intellectuals, whereas Lukács had argued it was only the proletariat who could gain the proper vantage point. At this point, then, Mannheim was only somewhat adrift from Lukács, and explicitly acknowledged his indebtedness to him. By 1929, however, with Mannheim's *Ideology and Utopia*, Lukács was relegated to a footnote, and with the 1931 essay 'Wissenssoziologie' which was appended to later editions of *Ideology and Utopia*, he singled out Lukács for attack, saying he failed 'to distinguish between the problem of unmasking ideologies on the one hand and the sociology of knowledge on the other'.[4] Mannheim had also in *Ideology and Utopia* developed his thesis that it was the intellectuals as a 'collectivity' that were able to gain totalistic knowledge. By this he meant that the partial validity of individual perspectives, gained from their diverse social origins and engagements with the world, and hence their 'relativism' individually, could be overcome and a truth appropriate to the period would be gained through what Jay calls a 'dynamic synthesis of partial truths' (Jay 1994 [1974]: 178).

This, to my mind, bears a striking resemblance to Hayek's concept of 'spontaneous order', which was echoed by Polanyi,[5] and which gave rise to the neoliberal notion that the 'market' synthesises partial perspectives on prices into an overall perspective that is appropriately 'true' to its time. However, staying with Budapest, we have seen so far that the emergence of 'knowledge', explicitly as a unit of analysis, was intimately bound to a particular set of critiques. First, it was a critique, shared by the Sprites, of the Hungarian Social Democratic Party, the Second Internationale, and their 'mechanistic' forms of organisation and government. Second, it was a critique of Lukács' particular later ideas about who, exactly, was able to gain the best view of the 'social totality'. However, these critiques had also emerged in the context of debates about what we will call here 'the ethics of intellectual activity', and debates about science. The Analytic philosophy of Bertrand Russell had assumed a particular ethics of intellectual activity, a positive ethics about which one could validly speak, just as one could validly speak about science, supported by Russell's 'theory of knowledge'. This analytic and 'pro-science' tradition was challenged in Germany by the neo-Kantians and the Heidelberg School, and Wittgenstein, Lukács and Mannheim each responded in particular ways. Wittgenstein used logic in opposition to science and the 'theory of knowledge' to argue that 'ethics cannot be put into words' and that it was possible to clearly establish what science could and could not say about the world; Lukács essentially abandoned the notion of any ethics of *intellectual* activity, and abandoned science, just as he abandoned his intellectual colleagues in favour of the Party; and it was left to Mannheim to attempt to preserve and maintain a valid role for intellectuals, and in other words to preserve a positive ethics of intellectual activity, whilst developing what was, in embryonic form, a 'post-positivist' sociology of knowledge.

Budapest – the Polanyi brothers

The Polanyi family was a radical, intellectual and influential family, hosting many drawing-room salons up till 1919, entertaining many of the leading intellectuals including Lukács and Oszkár Jászi, the founder of the journal *The Twentieth Century*. Between the establishment of the Gallilei Circle in 1909 until well into the 1930s the brothers shared a similar outlook. At first 'free-thinking, atheist, and anti-clerical', they both became interested in Tolstoyan Christianity in the aftermath of the 1914–18 war. However, Karl became more directly involved in politics with a 1909 essay in *The Twentieth Century*, 'The Crisis of our Ideologies' (which prefigured his notions of stages of capitalist development), and then helped to establish the National Radical Bourgeois Party with Oszkár Jászi in 1914. Michael, on the other hand, moved towards what he called 'The New Scepticism', publishing an essay of that title in the Gallilei periodical in 1919. This argued that 'scientists and artists, "men of spirit", must ... erect the church of the new scepticism, and await the coming of those enlightened ones who no longer believe in politics. It was politics which had entangled the world in war.'[6]

Michael visited the Soviet Union in 1933 and became concerned that state control was 'corrupting' the sciences, and in 1935 published an attack on the economic policies of the USSR (see Prosch 1986; Nagy 1994).[7] In 1934 a serious rift opened with Karl, initially over relations between Michael's wife Magda, and Karl's wife Ilona Duczynska, who was a scientist and political activist, and had been expelled from the Hungarian Communist Party for 'Luxemburgist deviation' (Dalós 1990: 38). The rift became more serious with Michael's 1935 paper on the Soviet Union. Before that, they still shared an interest in the 'Christian Left', and we can surmise that it was Karl who introduced Michael to J. H. Oldham, editor of the *Christian Newsletter*, who later formed a discussion circle called The Moot, which Michael attended, and which included Mannheim. Mannheim had by now also moved to Britain and begun 'his growing movement to the right' (Jay 1994 [1974]: 183), and the specific translation of *Ideology and Utopia* into English in 1936 'had moved it in a far more pragmatist direction than the German original' (183). The rift between the Polanyi brothers deepened along with the increase of Karl's sympathies towards the Soviet Union during the 1930s.

We shall return to the development in Michael Polanyi's political and philosophical thinking, his involvement with Hayek, and his invention of the concept of 'tacit knowledge'. However, we can already see a reflection, in this divergence of the brothers' views, of the debates between Mannheim and Lukács.[8] Michael and Karl were re-presenting and re-posing the necessarily inter-related arguments about who, exactly, was in the best position to gain valid understandings of the 'social-totality' – was it science, intellectuals, faith, or the proletariat – and how could political commitments and actions be integrated with particular positions about those valid understandings?

Vienna, calculation, and knowledge

We now turn to the Vienna of the 1920s, site of one of the most famous experiments in Municipal Socialism, and also of the emergence of the Logical Positivism which Michael Polanyi (along with Karl Popper and Hayek) later reacted so strongly against. It will be here that we see the origins – once again within political debates – of a quite separate problematisation of 'knowledge', where it becomes mobilised within debates about the possibility of a centrally-planned economy, and the consequences of such an economy for 'freedom'.

Rosner, introducing his discussion of Karl Polanyi's work on 'socialist accounting', argues that

> [After] the collapse of the political order in 1918 ... the quest for a new economic order arose; but it could no longer be confined to abstract concepts of a better society without exploitation. It had to demonstrate the feasibility of the economic organization of a socialist society. Unfortunately, there did not exist any basis for such a discussion.
>
> (Rosner 1990: 55)

Wainwright (1992) lends some support to this diagnosis. She points first to the earlier *Privatseminars* in Vienna, most famously those of Ludwig von Mises and Böhm-Bawerk, in which prominent intellectuals would debate problems and issues about liberalism, social democracy and socialism. She then argues that the ascension of 'socialist economists' to the first Austrian Republic in 1918, together with the 'socialisation programme' proposed by Bauer and Schumpeter, 'in effect made public the debates of the *privatseminar*' (Wainwright 1992: 8). Another key element was the work of Otto Neurath, advocate of a Logically Positivist brand of scientific Marxism, who served as Head of the Planning Department of the brief Munich Soviet Republic, and in 1919 argued, from the 'lessons of the war economy', for a centrally planned economy (or more precisely a 'natural economy' – *Naturalwirtschaft* – one without money or prices) in which economic calculations could be made without reference to prices, and could instead rely solely on *in natura* calculations based on statistics, technical production relations and input coefficients: 'Neurath considered the planned organization of the economy to be a purely technical question, not a political one' (Rosner 1990: 56).

Against this background Ludwig von Mises, then Secretary of the Vienna Chamber of Commerce and organiser of one of the most prominent *Privatseminars* which included Friedrich Hayek and Fritz Machlup, wrote a paper arguing that 'rational economic activity is impossible in a socialist commonwealth' and that 'he who expects a rational economic system from socialism will be forced to re-examine his views' (Mises 1935 [1920]: 130). The paper was a detailed and lengthy argument against Neurath, Bauer, Engels and Lenin, but it was also an argument against *any* state intervention in the economy, on the grounds that such intervention would inevitably lead to a completely centrally-planned economy, which would in turn be devoid of any 'rational economic system'. Many commentators have suggested that this paper held a pivotal role in subsequent debates about 'socialist calculation' and central planning of the economy (Mendell 1990; Rosner 1990; Wainwright 1992; Desai 1994a, b; Keizer 1994),[9] and Keizer (1994) suggests that its translation and publication in English in 1935 'transposed the hitherto Central European calculation debate to the Anglo-Saxon economic forum' (209).[10] Keizer also argues that Hayek's subsequent 1937 paper 'Economics and Knowledge' arose directly from his involvement in those debates.

Von Mises (1935 [1920]) argued that under 'simple conditions' it was possible to make a judgement of the value of goods and that theoretically a 'labour theory of value' and a socialist system would be feasible. However, when there are a variety of lengthy processes of production and 'a bewildering mass of intermediate products and potentialities of production' (103) other methods are required for the valuation of goods and the means of production. These other methods can only be based on private property, the personal incentives that it bestows, and an 'exchange economy' because 'the human mind cannot orientate itself properly' around that 'bewildering mass' (103).

This question of the 'bewildering mass' was later to reappear as a central theme of Hayek (1937), as was von Mises' argument about the benefits of an exchange economy in terms of making calculations about future uncertainty.

Karl Polanyi responded to the von Mises paper, and then again to the replies from von Mises, between 1922 and 1925.[11] He argued first, in common with von Mises and *contra* Neurath, that 'accounting' would be impossible in a centrally planned economy but he did not accept their common assumption that socialism implies a centrally planned economy, instead focusing on a decentralised society with multiple units of decision-making. His aim was to introduce the guild-socialist ideas of G. D. H. Cole and Robert Owen (Rosner 1990) whilst maintaining a 'principal focus on the means to satisfy individual needs: the basic human needs of Marx, not the narrow material needs implicit in neoclassical economic theory' (Mendell 1990: 68). He was in essence trying to effect a 'moderate' balance between the excesses of a rigid adherence to either Marx's theories of value, or those of classical political economy.[12]

There are two reasons for mentioning Polanyi's intervention. First, his method of achieving this difficult balancing-act was to strictly separate accounting from economic theory, which prompted a criticism from Hayek in terms of the 'knowledge' element in both accounting and economic calculation. Second, his later book

148 Richard Hull

The Great Transformation (1944) was seen as one of the three main challenges to 'liberalism'[13] that prompted the establishment by Hayek in 1947 of the Mont Pèlerin Society. Although Polanyi's ideas had relatively little influence on the socialist calculation debates, which were eventually 'settled' through the responses of Lange, Lerner and Dickinson and ideas about 'market socialism' (see Wainwright 1992 and Keizer 1994), his arguments clearly nettled von Mises and especially his ardent student Hayek. In 1935 Hayek published *Collectivist Economic Planning* which included Mises' original paper, two other papers on 'the problem of value' and 'the possibility of adequate calculation' in socialist societies, together with a long introduction and concluding essay by Hayek. And in the concluding essay we see the first move to delineate what others have since called 'the Hayek knowledge problem'.[14]

> In a centrally planned society this selection of the most appropriate among the known technical methods will only be possible if all this knowledge can be used in the calculations of the central authority. This means in practice that this knowledge will have to be concentrated in the heads of one or at best a very few people who actually formulate the equations to be worked out. It is hardly necessary to emphasize that this is an absurd idea even in so far as that knowledge is concerned which can properly be said to 'exist' at any moment of time. But much of the knowledge that is actually utilised is by no means 'in existence' in this ready-made form. Most of it consists in a technique of thought which enables the individual engineer to find new solutions rapidly as soon as he is confronted with new constellations of circumstances
> (Hayek 1935b: 210–11).

Hayek has here 'translated'[15] the arguments about calculation, accountancy and planning into questions about 'knowledge' – its nature ('ready-made' or 'technique of thought', echoing Veblen's 'technological', 'habitual' and 'commonplace knowledge'), its distribution ('concentrated' or not), and its utilisation. Hayek then builds on this argument in order to turn his attack on ideas, principally those developed by Dickinson between 1930 and 1933, concerning the introduction of competition and pricing into a socialist society.

To summarise this section then: commencing with debates in Vienna about the possibilities for 'socialist calculation', we have seen the emergence of our second strand in the problematisation of 'knowledge as a unit of analysis', the strand that poses 'knowledge' as an issue for economists, and more specifically those economists and other scholars with an active interest in the governmental questions of 'freedom and planning'. We now move to the UK between the 1930s and 1950s, then home to so many of the intellectuals who had fled from Central Europe.

London and Manchester

Those émigrés arrived to find a Britain still curiously locked into the Logical Positivism they had thought moribund. As Magee (1973) notes, the 1936 publication of Ayer's *Language, Truth and Logic* 'imported' the Vienna School's Logical

Positivism which then came to dominate philosophical and metaphysical thinking in the UK (and indeed the US) at least until the 1953 publication of Wittgenstein's *Philosophical Investigations* and the turn to 'linguistic analysis'. We might speculate then – with some justification, as we shall see below – that the people who concern us – Michael Polanyi, Friedrich Hayek, Karl Mannheim and Karl Popper – found themselves in a situation which they perceived as potentially dangerous, intellectually and politically. For they associated Positivism with Marxism and Totalitarianism, and they saw danger in the contemporary and closely related 'scientism' which attempted to apply positivist scientific methods to social and economic spheres. To allow Positivism and its cousin 'scientism' to go unchallenged was to open the door to the 'scientific Marxism' they had experienced in Budapest and more strongly in Vienna.

Their responses differed in some respects, but they stemmed from the same problematic – how to develop meta-theoretical positions (about Science, Economics, Sociology and Philosophy, respectively) which could challenge Positivism whilst retaining the validity of 'positive' (in a weak sense) understandings, descriptions and prescriptions for the world. In brief, the responses of Polanyi, Hayek, Mannheim and Popper were cast in terms of, respectively: the central role of 'tacit knowledge' in science; how 'problems of knowledge' repudiated central planning; how the 'sociology of knowledge' proved the importance of freedom for intellectuals; and how scientific objectivity could be gained through falsification rather than Positivism. The fact that these four men shared the same problematisation, the same dilemma, meant first that they were more inclined to read and borrow from each other's work. Second, it meant that their responses provided, by the late 1950s, a particular set of intellectual resources (such as 'tacit knowledge', the 'sociology of knowledge', the 'distribution of knowledge', and 'science's requirement for open societies') that could then be mobilised by those such as Daniel Bell and Fritz Machlup, who more firmly cast 'knowledge' as a unit of analysis, in the context of an overall separation of 'knowledge and freedom' from 'ideology and totalitarianism'.

In grouping Polanyi, Hayek, Mannheim and Popper in this way, we are not implying that they formed any sort of explicit group in the form which had been so popular in Budapest and Vienna, and there is no evidence of such a gathering or network. Nor are we implying that they were in agreement on all matters, and indeed some significant disagreements over the respective roles of the State and markets emerged later. They were however obviously known to each other, they did correspond, they did write publicly about each other's work, they were each sometimes funded by similar 'foundations' and similar sources of grants, and they did meet – each of these in various sub-group configurations. Mannheim is perhaps the most 'outside' of the four, and we have only found evidence of close contact with Polanyi, although Hayek and Popper were evidently well aware of his work. Polanyi met with Hayek and Popper in the early Mont Pèlerin Society meetings from 1947, and had earlier joined Hayek in 1938 at the 'gathering of liberals' in Paris[16] and invited Popper to speak in Manchester, whilst Popper encountered Hayek in 1936 at the Hayek–Robbins seminar at the London

150 *Richard Hull*

School of Economics (Cockett 1994: 80). Hayek was the first to move to the UK, in 1931, taking a chair at LSE; Michael Polanyi moved to Manchester in 1933, whilst Popper arrived at LSE in 1945, taking a post that had been secured for him by Hayek (85), and Mannheim moved to the UK in the mid-1930s.

A number of strands run through their intellectual development in this period. There was first what Cockett calls the 'crisis of liberalism' during the 1930s – the perception by liberal economists that Keynesian notions of planning dominated government policy and economic thought – and the various post-war activities directed at promoting the intellectual foundations of liberalism and combating Communism. It was also in this period that Hayek began explicitly to discuss the role of 'knowledge' within economic theory, which we shall discuss in more detail below. Finally there were Michael Polanyi's concerns about science being directed and planned by the State, and the consequent intellectual attempts to separate science from scientism, which we also discuss.

Economics and knowledge

In 1936 Hayek presented his paper 'Economics and Knowledge' as his Presidential Address to the London Economic Club. This was later published in *Economica*, and reprinted in Hayek (1949a). It focuses on the assumptions made by economists about the knowledge 'possessed' by members of society, but is also a discussion of the knowledge conveyed by economic analyses, and hence of the philosophy of economics. In other words, the paper mobilises arguments about the role of knowledge in (economic) society in order to argue for a radical shift in economic theory away from its preoccupation with equilibrium analyses. First of all we see Hayek's explicit acknowledgement to Popper in the very first paragraph, clearly signalling support for his attack on Positivism by replacing verification with falsification as one of the key principles of scientific method. With this critique of Positivist methods in economics, the direct assault on equilibrium analyses, and the context of Hayek's other arguments against socialist and Keynesian economists – who all at that time relied essentially on Positivist methods and equilibrium analyses – the paper is clearly an attempt to undermine the very foundations of prevailing mainstream economics.

The discussion first turns to foresight, planning, risk and uncertainty, to argue for a significant difference between analysis of the plans and actions of an individual, and analysis of the actions and plans of a group of individuals. With constant reference to the assumptions of equilibrium analysis, Hayek argues that the assumptions of such analyses are only a special case of 'the more general problem of how knowledge is acquired and communicated' (Hayek 1937: 46), with passing reference to different views on this between economists and sociologists. In the course of this discussion he executes a manoeuvre which shifts consideration of 'correct foresight' to consideration of 'relevant knowledge'.

Having made a distinction between 'knowledge' and 'relevant knowledge', he turns to 'the conditions under which people are supposed to acquire the relevant knowledge and the process by which they are supposed to acquire it' (48), and from there to discussion of 'how much knowledge and what sort of knowledge the different individuals must possess' (50). Here we see Hayek making an enormous interpretative leap from von Mises' discussions of the 'mental division of labour', to his own formulation of the 'problem of the division of knowledge'. Asking the question 'what is this relevant knowledge?' he states: 'Clearly, there is here a problem of the *division of knowledge* which is quite analogous to, and at least as important as, the problem of the division of labour.' The italicised 'division of knowledge' is accompanied by a footnote 'Cf. L. v. Mises' followed by a quote from von Mises in German: 'Die Verteilung der Verfügungsgewalt über die wirtschaftlichen Güter der arbeitsteilig Wirtschafenden auf viele Individuen bewirkt eine Art geistige Arbeitsteilung, ohne die Produktionsrechnung und Wirtschaft nicht möglich wäre.'

We have had this translated,[17] making reference to the linguistic sense in use in Austria at the time von Mises was writing: 'In a Social Economy, functioning on the basis of the division of labour, the distribution, among many individuals, of the power of disposition over economic goods, effects a kind of mental division of labour ("geistige Arbeitsteilung" – translator's note) without which the calculation of costs and the operation of the economy would be impossible.'

So here Hayek *creates* and *invents* the 'problem of the division of knowledge' from what are very flimsy foundations – the distinction between 'relevant' and other knowledge, and speculations about the 'mental division of labour' – and along with this problem he offers a number of solutions. Some have already appeared, by posing the questions of 'how much' and 'what form' of knowledge is required for particular situations. Others appear later, as Hayek briefly suggests that the correspondence between 'subjective knowledge' and 'objective facts' can best be addressed by '*verstehende* social science' (signalling support for Mannheim) rather than the 'behaviourist approach';[18] this suggestion is broadened to argue that a key problem is how the combined operation of collected 'fragments of knowledge existing in individual minds' can achieve superior results to any individually developed plan; and finally that this combined operation of collected fragments, this 'spontaneous action of individuals', provides an answer to the 'problem' of the 'social mind'. Hayek has succeeded here in mobilising the emerging concept of a 'sociology of knowledge' – the social science of the ways groups and societies produce and distribute particular types of knowledge – and giving it his own particular spin into the concept of 'spontaneous order', all in support of his particular political opposition to socialism.

Hayek's focus on 'how much and what sort of knowledge' was mobilised again in his 1945 paper 'The Use of Knowledge in Society' (Hayek 1945), where again the principal aim of the paper appears to be to refute collectivist arguments, this time Schumpeter's *Capitalism, Socialism and Democracy*. Here, he states more baldly that 'the economic problem of society is . . . a problem of the utilization of knowledge which is not given to anyone in its totality' (77–8); that 'the problem of what is the best way of utilizing knowledge initially dispersed among all the people is at least one of the main problems of economic policy – or of designing an efficient economic system' (78–9); and that 'the most significant fact about this [the price system] is the economy of knowledge with which it operates, or how little the individual participants need to know in order to be able to make the right decision' (86).

Michael Polanyi on science

In the 1964 Torchbook edition of *Personal Knowledge* Polanyi writes:

> [The] enquiry of which this volume forms a part started in 1939 with a review article on J. D. Bernal's *The Social Function of Science*. I opposed his view, derived from Soviet Marxism, that the pursuit of science should be directed by the public authority to serve the welfare of society. I held that the power of thought to seek the truth must be accepted as our guide, rather than be curbed to the service of material interests.
>
> (Cited in Prosch 1986: 16)

As Prosch (1986: 16) suggests, Polanyi at this time was considerably concerned with the 'tendency' of intellectuals to 'flirt with Marxist and other proposals for planned cultures'. In other words he shared Hayek's concerns, although from a quite different 'Christian Left' perspective. From 1935 onwards he wrote a series of articles and reviews on the value of autonomous science and the danger of attempting to plan it, and his chief target was what Prosch calls 'the concerted movement in the 1930s to deprive science of its autonomy' (15). Some of these numerous essays and articles were later republished in *The Logic of Liberty* (1951) – although it should be noted that in many other respects he supported Keynesian policies. He also, as Prosch notes, 'lent his support to various societies and conferences of scholars where efforts to plan science were exposed as death traps for science'. This included establishing, along with J. R. Baker, the Society for Freedom in Science in 1941 (Cash 1996), and later lending active support to the Mont Pèlerin Society, the Congress for Cultural Freedom (its reliance on CIA funds was not then known), and its English affiliate the Committee on Science and Freedom (Cash 1996). This support paid dividends, as Polanyi later received grants from the CCF, the Rockefeller Foundation, and the Volker Fund (Polanyi 1958: ix), which also supported the Mont Pèlerin Society (see Plehwe and Walpen in this volume).

This then forms part of the context in which Polanyi *invented* and *created* the concept of 'tacit knowledge', just as Hayek had invented 'the problem of the division of knowledge'. However, before elaborating on this we must mention another crucial aspect of the context, namely Polanyi's assault on objectivity. Starting with his 1936 paper 'The Value of the Inexact' in the journal *Philosophy of Science*, he addressed what he came to see as one of the two key causes of contemporary social and economic problems. This was the obsession with rationality, an obsession held by both scientists and planners alike with the goal of complete and perfect objective knowledge, the belief that this was the only reliable knowledge, and the concomitant belief that all personal and subjective elements of knowledge were merely disturbances and essentially unreliable. In 1953 (in a favourable review of Hayek's *The Counter Revolution in Science*) he dubbed this 'scientism', a 'waywardness, due to a deeper and indeed total instability of reason at its present level of consciousness' which required a 'curing [of] this basic disorder' (Polanyi 1953: 3).

This mission of 'curing this basic disorder' was precisely what Polanyi was then attempting with *Personal Knowledge* and his later works. There is however, a final aspect of the context for this work. As we have mentioned above, at some time in this period Polanyi joined the Christian Left group The Moot, convened by J. H. Oldham, to whom Polanyi gave acknowledgement in the Preface of *Personal Knowledge*. Mannheim was also a member of this group and, whether or not they met there or elsewhere, Polanyi and Mannheim certainly became friendly and corresponded regularly (Cash 1996). Polanyi had initially been hostile to Mannheim,[19] but later softened towards him, perhaps after Mannheim's shift away from Lukács and his amendment of the English edition of *Ideology and Utopia*. Polanyi clearly came to regard Mannheim's work with great interest and respect, as can be seen in Polanyi's reviews in *The Manchester Guardian* at precisely the time he was writing *Personal Knowledge*: 'Mannheim's thought ... has woven itself closely into the intellectual fabric of our time' (Polanyi 1952). The debt owed to Mannheim is also evident from the first pages of *Personal Knowledge*: 'Any attempt rigorously to eliminate our human perspective from our picture of the world must lead to absurdity' (Polanyi 1958: 3).

These then are the contexts for the *invention* by Polanyi of the concepts of 'personal knowledge' and 'tacit knowing', which later became transformed into 'tacit knowledge'. There is of course an extended and detailed set of arguments, which we need only mention briefly. Following an initial critique of objectivism, built on detailed discussions of the way that scientists actually work and conduct experiments, he mobilises Gestalt psychology to argue that the 'skills' which are necessary for all activities, but especially science, cannot be fully and explicitly specified.[20] This leads to extensive discussion of the 'moral passions' which motivate action and especially intellectual activity, and a brief discussion of his theory of 'moral inversion' – the hiding of those moral passions whilst in practice contradicting them – which is Polanyi's explanation of much of recent history, in particular the rise of 'Scientific Marxism'.

Of course by this time, 1958, Polanyi was to some extent pushing at an open door, at least with his attacks on Positivism and 'scientific Marxism', and the fashion in philosophy had turned towards linguistic philosophy in response to Wittgenstein's later work in *Philosophical Investigations* (1953) (although no doubt events and revelations from Hungary and the Soviet Union were also a factor).

In terms of the philosophy of science, the area Polanyi had initially embarked upon, it was now Popper's work that generally held sway, although it was of course about to receive the shock of Thomas Kuhn's work in the history of science, which also rested in part upon the 'new fashion' of linguistic philosophy. However, these are now peripheral to our main concern. Whether or not Polanyi was at the time successful in his attempted interventions into debates about the philosophy and planning of science, what is clear is that he did succeed in bifurcating 'knowledge', constructing an alternative schema to the traditional Positivist – and indeed the pre-positivist Analytical – division between true and false knowledge. He had, in other words, whether intentionally or not, reinforced Hayek's 'problem of the division of knowledge' and created a further intellectual justification for treating knowledge as an entity amenable to analysis by diverse experts.

The Mont Pèlerin Society (MPS) – under-labourers[21] for neoliberalism

The consequences of the above narrative, and of the continuing unfolding of the notion of 'knowledge as a unit of analysis', could easily occupy the same space again. They range from an ethical critique of the combination of positive ethics with post-Positivist concepts of 'knowledge' (Rose 1992), to a warning of the dangers inherent in the notion of 'knowledge as a unit of analysis' and attempts at 'correct' definitions of 'knowledge'.[22] In the context of this volume, however, what is chiefly of interest is that we have filled in the background to the emergence of some key neoliberal formulations within the MPS. Whilst Hartwell (1995) claims that the MPS 'has been important in developing and sustaining liberal ideas' (xiv), it is more correct to say that it and its members have been central to shifting the arguments towards neoliberal formulations, or towards what Nikolas Rose (1999) calls the 'advanced liberal' mode of governmentality. This has been in the form of arguing that the classical liberal separation of powers, *laissez faire*, with the state governing its realms and leaving the markets alone, was no longer feasible. The state should instead intervene to ensure that 'real' markets can flourish in as many areas as possible, without monopolies, oligopolies or unregulated trade unions, and without state intervention in the activities of firms or restriction of entrepreneurial activity. The rationale is first that only such real markets, composed of groups of entrepreneurs acting for their own interests, can ensure efficient resource allocation. Second, that the 'scientific planning' of resource allocation is impossible because: (a) such applications of science must always contain subjective and personal elements; and (b) modern production is now so complex, and the risks and uncertainties so various, that no one single authority can have complete understanding of all the relevant factors. Finally, in support of Rose's (1999) arguments, we can see more precisely how the particular combination of the works of Hayek, Polanyi and Popper helped to problematise existing notions of science and expertise, which established the foundation or the promotion of new forms of expertise such as management and accounting.

Notes

1 Hull (2001a): this chapter is a shortened version of Chapter 4 of my unpublished PhD thesis. That chapter is titled 'The emergence of "knowledge" as a unit of analysis in economic, social and political theory, 1900–1979'.
2 Further details, especially of Szabo and his relation to Lukács, can be found in Lichtheim (1970, but cf. Nagy 1994, and Jay 1994 [1974]; see also Múcsi 1990).

The great lie 155

3 See Annex E, The Pollacsek/Polanyi Family Tree, in Polanyi-Levitt 1990.
4 Mannheim (1936: 310) quoted in Jay (1994 [1974]).
5 Polanyi's 1946 'Planning and Spontaneous Order', a paper for the Manchester School of Economic and Social Studies, later formed a chapter in *The Logic of Liberty* (1951). However, the substantive aspects of his concept of 'spontaneous order' are quite distinct from Hayek's.
6 Nagy (1994: 88–9) paraphrasing Michael Polanyi's essay.
7 Additional details of Michael Polanyi's papers and correspondence are drawn from Cash (1996).
8 McRobbie (1994) suggests that Lukács was 'a friend of Karl's' (50) and that they had corresponded since 1908. In 1918 he invited Lukács to contribute to a special issue of a journal he edited (Litván 1990: 33).
9 Hayek certainly considered the paper to be central, and reprinted it in *Collectivist Economic Planning*; and both Hayek and Mises considered Karl Polanyi's responses to be among the most important – see Appendix B of *Collectivist Economic Planning*, 'Selected Bibliography'.
10 Cockett (1994: 26) quotes Lionel Robbins' (1971: 106) description of his 'conversion to economic liberalism' from his previously held belief in Guild Socialism: 'In reaching this conclusion I was considerably influenced by the examination by von Mises of the possibilities of economic calculation under total Collectivism.'
11 See especially Mendell (1990) on these debates, but also Rosner (1990).
12 Polanyi's idea of socialism was in fact attacked by a prominent Marxist of the time, Felix Weil, in 1924 (Rosner 1990: 61). Weil had by then financed the establishment of the Frankfurt Institute for Social Research in 1923 (Kellner 1994 [1973]: 44).
13 The other two challenges were seen to be Schumpeter's *Capitalism, Socialism and Democracy* (1942) and Beveridge's *Full Employment in a Free Society* (1944) – see Hartwell (1995: 15).
14 Keizer (1994: 215) citing Kirzner (1984).
15 To use a term from Actor Network Theory (Callon 1986; Green *et al.* 1999), in which actors translate between the interests of others and their own through devising intermediary terms and concepts.
16 'Le Colloque Walter Lippmann' (1938) – see Denord (2003) and Plehwe and Walpen, this volume
17 My gratitude to Theo Balderston, Department of History, Manchester University.
18 Page 52, footnote 18. 'Verstehende' social science at that time referred to the social study of the understandings and cognitions of groups, societies and cultures – precisely the format of Mannheim's work.
19 Jeremy Shearmur, personal correspondence, 24 September 1998, based on his researches into the relations between Polanyi, Popper and Hayek during this period.
20 This is in explicit opposition to Freudian and Behaviourist psychology and the cybernetic model of human activity. The explicit rejection of Behaviourism echoes Hayek's earlier opposition.
21 The term 'under-labourers' is an ironic reference to Hilary Wainwright's work, which argues that radical intellectuals should 'under-labour' to develop ideas, concepts, phrases and 'findings' that indirectly impact on progressive policy decisions. I find this notion dishonest.
22 See Hull (2001a) for a full discussion, and Hull (2000a, 2000b and 2001b) for summaries.

8 Frontiers and dystopias
Libertarian ideology in science fiction

Peter Josef Mühlbauer

Neoliberalism is rarely an immediately visible element of American popular culture. The Chicago Boys simply weren't sexy enough. Instead, neoliberal economics come through the backdoor of a sexier, more radical ideology that promises not only less state but also a lot more sex, more drugs, and more rock 'n' roll – libertarianism.

What is libertarian ideology?

Libertarian ideology is particularly important in the USA but relatively unknown in other parts of the world. In its current meaning, the term 'libertarianism' is an American creation. In nineteenth-century Europe, 'libertarian' was a common synonym for left-anarchist. After World War II, the American advocates of unregulated markets discovered the term for their own purposes. It excelled competitive designations and eventually entered American everyday language in the 1960s. The *Encyclopedia Americana* defines libertarianism as a philosophy based on the doctrine of the rights of the individual – put briefly; it's tantamount to absolute individualism. Out of the belief in an absolute and inalienable right to private property grows the libertarian postulation of a laissez-faire economy. Taxes are seen as an institutionalized theft of private property that the state uses to be able to intervene deeper and deeper into the lives of individuals. A popular definition of libertarianism is therefore 'anarchism for the rich'. Influential libertarian ideology is often relatively unsophisticated. It hardly caters to contradictions and is limited to a praise of the curative forces of self-interest and the market as well as a condemnation of taxes and governments. But this home-made-appeal seems to be an ideal for libertarian ideology.

In his 'Non-Libertarian FAQ' (2004), Mike Huben states that there is hardly any literature on libertarianism that does not come from within the movement. The discourse about libertarian ideology is therefore unhitched from other political discourses, which makes an analysis substantially more difficult. In this text, the author, obviously exhausted from the effort of refuting libertarian ideology, argues: 'Bumper sticker analogies are as poor a method of understanding libertarianism ... as science fiction. Too bad so many libertarians make such heavy use of those methods.' Although Huben's reservations are somewhat understandable, gaining insights from the most popular layers of a popular culture depends on the handling, not the source. This is because the popularity and the aforementioned homegrownness are not only inherently constituent, but also an ideal for an ideology which abhors academic elitism.

I intend to examine different expressions and modes of libertarian ideology in American popular culture and to point out their remarkable 'forerunner' role for ideas that became widespread in the 1990s. And will demonstrate the ideological patterns within a set of examples that bring to light different aspects of libertarian ideology. Specifically, I will examine the emergence of libertarian ideology in science fiction literature and films. The – sometimes hidden – emergence of libertarian ideology in this field will be demonstrated, analyzed, and put in context.

The role of science fiction in the development of libertarian ideology

The realm of science fiction literature and films was and still is significant for the development and distribution of libertarian ideology. Martin Morse Wooster (1998) estimates the proportion of the sympathizers of libertarian ideology within science fiction at up to a quarter of all authors. Among readers and fans alike, libertarians are an even smaller minority. However, many explicitly libertarian novels such as Robert Heinlein's *The Moon is a Harsh Mistress* (1966) or Poul Anderson's merchant novels are classics of the genre.

Although explicitly libertarian material appears in other genres, too, there's a special bond connecting the ideology with science fiction. Libertarian literature outside of science fiction (for instance Ayn Rand's 1957 novel *Atlas Shrugged*) is dependent on stylistic means from the genre. Also, connections between theoretical libertarian writings and science fiction are quite close. Science fiction authors frequently sketch a theoretical model in the form of a novel. Likewise, models from science fiction serve as an inspiration for academics. For example, libertarian theoretician and member of the Mont Pèlerin Society (MPS, see Plehwe and Walpen in this volume) David Friedman refers in his writings (i.e. 1989: 241–3) to Vernor Vinge's *The Ungoverned* (1985) and to Poul Anderson's *Margin of Profit* (1956). MPS founding member Milton Friedman compared health insurances to bets, just like Robert Heinlein in *The Moon is a Harsh Mistress* (1966), one of the bibles of the libertarian movement. Heinlein's slogan 'There ain't no such thing as a free lunch' was used by Milton Friedman as a book title (1975) and became a widespread proverb in libertarian circles. In addition, science fiction often plays an important role in libertarian projects, for example in the case of the millionaire and creator of the libertarian project 'New Utopia', who called himself 'Lazarus Long' after a literary figure created by Robert Heinlein.

There are roughly two areas of manifestation of libertarian ideology in science fiction, which are mutually supplementary: libertarian utopias and anti-utopias or 'dystopias'. The libertarian science fiction utopia is a place without taxes and government. This paradise is threatened from the inside (by regulation-crazy small minds and envious people) or from the outside (by authoritarian systems that stretch out, or by a motherland that wants to integrate colonists back into its realm of power). The inhabitants of the libertarian utopia now either defend their paradise or they rush on to new planets, to the new frontier, where they can lead a life without being kept on a leash. This basic plot is enriched with frequent references to American history, tax rebellions, the praise of the possession of arms, descriptions of possibilities to act out sexual deviation, and numerous entrepreneur-, merchant-, outlaw-, and smuggler-heroes. A separate literary topos is formed by quasi-religious narratives, in which an almighty market provides peace and justice.

Final frontiers

Mark Seltzer (1992: 3) realized that nothing shaped American identity more than the love of nature – with the exception of the love of technology. One of the characteristics of libertarian science fiction is the union of these traditional contrasts. The genre achieves this union with the concept of the 'frontier'.[1] The boundlessness of a frontier is a comfortable prerequisite of libertarian models. If there is no 'open' space, libertarian ideology can be imagined coherently only with difficulties. Therefore, very often libertarian ideology uses – in one form or another – a conception of the frontier, of the space that can still be conquered – and thus finds itself in a specifically American tradition. If 'unsettled' space, which is necessary for this conception, is no longer available on earth, then conceptions of technology (be it the conquest of the universe or the production of virtual worlds) serve the literary or cinematic creation of such free spaces.

In science fiction, the frontier almost always shows utopian lineaments.[2] This has several reasons. For one, unlimited space leads to the idea of unrestricted economic expansion, as Robert Heinlein briefly and concisely stated in a speech at the House Select Committee on Aging on 2 July 1979: 'Our race will spread out through space – unlimited room, unlimited energy, unlimited wealth' (1980: 502). Libertarian science fiction appreciates this economic potential as a prerequisite for self-realization. In James P. Hogan's eco-dystopia *The Multiplex Man* (1992), his heroine Kay explains why hope lies in the frontier, in space, with the 'Offworlders': 'What right could be more basic than the freedom to become whatever you're capable of? And that's just what the Offworld culture means: room for everyone to grow, and achieve, and become; with unlimited room to do it in and unlimited means to do it with' (170).

A further advantage of the frontier in libertarian utopias is the absence of governments. The hero Valland in Poul Anderson's *World Without Stars* explains: 'Tyranny gets unstable when a cheap boat can pace a warship and there's a wilderness for dissatisfied people to vanish into' (1967: 77). But what can a hero do if a state threatens to bed itself in the former wilderness? The science fiction author Brad Linaweaver describes such a 'market for statism' in *No Market for Justice*: Acephale societies develop into states. This takes place (among other things) through license fees and rents charged by private companies secretly tending to develop into taxes and thus open the gates for a second coming of the state (1997: 66). Therefore, a life without a government is only possible at the frontier. That is the reason why space and a nomadic way of life is an even more suitable conception of an eternal frontier than faraway planets, which are exposed constantly to the 'danger' of civilization. In Victor Koman's *Demokratus* (1997), for example, only the spacemen, traveling through space all of their lives, are really free (197–220). But why avoid government? Because in libertarian science fiction, government stands in the way of the heroes' self-realization. In *Gentlemen, Be Seated* (1948), Robert Heinlein characterizes his heroes as follows: 'Space men – men who work in space ... are men who like a few million miles of elbow room'(53).

Entrepreneurs have nothing to lose but their chains

Like in the historicism of former times, in libertarian science fiction progress is created by great men. These figures are described as sources of all progress. One fundament of the libertarian objection to state interventions is the faith in the rights of such an elite (Smith 1978: 137–71), which should – for the sake of progress – be unlimited. Robert Heinlein lets his figure Lazarus Long explain: 'Throughout History, poverty is the normal condition of man. Advances which permit this norm to be exceeded – here and there, now and then – are the work of an extremely small minority [...] Whenever this tiny minority is kept from creating [...] the people [...] slip back into abject poverty' (1973: 262). A recurring theme of libertarian science fiction is therefore the entrepreneur-hero, the 'rugged individualist,' like D. D. Harriman in Robert Heinlein's novels. For Harriman (designed after the American robber baron Edward Henry Harriman), the 'wild-west laissez-faire' capitalism (Stover 1987: 9) in Heinlein's *The Man Who Sold The Moon* (1950) is the natural environment he needs for his self-development. At the frontier, with all its potential challenges, the hero can develop without being disturbed by the less talented, precisely because these lesser folks are scared off by such challenges. This idea of freedom through the selection of a frontier environment shows itself very clearly in a contribution to the LIBFUT mailing list, dealing with early colonial America: 'What made the period so utopic was [that] the fool never thought of coming, the lazy never started the journey, and the weak died along the way' (Ryder 2000).

The enemies of a frontier hero are the government or dogs in the manger, who throw mines of regulation in his way, which he has to sidestep. The elite is constantly limited in its free development by the masses. From the admiration of such an elite results the anti-democratic lineaments of libertarian science fiction, the skepticism against compromises and majority decisions. Here, through the voluntary support of charismatic leaders, libertarian ideology goes hand-in-hand with authoritarian models (Orth 1990: 293–316).

The blueprint of these patterns appears in its purest form in the works of Ayn Rand. 'Man is a word that has no plural' reads one of the slogans she used to describe a self-made philosophy she propagated with religious eagerness (Baker

1987: 96). As a symbol of her movement she chose the $, for her the sign of free trade and, accompanying free trade, of free human beings (Toffler 1964: 36). The current chairman of the Federal Reserve Board, Alan Greenspan, was a member of the Class of 43, the narrower discipleship of Rand, and wrote for the periodicals published by her (Chairman's Favorite Author 1974: 53–4). In Ayn Rand's novel *Atlas Shrugged* (1957), the geniuses of the world disappear one after another to 'Galt's Gulch,' a 'utopia of greed,' when they become aware of their 'exploitation.' In a strike of the entrepreneurs, they refuse to give their services to the world any longer. Ayn Rand's archetypal entrepreneur hero, however, is architect Howard Roark in *The Fountainhead* (1943). As a sign of his will and his claims to his 'intellectual property', Roark blows up a low-rent housing complex, because it wasn't built the way he designed it. In court, he defends this act with a programmatic speech, in which he states the primacy of the right to his 'intellectual property',[3] to unrestricted individualism, and to self-realization. Ayn Rand's passion play is actually a post-capitalist utopia: Roark's only motive is not cash (which he refuses at the beginning of the story), but 'Werkgerechtigkeit' (justification by works). The behavior of Howard Roark in *The Fountainhead* inadvertently demonstrates a major contradiction of libertarian ideology: persons who want to be successful in markets must orient themselves toward others – via the inherent logic of the market. They must produce or do what others want to buy. This way, the community, the network, is automatically placed before the self (Treanor 1996: 121–6).

Adventure capitalism and merchant heroes

The merchant hero is a special incarnation of the entrepreneur hero. The best-known of these science fiction merchants is Nicholas van Rijn, the main protagonist in many of Poul Anderson's stories. Van Rijn is not only a successful merchant, but – similarly to Heinlein's Lazarus Long – a natural, informal leader as well. In libertarian science fiction the merchant has an additional natural potential for salvation: with the help of the market he can liberate people from the government. In Joan and Vernor Vinge's *The Peddler's Apprentice* (1975), a suppressive world government blocks technical progress for the sake of stability. This world is finally liberated by a time-traveling-merchant, because the government is bad for his business. In the Hugo-award winner *A Deepness in the Sky* (1999), the traders of the Queng Ho fleet want to win customers on another planet and thereby become the natural enemies of the Emergents, who want to subjugate the other people. Besides that, merchants keep peace in libertarian science fiction, because peace is (in the libertarian ideal) good for their business. In Jared Lobdell's *The Last Holosong of Christopher Lightning* (1997), the merchant's slogan is therefore: 'Make money, not war' (327 and 336).

In *Capitalism and Freedom* (1962), Milton Friedman claimed that the free market would reduce ethnic and racial discrimination, because consumers would always buy from the cheapest provider (110). This idea was adapted by Francis Paul Wilson in his novel *Wheels Within Wheels* (1978), in which an alien mongrel population with characteristics from Navajo and African-Americans is discriminated against by settlers. Their liberation (as well as that of women) is for Wilson not a question of laws, but of personal skills. When Wilson's heroine Josephine Finch asserts a personal regiment in her inherited company, this is commented upon with the words: '[...] others spent their time shouting about woman's equality to man; Jo spent hers proving' (74). In Heinlein's *Delilah and the Space Rigger* (1949), efficiency solves the problem of prejudices against a woman on a space station: After a view at the 'progresses charts' the former misogynists decide to immediately enlist a whole group of women (23). In Neil Smith's *The Probability Broach* (1980), the market even leads to the integration of anthropoids, whales, and dolphins into human society (98). Likewise, the market ensures military protection, like in Heinlein's *Red Planet* (1950). In this juvenile novel, Heinlein's protagonist Smythe helps the heroes, but requires cash payments for each of his services. Finally, when the going gets tough, Smythe volunteers for a military command, in order to protect his conferred cash – and thus indirectly the two heroes (190).

Besides farmers, entrepreneurs and traders, outlaws make good heroes for libertarian ideology in frontier settings. The outlaw is one of the classical frontier hero figures and appears in numerous Hollywood western movies. He is among the first at the frontier, but he cannot accept the standards of subsequent settlers and subordinate himself to the community. So he must start over and over, to the next frontier (Kopytoff 1999: 34). Among the standards the frontier hero cannot accept, sexual standards play an important role. Deviation from dominant sexual norms was practiced by numerous religious groups and utopian communities of the nineteenth century – one of the most common examples were the Mormons. This process found its artistic representations in the figures and in the literary and cinematic topoi of the frontier: in the western musical *Paint Your Wagon*, Lee Marvin tells us that he is always at the frontier before the law is there – and he is away, before the law can follow – that's why he can share his wife with Clint Eastwood. Sexual deviation is also a commonplace in numerous science fiction novels. One of the reasons why Robert Heinlein became famous and successful in the 1960s is the description of sexual liberties in his novels at that time. This feature shows up most prominently in *Stranger in a Strange Land* (1961), where Heinlein's heroes found 'nests' in which absolute sexual freedom prevails. The book met the spirit of the time and became a best-seller as well as a guide for Hippies.

The frontier permits personality structures that would in civilization be punished with prison or the asylum, for example the enormous aggressiveness of Øyvind Myhre's hero Bull Running (1990: 14). If their activities are directed against the state (i.e. if they are smugglers or tax rebels) these kinds of heroes are particularly suitable for a libertarian message. That's why in F. Paul Wilson's science fiction novel *An Enemy of the State* (1980), Robin Hood is redefined as a tax rebel: that he took from the rich and gave to the poor is – to the protagonist LaNague – only a governmentally distorted version of the legend: strictly speaking, the 'rich' were just the tax collectors of King John, the 'poor' in turn those from whom the tax was taken before – so Robin Hood didn't redistribute – he just gave tax refunds (101).

In connection with frontier scenarios, American history is repeated again and again in science fiction. That includes the emigration spaceship 'Mayflower' in Heinlein's *Farmer in the Sky* (1950), the use of pioneer characters, like Johnny Appleseed in Ray Bradbury's *The Martian Chronicles* (1950), and the Declaration of Independence of the moon, which is – in Heinlein's *The Moon is a Harsh Mistress* (1966) – a copy of the US model (205). In *The Probability Broach* (1980), L. Neil Smith sketches a libertarian utopia by means of an alternate time stream scenario in which the American frontier perpetuates itself into the present. In a parallel world to ours, history was the same up to the Whiskey Rebellion of 1794. But then (in the libertarian parallel world) the Swiss financier Albert Gallatin supported the revolting Farmers and persuaded George Washington's troops to switch sides. A march to Philadelphia followed. Alexander Hamilton fled to Prussia, George Washington was executed (91–4). In the then-developing North American Confederacy (Smith's scenario for seven further novels), the power of the state was drastically limited. Individual liberty was considered the single most valued property (245). It was therefore well protected from incursions of the state. For the defense of liberty, everyone carried a weapon (110). The only state organs were the Continental Congress (which rarely assembled) and a president. Neither the congress nor the president had real powers to force anybody to do anything: 'Everybody's got a right to ignore the state and be safe doin' it' (214). Government property, an official currency, taxes, and public control organs were unknown. Thus, technical progress developed far more unrestrained and faster: the average life expectancy exceeded 200 years and a colony on Mars was established in 1968. That parallel America knew neither unemployment nor poverty, and only one type of redistribution: 'New opportunities [...] new ventures! That's how wealth really gets distributed' (135).

The idealization of the frontier includes the glorification of craftiness and hillbilly culture. In Eric Frank Russell's *The Great Explosion* (1962), an inexpensive trans-lightspeed device is invented by a single civilian (7). This invention enables the individual settling of space. After this individual settling, the earth bureaucracy wants to re-integrate the 'colonies,' despite the fact that it does not have any contact to the settlements. A spaceship filled with bureaucrats, diplomats, and soldiers eventually fails on this mission because of the interventions of grouchomarxist hillbillys on a libertarian planet. The inhabitants of this planet take everything literally and mostly ignore the bureaucrats. With the phrase 'Myob,' which turns out to be an abbreviation for 'mind your own business,' the acephale settlers demoralize the bureaucrats from earth. The Flinters from F. Paul Wilson's LaNague novels are another hillbilly-like libertarian people, a mixture between a Ninja warrior tribe and the NRA, that particularly wants to remain undisturbed. Their philosophy is called 'KYFHO,' which is short for 'keep your fucking hands off' (1980: 127).

On the planet Flint as well as in most other libertarian utopias, weapons serve as protection from the dawning of the state. In Vernor Vinge's *The Ungoverned*

(1985: 200–54), an anarchist farm belt defends itself against the attempted takeover of a nearby republic with a combination of private security agencies, gun-craziness to the level of a private atomic bomb, and teenage hackers. At the science fiction frontier, the right to vigilante justice is closely associated with the right to bear arms. For example, the Americans of a parallel universe in Heinlein's *The Number of the Beast* (1980) hung all lawyers and oriented their laws on the simple principle of the *lex talionis*. Heinlein lets one of his heroes explain the effect: 'This place has no prisons, almost no crime, and it is the safest place to raise children I've ever heard of. We are having to relearn history' (384). Finally, the right to vigilante justice can be associated with protection from politicians, as in *A Planet for Texans* (1958) by H. Beam Piper and John J. McGuire, the winner of the Hall of Fame Awards of the Libertarian Futurist Society in 1999. On planet New Texas, the 'meat supplier of the galaxy,' a politician who wanted to introduce an income tax, is killed with a machete. The perpetrator is accused of 'excessive criticism' of the politician, but acquitted. The judge even calls him a hero. The New Texan girl Gail explains the situation to ambassador Cumshaw, who's freshly sent from the Solar League: 'That wasn't murder. He just killed a politician. All the court could do was determine whether or not the politician needed it [...]' (49).

Apart from the right to bear arms, tax evasion and tax rebellions are part of the founding myth of the USA. One of the most popular motives for libertarian utopias is the absence of taxes. And one of Heinlein's writing rackets, which most clearly expresses the refusal of taxes, is the already mentioned Lazarus Long. 'Taxes are not levied for the benefit of the taxed' (1973: 268) is one of his most famous utterances. In *The Moon is a Harsh Mistress* (1966) and in numerous other novels and short stories, we will find rants against the 'nonsense' of taxes (204). Through a debated tax on moon tunnels (that are the carriers of progress and help pushing the frontier forward), the act of taxation is presented as something particularly perverse. Apart from the refusal to pay taxes for the sake of one's own finances, libertarian ideology sees its application only in the extension of national interventions into the private lives of citizens. An example for this application is found in Francis Paul Wilson's *An Enemy of the State* (1980). 'Keep a government poor and you'll keep it off your back' (184) is the conclusion of Wilson's hero LaNague.

Looking closely, not only libertarian literature, but also libertarian theory in general, is difficult to conceptualize without such a conception of 'open' spaces. Thus, in *Free to Choose* (1979), Milton Friedman names not only the reduction of status privileges and government restrictions as well as a fertile cultural climate for innovation as prerequisites for the development of the USA in the nineteenth century, but also (even if somewhat ashamedly) an 'empty' continent, one that was available for settling (3).

About utopian dystopias and dystopian utopias

The frontier becomes particularly effective as utopia if it is directly contrasted with a – usually urban – dystopia. Consequently, another popular scenario in libertarian science fiction consists of a powerful and expanding government and a handful of heroes courageously defending their individuality. Beside the frontier, American science fiction in the twentieth century is characterized mainly by such dystopian scenarios. The two scenarios are not mutually exclusive, but – on the contrary – complete each other: the frontier is particularly clearly recognizable as utopia if it is confronted with a dystopia. For the development and mediation of libertarian ideology, both styles are well suited. In libertarian utopias, anarcho-capitalistic society models can be conceptualized, while in libertarian dystopian scenarios the fatal or even lethal influence of government can be described.

A direct comparison of utopia and dystopia is found in Robert B. Boardman's *Savior of Fire* (1991). A spaceship from earth lands on the planet Fire, whose inhabitants live in a libertarian paradise. They are so free that they do not know a word for freedom. An economist from earth, called 'John Maynard' – like John Maynard Keynes – wants to fight unemployment and to promote progress on the planet. Following the theory of the Austrian economist and MPS founding member Ludwig von Mises (1949), the inflation thus triggered is the basic cause of all evil and leads successively to price increases, a minimum wage, criminality, police, taxes, government, urbanization, pollution, and war. Finally, when the population stops believing in paper money, the system breaks down (Boardman 1991: 145, 168, 255 and 285).

But not every dystopia promotes libertarian ideology that directly. Often dystopias in science fiction are merely connected to an immoderately forbidding, controlling, conspiring, or de-individualizing and equalizing government and, circumventing these modes of control, open a free space for libertarian ideology. In 1924 the first important dystopia of the twentieth century was published – Evgenij Zamjatin's *We* (1924). Aldous Huxley's *Brave New World* (1932), George Orwell's *1984* (1949) and a multiplicity of genre-bound dystopian works followed. They were usually no mere criticism of Soviet communism, but a general critique of the Fordistic ways of life and of production (Adorno 1955). Already for the year 1939, cultural historian Bruce Franklin noted a change from the technology-enthusiasm of the 'Wow! Gosh! era' to a more dystopian view of earth's future in an investigation of the science fiction magazine *Astounding* (Franklin 1982: 40). Later, especially in the 1970s, most science fiction films are characterized by pessimistic, or apocalyptic scenarios (Franklin 1983: 48) – even if these are often connected with an escape to a frontier. According to Frederic Jameson (1982: 151ff.), science fiction restructures the present as history and can thereby enable reflection. What was felt as repression in twentieth-century America emerged as an extrapolated and more severe problem in the dystopian science fiction of these times (Schwartz 1974: 60). Although not openly political, science fiction films therefore revealed many problems and fears of their times. The disaster in these dystopias develops from the extrapolation of threats that were already visible: pollution (*No Blade of Grass*), overpopulation (*Soylent Green*), crime and the decay of inner cities (*Escape from New York*), or the threat of nuclear war (*Colossus: The Forbin Project*).

How the frontier is separated from the dystopia

The vast majority of anti-utopian extrapolations are located in cities. But the city was by no means automatically bound to dystopian scenarios. In the classical utopian literature it is – because of the protection that its walls offer – a prerequisite for the seclusiveness and thus the existence of the utopia. Only in the American history of ideas did the city become a threatening symbol. Thomas Jefferson and the most important American poets of the nineteenth century, Ralph Waldo Emerson, Henry David Thoreau, Herman Melville, Nathaniel Hawthorne and Edgar Allan Poe, used the city already as a dystopian place. Diametrically opposed to the city, rural life served as an ideal (Graaf 1971: 84–5 and 198, footnote 36). Dystopian restrictions were the opposite of the infinite space of the frontier utopia. The film *Soylent Green* takes place in the year 2022, in a hopelessly overpopulated New York. Food and dwelling are extremely scarce because of climate catastrophes and population growth: Charlton Heston plays a police officer who is constantly busy avoiding stepping on humans who sleep on stairways and shunning people aside. Overpopulation is one of the most important literary and cinematic topoi of dystopic science fiction of the 1970s. In Ira Levin's novel *This Perfect Day* (1970), humans must die at age 62 for efficiency reasons (121). In the disco-dystopia *Logan's Run*, this happens at age thirty. In the 1971 film *Z.P.G.* (Zero Population Growth), overpopulation causes serious air pollution, resulting in a law against births. Anyone opposing this prohibition is condemned to death. These dystopias offer solutions to problems not in the form of political measures, such as forced birth control (these are presented as ineffective or as inhuman), but only in the form of an escape from the cities. In *Logan's Run*, the hero saves himself, accompanied by a female rebel, into a non-controlled, non-urban outside world. In *Soylent Green*, the protagonist Sol Roth (Edward G. Robinson) can save himself only through state-sponsored suicide, accompanied by pictures of nature, projected in an exaggerated widescreen effect: here, death is the 'final frontier'.

The utopian dystopia

Libertarian dystopias are not always overpopulated but often clean, peaceful, and endowed with lots of rules and laws. So – how can they function as dystopias? Traditional utopias are usually static. Social problems and conflicts have been solved (Woodcock 1956: 81–3). In the twentieth century, this static condition was increasingly perceived as unsatisfactory. Dystopian authors like Huxley interpreted this change of perspectives as a result of the fact that humans had to decide between the barbarism of chance and 'culture' as an objectively higher status, that includes misfortune (Adorno 1955: 111).

In Marco Brambilla's science fiction film *Demolition Man* (taking place in the region of Los Angeles in the year 2032), roads are tidy, graffiti gets automatically removed from buildings, cars are noiseless, the air is clean, and the lawns are mowed. The inhabitants are – by standards of late-twentieth-century America – exaggeratedly friendly and even call each other by their full names. Swear words are forbidden, fatty foods and alcohol are outlawed. A group of rebels led by Edgar Friendly (Denis Leary) doesn't want to subject themselves to these regulations and prohibitions and therefore lives in the canalization. The rebel leader explains his desire for individualism and liberty, his desire to do unreasonable things to the hero John Spartan (Sylvester Stallone): '[...] I want fat, I want cholesterol! I wanna eat butter and bacon and buckets of cheese!' Peter W. Huber, in *Orwell's Revenge* (1994), lets his hero reason similarly: 'Freedom includes the freedom to be foolish, to be sick. Free choice includes the freedom to choose badly' (195). Material contentment and spiritual liberty are regarded as incompatible in those static-utopian dystopias. The element perceived as missing is often located in the irrational – like 'art,' or 'poetry'. Aldous Huxley's 'Savage' in *Brave New World* (1932) demanded his 'right to be unhappy' with the words: '[...] I don't want comfort. [...] I want poetry, I want real danger, I want freedom [...]' (163). Governmental concern is regarded as a danger to the individual, welfare as forced conformism. For their dystopian representation, governments are shown as forcing people to take anti-depressants or as treating deviating behavior with forced medical treatment. For example, in Ira Levin's novel *This Perfect Day* (1970), the entire population is constantly drugged with lithium (256).

The dystopian utopia

Whereas order and prosperity appear dystopic to many libertarians, opposite scenarios have utopian qualities to them. In libertarian circles, descriptions of economic decline, connected to lack of security and vigilante justice, as described in Neal Stephenson's novel *Snow Crash* (1992), count as utopias. Stephenson takes up many potential weak points of anarcho-capitalism and integrates them into his novel: 'This is America. People do whatever the fuck they feel like doing, you got a problem with that? Because they have a right to. And because they have guns and no one can fucking stop them. As a result, this country has one of the worst economies in the world' (2). In such terrible but exciting jungle and adventure settings, the libertarian hero can prove himself, can even actualize himself. What's a dystopia to the less skilled is a utopia to him.

The individual in peril

Neither in death nor in destruction, but in dehumanization, does film historian Carlos Clarens (1968) find the one instrument of science fiction that can produce the most fear (134). Besides the already mentioned works of Zamjatin and Huxley, a very early example of the fear of the perils to individualism is Ayn Rand's short story *Anthem*, written in the late 1930s, but published in 1946 for the first time. In her dystopian future there is no 'I', only 'We'. Likewise, in the late 1930s and early 1940s Robert Heinlein published the two stories *If This Goes On* (1939) and *Coventry* (1940). In these stories, he describes a pre-Orwellian suppressive system with thought-control, brainwashing, and camera surveillance, ruled by a theocracy. In Alfred Bester's novel *The Demolished Man* (1951), a dystopia taking place in the twenty-fourth century, the government is allowed and able to read thoughts. So-called 'Espers' (after ESP, Extrasensory Perception) can latch themselves onto the thoughts of other humans. Through this ability they represent the fear of the dissolution of the individual, of the absorption into a group consciousness.

In the science fiction film of the 1950s, disciplining of individualism is still predominantly affirmed. In these films, individualists that dare to stray too far from the community usually get killed. However, when sociology began criticizing the 'organization man' of the 1950s (see Whyte 1956 – the figure was perfectly embodied by Tony Randall as submissive advertising employee in Frank Tashlin's *Will Success Spoil Rock Hunter*), American culture got scared of itself and started a revival of individualism and the values of the pioneer times (Frank 1997). In the dystopias shaped by this fear, the individual is usually endangered either directly by physical or medical influences on his consciousness, or indirectly by advertising or propaganda. In *THX 1138*, a film George Lucas released in 1970 (and after which today's Lucasfilm sound system was named), life is regulated by the state. Individuals are forced to take drugs that adjust their sexual desires. Thoughts and actions are electronically controlled. All humans carry names that consist of a combination of letters and numbers. Optically, Lucas transfers the conformity through uniform white overalls and bald heads displayed by all actors. Humans who deviate from the standard beyond a certain tolerance level are reconditioned.

A further method for the production of conformity is constant surveillance. In Marco Brambilla's *Demolition Man*, the entire city is monitored by a camera-and-microphone system, which is used (among other things) to enforce adherence to the prohibition of cursing. All citizens have chips implanted into their skin that also serve monitoring functions. The fact that not only governments, but also markets, can limit free speech remains – particularly in explicitly libertarian science fiction – a widely ignored matter. In Larry Niven and Jerry Pournelle's *Oath of Fealty* (1981), for example, private monitoring in a gigantic Gated Community is regarded as voluntary security, not as forced surveillance.

The more direct the government restrictions of individual rights, the better suited they are for their representation in a dystopia. Neil Schulman developed a quite impressive dystopian scenario based on this formula in his novel *The Rainbow Cadenza* (1983). Schulman contrasts the libertarian moon colony Ad Astra with a dystopic future earth. In his novel, he extends government control into unusual areas. Due to the drug 'Adamine', which results in exclusively male offspring, there are seven times more men than women on earth in this novel. The state reacts to these changes with the introduction of a three-year conscription for women in the 'Peace Corps.' Using the old hippie slogan 'Make Love not War,' women are forced by the government to provide sexual services for needy men. This canalization of the libido is intended to prevent wars. The forced sexual activities during this national peace service do not fall under the legal definition for rape, valid on Schulman's earth, since the involved partners must pledge allegiance – and that oath includes acquiescence to officially exercised sexual intercourse. In contrast, intercourse with a deserter automatically counts as rape, because here the necessary consent of the government is missing. By means of this institution, Schulman caricatures both the military service, where the state has command over the bodies of young men, as well as other governmental actions: 'If you find this whole set-up unlikely, then consider that property taken from a person without that person's consent is theft – unless it is taken by a government tax collector to hire police to protect us from robbery – and consider that taking another person's life is murder – unless it is taken by a government executioner to prevent us from being murdered – and consider that forcing servitude on another person is slavery – unless it is done by a government draft board to save us from those foreign enemies who would, if they conquered us, reduce us to involuntary servitude. Government never outlaws these crimes: it merely claims a monopoly on them – so why should rape be any different?' (Appendix II).

The bureaucracy as sovereign

These threats to the individual are exercised not so much by individual villain politicians, but by a faceless bureaucracy. The state conspiracy can emanate not only from politicians, but rather from the same faceless bureaucracy. In the *John Franklin Letters* (1959), America is the victim of a UN conspiracy that begins with regulations and taxes and ends in genocide. In this narrative, the administrative elite in power is only called 'Buros' (short for 'Bureaucrats') by the rebels and completely lacks any charismatic leader figure.

During the New Deal and the Cold War, the US went through crucial changes. The New Deal brought regulative interventions in economics and culture, while the Cold War let the military–industrial complex (with its enormous defense budgets) grow and demanded intensified conformity under the auspices of anti-communism and the 'organization man' culture. Between these vertices a plant prospered that was increasingly perceived as an evil by many Americans – bureaucracy. Demands for more efficiency and control of the welfare state only created an ever tighter bureaucracy. In the 1950s, science fiction already mirrored experiences with and fears of increasing bureaucracy in dystopian scenarios. The structure of governmental organizations (including the army) was viewed with a basic skepticism, even if they were regarded as necessary for protection, as in the movie *Them*.

From bureaucracy to state conspiracy

None of the 50 Hollywood science fiction films between 1970 and 1982 shows a functioning democracy. The political system in these films is usually a totalitarian apparatus or a conspiracy (Franklin 1990: 22–3). Often, the conspiracy is shown as an intermediary step to totalitarianism. Measures of an apparently harmless welfare state are covert preparations for total control. Thus, the eco-regime in James P. Hogan's *Multiplex Man* (1992) operates only superficially with repressive tolerance – in reality, a bureaucratic conspiracy plans the modification of the personalities of dissidents (227). From the 1970s on, these plots became so popular that they could establish themselves as an independent genre. With films like *Rambo: First Blood Part II* and television series like the *X-Files*, the pattern of a government conspiracy gained such a firm foothold that a special iconography of government conspirators with dark suits and black helicopters developed.

The communion of the prohibited

In contrast to the conspiracy of the bureaucrats, the cooperation of individuals in science fiction dystopias is usually created through the widespread infringement of government prohibitions. The community needs the communion of the prohibited to come into existence. Other worlds and future scenarios are excellent means for representing the relativity of national prohibitions. In *If Pigs Had Wings* (1998) by William Alan Ritch, 'crime-cubes' (or films) are called 'pornos', and they are forbidden (254). Another stylistic device is the expansion of existing prohibitions into dictatorship. In *Day of Atonement* (1998) by J. Neil Schulman, for example, a theocratic dystopia developed from the numerous religious prohibitions in Israel. Finally, the third method is the design of functioning libertarian utopias without the prohibitions that exist in twentieth-century America. These prohibitionless utopias are then endangered by regulation raging rooks. In *The Moon is a Harsh Mistress* (1966), Robert Heinlein ridicules a lot of regulations existing in many American states and towns as excesses of a 'perverse' regulation rage: 'One female [...] had a long list she wanted made permanent laws – about private matters. No more plural marriage of any sort. No divorces. No "fornication" – had to look that one up. No drinks stronger than 4% beer. Church services only on Saturdays and all else to stop that day (Air and temperature and pressure engineering, lady? Phones and capsules?). A long list of drugs to be prohibited and a shorter list dispensed only by licensed physicians [...] She even wanted to make gambling illegal' (204). Heinlein emphasizes the bureaucratic character of such prohibitions through the use of German words. The application of a foreign language serves him as symbol. In *The Cat Who Walks Through Walls* (1985), he uses the German word 'verboten' to signify developments indicative of a Prussian 'Ordnungsstaat' (194).

Conclusion

Popular Culture in general and science fiction in particular reveal not only some central means of neoliberal ideology, but also some basic contradictions: The means are promises of a benevolent god-market that distributes an ever growing wealth without constricting individual liberties even in the slightest way. And the horrors of a dystopia of subordination to society, that leads from a merely annoying bureaucracy straight into totalitarianism and dictatorship.

The first important contradiction within these means is that the utopia needs the vision of a frontier. When there is no frontier in sight, more or less improbable or remote literary anticipations have to be created in order to recover the utopian spirit. The second contradiction is the problem of private or corporate power that leads not only to monopolies (that contradict the image of the god-market) but also to the development of corporations into state-like entities that can collect license fees like taxes and restrict individual rights as well as states – but without any form of democratic control. The most important battlefield with regard to these contradictions is the area of 'intellectual property', that is not only part of science fiction novels like Greg Egan's *Distress* (1997), but becomes more and more part of everyday life.

Notes

1 For further information on this term see Turner (1894: 199–207) and Petersen (1996).
2 An example for one of the few negative representations of the frontier is Philip K. Dick's *Three Stigmata of Palmer Eldritch* (1965). In this novel, the frontier is settled by force of the UN and a military-like conscription-system. Dick compares the settlement in his narrative not with the successful settlements in American history, but with Roanoke – a colony that died out completely.
3 This primacy of 'intellectual property,' that shows up especially clear in Howard Roark's final speech, is contradictory to large parts of the brand of libertarian ideology present within the Open-Source-movement and is (along with the problem of monopolies) one of the two most visible contradictions of libertarian ideology.

9 The education of neoliberalism[1]

Oliver Schöller and Olaf Groh-Samberg

In this chapter we will examine educational reform efforts to shed light on strategies to obtain and consolidate neoliberal hegemony. We start from the premise that neoliberalism to a large extent owes its hegemonic position and its political influence to the significance of the technocratic knowledge of experts and of knowledge-elites, who succeeded in organizing themselves effectively in a worldwide web of the neoliberal think tanks. We will devote our attention to the mechanisms by which the power of knowledge-elites and the power of elitist knowledge mutually generate, stabilize and build on each other. As a first step we will reconsider reflections by Pierre Bourdieu on the sociogenesis of neoliberal technocracy. On this basis, we then argue that the formation and assertion of neoliberalism came about by means of the successful adjustment strategies that constituted the reaction of the ruling class to the challenges of the educational expansion.

Taking the Bertelsmann Foundation, the corporate think tank of Germany's transnational media conglomerate Bertelsmann AG, as a concrete example, we want to show in the second part how the organization of think tanks contributes to the consolidation of the enormously powerful position of technocratic knowledge-elites. The hegemonial power of neoliberalism is based to a great extent on this elitist and technocratic organizational form of expert-knowledge, which exerts more and more influence on political decisions without being subject to democratic control mechanisms.

In the third part we take a look at neoliberal educational politics in Germany. Here, the wheel of knowledge and power comes full circle: By transforming the educational system entirely and permanently, according to the principles to which they owe their superior education and the legitimacy of their exclusive position of power, the neoliberal knowledge-elites gain ever more institutional control over recruitment into the system, while safeguarding their own reproduction.

Neoliberalism, intellectuals and power

Bourdieu observed that the traditional antagonism of economical and intellectual factions within the ruling classes has been almost overcome since the rise of neoliberalism. The novelty of neoliberal hegemony according to him consists in the fact that it is exerted by a new *ruling* faction within the ruling class, which is no longer based on the dominance of its economical power alone, but asserts itself via *intellectual* superiority and the authority of its *cultural* capital. In other words: the neoliberal knowledge-elites promote a new variety of cultural capital, which intellectually refines and legitimizes their economical capital instead of contrasting with them.

The 'New State Nobility' and the neoliberal technocracy

In his political writings Bourdieu repeatedly refers to the dominance of neoliberalism as 'technocracy', or the power of a 'new state nobility'.[2] A small group of academically educated elites feels entitled to rearrange society top to bottom because of its superior knowledge and its economist approach.

> This state-nobility, preaching the retreat of the state and the undivided rule of market and consumer – this commercial substitute of the citizen – has monopolized the state. It has transformed public into private property and made the public matter of the republic its own private concern. What matters today is the reclaiming of democracy and its victory over technocracy.
> (Bourdieu 1998a: 35)

The central new way to warrant social supremacy and inequality is the claim to superior knowledge. Bourdieu writes about an 'ideology of competence' (51) or even a 'racism of intelligence' (Bourdieu 1993): 'In fact, the power of neoliberal hegemony is based on a new form of social Darwinism: In the words of Harvard, "the best and the most remarkable" win the race' (Bourdieu 1998a: 51). Education, in the sense of knowledge and competences accumulated through life, is the main means of justifying social inequality. Thus it does not merely justify that the bearers of the most respected titles of education guide the state and its society in the manner of a technocracy or a state nobility, but also serves as an argument for why the least qualified should remain unemployed and without social support, being after all useless for society. The rule of neoliberalism is based on the power of neoliberal knowledge. The ambition of neoliberalism thus consists less in being right in its view of politics but in being scientifically 'true', i.e. that it should be able to claim the authority of scientific truth based on 'economic science' when political goals are being defined. Nearly all important neoliberal reforms are legitimized and accepted by the public when the argument of 'specific obligations' is called upon.

This also helps to understand the exceptional role of *think tanks* as networks of neoliberal knowledge production. The knowledge produced and disseminated here is not monopolized by a dominating faction of intellectuals who dissociate themselves from the money-bourgeoisie because of their cultural capital and distinction. It is rather a younger faction of the ruling class who has the right of disposal of this knowledge. It owes its social leadership as much to its economical as to its cultural capital and has asserted itself in intellectual debates even against the classical intellectuals – not to mention those positioning themselves as left-wing – with their respective knowledge.

The fight for education and the adjustment strategies of the ruling classes

Marxist class theories assume the possibility of independent political action and articulation by the working class. Bourdieu on the contrary never wearies of emphasizing how much the political effectiveness of statements depends on the educational capital of the speaker, if not his economic status (Bourdieu 2001). According to Bourdieu, the fiercest symbolic class struggles do not rage between ruling and ruled classes, but between the various factions *within* the ruling classes. Only the faction of the very highly educated has the chance to wage an effective war against the economic bourgeoisie at the head of the ruling classes. The history of the ruling classes and the class struggles of highly developed societies are characterized by the split of the ruling power into two poles, one economic, one intellectual. The relations of clerical and secular powers are predecessors of this division. From the nineteenth century until a short while ago the chasm was most marked in the relations between the economic and the educated upper classes.

This cleft in the structure of the ruling classes is naturally subject to historic modifications. In their social and symbolic fights, the representatives of the different factions always try to establish a balance of power in accordance with their own type of capital. The growing importance of the historic-secular trend of expert knowledge, i.e. the educational expansion, causes a continuous imbalance of social powers. The process of educational development is accompanied by permanent fights within the ruling classes about the re- or devaluation of the various forms of cultural, social or economic capital. The exceptionally fast and intense educational expansion of the 1950s and 1960s created unrest among the ruling classes. From the beginning, all their factions tried to make use of the growing importance of educational titles and to prepare themselves for the intensified rivalry for the best respected educational titles. Members of the middle and lower class also took part in this competition, their numbers rapidly declining with their social status. Intense social debates concerning the social definition, evaluation and meaning of education evolved and continue to this day. These changes and debates eventually led to a completely new evaluation of cultural capital among the classes which owned inherited wealth.[3]

The reformers of education and the inclination to revolt

In his work *Homo academicus*, Bourdieu (1992) looked intensely into the developments of the educational expansion, which were to lead to the movement of May 1968. His analysis is characterized by the peculiar scepticism he already showed in the early 1960s for the 'pseudo-revolutionary' trends in the debates on educational reforms.[4] Although Bourdieu was unable to sympathize with the student protests and the emotions and ideals that accompanied them, he developed an interesting socio-educational and class-sociological explanatory background for the outbreak and the failure of the revolt.

According to his views, two social groups can be seen as the most important initiators of this uprising. First, the educational climbers of the middle and lower classes, who had associated social advancement with the acquisition of high educational titles, and felt cheated by the inflationary devaluation of these titles. According to Bourdieu, the inclination to revolt results from this frustration, together with the tendency to question the entire institution of higher education and all institutions which owe their prestige to issuing certificates of education like entrance tickets.

> It is the disillusionment resulting from the structural gap between aspirations and prospects which causes disinclination and aversion to work and the manifold manifestations of disapproval of social effectiveness. These are the roots of all 'alternative-culture', the growing constitutive escape attempts and phenomena of denial.
>
> (Bourdieu 1982: 242)

The second group is much more important for the emergence of the protest movements because of its greater inherited funds. It consists of the offspring of the ruling classes whose success in changing the family mode of reproduction to school-mediated strategies was inadequate, or who in the intensified competition for academic titles were pushed into less prestigious fields. Bourdieu interprets these individual cases of failed adaptation to a new mode of reproduction as 'sacrifices' the ruling class has to make for preserving its 'statistic reproduction' (Bourdieu et al. 1981: 44ff.). The less prestigious fields in turn provided an opportunity for the less successful offspring of the ruling classes to distinguish themselves as heretics, and to set themselves up as spokesmen or -women of the protest movements.

Bourdieu's 'class-sociological hypothesis' explaining the protest movements and the policies of educational reform of the 1960s and 1970s still has to be tested by way of international comparative research. We do think that Bourdieu tends to underestimate these reforms and to polemically simplify their motives and driving forces. For instance, he ignores the experience of *emancipation by education*, which is so decisive for the group of educational climbers. The expectation and real prospect of professional advancement via education and of being able to exchange the physically hard and monotonous work of the parents' generation for an intellectually sophisticated occupation was surely very important for such social aspirations. Such expectations are often accompanied by the expansion of one's personal horizon and the emancipation from a traditional and authoritarian background (cf. Giegel 1989). This experience of social emancipation via education is precisely the reason why educational climbers tend to define education as well as politics primarily through 'changes in outlook.' In his analyses of the 'new petty bourgeoisie' Bourdieu depicted this disposition vividly, if again disparagingly (Bourdieu 1982: 561–72).[5]

Later, the new right-wing criticism of reform policies and protest movements would aim precisely at their weakest and most sensitive points as pointed out in Bourdieu's analyses. Even in the form of a critical and emancipatory educational ideal, the cultivation and extolling of education and of cultural capital carry with them aspects of power and distinction. In times of intense fights for academic titles these aspects point at the lead the children of the ruling class have over those of the dominated class that hitherto has been ignored. The neo-conservatives inveighed against just this chasm between the bourgeois left-wing intellectuals and, in Helmut Schelsky's (1975) famous words, 'the others who do the work'. But Bourdieu fails to see that the reason for this effect of power and for the repressive competition for profitable academic titles is not an objective shortage of prestigious titles or leading positions, but a scarcity of well-paid, secure, respected and fun jobs, induced by economic powers. *The gap between the dominating and the dominated can be reduced by the expansion of education and educational reforms, if they are accompanied by emancipatory processes that can be lived and experienced by the disadvantaged groups of society.* In our view, the intensity and the successes of the protest movements of the 1960s and 1970s are explained more by the fact that there have been such experiences of emancipation than by the experience of being cheated.

Bourdieu's central argument in any case is that the economic–technical modernization makes an educational expansion necessary. The economically ruling classes react to this by adjusting the mode of social reproduction, which is displaced from the realm of the family on to the educational system. This is connected with Bourdieu's diagnosis of a change in the lifestyle of the ruling class, the emergence of a 'new bourgeoisie', the most remarkable feature of which is the attempt to overcome the old contrast of economic and cultural capital. In the following we will sum up the socio-genesis and effects of this new form of power and hegemony of the bourgeois classes, which mainly arose from the battlefields of education.

The 'New Bourgeoisie' and the school-mediated mode of reproduction

Those social class factions who achieved the shift from the family mode of social reproduction to a school-mediated mode used their broad education not for the purpose of emancipation but with the object of preserving and consolidating their leading social positions. This process, as already detected by Bourdieu in the early 1970s, takes place via homologous changes in the economy, in the sector of elite universities, and finally in the formation of classes. Changes take place in the universities for the elites so that a selection process for leading positions in economics and politics becomes an implicit aspect of university education. This is motivated by changes in business practices, especially by personnel cuts, the restructuring of management and changes in recruitment (Bourdieu 1996).

At first, the school-mediated mode of reproduction is accompanied by a legitimization of power. It consists of the 'formally entirely faultless competition' (Bourdieu 1982: 495) in which the children of the ruling classes prove superior. Presumably, this very experience of competition in school has a strong formative influence on the careers of the new bourgeoisie, and predisposes this class faction for idealizing competition, achievement and the market. *Competition is associated with pleasure.* In addition, the faith in fair competition serves not only to justify one's own leading position towards others, it is also a source of the subjective feeling that one has the capability and even vocation to maintain this position. This belief becomes the psychological basis of the entire personality and the core of its world view (cf. Bourdieu 1982: 487ff.).

Consequently, it is understandable why changes in educational and professional careers or the modes of recruitment result in 'eventual differences in disposition' (488). The 'metamorphosis of disposition' (Vester *et al.* 2001: 324–7) of the ruling and ascending classes, accompanying the educational expansion and the move to secure one's continuity through schooling, finds expression in new lifestyles, new ways of distinction and new forms of domination. In this way the traditionally bipolar structure of the dominating taste becomes destabilized. 'The power and circumstances of the new avant-garde depend on the structure of their capital which openly manifests itself in their lifestyle' (Bourdieu 1982: 494). Bourdieu emphasizes three characteristics in particular: first, the 'cosmopolitanism' of the new bourgeoisie, consisting for example in numerous foreign diplomas, international business flights and jobs in multinational corporations; second, the new human skills of a modern executive, such as team work, autonomy and communicative skills; and eventually a 'modern lifestyle', to be discerned by the preferred sports, typically sailing, skiing, water sports and tennis, or by the tanned, athletic body, or by such details as preferring whisky to champagne. This group is the 'new bourgeoisie' seen by Bourdieu as inherently connected with neoliberal knowledge production. He characterizes the group as 'totally saturated with the education of economic politics and its modern view of economy and society, that is taught in political institutes and business schools, a view to which they in turn contribute in colloquia, committees and seminars' (495) or, pointing out their interest in business magazines and economic education:

> The education of the modern executives strengthens their feeling that they are holders of an intellectually legitimised authority, valid for society as a whole. The contrast between the 'altruistic education' of the intellectual and the 'lack of education' of the 'bourgeois', caught up in his ordinary, practical interests, is now replaced by the contrast between the pointless, unrealistic education of the intellectual, and the economic or polytechnic education of the 'modern executives', which seeks to be practically orientated, but not to be reduced to 'practice only'.
>
> (Bourdieu 1982: 495f.)

Educational strategies and class struggles – stages of the neoliberal counterrevolution

To sum up what has been said so far, according to Bourdieu the strategies of acquiring education and of increasing its value can be seen as the central strategies of class struggles in modern societies. The emergence and implementation of the neoliberal hegemony can be comprehended as a top-down class struggle, taking place not least thanks to the assertion of a particular kind of education with its own ways of acquisition and usage. Following Bourdieu we developed the central hypothesis that the younger generations of the ruling and rising classes with their elitist and authoritarian view of economic education were able to assert themselves against the more democratic varieties of a socio-scientific education, mainly represented by educational climbers and left-wing intellectuals.

Still, the intellectual and social battlefields and the hegemony of neoliberalism are not homogeneous. In the 1970s a new discourse of neo-conservatives and right-wingers had established itself in a direct reaction to the increased strength of the old and the new Left. At the same time, parallel to the worldwide economic crisis of the 1970s, the neoliberal economists made their appearance (cf. Dixon 2000a, b). The campaign of monetarism against Keynesianism ran parallel to the campaign of the neo-conservatives against the reform and protest movements, and both met on the battlefield of the criticism of welfare state and trade unions.

But neither the economic education Bourdieu had pointed out as specific for the new 'state nobility', nor the particular cultural capital he considered typical for the new bourgeoisie, were immediately transformed into the currency of power. First, the authoritarian, anti-modern traditions that the neo-conservatism had mobilized and cultivated in its battle against the (new) Left had to be shed. The defensive stage, marked by strategic actions (until the beginning of the 1970s), and the offensive stage, dominated by the neo-conservatives, were followed (in the 1990s) by a third stage of neoliberalism, interpreted by Plehwe and Walpen (1999) with Gramsci as 'positional warfare'. Typical for this stage is the gradual merging of alternative with yuppie cultures, the conciliation of making a career for oneself and self-realization, and the ideological enrichment of neoliberalism with the emancipatory traditions of civil society as well as with communitarian and neo-corporatist ('competitive corporatism') elements. Thus, neoliberalism loses its dogmatic severity on the one hand, but on the other becomes less open to attack, being disguised by the ideology of a so-called 'Third Way' (Ryner 2002). It acquires a modernistic image, welcoming economic, technical and cultural progress. That makes neoliberalism attractive for the young, highly-qualified, open-minded and reform-orientated factions of the ruling classes as well as for the disillusioned factions of alternative and left-wing intellectuals who gave up their previous ideologies and are reformed by political realism.[6]

The new state nobility in power – the example of the Bertelsmann Foundation

The Bertelsmann Foundation was founded by the family corporation of the same name. With 81,000 employees in 51 countries and a total turnover of 20 billion euros, the company ranks fourth among the world's biggest media enterprises (Lehning 2004). In 1993, 70 per cent of the capital loans of the entire corporation were transferred to the corporate foundation, founded in 1977 by the patriarch of the family of entrepreneurs, Reinhard Mohn.

Today, it is the largest German corporate foundation; with a total budget of 65 million euros financing 300 employees in charge of 100 projects (Anheier 2003; see Schöller 2001, 2003 for further information). The Bertelsmann Foundation works operatively, independently devising projects and consistently attending to their realization, with the intention of initiating social reform processes. It sees itself as an independent thought factory consciously taking up the US tradition of political consultancy mediated through think tanks.

The self-assessment of the foundation and its image in society has been outlined in several programmatic papers. It shows three central attitudes of the modern state nobility, peculiarly combining neoliberal programming with communitarian rhetoric (compare Bieling in this volume). In the *first place*, the foundation systematically criticizes the welfare state, maintaining that the hierarchical and ossified structures of the state's over-regulation suppress the individual's creative potential and hinder the progressive development of society. *Second*, the foundation has for a long time been propagating a participative business culture, developed by the mother company in Gütersloh. The language of flat hierarchies and possibilities for participation, however, obscures rather than illuminates the owner's limited understanding of 'participation'. He did not mean workers to obtain a role in powerful decision-making processes in support of work-place democracy (compare Mohn 1986: 18). *Third*, the Bertelsmann Foundation postulates the fundamental claims to leadership of 'charismatic entrepreneur-personalities' (Bertelsmann-Stiftung 1997: 10). This right is deduced from the exceptional social position of economic leaders and the resulting responsibility. Their prominent social position on the other hand is explained by the special intellectual abilities of this obviously particularly talented elite. Here, the immense significance placed on education in order to entitle economic leaders to their social position becomes apparent. This importance is further underlined by the corporate-owned university, set up especially for the management elite obliged by the directors to constantly further their education by means of international training courses. The modernized commercial class does not see itself as a ruling elite pursuing its particular interests, but presents itself as a competent functional elite legitimized by titles of education, and furthermore as an elite of values, as mediators of meaning, serving the public good.

In the following we will try to elucidate how the new state nobility systematically uses its international networks to secure its ruling position, taking the Bertelsmann Foundation's strategy of educational politics as example.

Transnational discourse communities

> It is the job of politics and the media to make society accept the new definition of the state's responsibility.
>
> (World Bank 1995c)

In the past, activities of international organizations mostly concerned specific national interests, but recently the relative independence of global actors has been stressed (Higgott 2000). The theoretical concept of *transnational discourse communities* provides a useful instrument to explore the contribution of private actors in global arenas. These communities display international network structures with their own agenda, feeding their propositions into international and national discourses. In this way, transnational discourse communities do not exert direct influence on policy-makers. Their main effect is rather seen as justifying reform politics. While transnational discourse communities attached to the United Nations complex (World Bank, IMF, etc.) or the OECD complex have already received a considerable amount of attention, a third and less structured landscape of organizations involving groups of experts joining to discuss a broad range of topics, to facilitate international exchange and to develop programmatic concepts, remain understudied. We are talking about foundations in particular as a preferred type of organization to empower transnational discourse communities.

Among the various protagonists of the third organizational complex, globally active media corporations like Bertelsmann have a special position (see Barnet and Cavanagh 1994). Bislev *et al.* (2002) investigated the activities of the Bertelsmann Foundation's project 'Cities of Tomorrow' more closely to distinguish transnational discourse communities from the more limited concept of epistemic discourse communities. In Germany, the Bertelsmann Foundation initiated the introduction of new control mechanisms of local governments according to the concept of *New Public Management* (NPM). The Bertelsmann Foundation started its project in 1993 by presenting the internationally renowned Carl Bertelsmann Award[7] for successful local reforms to the cities Phoenix and Bremen, according to their own words aiming at fighting immobility, rigidity and backwardness in our society and triggering impulses for considerations, discussions and, last but not least, activities orientated towards a socially wholesome shaping of the future (Carl Bertelsmann-Preis 1990a: 10). In the meantime, the Cities of Tomorrow network comprises 16 cities from Europe, the USA, Canada, New Zealand and Japan. By now, NPM (as well as PPP, public–private partnership) has become a globally accepted instrument for replacing bureaucratic structures with procedures fulfilling the criteria of economic efficiency (see Pelizzari 2001). Well into the 1990s, the situation of local government in Germany was marked by a generally lamented delay of reforms. The activities of the Bertelsmann Foundation are frequently stressed – even in textbooks on local politics (see Kleinfeld 1996: 162) – as a crucial factor for the alleged success in starting and speeding up reform processes.

Bislev *et al.* deduct two central insights from this example of successful manipulation of political reforms at the local level:

> First, as evidenced by Phoenix and Bremen, the Bertelsmann Network has not only been capable of diffusing its managerialist messages into rather dissimilar places in very distant countries. It also orchestrates a whole number of criss-crossing links and overlapping fora which enable those associated

with the network, either as full members or as participants in events and projects open to non-members, to engage in its activities to varying degrees, in different policy areas. Importantly, though, all the programmes, events and activities organised under the auspices of the network aim at the exchange of experience, mutual learning and the search for exemplary practice orientated solutions. Second, our material indicates that at no point during the events that led to the two cities becoming part of the Bertelsmann family were the respective national governments involved as 'facilitators' or 'opponents'.

(Bislev *et al.* 2002: 205)

Objective: a new market of education

Twice already, the Bertelsmann Foundation has awarded the renowned Carl-Bertelsmann-Preis for educational achievements, once in 1990 for the successful introduction of new governance mechanisms of universities, then in 1996 for similar innovations for schools. The education activities of the foundation like local government activities are carried out in the program on 'Government and Administration'. These projects aim at 'making the quality orientated control primarily of communal, but also of national, areas of responsibility more efficient and effective' (Carl-Bertelsmann-Preis 1996a: 11).[8]

Much like local government the education sector is supposed to be invigorated by way of introducing NPM-structures and the cooperation of institutions of education in PPPs. The main aim is to reduce political influence on the shaping of educational organizations, to be replaced by economic rationalist criteria. The Bertelsmann Foundation awarded the 1990 prize to the British University of Warwick. According to this university, its successful restructuring was prompted by the financial cuts in public sector spending in the 1980s. As a result, the university was able to tap into non-governmental financing opportunities. It was acknowledged that 'probably earlier than any other university in Great Britain, this university realized that its future was inseparably linked with its external relations achieved by cooperating with the industry as well as by playing an innovative part in the local economy' (Carl-Bertelsmann-Preis 1990a: 63f.). The international dimension is crucial: as early as 1990 the Bertelsmann Foundation held up the USA, Great Britain, Switzerland, the Netherlands, Belgium and Norway as examples in its search for excellent universities (see Carl-Bertelsmann-Preis 1990a, b). So-called expert committees were established in 1996 in New Zealand, the Netherlands, Norway, Canada (Ontario), Switzerland, Scotland and Hungary to assess examples of Best Practice in schools.

> The Bertelsmann Foundation has declared it its goal to join together representatives of the different school systems and of the schools themselves in a network for a systematic exchange of experience. Moreover it plans to make its own contributions for the network concerning research and development

on reform sectors that are particularly important internationally. The point of the network is to promote innovation and efficiency of the school systems.
(Carl-Bertelsmann-Preis 1996a: 177)

Both with regard to structure and content, parallels to the foundation's activities concerning local politics can hardly be missed. Just as the local administrations are supposed to work more 'independently' in the future, freed from political influence and without the permanent meddling of higher-level political representatives, the educational institutions should see to their own affairs as autonomously as possible. The proclaimed objective of democratization achieved in this way, though continuously emphasized by the foundation, is rather limited and not without traps. Academic staff enjoy somewhat more freedom to shape activities due to global budgeting, but more likely than not under financial constraints of frozen public spending. Resources will have to be secured elsewhere: 'Along with empowerment in the classroom goes the empowerment of the management' (Carl-Bertelsmann-Preis 1996a: 173). Again, the foundation aims to make solutions from other countries available to stimulate the German discussion (Carl Bertelsmann-Preis 1996a: 177).

The following analysis of the evolution of the German educational discourse in the 1990s shows to what extent the Bertelsmann Foundation has been able to influence the trajectory of educational reforms.

The establishment of a hegemonic discourse of (financing) education

In the mid-1980s, the German *academic council*[9] started the debate on competition in the German university system. At that time, competition was neither seen as an end in itself nor did it aim at commercializing universities to provide 'educational services' in an economic sense. Rather, academics warned of the risks of disordered competition (see Wissenschaftsrat 1985: 8). Universities were not to be transformed into production centres, but to focus on excelling in a small number of fields and compete in this way for public funds. Competition in the context of the academic council of the time stood primarily for the strengthening of the mechanisms of academic selection against the forms of political regulation and participation of the so-called participatory 'group-university' established in the reform era of the 1960s–70s.

Since the beginning of the 1990s, the Bertelsmann Foundation on the other hand has been interested above all in a transformation of the understanding of the role of competition. It favours the introduction of the conditions of free enterprise and the control mechanisms of business management. Even the financing of individual education via educational vouchers and a corresponding diversion of national resources was briefly considered, though later rejected on grounds of practicability. At the time, the social resistance to such structural changes was generally expected to prevail. The only salutary way to achieve a paradigmatic change was seen in the traumatic shocks triggered by national budget cuts, like the ones experienced in Great Britain in the 1980s (Carl-Bertelsmann-Preis 1990a: 140).

In the course of the 1990s, the German discourse on educational reforms has been more and more characterized by financial concepts devised by so-called committees of education, all orientated towards the dogma of the empty public purse. In 1992, the educational committee of North-Rhine Westphalia (NRW), in which the founder of the Bertelsmann Foundation, Reinhard Mohn, played a prominent role, was the first to set this process in motion. The aim was to reorganize the public school system. At that time, pedagogical considerations still loomed large in the discussion of envisioned reforms. However, the committee eventually proposed new forms of financing and managing education. The already familiar organizational principles of autonomous self-administration of educational institutions propagated by the Bertelsmann Foundation served as the model. Educational organizations were supposed to get a generous flat rate to be administered at the local level, effectively decentralizing budget authority and responsibility. The authors stressed that they wanted to maintain state and local government financing, and insisted that the financial problems of public households should not be used as a pretext for cuts in the flat rates. They even rejected resolutely a commercial control of financial resources for the educational system. Nevertheless, the description of the situation of public expenses for education allegedly necessitated greater management efficiency (Bildungskommission NRW 1995: 204 ff.), and first cracks appeared with regard to the traditional understanding of public responsibilities in the field of education.

Two years later the Bertelsmann Foundation took a further step in reforming the educational system, this time at university level. It succeeded in winning over the advisory committee of the presidents of German universities (Hochschulrektorenkonferenz or HRK), to jointly found the *Centre for the Development of Higher Education* (CHE) (Bennhold 2002). CHE's director, Professor Dr Müller-Böling, teaches business management at Dortmund University. His book *Die entfesselte Hochschule* (University Unbound) succinctly sums up the reform goals of the CHE. The liberated university will be an autonomous service company, pursuing high-powered knowledge production for national and international educational markets, in competition with other suppliers. To that end the former political control mechanisms are to be replaced by methods of economical self-regulation (Müller-Böling 2000).

The apparent tendency to de-politicize education – Müller-Böling has nothing to say on the political, let alone democratic, constitution of the liberated university – has henceforth been characteristic for all politically relevant concepts for reforms in education. As early as 1996 the HRK (in close cooperation with the CHE) propagated the financial conditionality of future university funding by the state. Thus instead of concentrating on the fight over public budgets, the university directors started to voice the University of Warwick opinion, according to which restrictive public finances open up possibilities of tapping into new private sources of university funding. The universities were recommended to open up to the financial markets and to offer investment possibilities (to university building contractors, for example) in order to ease the financial burden on the public (see HRK 1996:2). Eventually, it was publicly suggested for the first time that the students themselves should contribute to the expenses of their studies. This demand was tied to an emphatic demand for progressive reforms of financial support by the state (BAFÖG, grants), to ensure that the students' costs of living be covered. But later in their report, the HRK advocates quite a different form of financial help more concretely. It comprises of a basic charge, independent of parents' income, to be financed individually by a model of tax exempted and possibly subsidized 'educational saving accounts' (analogous to home ownership saving accounts).

The *committee of experts for education of the trade union based Hans-Böckler-Foundation* also expects educational reforms to benefit from a new role of semi-private financing. The system combines educational accounts, education vouchers, educational savings and educational loans with a basic scholarship from the state. The amount of subsidies to the individual educational accounts is dependent on income (see Schöller et al. 2000). This committee of experts wants this model to start after graduation from the compulsory tenth grade ('Sekundarstufe I'). This would mean that 'Sekundarstufe II' (tenth to twelfth or thirteenth grade), so far fully financed by the state, would already partly have to be paid privately like higher education at university level.[10]

The committee expects this to have a *pedagogical* effect with regard to using one's time as well as using the educational possibilities on offer in a responsible way. This constitutes a new way of combining politico-economic elements with business management and moral education. In this manner, people interested in education are attuned to a commercially organized educational system. 'The individual right of disposal of educational credits and vouchers increases the quality of the education on offer, because the suppliers of education need to compete for them, the institutions being only partly financed with a basic sum from the state, the rest of the money is provided by the vouchers. If an institution doesn't get enough educational vouchers, its existence is at risk. Suppliers would be punished for a lack of quality and rewarded for excellence' (Sachverständigenrat Bildung 1998: 49). In the long term, the expert committee wishes to extend the resulting increase in competition to the entire educational system.

Among the authors of the financial paper of this expert committee are Klaus Klemm and Jürgen Lüthje who also participated in the joint team of the Founders' Association for German Science[11] and the CHE (1999), which in turn is in close contact with the Initiative for Education of the Bertelsmann Foundation (see 1999). Considering this linkage it is not surprising that the financial concepts are nearly identical. The same is true of the Committee for Education of the Heinrich-Böll-Foundation (2001), affiliated with Germany's Green Party. The foundation's chair Sybille Volkholz had previously participated in the Hans-Böckler-Stiftung effort while the chairman of the Hans-Böckler-Stiftung committee, Dieter Wunder, has been invited to join the Heinrich-Böll-Foundation effort. Moreover, Wunder also supported the Initiative for Education of the Bertelsmann Foundation, while Cornelia Stern of the Bertelsmann Foundation took part both in the Committee of Experts for Education and in the committee for education of the Heinrich-Böll-Foundation. And eventually, part of the regular personnel can be found in the so called Network European Learning Processes (NELP) jointly developed by the Hans-Böckler-Foundation and the Institute of Sociology of the University of Freiburg. In the beginning of 2002, NELP started to advocate a more radical version (with regard to the commercialization of education) of the previous trade union foundation reform proposal, the so-called manifesto 'Education for a Society of Work and Knowledge' (NELP 2002). While the position of the trade union foundation sponsored committee was not regarded as the foundation position – several trade unionists in fact disagreed with the partial 'privatization' and commercialization perspective and withdrew their support – the responsible executive director of the Hans-Böckler-Stiftung, Nikolaus Simon, now signed legally responsible for the NELP manifesto.

Finally in 2004 the committee of experts for 'financing lifelong learning', which was installed in 2002 by the Minister of Education, published its report (Expertenkommission 2004). The report summarizes the foregoing debate and pleas again for a semi-private financed system of educational saving accounts.

While there clearly was a lot of repetition with regard to the reform proposals by the various organizations representing different social forces in German society, and considerable overlap with regard to the experts involved in developing the positions, we are not just dealing with a repetition of the same by the same people. The different committees of experts that appeared halfway through the 1990s have to be seen in a specific translator role, organizing the channelling of previously developed arguments and the world of trade unions and (Green) party politics with their particular ways of thinking, traditionally opposed to (partial) privatization of public sector education.[12] A reliable connection has thus been successfully established between the original private sector think tank effort and crucial social and political institutions not easily to be convinced of neo-liberal solutions.

A globally orientated competitive corporatism

The closely woven international network of the Bertelsmann Foundation is reproduced on a national level in form of various cooperating institutions and personal connections. The foundation pursues a corporatist (integrative) approach, and thus succeeds in the systematic involvement of very different social protagonists in its strategies. This holds especially true for public institutions and their staff, deliberately integrated into the foundation's network. By now, for instance, the foundation attends to a multitude of school projects in 16 German states. One hundred and fifty-two schools are involved in the pilot project 'Schule & Co.' alone, which was realized together with the ministry for education of NRW (Klausenitzer 2002). In the new multi-year project (until 2008), 278 schools are involved. And the Bertelsmann Foundation maintains the CHE as an important channel of influence. Secret negotiations of the CHE with Munich's Technical University regarding the introduction of student fees recently came to light (Bartz 2002). For the CHE, the TU serves as an example for a Best-Practice-University.[13] By now, the concept of 'contributions to education' – that is, tuition fees – has been published and aggressively promoted by the president of the TU. It is emphasized that these 'contributions to education' are a first step to the acquisition of other forms of private funding such as loans, third-party funds and grants from industry. The concept is explicitly connected with 'converting the university from an institution for free education into an entrepreneurial solidarity committee' (Hermann 2002: 5f.).

Consequently, Frank Nullmeier is right in describing the processes of educational reforms since the 1990s as new forms of subpolitics:

> Reforms below the level of legislative changes are intensified by financial constraints and the necessity of consolidation. They are supported by the chairmen and presidents of universities ready to tackle changes, and by individual governments and several foundations who have become aware of universities as organizations.
>
> (Nullmeier 2000: 220)

After international preparation and exemplary presentation, the reform ideas of the Bertelsmann Foundation – Public–Private Partnership, New Public Management and 'client/supplier' relations – are thus introduced at the national level.

Aporia of neoliberalism

There is a broad consensus on education being the central resource of the knowledge society. It seems to be acquired individually, depending on one's

Table 9.1 Chronology of education reform activities: a new perspective of competition

1985	Academic Council (Wissenschaftsrat) opens the debate
1990	Bertelsmann Foundation Initiative
1992	Educational Committee of North-Rhine Westphalia
1994	The Advisory Committee of the Presidents of German Universities (HRK) and Bertelsmann Foundation found the Centre for the Development of Higher Education (CHE)
1996	Advisory Committee of the Presidents of all German Universities (HRK) advocate new position
1998	Committee of Experts for Education of the Hans-Böckler-Foundation (trade union affiliated foundation) adopts position
1999	A common report of the Founders' Association for German Science and the Centre for the Development of Higher Education (CHE)
1999	New Education initiative of the Bertelsmann Foundation
2001	Committee for Education of the Heinrich-Böll-Foundation (Green Party foundation) adopts position
2002	Network European Learning Processes (NELP) (joint initiative of the trade union foundation and Freiburg University's Sociology Department) propagates radicalized trade union expert committee recommendations as official trade union foundation position
2004	The government committee of experts for 'financing lifelong learning'

specific abilities. Allegedly, only the qualification acquired in accordance with a person's natural talents decides nowadays his or her position in society, independent of material wealth, class, and social status. What counts is the emancipation of the autonomous consumer of education through her or his unlimited access to the educational merchandise on the free market. To realize this vision, relics of spoon-feeding by the state have to be removed in order to free the individual's educational biography.

This emphatic Individualism and economist view of education is rarely confronted with a reference to its authoritarian character. In his functional analysis of cultural assets, Pierre Bourdieu has expounded thoroughly on the particular significance of academic titles for keeping up a society's hierarchy of power. In doing this, he uncovered the close interrelation of economic and cultural capital as well as the new part education plays for the ruling economic class to legitimize its social position and the mutually beneficial relations between the state and education. By having the public education sector systematically commercialized under the influence of civil society institutions closely related to the corporate sector such as the Bertelsmann Foundation, the new state nobility further obscures its existence through social selection mechanisms that work subtly, because they will be effectively mediated by an allegedly 'neutral' and 'objective' market of education.

Notes

1 Translated by Marianne Henry.
2 The term 'state nobility' (*noblesse d'état*) denotes two closely interrelated phenomena that are of central significance to Bourdieu: the magic effect of academic titles and the close relation of education and state. Academic titles created by the state bestow authority to the educated nobility, which in turn has a special interest in expanding the state's power and its symbolic capital. Consequently, the genesis of the modern state is inseparable from that of the state nobility which runs its business (Bourdieu 1998b: 38ff.; also compare earlier contributions: Bourdieu *et al.* 1981: 23–53; Bourdieu 1982: 210–76, 462–96).
3 According to Bourdieu's analyses, two dominant developments can be discerned that proved decisive for the (preliminary) outcome of these fights. On the one hand the educational climbers of the middle and lower class together with the 'dissidents' of the bourgeoisie were able to initiate and implement reforms in educational politics, aiming at the democratization and social opening of the educational system. Humboldt's classical ideal of education, consisting in the full evolution of the personality, free from authoritarian and socially discriminating structures, was shown off to new advantage. On the other hand, the economic factions of the ruling and the middle classes very successfully adjusted the mode of social reproduction by focusing on the education sector. This process seemingly took place in the shadow of the turbulences of 1968 and was consequently less public and vociferous, but seems to have been victorious over the policies of reform on the educational sector.
4 He had expounded these considerations in his early socio-educational work 'The Illusion of Equal Chances' (Bourdieu and Passeron 1971: 13–45).
5 The social climbers who have been swindled out of higher aspirations find their professional niches mainly on the sector of medical and social services. They represent to a great extent the 'left hands' of the state, talking education and supporting

the expansion of the welfare state, soon to be drained financially and bitterly subjugated by their adversaries, the 'right hands' of the state, that is, the new state nobility (see Bourdieu 1997).
6   Competing ideologies do not completely disappear, of course. On new conservative severity with regard to 'authoritarian education' compare Keller and Schöller (2002).
7   The Carl-Bertelsmann-Preis has been awarded since 1987. According to the preamble, the ambition is to 'distinguish innovative ideas and promising initiatives, which make an important contribution to structuring the evolution of a constitutionally democratic society, especially institutions and structures of economy and communication ... to promote the development of our own as well as foreign societies.'
8   Foundation activities are divided into nine sectors: Government and Administration, Economy, Media, Foundation-Management, Medicine and Health, Public Libraries, Culture, Politics and Universities.
9   The academic council has been a division of the federal government's planning commission for science in cooperation with the leading science associations since 1957. Members are envoys of all the relevant ministries (political commission), but especially top-class professors on whose appointment the HRK, the DFG, the Max-Planck-Gesellschaft and the 'Association of Large-Scale Institutions for Scientific Research' reached common agreement (scientific commission). The 'specific gravity' of the respective recommendations results from this committee.
10 The public–private ratio suggested is 90 to 10 ('Sekundarstufe II') and 70 to 30 (university) (see Bulan 1999: 22).
11 The Association of Foundations was established in 1949 as Society for the Support of the German Economy, and today consists of 21 foundations. It is essentially a lobby organization managing almost the entire budget of private sector foundations.
12 When the recommendations for funding education were presented, Sybille Volkholz (Green Party) explained this clearly. She observed that everything about the subject had been said, but not yet by all. Accordingly, the Böll Foundation considers it an important task to make a special clientele understand the already familiar contents by using the appropriate language of its own constituency. The declared aim is to contribute to a greater social acceptance of the intended educational reforms.
13 The CHE strengthened its influence on the universities in order to support experimentation with innovative solutions and lighthouse projects for future reforms by admitting Wolfgang Hermann, the president of the TU-Munich, to the CHE's expert committee. In this function he will work together with Gerd Schulte-Hillen, one of the leaders of the Bertelsmann Foundation, and with the president of the HRK.

10 Gender mainstreaming

Integrating women into a neoliberal Europe?

Susanne Schunter-Kleemann and Dieter Plehwe

With the dawn of the new millennium, the debate on 'gender mainstreaming' has fully taken off in Europe. Gender mainstreaming has become a new topic of academic and political conferences. Academic journals are devoting their issues to gender mainstreaming. This apparent shift in the discussion of gender raises a number of fundamental questions. In view of the slowing and even retrograde developments in the efforts to achieve gender equality, has perhaps the time come, in terms of women's rights and politics, to give up the burden of old mottoes of the women's liberation movement? Given the changes in the political environment, driven by the developments toward a service society, internationalization and globalization: is gender mainstreaming a more appropriate means to the end of gender equality? Do the political scope and impact of gender mainstreaming actually go beyond the earlier approaches toward women's emancipation? Is it thus a step forward since the issue of women's rights is regarded not simply as an isolated problem of women, but rather as one that encompasses all political fields and affects women and men alike? Has the concept of gender mainstreaming, as it is now being promoted worldwide by numerous governments and organizations, led to the long-sought common political orientation and perspective that could contribute to the more effective networking of the international women's right movement? Finally, does the attack on 'gender mainstreaming' led by right-wing, anti-socialist women groups overlapping with (predominantly male) global neoliberal networks (see Plehwe and Walpen in this volume) support a progressive reading of gender mainstreaming?[1]

In this chapter it will be argued that the concept of gender mainstreaming does not provide a miracle solution to the problems of gender inequality, nor does it constitute an unequivocally progressive innovation or idea. Gender mainstreaming is far better understood as a highly ambiguous concept, a Janus-faced approach characterized by many hidden catches and providing some opportunities as well as many risks. Furthermore, gender mainstreaming can be interpreted in quite different ways. In our opinion, the gender mainstreaming discourse is marked by conflicting positions and contradictory expectations creating ample room for an uneven ideological and political battleground. One can say that those on the 'top' most certainly have other interests and aims when they promote the idea of gender mainstreaming than those at the 'bottom'. For this reason, the various pitfalls that may appear in the implementation of the gender mainstreaming process are highly important.

We develop this argument in three steps. First we reflect on the historical origins of the concept of gender mainstreaming. The new philosophy is best understood as an outgrowth of a management concept developed in the US under the rubric of 'Managing Diversity'. Second, the adoption and adaptation of this managerial concept by international and supranational organizations is examined. Of particular note is the prominent role of organizations such as the World Bank and the European Commission – which have historically been rather closed bastions of male power – in promoting the discussion on gender mainstreaming. Since both supranational organizations are power centers of contemporary capitalism not previously known as the avant-garde of the women's rights movement and other progressive campaigns in support of industrial democracy and the welfare state, their recent efforts on behalf of women deserve a close, critical look. Third, we discuss the application of gender mainstreaming concepts in European labor market policy development. In this context we look more closely at the question: which groups of women are likely to benefit from gender mainstreaming, and which ones will not.

The origin and the historical context of the 'gender mainstreaming'

The origins of gender mainstreaming can be traced back to the development of a new concept in organizational theory and behavior in the US in the 1980s. This concept was generally placed under the heading of 'managing diversity' or, in some cases, 'the multicultural enterprise'. The concept is based on the idea that a diverse workforce, i.e., a workforce diverse in terms of ethnic background and gender, might confer an important competitive advantage to the firm. In practice, managing diversity is seen as a set of measures employed by management to establish equal opportunities for all employees, irrespective of their ethnic backgrounds or gender. The managing-diversity approach is aimed at creating a working environment in which all employees can be motivated to fully develop their potential (Krell 2000: 29).

As such, the idea of managing diversity represents a top-down management approach. It is a new managerial paradigm designed to utilize more effectively the existing human resource potential of the firm for the benefit of the organization. In order to achieve this, the individual employees involved are partially drawn into the decision-making process at the organizational level. The need for human resource development is not seen exclusively or even primarily in terms of the conditions and requirements of female employees, but it is cast in terms of a change in organizational culture. The aim is to create an organizational environment that does not focus only on the interests and needs of the white middle-class American male, but rather on the needs of all employees.

Management consultants cite a number of competitive advantages that such 'multi-cultural' or culturally diverse firms have over more traditionally managed so-called 'mono-cultural' organizations. These include:

1 *The cost advantage*: With the inevitable increase of ethnic and gender diversity in organizations, inefficiencies or outright failures in the integration of human resources will lead to an increase in cost for the firm.
2 *The personnel recruitment advantage*: Organizations with good reputations in managing diversity will be in the best position to compete successfully for the most qualified women and ethnic minorities in the labor pool.
3 *The creativity advantage*: Greater diversity in viewpoints and perspectives among employees will contribute to higher levels of creativity.
4 *The system flexibility advantage*: Mono-cultural organizations tend to be rather resistant to change. In contrast, multi-cultural organizations appear to be much more flexible, and to adapt more easily to changes in the operating environment.
5 *The internationalization advantage*: If a firm succeeds in establishing a multi-cultural environment – that is, if the employees have learned to respect and value diversity and to work effectively with others of different ethnic backgrounds and gender, free of prejudices, cultural bias and conflicts – it will have a competitive edge in successfully internationalizing its operations (Cox and Blake 1991: 47; Krell 1997).

The concept of managing diversity is an outgrowth of a liberal market philosophy that places great emphasis on harmony. It is a so-called 'win-win' approach. The organization as a whole 'wins', as do the women and the men in the organization. Within this model there are no structural conflicts of interest between capital and labor, nor between men and women. In promoting equal participation of men and women, it is argued, the organization gains access to untapped reserves of human resource potential within the firm, thus producing greater innovation and employee motivation. Women, previously viewed as a relatively unexploited talent source, are now – because of their emotional intelligence and social skills – regarded as an important asset for the firm. In addition, they are seen as likely allies with management on the issue of flexible working hours. Thus, it should be in the self-interest of management to overcome dated gender and ethnic divisions within the firm in order to mobilize the full potential of all members in pursuit of organizational goals under conditions of intensified global competition.

Adopting gender mainstreaming to suit the European environment

In the mid-1990s, the European Union Commission (EUC) adopted this management approach to promote EU-wide gender mainstreaming. This adoption represented an innovative third focal concept on the issue of equal opportunity following as it did preceding concepts of 'equal treatment' (1970s and 1980s) and 'positive discrimination' (1980s and 1990s). What were the reasons for the EUC's adoption of this approach?

The answer might well be that this new attempt to promote gender equality can be seen as a response on the part of the EUC to the growing skepticism among women about the European integration process. Such skepticism grew out of what was perceived by a growing number of women as a failure of European institutions to express a clear commitment to European social policy and welfare objectives. Quite surprisingly, women turned out to be the crucial electorate in 1992 and 1994 referenda on European integration. By first rallying a majority to turn down approval of the Maastricht Treaty in Denmark, and then rejecting the European Economic Area (EEA) Treaty in Switzerland, women were instrumental in pushing the pressing issue of democratic and social deficits higher on the political agenda of European institution building. One of the most interesting aspects underlying these results was barely mentioned in the European media: in almost all European countries, women displayed a far more skeptical attitude toward the Single Market and the Economic and Monetary Union (EMU) than men. Skepticism on the part of European women was reaffirmed in the 1994 referendum in Norway that rejected the country's entry into the EU), and in many Euro-barometer survey and opinion polls. In fact, on no other public policy issue is the difference between men and women as pronounced as on the topic of European integration. Responding to these differences, the European Commission identified women as a 'priority target group' for European Union information and communication policies (FAZ, 1 July 1993: 5).

It was not until the preparation of the United Nations' women's conference in Beijing in 1995 that the term 'gender mainstreaming' was coined. EU officials hurried to adopt, adapt, and promote the new concept by emphasizing positive terms such as 'participation' and 'transparent policies,' with the clear objective of creating a new partnership and dialogue between the EU Commission and Europe's female population. The declared aim was to reduce the acknowledged gender deficit with regard to democratization of the EU. Thus, EU gender mainstreaming strategies can be considered primarily as a consensus and integration strategy specifically aimed at women, despite the concept's original targeting of both men and women. They are intended to win back and renew the trust of European women. In order to gain further insights into the nevertheless ambiguous nature of the new European Commission strategy with regard to substantive elements of gender mainstreaming, we must first ascertain the predecessor concepts of gender mainstreaming. What are the philosophical origins of 'equal treatment' and 'positive discrimination', and what can be said about both their potential and weaknesses?

From equal opportunity to affirmative action to – gender mainstreaming?

The equal opportunity approach or 'equal treatment' of men and women is firmly rooted in the eighteenth-century liberal philosophy of citizens' rights; it can be directly traced to Mary Wollstonecraft writing at the time of the French Revolution. The 1957 Treaty of Rome mandated the principle of equal treatment for women and men with respect to employee compensation, but progress with regard to the implementation of European *primary law* (treaties) was in short supply until a series of European Community Directives (on equal pay, equal treatment, social security, occupational pension, part-time and others) were issued in the 1970s, 1980s and 1990s. Such European *secondary law* (regulations and directives) is immediately binding law in the member states in the case of regulations, and obliges member states to introduce national legislation in compliance with the core stipulations of what can be understood as a framework law in the case of directives. The Commission can also execute supranational powers to secure national commitments to enforce European secondary law. Still, European law remains a blunt instrument, incomplete and insufficient to address the complexities of the equal opportunity challenge and although arguably some ground was gained in the legal field, equal treatment did most certainly not lead to equal outcomes.

While equal treatment seeks to treat people that are marked by important differences in the same way, 'positive' or 'affirmative' action was developed foremost to recognize the importance of difference. With regard to gender, affirmative action attempts to address more fully the structural disadvantages women experience because of their differences to men. Historical patterns of systematic discrimination are used to justify special support for the less favored group in order to facilitate a catching up process. Specifically, affirmative action was developed to deal with the impact of the breadwinner/homemaker gender contract, which disadvantages women in the labor market. Affirmative action programs include measures such as training courses designed to attract women to new technological fields and other typically male areas of work, such as high-level management. The aim is to generate more equal (and visible) results at the aggregate level of labor markets.

The 1990 New Opportunities for Women (NOW) initiative is one example of a European affirmative action program. The project was designed to address women 'where they are' and thus managed to better respond to specific needs such as childcare, family-friendly working time, confidence building and so on (Rees 1998: 57). The major weakness of positive action plans such as NOW lies in the fact that projects often tend to be small, piecemeal in character, and precariously- or under-funded. Moreover, the systems and structures that produce and reproduce the discrimination women experience remain unchallenged. Finally, positive action programs as developed by European institutions are highly contentious, and consequently are rarely utilized as a strategy. Similar to affirmative action debates in the United States, critiques regard programs as costly and potentially illegal due to inherent dangers of 'reverse discrimination'.

How does the new approach of gender mainstreaming fit into this landscape? Similar to the (arguably more progressive) 'affirmative action' concept, gender mainstreaming does recognize fundamental differences between men and women.

The declared aim is to change the systems and structures that disadvantage women. Gender mainstreaming proponents seek to pro-actively transform organizations and procedures to allow women and men to participate on an equal footing. In this respect, it is based on the 'philosophy of difference'. Rather than simply seeking to correct inequalities arising from difference as affirmative action policies do, gender mainstreaming casts differences as constituting a potential benefit. Gender mainstreaming, however, shares a major weakness with equal treatment concepts, a shared problematic that can be traced to their common origin in the liberal equal rights tradition: unlike affirmative action concepts, both gender mainstreaming and equal treatment concepts are more concerned with procedural equality than with substantial equality as evidenced in results (Walby 1998: 6). As a result, even though the field of gender policy has been extended beyond the narrow confines of labor market, employment and vocational training policies, many urgent problems of female exclusion and oppression (such as prostitution, gender-based violence, abuse and women trafficking) have not become policy issues, let alone subject to penalties.

The concept of gender mainstreaming was formally introduced in 1996 in a memorandum released by the EU Commission, entitled 'Integrating a Gender Dimension into All Political Concepts and Measures of the EU'. Former EU Commissioner Flynn stated that gender mainstreaming was to acknowledge the fact that despite the absolute and relative growth in the number of women participating in the labor market, inequality between men and women in terms of employment, wages and working conditions remained significant and along some dimensions, had even increased (Flynn 1998: 1). From the point of view of the European Commission, the term 'gender mainstreaming' was meant to convey the idea that equal opportunity for men and women was no longer an issue at the periphery of the political agenda, but had emerged as a central conception of 'mainstream' European politics.

With its authorship of the third equal opportunities approach, the European Commission has taken the lead in promoting women's issues, an ascendance that comes at the expense of the European Council and the European Court of Justice (ECJ), which are no longer driving forces. In a time of disappointment about the low impact of the equal treatment law and only modest effectiveness of affirmative action programs, the EU Commission's entrance into previously unclaimed territory marks an effort to further expand its competencies and enlarge its constituencies in civil society (Schunter-Kleemann 1999: 19). As a result of its competition-oriented nature and its insertion into European employment strategy, the concept of gender mainstreaming holds a two-dimensional promise: that more effective organizational and political utilization of (previously underutilized) female human capital will improve performance at the micro-level, and that these micro improvements will improve Europe's overall – i.e., macro-level – competitiveness.

While the 1997 Treaty of Amsterdam does not feature the term 'gender mainstreaming', the concept of equal opportunity has been propelled to a more prominent position in Articles 2 and 3. In addition, the new Article 13 has been introduced to combat discrimination based on sex, racial or ethnic origin, religion or belief, disability, age or sexual orientation. Unfortunately, the treaty revision is neither satisfactory politically nor legally, since the provisions are not actionable and do not provide for sanctions in case of violations. Thus, in spite of all the manifold expressions of intent by the European Commission, it is important to remember that there is still no legally recognized and binding definition of the term 'gender mainstreaming,' either at the EU or national level. Most publications and legal sources appear to simply presuppose the legal validity of the term (Mückenberger *et al.* 2000: 7). Simply put, the idea of gender mainstreaming is at this point not binding in law or policy, and as such, it eludes legal challenges. There are no grievance or sanction mechanisms in place in case a particular administration does not abide by the new policy orientation toward gender mainstreaming. In contrast to equal treatment, then, the regulatory power of the mainstreaming approach has to be considered weak.

Thus we are faced with the fact that although 'gender mainstreaming' is strongly promoted by the European authorities, as well as by national governments, social democratic parties, and a number of trade unions and professional associations as the key program to promote gender equality in the twenty-first century, it is at the same time interpreted and implemented in quite different ways, varying from country to country and from organization to organization. Due to this diversity, no critical analysis of gender mainstreaming rhetoric and practice should subscribe to an interpretation of the concept as unequivocally progressive in nature without further empirical investigation. To further deepen the understanding of the highly ambiguous character of gender mainstreaming, we will discuss a number of real or potential pitfalls related to the new strategy, and then turn to a critical discussion of implementation experiences in the field of EU labor market and employment policies.

Pitfalls of gender mainstreaming

Skeptics and critics of the gender mainstreaming concept argue that it is a problematic means to achieve the goal of gender equality for a number of reasons. At least five traps can be identified.

Pitfall number 1: Gender mainstreaming is too vague a concept to be utilized as a catchy slogan in the fight for gender equality

From a German language point of view, the term gender mainstreaming represents a rather unfortunate choice. The women's movement certainly has created more exciting and original slogans in the past. Catchy and provocative slogans such as 'equal pay for equal work' or 'my belly belongs to me' had much more visceral appeal and readily served as rallying cries for women's groups. The term 'gender mainstreaming' on the other hand cannot shed its bureaucratic origins and represents a rather technocratic perspective on gender issues.

Pitfall number 2: Different positions on usage and meaning of gender mainstreaming as a political approach

Gender mainstreaming allows for a wide range of possible approaches and can mean quite different things to different groups and people. In the broadest sense, gender mainstreaming means that a gender sensitive-thinking should be promoted and practiced not only in certain narrowly defined areas of organizations, but should be seen as a responsibility of all involved governments, as well as unions and management. This is, of course, a good and important idea. However, this idea is not completely new; it has been an integral part of the women's rights movement since the early 1980s. It just appears that now this idea has been elevated to higher levels of recognition and acceptance.

In other publications and statements the maxim of gender mainstreaming is also viewed as a *useful concept to be applied in personnel recruitment and gender awareness and sensitivity training programs*. Others argue that gender mainstreaming should be concerned with gender equity and the *fair distribution of financial means, budgets and affirmative action funds*. And again, others see gender mainstreaming as a principle directed toward the *balanced participation of men and women in organizational decision-making processes*. Given the widespread confusion whether gender mainstreaming could be defined as the goal itself, as an instrument or method, or as a value orientation and guideline, female members of the European Parliament also considered the term to be too 'vague' and 'unclear' and thus 'unfortunate' (Frauen Europas Info, no. 71, June 1997; EP-Kokkola Report 'Statement of the Institutional Committee' 1997). Women's groups warned that with the incorporation of a 'gender dimension' in all political areas, the more directly relevant focus on 'women issues' in politics could be pushed back, possibly even completely eliminated.

Pitfall number 3: 'Gender is in – feminism is out'

In a statement by the Committee for Social Issues in the European Parliament (24 July 1996), concern was voiced about the danger of undermining existing affirmative action programs for women:

> The principle of gender mainstreaming should, on the other hand, not be used as a justification to abolish specific measures designed to promote gender equality. Gender mainstreaming does not infer that demands for gender equality can be turned down on the ground that the work toward gender equality has now been incorporated in all other areas and activities. In addition to integrating gender equality as an integral part of all political measures, we still need very specific measures to promote gender equality, as well as offices for equal rights and equal opportunity issues, women's representatives and funding. It is only under such conditions that we will actually be able to implement the principle of gender mainstreaming.
>
> (European Parliament 1997: 20)

A case in point to illustrate the above mentioned concern is the decision in 1998 of the German Chancellor Schröder, back then still the prime minister of Lower Saxony, to terminate the Ministry of Women's Issues in the state of Lower Saxony. To justify his decision, Schröder argued that in the future all ministries of the state government would be addressing the issues of women's rights and women's politics. This political leader is not the only one who interprets the idea of gender mainstreaming along the principles and requirements of a 'lean state' that leads to the next trap.

Pitfall number 4: The employment of gender mainstreaming as a cost-cutting vehicle

The major threat inherent in the gender mainstreaming approach is that decision makers will use it simply as a vehicle to cut costs. The ongoing restructuring and modernization efforts in organizations, universities and in public administration pose the threat that women's representatives and women's offices will be eliminated. The approach can also be used to turn down long-voiced requests to set up specific affirmative action programs for women with the convenient argument that financial programs aimed solely at women represent an obsolete and dated strategy.

The expectation on the part of women groups that gender mainstreaming should lead to the fairer distribution of financial means and funds in favor of women has up to now remained chimerical. An examination of the various EU-Policy programs has revealed some serious weaknesses in this regard. The Women's Rights Committee of the European Parliament has assessed the most important future directed political programs of the EU. In a list of shortcomings, the committee complains that the principle of gender mainstreaming has not been adequately integrated into EU financial programs. Even the EU Commission admits to this fact in its first follow-up report (1998). The report notes that a paradoxical side effect of gender mainstreaming has been its use as a pretext to cut particular budget items and use up the reserves that have been built up to finance specific women's labor market projects (Progress Report of the EU Commission 1998: 11).[2]

Pitfall number 5: Incoherent implementation

A recent study also shows that the attempt to integrate the gender mainstreaming approach within the financially significant European Structural and Regional Policy, for example, can presently be regarded as a mixed success at best. While the European Commission issues statements to the contrary, a 2001 study undertaken by the German state of Brandenburg arrived at the following, rather pessimistic conclusion:

> The listing and the specific definition of the main objectives aimed at equal opportunity can generally be found within the framework of the European Social Funds (ESF) – Directive, it can only be partially found within the

European Regional Funds (EFRE) – Directive, and it can only be found to a minimal extent within the European Agrarian Funds (EAGFL) – Directive. The attempt to integrate conceptually gender equality policy objectives from the beginning within all programs has been counter-productive. (...) The financially extensive, and even in terms of economic structural policy significant funds EFRE and EAGFL, remain on a general level – even though 'mainstreaming' is also referred to as an objective within these funds.

(Ministerium für Arbeit 2001: 6)

At the European Social Funds Conference in Vienna in September 2003 (in which the author Susanne Schunter-Kleemann took part) participants confirmed the general lack of implementation of gender mainstreaming. It still remains a concept for narrow areas of education, health and labor market policies. Implementation in the areas of economic and agricultural politics has not been started. In the fields of European trade, transport and environmental policies, the debate on employment and gender impact did not even begin.

Taken together, recent European experiences suggest that the gender mainstreaming approach can be played off against labor market programs and measures focusing on women, programs the European women's movement fought hard to achieve. These programs, designed specifically for women in the light of structural disadvantages in the labor market, aim at opening up new employment areas and providing women with the opportunity to obtain necessary training and qualifications. In order to carry out such affirmative action programs, it is essential that such projects have access to their own staff and facilities and are supported by specific budget provisions.

Experiences with the implementation of gender mainstreaming in the EU labor market and employment politics

It is evident that gender mainstreaming can only counter prevailing gender inequality in the labor market if it is embedded in a coherent welfare state oriented strategy. Gender equality promoting mainstreaming simply cannot work to promote substantive equality if it is restricted to or overridden by a neoliberal political approach that serves to increase rather than to decrease inequality. Currently, however, precisely this appears to be the case. As British labor market politicians Rubery and Fagan (1998) have shown, EU-employment guidelines have counter-productive effects on women's employment even though these guidelines explicitly refer to the ideas of equal opportunity and gender mainstreaming. The reasons for these counter-productive effects can be found in the shortcomings and flaws of the EU policy decisions on the coordination of the EU labor market policies made in Luxembourg in 1997. These decisions were simply poorly thought out in terms of their gender impact. In practice, EU labor market policy is directed toward the situation of the average male employee, an orientation that results in the widening of the existing gender gap in the labor market

(Rubery and Fagan 1998: 113). Stated more pointedly, it is simply not enough to promote the idea of gender mainstreaming when concurrent policies have a detrimental impact on efforts to promote equal employment opportunities for women. The policies at issue include attempts to further privatize the public sector, to achieve more deregulation and flexibility in employment arrangements and contracts, to lower wages, to introduce low-wage sectors, and to encourage the further decentralization of trade union collective bargaining. These practices, all of which are inspired by neoliberal ideas and are currently implemented throughout the EU, come at the expense mostly of already disadvantaged women (who constitute the bulk of the temporary and contingent workforce), and cannot possibly be cushioned or offset by the implementation of gender mainstreaming, no matter how effectively this might be done.

In the EU guidelines on employment, for example, the ambivalent nature of part-time work for women has not even been considered in terms of its socio-political consequences. The rapid expansion of part-time employment is seen to have strong positive effects on the labor market and is viewed as a perfectly acceptable form of working time reduction despite of the lack of legal protection for part-time employees in most of the European countries. Proposed alternatives to contingent (and predominantly female) part-time work such as a general reduction of working hours in the full-time (and predominantly male) employment segment are strictly opposed in the EU bodies. In the final analysis this means: while the redistribution of labor among women is intentional, this is not the case between men and women, and definitely not between paid and unpaid work. As a result of neoliberal strategies that promote greater flexibility in the labor market, there has been a dramatic increase in the number of female employment situations that lack adequate legal and social security protection, compensation and benefits across the EU.

Additional threats to the concept of a sustainable and welfare (state)-based concept of gender democracy come from other political areas, such as European monetary policy. The commitment on the part of national governments to the goal of the Economic and Monetary Union (EMU) and the Agreement on Stability and Growth signed in 1997 must be viewed as counter-productive. These agreements on monetary policy have created additional barriers to the pursuit of a policy of gender equality in the family work environment largely because of the highly restrictive deficit criteria to be met by EMU members. Over recent years it was possible to observe in all EU member states that the Maastricht convergence criteria have been used as an argument to justify a deflationary policy of fiscal austerity. The continual pressure on the member states to cut back on their national debts and budget deficits has lasted for an entire decade now, and has led primarily to cuts in welfare benefits and the privatization of public businesses and services, which in turn has led to a dramatic decline in public sector employment figures. In all member states women have been negatively affected by these measures in a two-fold way: first because the number and the quality of available jobs have deteriorated, and second, because major cost-cutting measures in the public sectors have reduced provision of services that are essential for balancing job and family responsibilities. According to a 1999 OECD study, Germany alone eliminated approximately 1.3 million public service jobs in the 1990s. A closer look at the different categories reveals that 700,000 jobs were lost in the (lowest) blue collar segment, and 600,000 jobs were lost in the medium segment (usually not requiring higher education as well). The only jobs that were added in the same period accrued to the higher and highest service segments (15,000 and 20,000, respectively) traditionally dominated by men (Goffart 1999: 13).

Given this situation, the critical question that has to be considered is the following: is the concept of gender mainstreaming suited to respond appropriately and effectively to violations of the central interests of women, as they manifest themselves in the manifold mechanism of discrimination against women in the labor market and workplace today? Or does the concept deflect attention to peripheral issues of equality politics that might bring advantages to a small number of women, but demand so much public attention that there might be not enough energy left to fight against the concrete deterioration of the situation of a larger number of women?

In an attempt to answer this question we will now take a brief look at the situation in Germany. Politicians and unions placed high hopes on the concept of company-based affirmative action programs for equal opportunities. Numerous and quite diverse company agreements have been negotiated, but only a few union contracts have been signed. Today we know that the voluntary company programs did not go far enough and that in reality only a very small group of already qualified women benefited from these initiatives. The way company positive action programs have been designed and realized so far suggests that they have been reduced to mere instruments for corporate image promotion. Moreover, affirmative action programs have been primarily run in more successful larger enterprises. In the many small- and medium-sized firms in the service sector, where the share of unskilled women, and women trained on the job, is very high, and in sectors that traditionally have employed large numbers of women but are currently suffering from structural crises, company-based programs for equal opportunities have remained exceedingly rare. Certainly, large numbers of women who have lost their jobs as a result of rationalization and restructuring measures have not been reached through affirmative action programs.

The results are not better if we look at the regulations governing company-led schemes for equal opportunities. One focus that has emerged in recent years is the creation of guidelines on the compatibility of family and work; here, some progress has been made on parental leave entitlements for both men and women (e.g., job guarantee, parallel part-time leave options, etc.). Female union members and others, however, have criticized that programs are by and large limited to the field of family policies. At the same time, flagrant violations of basic women's rights have been completely left out of the company-led programs. Key issues here are wage discrimination, the disproportional number of women affected by unemployment, exposure to unhealthy working conditions and working hours not easily reconciled with family needs, such as weekend and overtime work.

These critical areas have been left untouched because they would challenge the central structures that suppress women in the capitalist system.

Recognition without redistribution?

Structural features of the gender gap in the labor market have persisted for decades and are extremely resistant to change. Measures such as consensus talks and attempts to raise gender sensitivity and consciousness levels of management and administration – both suggested by the gender mainstreaming approach – will have a limited impact at best. This is not to deny the fact that due to some innovative management models, new possibilities in organization and human resources development are and will be opening up for some women. However, the potential of these new developments is greatly exaggerated. They ignore precisely those deeply rooted socially and culturally institutionalized regulatory patterns that have led to the uneven distribution of power in terms of decision making, control, and assessment in business and in society at large.

Viewed critically, the gender mainstreaming approach appears to imply that the decade-long efforts to achieve gender equality have failed because women themselves did not come up with the right arguments. Today, strong attempts are being made to integrate women by introducing a corporate rhetoric and the language of marketing and competition into the political discussion of gender issues. Earlier socialist justifications for gender equality, which are grounded in an analysis of structural social injustice and violations of basic rights and laws, are at the same time dropped like hot potatoes. Gender mainstreaming is thus used as a powerful alternative discourse to promote certain liberal ideas of equal opportunities in public administrations and organizations. It is presented as a concept that combines gender equality with all the corporate advantages to be gained by better 'managing diversity', namely cost saving, higher creativity, more effective marketing and greater efficiency.

If gender mainstreaming as a model of reorganization is as effective and advantageous as heralded, however, it seems perfectly legitimate to ask why in spite of the claimed gains in efficiency, there has been no noticeable transfer of women into men's positions? Is the discrimination of women in the labor market indeed merely the result of a management oversight and mistakes in operational cost planning? Such a rather narrow 'human failure' explanation is far too limited in consideration of the larger picture of the economics of gender discrimination.

As a top-down technocratic approach, gender mainstreaming cannot offer a coherent strategy to develop the conditions necessary to realize 'participatory parity' (Fraser 2003). Fraser distinguishes the 'objective condition' – 'the distribution of material resources must be such as to ensure participants' independence and "voice" from the "intersubjective condition" exclusively addressed by gender mainstreaming, namely efforts to stop burdening specific status groups (such as women) "with excessive ascribed 'difference' or by failing to acknowledge their distinctiveness"' (Fraser 2003: 36). The first condition cannot be met since gender mainstreaming follows an underlying logic of the beneficial laws of the free market and as such subscribes to a social harmony perspective that fails to consider issues of power and control in social organizations, social conflicts of interests, asymmetrical power structures, and the unfair distribution of financial means and benefits between men and women (Regenhard 1997: 42). Gender mainstreaming proponents claim instead that by implementing practices such as information sharing, consciousness raising and on-going training of the human resources staff, the implementation of gender democracy can be effectively managed. In line with neoliberal particularism, the approach leaves it to individual organizations to decide on which measures within the range of gender mainstreaming programs will be implemented. Proponents of women's rights should be concerned that organizations will limit their subscription to gender mainstreaming program elements to those most suitable for the promotion of their image.

Since the long history of discrimination against women is deeply rooted in the structures of the market economies *and* male power interests that allow advantages from segregation, to accrue to men, gender equality requires a different and more forceful approach than the non-binding and non-committal concept of gender mainstreaming. Gender democracy needs welfare measures and clear legally-binding regulations, such as quota-systems, that put specific target numbers on administrations and firms and enforce these with sanctions, if necessary. The gender mainstreaming concept does not include such clear-cut stipulations, quota-systems and sanction requirements, but simply passes all these issues down the organizational hierarchy. This in turn means that the European welfare states have found a convenient mechanism for abdicating political responsibilities to actively support gender equality.

Gender mainstreaming: feminism and neoliberal hegemony

Gender mainstreaming clearly must be understood in the liberal tradition of human rights, albeit a certain analytical overlap with affirmative action programs that take structural dimensions of inequality into consideration does exist. Unlike affirmative action approaches, however, structural inequality is reinterpreted as diversity, which can be regarded as potentially advantageous for organizations. The 'women are a potential resource' perspective is not exactly new, however, since male-dominated organizations were eager to exploit women in an effort to reduce wages both at the workplace and by way of soliciting unpaid (family) work. In addition, a case is now made for better utilization of a wider spectrum of female human resources in the competitive race. At the same time, contradictions of the European neoliberal development path have forced leaders in both the public and private sectors to more strongly consider women as a constituency to shore up the legitimacy of the neoliberal project. Faced with the evident loss of legitimacy for the more or less dramatic cutbacks of the welfare state as a result of the 'destructive phase' of neoliberalism, the attempt is made to create a new social basis for neoliberalism through a 're-constructive policy'.

'Competition-oriented company corporatism' and wage moderating 'alliances for work' are among the new manifestations of such social democratic consolidation of neoliberalism in Europe. Similarly, the gender mainstreaming strategy can be viewed as a manifestation of the dynamics of the 'third way' of neoliberalism shored up with communitarian language, a consensus-based project aimed at women in Europe, but designed to support the market-oriented modernization strategies (see Bieling in this volume). In this process, certain loopholes are created for progressive discourses and women's rights activists due to the widening of the arenas of women's rights discussions. Notwithstanding such ambivalences, right-wing attacks on gender mainstreaming (see Note 1) appear to confuse the passionate language for gender equality with substantial practical steps in advance of a truly progressive transformation of gender regimes and gender democracy. With regard to women as a group, the findings of this chapter offer a rather chilling perspective on the question of greater unity of the women's movement: specific concerns of more privileged women appear to find more room in the gender mainstreaming discourse ('female entrepreneurship', female consultants), while programs previously designed to ameliorate the plight of lower-qualified female workers and family women are subject to cutbacks. Equal opportunity programs might thus be considered selective opportunity programs. Needless to say, higher-qualified women frequently are more vocal with regard to representing their cause than the victims of downsizing and cutbacks. The emergence of a neoliberal wing of individual 'feminism' that vocally rejects affirmative action and claims to radically defend individual rights (including the right to prostitution, etc.) speaks to a certain success in widening the hard-core constituency of neoliberal hegemony. This development is more strongly based in the US than Europe, but the very same structural transformations of gender patterns that increased inequality between women and men and between groups of differently situated women are well under way in European societies, a trend that can be traced to the successful undermining of the welfare state.

Notes

1 See www.iwf.org, www.zetetics.com/mac/index.html, for example. Libertarian feminist Wendy McElroy (2000) has the following assessment of the EU efforts with regard to gender mainstreaming: 'The European Parliament has announced its intention to impose gender mainstreaming on "all relevant areas of EU policy." In short, the EU will impose equality for women on all the policies it implements. This goes far beyond equal treatment under the law and creates privileges that extend into every area of human endeavor. For example, consider employment: women by law would receive the same pay as men and be hired in equal numbers, which amounts to a quota system. Foreign policy – African nations that practice female genital mutilation would be denied foreign aid. Education: there should be as many women scientists graduating from universities as male scientists. Government: a quota system must ensure equal representation of the sexes in commissions, committees etc. There is no area or issue that gender mainstreaming does not impact' (www.zetetics.com/mac/talks/eu.html, accessed 5 August 2003, compare also her interpretation of United Nations policy documents at www.zetetics.com/mac/articles/unfamily.html,

accessed 5 August 2003). As we will show in this chapter, gender mainstreaming certainly does not go far beyond equal treatment under the law in the case of EU policies. Otherwise and unfortunately with regard to the individual rights potential of a radical libertarian message, McElroy seems to be more concerned about any type of intervention than about the fate of girls suffering from genital mutilation.

2 Similar experiences and insights were reported at a conference on labor market policies in Vienna in 2000 that the author S. Schunter-Kleemann attended. Participants at the conference emphasized that there was a strong rhetoric in favor of gender mainstreaming in labor market policies in Austria. The primary effect, however, appears to be increasing difficulty in justifying labor market policy measures that deal specifically with the situation of women. Such measures might become entirely unfeasible in the long run.

Part IV
Major hegemonic battle lines

11 Neoliberalism and communitarianism

Social conditions, discourses and politics

Hans-Jürgen Bieling

Introduction: neoliberalism and its context

Since the early 1980s, critical left-wing intellectuals have undertaken great efforts to deconstruct the world-wide neoliberal ideologies in ascendance. Most analyses dealt either with the social or class character of neoliberal politics, with the ideological impact of more comprehensive neoliberal concepts and ideas, or with the history of neoliberal intellectuals and think tanks operating in an increasingly ramified network of collaboration. Not a few are inclined to regard the history and present networks of neoliberal communication as paramount for a better understanding of the overall success of neoliberal ideas and strategies (see Cockett 1994; Plehwe and Walpen 1999; Dixon 2000a). And some go so far as to see the emergence of neoliberal thought as a model for the re-emergence of alternative left-wing concepts and socialist ideas. Eventually, this would mean building a counter-hegemonic network of critical think tanks to provide the ideas that might trigger a fundamental shift in public discourses, perhaps during a fundamental crisis somewhere in the future.

Indeed, it seems to be very alluring to adopt a view that emphasises the prominent role of intellectual leadership in social and political struggles. Nevertheless, from a Gramscian perspective (see Gramsci 1975: 1396–401 and 1513–40), leadership is only poorly understood, if it is seen primarily as a 'top down' application of a fairly comprehensive and coherent set of theoretical concepts and ideas. The basic structures, power relations, contradictions, and conflicts inherent to the given mode of capitalist societalisation are by no means simply secondary. Neither are the ideas and perceptions – the content of common sense – which emerge from the 'bottom up' in these processes. To put it differently, to beware of the pitfalls of idealist reasoning, it is always important to place competing theories, concepts, and ideas in the general context of capitalist reproduction. How this should be done, however, is far from clear. Ideational factors cannot immediately be ascribed to particular social forces. Likewise, it would be misleading to take them as completely autonomous causes detached from material conditions and power relations. To avoid both forms of one-sided analysis, this chapter will argue that the focus should be on the particular – socially mediated – articulation of the material and ideational dimensions of societal reproduction. This means, in terms of political strategies, that they are always influenced and shaped by a whole set of different factors: by the structures, requirements, and contradictions of the particular mode of capitalist reproduction, by the structural power relations inherent to it, by multi-level discourses of intellectuals, politicians, journalists and the people, and, of course, by particular dynamics in the political field itself.

In the following, it should be clarified what this implies with regard to the relationship and competition of neoliberal and communitarian ideas. To do this, the chapter starts with a very brief outline of the overall 'societal configuration' supportive or non-supportive of current political concepts and ideas. Then, in a second step, it will turn towards social philosophy in order to illustrate that on this level neoliberal and communitarian ideas are fundamentally contradictory. But eventually, when they become practically relevant on the level of political strategies, the comparison is less contradictory as the stark philosophical controversies may suggest. Hence, in a third step it will be shown that in terms of practical politics many differences between the two discourses are rather blurred. This applies above all to the 'third way' approach of new social democrats, an approach that represents an attempt to reconcile or even create a new synthesis between the opposed principles of neoliberal market competition and a responsive society based on strong communitarian commitments, identities and community bonds. Finally, this brings us back to the question raised in the beginning: how should we understand and analyse neoliberalism from a critical point of view?

The societal configuration

Competing social discourses emerge and develop in a relationship with the basic structures, features, contradictions and conflicts of the overall societal configuration. In principle, there is a broad consensus that the process of capitalist societalisation was subjected to a fundamental break from the mid-1970s onwards. There is a great deal of critical analyses that provide instructive frameworks of interpretation. With few exceptions, all of them share the phasing offered by regulationist approaches, which demarcate various stages of capitalist development: the period of 'Fordism' (from the end of the Second World War to the mid-1970s), the 'crisis of Fordism' (from the mid-1970s to the mid-1980s), and finally, a new mode of capitalist reproduction, often called 'post-Fordism', 'flexible capitalism', 'transnational high-tech capitalism' and the like (see on this Bieling 2000: 197ff.). Although the details of these sometimes very complex debates will not be engaged here, it is of critical importance to recognise that the transformation of the mode of capitalist reproduction represents the basic background against which changes of the prevailing political concepts took place on different levels: on the level of collective intellectual spaces in the form of epistemic communities, think tanks or strategic planning bodies, on the level of political organisers (e.g., governments, parties, associations or the media), and also, depending on social conditions and circumstances, on the level of general public opinion or common sense.

1   With respect to such considerations, the period of 'Fordism', or, as some call it, the 'golden age' of capitalism (Marglin and Schor 1991) basically represented a 'Keynesian configuration'. This does not simply mean that on the international and domestic level Keynes' economic policy concepts and prescriptions were consciously applied during this period. Historical accounts of the global Bretton Woods System and domestic economic policy strategies tell us something different (Kuttner 1992: 25ff.). Nevertheless, it is legitimate to call the age of 'Fordism' a 'Keynesian configuration', since many factors – the socio-economic mode of reproduction, the balance of forces and the set of public beliefs that emerged out of the Second World War – were generally advantageous for strong political regulation and state intervention in economic affairs. Under such conditions of 'corporate liberalism' (van der Pijl 1984) or 'embedded liberalism' (Ruggie 1982), orthodox approaches of laissez-faire economics were rather marginalised, while Keynesian approaches seemed to rule the scene. In this sense, in developed capitalism there was an enduring basic consensus that 'full employment' and 'extensive social security provisions' should be the top priorities of political decision makers. In order to realise these goals, it was generally acknowledged that international economic co-operation and regulation, anti-cyclical economic state intervention, industrial policy programmes, strong trade unions, and an encompassing welfare state – in short, the institutions and instruments of a 'mixed economy' – were essential.

2   During the crisis of Fordism this broad consensus on the operation and reproduction of developed capitalism was undermined. First emerged the increasing criticism on the part of 'new left' movements: the 1968 students' movement and its protest against the one-dimensional – materialistic and growth oriented – mode of capitalist development and encompassing state control, as well as growing trade union militancy aimed at increasing incomes and autonomy in the workplace. Both movements were characterised by a strong impulse to democratise capitalist societies. Their ambitions came to a hold with the world-wide recession of the mid-1970s, which created a new problematic for developed capitalist societies. After the collapse of the Bretton Woods System, low or even negative economic growth, rising unemployment, increasing public debt, and high rates of inflation it seemed very difficult to adhere to the priorities and political strategies ascribed to the 'Keynesian configuration'. Moreover, neoliberal forces that criticised trade unions as too powerful and welfare state regulation and intervention as too extensive, gained ground (Dixon 2000a: 46ff.). With different rigour, right-wing political parties, market-oriented economists and intellectuals and, of course, the business community, pressed step-by-step to loosen political control of the capitalist economy by demanding policies of deregulation, privatisation and flexibilisation combined with tight budgetary policies. These, in turn, implied both increased differentiation of incomes and reduced social service provisions.

3   Everywhere in the developed capitalist world, the economic and financial policy strategies of the 1980s were marked by a new orientation towards

market-led restructuring and monetary stability (see Anderson 1997). Of course, this shift was more pronounced in the Anglo-Saxon world. It also took hold, however, in more consensus-based and corporatist mediated societies in continental Europe, where public discourses were increasingly influenced by neoliberal reasoning. The defeat of the neo-Keynesian strategy of the left-wing government in France in 1982–3 (Helleiner 1994: 140ff.; Smith 1998: 70ff.) signalled very clearly that the societal configuration was in a process of fundamental change. From then on, market-led restructuring and monetary stability – and implicitly, ongoing modernisation of national regimes of regulation and redistribution – represented the backbones of the major projects of European integration. They were not only inscribed into the Single Market Programme, EMU (Economic and Monetary Union) and recent initiatives to create a truly integrated financial market, but also in the broader context of economic globalisation in terms of trade, services, finance and investment. What emerged was a 'transnational high-tech capitalism', fundamentally different from the Fordist mode of reproduction. The new regime of capitalist accumulation is based not only on globalised finance and investment relations, transnational production chains, and amplified market-competition, but also corresponds with significant cultural changes within state–civil–society complexes such as an emergent market civilization based on property-based individualism and consumerist preferences. Moreover, the main objectives of 'economic imperialism' have been 'locked in' – step by step – via a process of global and European 'constitutionalism' (see Gill 1998), so that the new mode of capitalist development can be conceived as principally 'neoliberal'.

There is no paucity of descriptions of the main elements of the 'neoliberal configuration'. One of the earliest and most pronounced attempts to grasp the fundamental socio-economic change was written by Ralf Dahrendorf (1983). He proclaimed the 'end of the social democratic century', since in public debates the most decisive themes and objectives have altered significantly. Whereas the old themes had been 'growth', 'equality', 'work', 'reason and progress', 'state' and 'interventionism', from the late 1970s onwards the new agenda was primarily about 'globalisation', 'competition', 'risk', 'flexibility' and the like. All these issues, by and large, are firmly rooted in new modes of capitalist reproduction. Hence, it is no surprise that even if radical neoliberal approaches and political concepts are not immediately instructive to political decision making, their most fundamental objectives – market-led restructuring and monetary stability – are pervasive. In other words, they represent the basic features of a 'passive revolution', i.e. of the self-adapting transformation of capitalist societies from above; and as long as emerging social and political criticism articulated by different groups and intellectuals is not able to question neoliberal objectives directly and practically, it will tend to be absorbed and neutralised by the transformative capacities of a transnational bloc of neoliberal social and political forces.

Competing conceptions and ideas: the neoliberal versus the communitarian paradigm

How this process of incorporation takes place can be illustrated by means of the relationship between neoliberal and communitarian ideas. Principally, neoliberal concepts have not been the only, but the most important and influential ones shaping the transition towards the formation of 'transnational high-tech capitalism'. Neoliberal arguments buttressed the most crucial position of points on two fronts. In terms of international economic relations, they supported and justified the ongoing liberalisation of trade, the abolishment of capital controls and the transition towards a global regime of floating exchange rates (Helleiner 1994; Scherrer 1999: 193ff.); and in terms of domestic policies, they vindicated all attempts to deregulate and flexibilise market relations, to limit state intervention, to privatise the public infrastructure and social service provision, to restrain the influence of trade unions, and to enforce monetary stability and sound budget policies. These elements are more or less inscribed into the new societal configuration. They are the pivotal elements of a supply-side economics agenda that privileges a particular – market-centred – conception of competitiveness. Its salient features are pronounced world market orientation, strongly market-determined decisions on investment and political regulation, a strong focus on particular high-technology products, the realisation of short-term gains and the loosening of long-term co-operative bargaining structures and socially oriented network relations. All this demonstrates very clearly that the power of neoliberal concepts is strongly linked or even goes hand in hand with the changed orientation of an increasingly internationalised business community – industrial TNCs, big banks, financial conglomerates and other investment-related firms – or as some call it, of an expanding 'transnational managerial class' (Cox 1987: 359ff.; Strange 1994: 138).[1]

This embeddedness of neoliberal conceptions into the given mode of capitalist development – their tendency to reinforce unequal power relations, but simultaneously stabilising them by compromising on the basis of the requirements of market-led competitiveness – is often underestimated by critical analysis. Many of them tend to take the 'free market' ideology too literally, i.e. they focus extensively or even exclusively at the level of elaborated theoretical conceptions provided by both neoliberal economists and social scientists.

The propositions provided by economists, of course, are predominant within the neoliberal discourse so far. They emerged first out of the critique of a fairly encompassing political and social regulation of post-war Fordist capitalism. In general, it was argued that 'new deal' or Keynesian politics and state interference in market affairs would obstruct competition, innovation, economic productivity gains and growth expectations. This general view became then differentiated and diversified by different particular contributions (see on this Plehwe and Walpen 1999). Friedrich Hayek elaborated on the pivotal role of the price mechanism as the only adequate and superior instrument to provide a most efficient and decentralised organisation and distribution of knowledge. The 'free society' for him was therefore a society based on a constitutionally guaranteed extensive application of market competition. Ronald Coase argued that apart from particular intra-firm operations, the market mechanism would be the mode of co-ordination with the lowest transaction costs. Public choice economists developed a range of models in order to show that even the operation and calculation of political institutions – parties and governments – can be explained and remodelled in terms of rational economic interests, and that the welfare state would inescapably lead to political failure, because it systematically creates and reinforces 'rent seeking' behaviour. Finally, there has been also the 'human capital' approach complementing individualist economic reasoning by application to the reproduction of the labour force.

Of course, this very short list of neoliberal concepts and arguments is far from complete. However, it gives sufficient evidence of the common features of neoliberal thought. First, in terms of the central message, neoliberals maintain that – with very few exceptions – market-relations are generally more efficient and superior to all forms of collective co-operation, whether mediated by the state or by other political organisations as trade unions. Non-economic principles like solidarity, social fairness and social redistribution are therefore totally inappropriate criteria for an optimally organised capitalist society. Moreover, following the logic of 'economic imperialism', neoliberal concepts argue that many political and social institutions can and should be rearranged or replaced in accordance with the criteria of market competition. Second, in terms of the underlying ontology, neoliberal arguments are based on the assumption that the capitalist economy is a market economy which requires a certain constitutional framework, but consists above all of rationally oriented individuals – producers, consumers or voters, provided with particular knowledge – striving to maximise their individual benefits to the benefit of the whole society. Third, this more or less explicit utilitarian ontology goes often hand in hand with a distinctive methodological individualism. This implies the assumption that the rational individual – above all the economically rational individual – represents the starting and ending point and only reliable unit of analysis.

This latter aspect of methodological individualism is common to all rational choice analysis. Rational choice is, however, not automatically neoliberal, since the criteria of rational behaviour must not necessarily be market-determined and also the social context can be seen in completely non-neoliberal terms.[2] Yet this is not the case for Hayek (1949a), whose theory of knowledge is part of a broader neoliberal social theory. Similarly, the public choice approach as applied by James Buchanan (1979) is beyond doubt linked to a neoliberal understanding of the state and the political system. Besides these still primarily economic views, there has also emerged a body of socio-scientific and philosophical papers, of which Robert Nozick's (1974) utilitarian conception of the 'minimal state' was probably most influential.

The communitarian approach came into existence after Michael Sandel (1982) and Charles Taylor (1992) developed critiques of the individualist assumptions of recent social theory and philosophical discourses. Since then many other philosophers have become engaged in this debate. The communitarian critique put forward, however, did not focus on the particular conceptions provided by the proponents of radical market theorists; rather, the focus was both much broader and narrower at the same time. It was broader insofar as it was directed primarily against the ontological and methodological assumptions of much of contemporary contract theories. It was narrower, as well, with Rawls' (1972) *Theory of Justice*, which provided not a neoliberal but a social-democratic argument, taken as the most prominent example of neo-contractual ways of thinking.

In this context, the communitarian critique was based on the following arguments: first it was noted that the individualist methodology applied by Rawls suggests the ontological view of a personality not situated in a specific historical social context – of culture, values and norms determined by particular community bonds – but one totally unencumbered by all this.[3] Besides this critique of the atomistic anthropology, the second communitarian argument addressed the universalistic orientation of liberal thinking. It was held that the focus should be on concrete ethical considerations, instead of the procedures of an allegedly universal morality. Finally, communitarians argued that not only political institutions but also the republican virtues in civil society on which the political system is based are important for the quality of democratic organisation of modern societies.

In principle, philosophical communitarianism cannot directly be seen as a counterpart to neoliberal approaches. At least initially, most philosophical communitarians did not deal immediately with the neoliberal claims to extend the sphere of market competition. Instead, they questioned primarily the individualist ontology and methodology of contemporary liberal neo-contractualism. Hence, the focus of the critique was less on (neo)liberal political concepts and suggestions and more on the general direction of scientific modelling based on ahistorical individualist and rationalist assumptions.

In a way, this changed after more social and political scientists joined the communitarian camp. This second group of communitarians paid more attention to the socio-economic and political development of capitalist societies (see Bellah *et al.* 1985; Etzioni 1993; Barber 1995). In doing this, they provided – first in the US, but also then in Western Europe – a particular diagnosis of societal problems typical of the late 1980s and early 1990s. For communitarians the most fundamental problem consists in the weakening of middle-class-based community ties, i.e. the decay of values, norms, and identities that are reproduced and stabilised by particular social networks, kinship relations, or neighbourhood structures. From their point of view, this weakening is caused by two complementary tendencies: On the one hand they expound the problems of too much state intervention, too encompassing administrative regulation and control, and too extensive bureaucracy apparatuses. On the other hand they criticise the devastating impact of too far-reaching market relations and the thorough commercialisation of social life.

At least insofar as the latter is construed as the 'imperialism' or 'tyranny' of the market, communitarianism can be seen as a product of and reaction against the process of neoliberal restructuring. It is no accident that communitarian ideas became influential above all in those countries – United States and Great Britain – that suffered most from a radical deregulation of labour markets, social services and public infrastructures. In the Anglo-American world, federal structures, trade unions, and forms of corporatist interest mediation have been too weak to moderate this process, while the dynamics of financial markets proved too strong to be kept under political control. The result of the changed power configuration was a transition towards a finance-led mode of capitalist accumulation subjecting the process of socio-economic reproduction – e.g. corporate governance and employee participation, economic and financial policies, but increasingly also social security regulation and provision – to its discipline. In combination with rigorous neoliberal strategies, the new mode of accumulation brought about an extensive commodification and commercialisation of many areas – large parts of social reproduction – formerly shielded from market competition by extensive social regulation (van der Pijl 1998: 43ff.). Eventually, this caused – or at least reinforced – many negative effects for community-based social networks and the values and identities reproduced by them. In the 1990s this also became evident in continental Europe. Hence communitarian ideas spread there, too.

The new political synthesis: 'Communitarian Neoliberalism' and 'Third Way Politics'

In principle, the diagnosis of communitarian approaches represents a critique of neoliberal socio-economic restructuring from a community-centred point of view. As suggested by the wide application of terms such as 'anomie', 'problems of social cohesion', 'fracture sociale' and 'social exclusion', it emerged as a widely accepted view of the 'new social question'. In the late 1980s and early 1990s, many intellectuals, above all social scientists, but also many writers and journalists, joined – more or less explicitly – the communitarian camp. In the US, they are grouped around the 'communitarian network' and its journal *The Responsive Society*, while in Great Britain, some quite influential think tanks close to New Labour – for instance, Demos, Nexus, the Institute for Public Policy Research or the Fabian Society – and journals such as *Renewal* embraced and promoted communitarian ideas (Dixon 2000b: 46ff.). These new think tanks, networks and journals contributed not only to the formation of a new 'epistemic community'. They also stimulated a broader discourse centred on community and civil society issues, which then became more and more adopted by social democratic parties in order to rework their general programmatic orientation. In this context, some prominent intellectual figures promoting the communitarian discourse have built up close linkages to the new generation of social democratic party leaders. Among the most important political advisers have been, to name just a few, Benjamin Barber (1995), Amitai Etzioni (1996) and Robert Reich (1991) in the US, and Anthony Giddens (1994) and John Gray (1998) – a former proponent of Thatcherism and member of the Mont Pèlerin Society – in Great Britain. Their ideas became reference points of many debates in both social sciences and public discourses. In continental Europe this turn towards communitarian arguments was less demonstrative. But even there, at least gradually they invaded public debates.

What have been the main arguments and ideas provided by these groups of – communitarian inspired – intellectuals? The general view, taken by most of them, sees the 'modern society' subjected to a range of transformations, all changing the mode and character of the forms of societal reproduction. They referred to the ongoing process of globalisation, post-traditional social relations, new forms of risk production and generalised insecurity – some mention also a new kind of reflexivity inherent to the new information society – in short, to a fundamentally changed context of political regulation and decision making. In this context, it was acknowledged that the most important transformations are propelled by globalising market-forces and that this dynamic is both unavoidable and principally advantageous for societal development in terms of economic growth, productivity, innovation, etc.

At the same time, however, communitarian intellectuals mention the potentially 'dark sides' of this development. They are concerned about the undesirable effects, which tend to become predominant, when market-led restructuring takes place as an unbridled process that ignores the elementary needs of society. For when one-dimensional orientation towards economic growth and competition undermines ecological reproduction, social community ties, solidarity structures and civic liberties, in short, self-organised forms of social cohesion, this also endangers the very foundations of democratic capitalist societies. Moreover, the disembedding tendencies of globalisation create conditions favourable to those forces – nationalist, racist or atavistic – which aim to blockade or even roll back all the progressive elements established so far in the transition to an open transnational society based on respect for particular communitarian cultures and cosmopolitan principles.

For liberal communitarians such dangers can only be avoided by a proper handling of the new social question, which is primarily a two-fold process of social exclusion (see Giddens 1998). At the bottom end of society, exclusion takes place as the solidified marginalisation of all those groups who suffer from poverty and long-term unemployment, while at the top, globalised elites become increasingly detached from society by avoiding or rejecting social responsibilities, for instance, paying taxes. To overcome this two-fold exclusion, communitarian-inspired proponents of a new 'third way' strategy, however, do not propose strengthening of the old welfare state (see Gray 1996). They are rather sceptical and critical of all suggestions pointing in this direction for a couple of reasons. First, they see the welfare state itself as a form of 'big government' undermining – more or less – self-organised community ties and civil society relations. Second, they are worried that more central state control would do harm to a dynamic market-led reorganisation of the capitalist economy. Third, they deny that traditional social policy measures that utilise welfare state redistribution are still possible in an increasingly globalised world economy, since more progressive taxes, for instance, would stimulate capital flight. Finally, it is argued that the old welfare state will probably only administrate the given inequalities without actually enabling the excluded to participate once again in economic and social life.

In as much as communitarians are in favour of the new 'third way' strategy, they adopt a completely different – programmatic and practical – approach. On a very general level, they suggest modernising the entire set of social democratic values by adjusting them to the changed mode of capitalist reproduction. Instead of adhering, at least programmatically, to the socialisation and public control of the means of production, proponents of the 'third way' approach stress first the need of a 'dynamic economy' and a 'thriving private sector', before mentioning that these are the bases for 'high quality public services', a 'just society', democratic structures, a 'healthy environment', equal opportunities, a cohesive civil society and solidaristic social relations, or even claim that solidarity is important and beneficial (Sassoon 1997: 739f.). It is no accident that in support of this overall orientation, communitarian terms such as responsibility, obligation, mutual trust and respect, a sense of belonging, common work and co-operation are stressed again and again (see Blair 1997). They represent an appealing formula:

(a) to keep key values of the labour movement on the programmatic agenda of new social democratic parties;
(b) to facilitate thereby, however, their profound transformation – for instance, 'solidarity' transformed from a term of class struggle towards a term of social cohesion;
(c) to make traditional social democratic values acceptable for the 'new middle classes'; and
(d) to utilise them also as a means and resource in global economic competition (see Bieling 2003).

On a more concrete and practical level, the 'third way' approach has developed a myriad of concepts for almost all policy areas. Most important, particularly as far as the fight against the new social question is concerned, are its suggestions to modernise social and welfare state policies (see Giddens 1998). Supported by corresponding policies – economic, financial, industrial, and labour markets policies – the modernised welfare state is not primarily seen as an agency for social redistribution, but above all as a means to invest in human capital and to promote social inclusion. In this sense, the welfare state should be transformed into an institution actively shaping the process of ongoing economic modernisation. This pro-active policy stance can, however, only partly be achieved by means of administrative measures and prescriptions. Therefore, it should also be accompanied by ideological public campaigns generating a changed public culture more sensitive to the competitive resources rooted in social community networks.

In the meantime the transposition of this communitarian-inspired third way approach into concrete political strategies can be analysed with respect to a range of countries. So far, the experiences with the New Democrats in the United States and with New Labour in Great Britain are most informative (see Smith

1997). The Clinton administration, as well as the Blair government, has shown very clearly that third way politics represent no fundamental departure from the former neoliberal strategies of capitalist reorganisation. Nevertheless, it is characterised by at least two significant modifications. First, the head-on neoliberal struggle against the welfare state and social regulation has been abandoned and replaced by more co-operative strategies stressing the need of a more balanced form of state regulation and the involvement of civil society such as organised interests and social movements. Second, instead of the conservative – often nationalist or even racist – arguments that accompanied neoliberal strategies, the third way approach is supported above all by communitarian ideas. Compared with neo-conservatism, its emphasis of decentralised units of social reproduction – of families, neighbourhoods, local networks and infrastructure – is, in principle more liberal and therefore also more in line with the beliefs and values of cosmopolitan-oriented middle classes.

In continental Europe the communitarian perspective corresponds to a more competition-oriented and network-based approach of corporatist interest mediation. Here, it is seen that an accelerated modernisation of the welfare state requires the involvement, participation and responsibility of certain civil society groups and their associations. The recent Lisbon strategy, which includes an inter- or transgovernmental co-ordination of the processes of welfare state modernisation, points also in this direction. In a way, it represents the attempt to Europeanise the 'third way' approach (see Aust 2001): on the one hand, it is based on the method of open co-ordination with the collaboration of representatives of an emerging European civil society. On the other hand, in terms of its content, it is strongly influenced by the idea that the welfare state and social security systems should be reorganised in a pro-active manner that increases the rate of economic participation of the labour force. The Lisbon strategy is therefore the attempt to promote the objective of 'employability' – a core feature of the European employment strategy promoted by the proponents of the third way likewise – by re-adjusting the criteria of the whole system of welfare state regulation.

This programme of a market- and competition-oriented reform of the welfare state vindicates that the programmatic of a new 'third way' can be seen as the condensation of a third wave of social democratic revisionism. The first wave of revisionism (after the First World War) has been characterised by giving-up straightforward revolutionary strategies and by embracing representative democracy. The second wave (after the Second World War) allowed, under conditions of full employment and welfare state expansion in general, acceptance of the basic elements of capitalist reproduction, e.g., free markets, private property rights, etc. Now, the post-Cold War third wave is driven above all by the insight that all national paths to social democratic modernisation are practically impossible, and that there is no alternative other than accommodation to the processes of globalisation and European integration (Sassoon 1997: 730ff.). This makes clear that communitarian ideas, if they become relevant for centre-left-wing parties, are normally not more than a programmatic backing in order to smooth the social

218 *Hans-Jürgen Bieling*

democratic acknowledgement of the new societal configuration. Eventually, their basic principles, norms and values become subordinated to prevailing neoliberal objectives such as the promotion of market competition, improved competitiveness and the primacy of sound budget policies.[4]

Rethinking neoliberalism

The argument provided so far has been that the relationship between communitarian and neoliberal discourses turns out to be different depending on the analytical level and focus of dispute.

With respect to the philosophical dispute, the focus has been on different ontological and anthropological assumptions, as well as on the methodological concepts applied. Whereas the neoliberal view takes, in principle, the individual as the basic unit and starting point of analysis, communitarians counter radical individualist thinking by emphasising the embeddedness of individuals in particular historical and community contexts characterised by specific social bonds, obligations, values and identities. At least in this regard, the discourses are contrary to each other. This is supported by the fact that neoliberals tend to refer to John Locke or – if more socially oriented – to Immanuel Kant, while communitarians represent rather a community-centred strand of Hegelian thinking.

This controversial relationship persists also in terms of the diagnosis of the most serious problems of contemporary capitalist societies. Whereas neoliberals still see too many hindrances for the free operation of markets for goods, capital, services and labour markets, communitarians criticise unfettered and commercialised market relations as one cause for the weakening and dissolution of social communities. At the same time, however, they share a common adversary: the centralised and bureaucratic state, which generates forms of 'big government' that impede both the operation of free markets and the reproduction of self-organised community structures.

It is this latter point that the discourses converge in terms of practical politics. Specifically, the conception of a 'new third way' aims at synthesising the neoliberal view and communitarian ideas. It argues for a market-led process of capitalist restructuring in consideration of revitalised community bonds and sound civil society structures. In other words, proponents of the third way discourse repeatedly emphasise that the market-led modernisation of the state and society should be pursued in a more co-operative manner, by taking also into account non-economic – above all cultural – aspects of societal reproduction.

Yet what does this differentiation conceptually imply for the understanding of neoliberalism? First of all, it seems necessary to elaborate an even more differentiated analytical concept, in order to avoid the trap of terming all and everything that happens nowadays as 'neoliberal'. For only this enables critical analysis to take the motives of social forces seriously, which might represent a potential source of counter-hegemonic transformation, even if they are – unintentionally – in favour of certain elements of neoliberal restructuring. In this regard, it seems to be useful to draw the following distinctions:

1 As already outlined in the beginning, the first level of analysis should refer to the general mode of capitalist reproduction. It is on this level that the terms of macro-economic development and market competition, as well as the broad framework of societal and political regulation, are relevant. The character and operation of all these dimensions is largely determined by the given socio-economic, political and ideological power structures. In the era of Fordism, these tended to be in favour for a Keynesian, state-interventionist management. This changed then with the crisis-led transformation of the capitalist mode of production and accumulation, with alterations in the social structure and the organisational structure of capitalist societies, the transnationalisation of trade and investment, and the transition to a flexible global currency regime and the re-emergence of global finance. All this gave transnational economic forces – transnational corporations, big banks, institutional investors – more leverage *vis-à-vis* national governments and domestically rooted social groups and political organisations. In this sense, the new 'transnational high-tech capitalism' represents a 'neoliberal configuration' in which alternative Keynesian or even socialist strategies have no chance to become successfully implemented on a national level alone.

2 Competing social discourses in the public realm only partially pick up these fundamental socio-economic relations as a central theme. In principle, there are many different focuses that cannot and should not be squeezed in the rather crude alternative between a neoliberal or anti neoliberal orientation. This concerns particularly debates centred on questions of a theory of knowledge or the applied methodology. Such questions have a merit of their own, and should not immediately be assessed by their potential political impact. The latter is, however, relevant, if social theories provide a particular ontology – a society of market-oriented individuals *vis-à-vis* a society as a network of particular communities – and a comprehensive diagnosis of given societal problems: too many hindrances for the free operation of markets *vis-à-vis* the dissolution of community ties. This contradictory relationship between the neoliberal and communitarian discourse is, however, far from symmetrically balanced. In general, neoliberal arguments dealing with the operation of the economy, the state, and world politics seem to be far more influential in the public realm and in the process of political decision-making, whereas communitarian arguments dealing with social and cultural issues are rather secondary.

Besides this structural asymmetry between the discourses, each discourse is internally hierarchically structured, too. To put it very crudely with respect to the neoliberal discourse: on the top, there are the 'great' or 'conceptual' intellectuals elaborating a fairly comprehensive and coherent 'grand design' to understand and shape the development of societies. If they are part of scientific networks and think tanks, they may form a broader neoliberal 'epistemic community'. On a second level, the world view – the explanations and ideas – provided by conceptual intellectuals is taken up by mediators in public communication. This can be teachers, journalists or academics of different kinds or also politicians and their advisers. This group can be called 'intellectual mediators' or in the words of Hayek 'second hand dealers in ideas' (Hayek, cit. after Cockett 1995: 159), all involved in a process of 'practical neoliberalism'. If the discourse is already more incoherent and fragmented on this second level, this is even more the case on the third or 'bottom level' of the common sense. Common sense is shaped by the many different, often contradictory experiences of everyday life. On this level therefore the social positions – the material interests, expectations and life chances – in the general reproduction of the societal configuration are particularly relevant. In this regard it seems to be appropriate to speak of 'everyday neoliberalism', which although influenced by intellectual discourses, is rooted also in the concrete experiences and expectations of different social groups and classes. It is probably this level that best explains why neoliberal and communitarian discourses, despite their apparent contradictions, can manage to co-exist in the more focused programmes and strategies of political parties.

3 A last differentiation, which might also be helpful for understanding neoliberalism, refers to different phases of its practical realisation (see Bieling and Steinhilber 2000). The transformative capacity of neoliberal ideas was driven first by the critique of the Keynesian welfare state and trade unions, above all in course of the crisis-ridden 1970s. Due to its rather fundamental stance, this critique triggered a first phase which might be called 'aggressive neoliberalism'. This aggressive attitude prevailed even after the right-wing parties took office. Moreover, it was generalised throughout Western Europe with the Single Market programme launched in the mid-1980s, which raised many expectations – in terms of economic growth, productivity, investment and employment – in the public at large. Since the Single Market was received rather enthusiastically, it led to the second phase which might be dubbed 'euphoric neoliberalism'. Most of these expectations then became dashed due to intensified economic restructuring, rising levels of unemployment, a world-wide recession in the early 1990s, and the foreseeable austerity programmes enforced in preparation of Economic and Monetary Union. As the public climate changed again, another phase, 'disciplinary neoliberalism' (see Gill 1998), emerged. To a large degree, the electoral success of new social democratic parties and the formation of new centre-left governments was part of the reaction against the negative effects of socio-economic restructuring and the crisis of political legitimacy. The main modifications brought about by this have been, however, far from fundamental. Above all, the new social democrats aimed at consolidating the given neoliberal framework by strengthening corporatist forms of socio-economic co-operation. Programmatically, communitarian ideas ranked high in the ideological flanking of this process. For this reason the more recent phase of neoliberal consolidation might be named 'communitarian neoliberalism'.

Finally, from this outline of a framework of differentiation, two conclusions might be drawn. The first one refers to the hegemonic capacity of neoliberalism to absorb and neutralise potentially counter-hegemonic forces and ideas. In this regard, the distinction of different phases and the handling of the communitarian discourse represents a very good example of a strategy of 'trasformismo' (Gramsci). This strategy is, however, not primarily due to the superiority and organised proliferation of neoliberal think tanks, but to the socio-economic power structures backing neoliberal restructuring. The second conclusion is less analytical than political. The emergence of the communitarian discourse – and its articulation on the level of the everyday common sense – is not necessarily linked with neoliberal and authoritarian attitudes. As much as the dissolution of solidaristic community relations is concerned, it might also entail some progressive elements. These progressive elements will, however, only realize their potential if the material dimensions of the social and cultural crisis – i.e. socio-economic inequalities, hierarchies and power relations – are not ignored but forcefully addressed in order to overcome the neoliberal configuration.

Notes

1 Eventually this transnational bloc of social forces is more extensive as it seems at first glance:

> The transnational managerial class is not limited to persons actually employed among the managerial cadres of multinational corporations and their families. It encompasses public officials in the national and international agencies involved with economic management and a whole range of experts and specialists who in some way are concerned with the maintenance of the world economy in which the multinationals thrive – from management consultants, to business educators, to organizational psychologists, to the electronics operators who assemble the information base for business decisions, and the lawyers who put together international business deals.
> (Cox 1987: 359–60)

2 In this sense, it would be quite too crude and simplifying to classify even 'analytical Marxism' or all post-modern and post-structuralist work which aims at the decomposition of social structures and puts the emphasis on the decentralised subject as neoliberal.

3 The problem is that this communitarian argument is based on a short circuit. It does not take into account that the 'veil of ignorance', a primitive state of a-historical individuals invented by Rawls, is a methodological abstraction not necessarily implying a certain ontological view of society.

4 The subordination of communitarian thinking to neoliberal or third way conceptions, of course, applies not to all variants and proponents of this discourse. Nevertheless, it seems to be rather easy for other discourses and concepts to seize and use communitarian suggestions without being disposed to change major elements of the overall perspective. The reason for this facile utilisation is quite simple: in general, communitarian thinking is not based on a deeper analytical understanding of societal reproduction, since it forgoes to critically analyse social and political power structures. This implies in turn that it is susceptible for a certain – community-centred – way of authoritarian thinking and/or can be easily functionalised by other social discourses and theories (Bieling 2000: 158ff.).

12 Neoliberalism and cultural nationalism

A *danse macabre*

Radhika Desai

'The Great Moving Right Show', as Stuart Hall had dubbed the rise of Thatcherism in the late 1970s has been running in political theatres across the world for nearly three decades now. When Hall (1983 [1978]) initiated the Gramscian analysis of Thatcherism, when neoliberalism's anti-state, free-market and anti-union nostrums could still sound unfamiliar, it may still have appeared to many as a freakish side-show in a declining industrial democracy. In the decades since then the might of the New Right has swept all before it, *making* right its insistence that 'There Is No Alternative' (TINA). Of the many facets of the New Right – social, political, cultural, ideological and economic – analysts have tended to emphasise its ideology. Though understandable – it was unusual for right politics to be ideological and intellectual as the New Right appeared – it conveyed the impression that the New Right's political advance rested mainly on the intellectual merits of neoliberalism, and on the political influence its exponents deftly acquired through their now famous networks and think tanks – the 'world wide web of neoliberalism' as the title of the conference originally stimulating this chapter has it.

This is, at best, a partial view. Market dogma may be well entrenched in capitals around the world, but its intellectual vacuity and practical failures have been documented in a vast literature. It would be truer to say that neoliberalism's intellectual pretensions are designed to provide a fig leaf of intellectual respectability to the most naked pursuit of the interests of capital and property than that neoliberalism has motivated this pursuit by its intellectual force and political influence. A combination of the exhaustion of left and social democratic politics and outright electoral and political manipulation have entrenched neoliberalism in power, whether in its English-speaking homelands or farther afield in countries where it has either been clearly imposed from 'without' by international agents of neoliberalism such as the International Monetary Fund (see Murrell 1994 on 'Russian' Shock Therapy), or adapted to 'centrist' (Congress in India, PRI in Mexico, or LDP in Japan) or social democratic ('Third Way') politics. In being so adapted, neoliberalism demonstrated an endurance greater than the parties of the New Right which had first brought it to power. As they lost power in one Western capital after another in the 1990s, Perry Anderson (2001) discerned a new stabilization of neoliberalism's power in social democratic neoliberalism: a 'Formula Two' had succeeded the neoliberalism of right parties in the 1980s. However, as the century turned: right wing parties in many countries – France, Austria, India, the US, Spain and Italy, most prominently – reappeared in power, and in others seemed to be regrouping. Three decades of neoliberal policies had also re-made the world so substantially that isolated instances of resistance to them, whether springing from its injustices – Chiapas, Chavez, or Lula – or its contradictions – Iraq, Afghanistan – faced being worn down by the 'dull compulsion of economic relations' or mown down by the blunt and brute military force of the power – the United States – presiding over the neoliberal world. The second term granted George W. Bush in the US confirmed even more clearly the weight of factors other then neoliberalism in the success of the New Right: the mobilisation of the social authoritarian tendencies such as the Christian right, the disorganisation, intellectual and political, of the Democratic Party and the creation of a climate of fear to an extent that it largely eclipsed strictly economic issues almost completely.

Three major strands of scholarship on the politics and policy of the New Right can be identified. The analysis of the New Right as a Gramscian struggle for hegemony inaugurated by Stuart Hall was theoretically the richest approach. It generalised the use of 'hegemony' and associated Gramscian concepts across the social sciences and humanities, and practically single-handedly gave rise to a whole new discipline: Cultural Studies. The second approach, originally an offshoot of the first, focused on the apparently novel role of think tanks in the rise of the New Right. Initially spotted and analysed in Britain,[1] it soon became clear that British think tanks were part, and in the case of the Institute of Economic Affairs (IEA), the hub, of an international network of neoliberal scholars, think tanks and policy institutes. Over the next decade and a half, studies of think tanks in national and international contexts proliferated and the creation of the Mont Pèlerin Society at the initiative of Friedrich von Hayek in 1947 was widely identified as the *fons et origio* of contemporary neoliberalism. Naturally, with all this attention being showered upon them, the think tanks got into the act themselves, alternating between sober reflection on the extent and limits of their own role and influence (Gamble *et al.* 1986), and a conceit which emphasised particularly a lonely heroism of the early years (Harris and Seldon 1977, 1981; Seldon 1985). Studies of think tanks highlighted the intellectual function in politics. Think tanks became all the rage, not only as objects of social-scientific scrutiny but also as *the* new form of politics, slated to replace 'old' forms such as parties, memberships and canvassing. As I had occasion to note a decade ago:

> Nowadays, think tanks seem in vogue, the Labour Party makes sure everyone knows it's on the lookout for the 'big idea', and Demos – the bold new post-Thatcherite, postmodern, indeed, post-party venture – even while declaring the old political mould obsolete, underlines its acceptance of this as a lesson of Thatcherism in its declared aim to 'draw on the most advanced

thinking from throughout society and across the world' and 'reinvigorate political thinking'.

(Desai 1994a: 28, quoting from Geraldine Bell, 'Geof and Martin's Big Idea', *Independent on Sunday*, 24 January 1993)

There was a double irony in this 'Learning from Thatcherism' (Hall 1988). On the one hand, the focus on think tanks, and by extension, of the intellectual role in politics, seemed to come at precisely the historical moment of a major crisis of this role. Diagnosed variously by observers of the left and right alike,

> [a] list of [its] symptoms ... include[d] the institutionalisation of intellectual life in the Academy, its consequent isolation from wider social currents and its attendant disciplinary specialisation; the domination of intellectual life by the media; the substitution of market-driven decisions for any independent judgement intellectuals have had in culture and politics; and the replacement of a generally educated public, interested in social and political ideas, by a plurality of more specialised and disparate audiences.
>
> (Desai 1994b: 27)[2]

The centrality of think tanks, rather than more established institutions, in politics was a symptom of the critical condition of intellectual life. In these conditions, an analysis of the *intellectual* role of think tanks was only possible with, and underlined more than ever the truth of, a sociological rather than an intrinsic concept of intellectuals. New Right intellectuals were not necessarily original thinkers but those who had a hold on the public credulity through their access to various media, often of their own devising (such as the think tanks themselves). Moreover, they aimed to convince 'effective publics' – not the public as a whole, but strategic elements of it. Indeed, the label 'think tank' turns out to be 'a misnomer. Most think tanks, and certainly all Thatcherite ones, were set up not to "think-up" bold new ideas but to elaborate and peddle a single, already fairly well worked-out ideology. They were and remained in essence proselytisers, not originators' (Desai 1994a: 62). On the other hand, the focus on ideas and intellectuals in the politics of the New Right and neoliberalism tended to draw attention away from the wider historical – economic and social – determinants of the success of neoliberalism which are central to any critical account of it, an account which would caution against the idealist emphasis on ideas and intellectuals to the exclusion of other determinants of historical change, which is implied in Hall's injunction that the Left 'learn from Thatcherism'.

If the politics of the New Right were a struggle for hegemony – a struggle of intellectuals and ideologies for 'hearts and minds' – its success was equivocal at best. Ivor Crewe's surveys of British public opinion clearly demonstrated that the values and principles of Thatcherism – whether 'free market', 'small state', or 'Victorian values' – were not accepted by the public more than a decade into that struggle, notwithstanding back-to-back election victories and the Labour

Party's intellectual and ideological submission. This finding would probably be replicated in country after country (Crewe 1989). As the right-wing and neoliberal National Democratic Alliance government in India was defeated in 2004, it only joined a succession of political formations in New Delhi who have failed to win re-election since the cross-party acceptance of neoliberalism:

> A succession of different political formations ruling at the centre – the Congress majority government under Rajiv Gandhi, the National Front minority government of 1989–91, the Congress minority government of 1991–6, the United Democratic Front coalition Governments of 1996–8, the two NDA coalition governments of 1998–9 and 1999–2004 have been succeeded by yet another one, the UPA government.
>
> (Desai 2005)

Nor did the New Right succeed in taking over the intellectual or bureaucratic (policy-making) worlds and here too the British case is exemplary: both the academy and the civil service in Britain were never converted to neoliberalism. While the think tanks were never right in their estimate that the civil service was a 'bastion of socialism' which would subvert their project, and on the whole Whitehall, Britain's higher civil service, settled down to serving its new political masters (Henessey 1989: 623–82). However, it also proved impervious to ideological takeover. Mrs Thatcher's terms in office featured several episodes of conflict between the regular civil service and irregular and ideological 'advisers' drawn from the world of the think tanks such as Professor Alan Walters and John Hoskins, formerly at the Institute of Directors. Thatcherite and more generally neoliberal treatment of the universities has led, at best, to sullen resignation in the academy and in intellectual circles.

Finally, a third approach to the study of the New Right consisted in examining the extent to which policy – whether of national governments or international organizations – actually bore the stamp of neoliberal ideology, and whether or not it could be traced back to particular intellectuals or think tanks (Marsh and Rhodes 1992). Remarkably, these examinations also delivered highly qualified verdicts. In the British case, the limitations of the neoliberalism of the think tanks became clear in its inability to reverse Britain's economic decline (Gamble 1985). Nor has it sped up economic growth world-wide. These economic crises – British and global – had given the New Right its historic opportunity as they unravelled post-war settlements – welfarist, Communist or developmental – in country after country. The age of the New Right may have witnessed the dismantling of the 'Fordist' regime of accumulation world-wide but has yet to see its replacement by any relatively stable new configuration of growth conditions, or 'regime of accumulation', as several other contributions to this volume also aver. Finally, if the success of the New Right was to be gauged from the extent to which public policy had become ideological, it appears that considerations of the electoral cycle, fiscal limitations and sheer pragmatism have weighed at least as much as ideology (Marsh and Rhodes 1992).

It should be clear then, that the success of the New Right is due to more than just intellectual theories and think tanks. These had an undeniable role and volumes such as the present one exploring this aspect are critical to the understanding of the New Right. In this chapter, however, I attempt to map the wider field of the New Right's political victories in a way which complements the other contributions to this volume. It is a perspective which I have developed in the course of a sustained involvement in the study of the New Right only the starting point of which was neoliberal think tanks. Looked at historically, the distinctiveness of the New Right as a political formation lies at the intersection of four developments: the passing of conservatism as a distinct element of the historic formation of the Right; the expansion of the primary social basis of the Right as propertied classes themselves expanded; an increase in its power relative to non-possessing social sectors; and finally, an intensification of its proclivities for the extremes of Right-wing politics. I outline these in the next section.

In the final section, I examine the ideology of the New Right which, in this fuller account, consists not just of neoliberalism, but also of an authoritarian socio-cultural complement. Beginning with some of the earliest analyses of the New Right (Hall 1983; Levitas 1986; Gamble 1988; Leys 1980), the presence of this latter component was noted. However, as the analysis of the New Right focused more and more exclusively on its economic component, namely neoliberalism, this socio-cultural component was ignored. Or it was considered only in analyses of extreme right parties and groups which emerged in Europe, as also elsewhere. Such a division of analytical labour implied that the ideology of the 'mainstream' New Right was confined to neoliberalism alone and that it was the radical or extreme right which, almost exclusively, displayed authoritarian social and cultural attitudes. It has also become a convention in the study of the right that these two political tendencies had little to do with each other. Sadly, it is wishful thinking. Herbert Kitschelt, for example, has demonstrated that the rise of parties of the New Radical Right (NRR), as he calls them, is predicated upon the politics of the mainstream right: the closer the mainstream right is to the political centre, the larger the space – a space which has come into existence since the 1960s – for the parties of the NRR to emerge and establish themselves (Kitschelt and McGann 1997). To the extent that the mainstream right itself occupies this space, and adopts NRR issues as its own, it stifles the emergence of separate parties of the NRR. One way or another, these issues find their articulation.

These authoritarian cultural politics, here dubbed 'cultural nationalism', are an integral component of the wider politics of property of the New Right. As neoliberalism has travelled across the political spectrum to encompass parties of the centre and left, and to be adapted by them with minor variations, so have the New Right's politics of cultural nationalism. While on the right they may be articulated as the expression of the cultural superiority of the national culture, and on the 'left' in terms of a 'multi-culturalism', they commonly privilege the dominant 'national culture' as 'normal'. The dynamic interaction of neoliberalism and cultural nationalism – their *danse macabre* – is the focus of the final section (see also Desai 2004).

The New Right in historical perspective

The right's main political task – the preservation and adaptation of the order of private property, and its cultural, social and political arrangements – has been performed in different ways through its history. Changes in the order of property as capitalism developed, and challenges to it, have been the motors driving the history of the Right forward (Girvin 1994). What marks the New Right out as a distinctive phase of right politics is the disappearance of the social basis of Conservatism. The politics of the New Right is *post-Conservative* Right politics. Ironically, scholars and observers of the New Right were so mesmerised by the drama of the New Right as a vanquisher of *social democracy*, a *left* project, that the passing of the hitherto most enduring element of Right politics went unnoticed and unacknowledged.

Conservatism was never synonymous with right politics but a distinct historical element of it. Originally it was a defence and adaptation of pre-capitalist forms of landed property, and its habitual modes of surplus extraction, amidst emerging industrial capitalism. But, by the latter half of the nineteenth century, when the bourgeoisie with its liberal ideology ceased to be a historically progressive force, and as the franchise covered lower socio-economic strata, liberalism and (religious and nationalist) populism also became elements of right historical blocs. Conservative politics also changed as landed property formed links with capitalist property and became capitalist. Naturally, it was never easy to pin it down in any clear doctrinal fashion (Honderich 1991). Given its formative association with the aristocracy and its cultural and political élan, the distinction between Conservatism and more authoritarian, reactionary and plebeian forms of right politics is frequently useful. But it was never an unbridgeable divide. Conservatives determined to retain political purchase on fast-changing contexts of political crisis have been known to come around to these normally despised forms of politics as they did everywhere in Europe with the rise of fascism (Blinkhorn 1990). Indeed, as Arno Mayer (1981) analysed it, Conservatism as an authentic political vehicle of the defenders of landed property reached its historical terminus in precisely that crisis, and its passengers had to board other much less sumptuously appointed trains for their further journey through history.

Up to 1914 the 'persistence of the old regime' (Mayer 1981) – based on land's dominance over capital as a source of wealth – meant that Conservatism remained the dominant partner in the coalitions of the propertied which formed the social basis of Right politics. During the Thirty Years' Crisis which followed Conservatism's material basis eroded considerably as capital finally constituted a source of greater wealth than land. But Conservatism persisted a little longer, even enjoying a brief and final efflorescence. Since power in the centres of advanced capitalism came to be based on capitalist private property after 1945, logically, Conservatism could no longer be adequate to the task of preserving this order of property and enabling its future accumulation. With its exclusively cash and commodity relationships, and fast changing production and consumption patterns, this purer capitalist order, now neither sheltered nor burdened by the overlay of feudal nobility, could neither affect nor effect a politics of continuity, pragmatism and deference. However, for roughly a quarter century after 1945, the new purely capitalist right politics wore a moderate and organicist appearance which could be taken for Conservatism, particularly in the new context of welfare capitalism. The old regime had persisted until 1914 by in part organising a symbiosis and interpenetration of the landed and industrial possessing classes, under the cultural supremacy of the former. The leaders of the mid-century Right, even as they became bourgeois could, for some time longer, claim a social distinction and deference which had been the hallmark of Conservatism hitherto.

> In the political realm, substantial figures like Adenauer, De Gasperi, Monnet embodied this persistence – their political relationship to Churchill or De Gaulle, grandees from a seigneurial past, as if an after-image of an original compact that socially was no longer valid.
>
> (Anderson1998: 84–5)

However, the post-Second World War ruling class soon succumbed to the logics of the very capitalist accumulation and attendant commodification, including that of culture, which it fostered as the basis of its prosperity. Beginning with the late 1960s, came an '*encanillement* of the possessing classes'. Its 'starlet princesses and sleazeball presidents' were the symptoms (Anderson 1998: 86). The New Right, with its miserly and punitive ideology, its open racism, social authoritarianism and cultural nationalism, the commoner social origins of its leaders, its mediatised relationship to the electorate, its rationalised organisation and its undeniable reliance on shock troops of the lumpen was surely the first purely and unabashedly capitalist right emerging in all its Brechtian glory. The brazen class biases of such politics made a sharp contrast to the mid-century Right which at least wore the appearance of organicism, whether of the patronage or the welfare variety. Neoliberalism's political accompaniment was an anti-democratic, often anti-constitutional right discourse of the Hayeks and the Huntingtons; its ideological accompaniment, a more or less punitive cultural nationalism.

With the final disappearance of Conservatism, the sole 'human' face (and it was more usually a mask) of right politics was lost, and this at a time when the primary social basis of right politics expanded enormously in absolute terms and became more powerful in relative terms. On the one hand, there was an enormous increase in wealth and incomes in the second half of the twentieth century, and on the other hand, particularly in the latter half of the period, they were more and more unequally distributed. This absolute expansion of the classes of property and the massive increase in their relative power against the propertyless classes was a global phenomenon.

In countries of advanced capital the expansion of the classes of property may have been less marked. But its true extent was also masked. Many of the claims to the new wealth, which were mediated through new financial structures such as pension funds and mutual trusts, were what Robin Blackburn called 'grey' – 'not only because it refers to provision for the old, but also because the property rights of the policy holders are weak and unclear' particularly under the present regime of trustee law where they are held in trust funds.[3] The phenomenon of the new 'grey' wealth was stronger in the two economies where the fruits of growth over the last two decades of the twentieth century were most unequally distributed, the US and the UK. Not surprisingly, for it was one of the chief instruments of this unequal distribution of wealth.

The political reflux of this modification of the class structure was to expand and consolidate support for the right among professionals and salaried workers reliant on the corporate sector for their incomes, and such property as they had or hoped to have. Privatisation and the contracting out of many functions formerly performed by the state bureaucracy to private agencies also worked to increase the numbers of those reliant on private capital, and thus expanded the core social basis of the right. On the other hand, those professionals who are in the state and NGO sectors formed the basis of the move of Social Democracy to the Right.[4] Having given up its central emphasis on economic egalitarianism, this new social democracy of the 'Third Way' functioned, instead, to integrate elements of newer propertied groups into wider ruling elites, politically recognising new wealth and power. They too represented a politics of property, but with important differences with established parties of the right. The following assessment of the differences between the Republicans and Democrats in the US applied more widely. It also accounts for both the attraction and limitations of the 'politics of recognition' which the 'third way' parties stood for as they abandoned those of 'redistribution'.

> [T]he Democrats remain more inclined to limited concessions – fiscal credits, affirmative action, medicaid – to the poor, and the Republicans to further largesse – tax breaks, deregulation, vouchers – for the rich ... These are differences that make it entirely rational for hard-pressed workers, defenceless Blacks, immigrant Latinos to vote Democrat, in the absence of any alternative within reach. Without their hopes and energies, the party of Jon Corzine and Terry McAuliffe would not be competitive. The mechanism that traps them depends on the integration of those who could create an alternative, the educated and organized of each constituency, into the system. In the Clinton era the social rewards for cooperation, long available to union leaders, have been extended to black politicians across the country. Little is granted the mass of the coloured or poor; but much has been gained by those who speak in their name. It is the domestication of wide swathes of this stratum that closes the lid of the two-party system on the least advantaged. In practice, the only means of escape for them is a numbed indifference – the greater part never lodging a preference at all.
>
> (Anderson 2001: 5–22)

Neoliberalism was the common commitment of this new politics of property which acquired its own 'right' and 'left'. The political potential for any alternatives to this neoliberal consensus emerging was blunted. The casualisation of the work of many corporate and state employees, professional and manual, increased personal uncertainty and expanded the potential basis of a more right-wing form of politics among the working classes as well. It was unlikely, however, as Herbert Kitschelt noted in his study of radical right-wing politics in Europe, that anti-neoliberal 'welfare chauvinist' appeals to which these constituencies can be expected to respond would emerge as strong political forces. They lacked a 'structural location in advanced capitalism in which to entrench themselves':

> short of a major economic catastrophe, it appears unlikely that the gradual transformation of Western economies will ever threaten or actually cut free a sufficiently large section of the workforce into unemployment to provoke the rise of significant authoritarian welfare-chauvinist parties. Parties with such appeals may do well for a while in depressed industrial areas or in regional protest elections but rarely on a national scale or for an extended period of time.
>
> (Kitschelt and McGann 1997: 23)

Such 'welfare chauvinism' was, in any case, out of the question in the vast majority of the countries that lacked welfare states in the first place. Right parties, including extreme right authoritarian ones, were generally anti-statist and neo-liberal.

This larger and more powerful right was also meaner. As a 'cartel of anxiety', as Arno Mayer (1971: 42) called it 30 years ago in a penetrating but now little-read study of the right, it was a lot more prone to the extremes of right politics because of the high levels of uncertainty and insecurity generated by the neoliberal order. On the one hand, the increased social inequality over which it presides inflicted on the propertied a political vertigo: an uneasy sense that, despite the disorganisation of the left, the order of property was vulnerable to challenge. The protection costs of the neoliberal order increased – from the proliferation of local laws to curb 'anti-social' behaviour such as begging and the mushrooming of private and public security forces to the war on terrorism – as states, firms and individuals sought to protect their interests and property. On the other hand, low economic growth, low growth expectations and a generally listless economic climate made relations amongst blocks of property volatile and competitive. Contrary to what neoliberal anti-statism might lead us to expect, competition over state largesse and support for this or that capitalist interest was sharper than ever before.

The dynamic interaction of neoliberalism and cultural nationalism

This is where cultural nationalism comes in. Only it can serve to mask, and bridge, the divides within the 'cartel of anxiety' in a neoliberal context. *Cultural* nationalism is a nationalism shorn of its civic-egalitarian and developmentalist thrust, one reduced to its cultural core. It is structured around the culture of the economically dominant classes in every country, with higher or lower positions accorded to other groups within the nation relative to it. These positions correspond, on the whole, to the groups' economic positions, and as such it organises the dominant classes, and concentric circles of their allies, into a collective national force. It also gives coherence to, and legitimises, the activities of the nation-state on behalf of capital, or sections thereof, in the international sphere. Indeed, cultural nationalism is the only ideology capable of being a legitimising ideology under the prevailing global and national political economy. Neoliberalism cannot perform this role since its simplicities make it harsh not just towards the lower orders, but give it the potential for damaging politically important interests amongst capitalist classes themselves. The activities of the state on behalf of this or that capitalist interest necessarily exceed the Spartan limits that neoliberalism sets. Such activities can only be legitimised as being 'in the national interest.' Second, however, the nationalism that articulates these interests is necessarily different from, but can easily (and given its function as a legitimising ideology, it must be said, performatively) be mis-recognised as, nationalism as widely understood: as being in some real sense in the interests of all members of the nation. In this form, cultural nationalism provides national ruling classes a sense of their identity and purpose, as well as a form of legitimation among the lower orders. As Gramsci said, these are the main functions of every ruling ideology.

Cultural nationalism masks, and to a degree resolves, the intense competition between capitals over access to the state for support domestically and in the international arena – in various bilateral and multilateral fora – where it bargains for the most favoured national capitalist interests within the global and imperial hierarchy. Except for a commitment to neoliberal policies, the economic policy content of this nationalism cannot be consistent: within the country, and internationally, the capitalist system is volatile and the positions of the various elements of capital in the national and international hierarchies shift constantly as does the economic policy of cultural nationalist governments. It is this volatility that also increases the need for corruption – since that is how competitive access of individual capitals to the state is today organised.

Whatever its utility to the capitalist classes, however, cultural nationalism can never have a settled or secure hold on those who are marginalised or subordinated by it. In neoliberal regimes the scope for offering genuine economic gains to the people at large, however measured they might be, is small. This is a problem for right politics since even the broadest coalition of the propertied can never be an electoral majority, even a viable plurality. This is only in the nature of capitalist private property. While the left remains in retreat or disarray, electoral apathy is a useful political resource but even where, as in most countries, political choices are minimal, the electorate as a whole is volatile. Despite, or perhaps because of, being reduced to a competition between parties of capital, electoral politics in the age of the New Right entails very large electoral costs, the extensive and often vain use of the media in elections and in politics generally, and political compromises which may clash with the high and shrilly ambitious demands of the primary social base in the propertied classes. Instability, uncertainty and disorientation characterises politics despite, or rather because of, the triumph of neoliberalism.

Cultural nationalism provides some means for dealing with this situation. Various degrees and varieties of inclusion in, and othering from, the dominant culture are employed to create viable electoral majorities. In these electoral coalitions of support, the proportion of economic to merely psychological rewards decreases as one goes down the economic ladder and from the centre to the periphery of the dominant coalition of interests. There are at least two sources of instability in this strategy, both of which contain the potential for violence. First, there is a potential for controlling – stopping or slowing – the upward trajectory of the propertied from othered groups, the 'minorities'. Their general cultural othering is a threat to make these groups amenable to the terms of the dominant groups. But since the positions of the dominant groups are necessarily, either relatively or absolutely, adversely affected by the rise of such groups, these terms may exhibit an irrational and escalating character. The recent call from the votaries of Hindutva that Indian Muslims 'nationalise' or 'Indianise' themselves (which is to say, accept, and not seek to disturb, the cultural, and therefore economic superiority of the predominantly Hindu capitalist classes), or the demands of the German Christian Democrats that immigrants accept the notion of a *Leitkultur* – a leading culture – are examples. The usually unspoken threat is that not complying may leave them open to violence and the state may, at the time, have better things to do than protect the victims.

Second, among the socio-economically lower sections of the 'dominant' national community, the proportion of psychological to economic rewards of belonging must, of necessity, be high for they are numerous and their economic demands prove hard to fulfil within the current neoliberal context. These psychological rewards – such as pride in one's whiteness or Hindu-ness, and the privilege of being mobilized, more or less frequently, often with the tacit complicity of the state, for symbolic or violent demonstrations – form the very substance of the relationship between the propertied classes and the poor of the 'dominant' community.

Cultural nationalism also operates through the ethnic segmentation of the labour market, putting greater obstacles in the path of class mobilisation among the poor and propertyless creating division between them in a way which allows the absorption of at least some of them into the electoral coalition of the Right. The ideology of cultural nationalism, and particularly the relative positions accorded to various working-class groups within the nation constitutes, as Etienne Balibar so clearly noted for Western Europe, a 'mechanism for differential reproduction of the labour force'. There is

> a match between (a) skill grading; (b) proportion of foreign workers; (c) the various modes of work-force reproduction which allow capital to reduce training and upkeep costs on unskilled workers by bringing them from dominated ('peripheral') regions of the world economy, where non-commodity modes of production [but more to the point less commodified forms of

reproduction] partly prevail and which lack those 'social rights' that the labour movement of the 'advanced' countries has been able to impose for more than a century.

(Balibar 1991: 13)

Balibar further argued that this type of 'cultural' politics denatures the universality of the state and the equality of citizens to serve the interests of a certain order of property and its reproduction: the state loses its 'public' character.

> The state in Europe is tending to disappear as a power-centralizing institution, one to which responsibility for policy can be ascribed and which exercises 'public' mediation (in both senses of the term) between social interests and forces. We might also express this by saying that we have entered a phase of a new-style 'privatization' of the state, but in the guise of a multiplication and superimposition of public institutions.

(Balibar 1991: 17)

Of course, it is not only the activities of the state in relation to workers but also, as we noted above, its activities in mediating the interests among the capitalists themselves which imparts to it this 'private' character. The neoliberalism of the New Right is oxymoronic in that New Right politics is premised on the violation of liberalism's political aspect: its constitutionalism.

The economic and social costs of this form of political economy are borne by the lowest strata in each country and the level of social and economic distress and disorganization that result mean that there are sizeable constituencies, and not just of the lumpen and the discouraged, who can be organised for reaction and extreme-right politics. It would be useful to see these forces in Arno Mayer's terms as 'counterrevolutionary'. Most attempts to understand the activities of contemporary extreme-right groups focus on their similarities, or otherwise, to fascism and Nazism in terms of their internal characteristics as movements. These writings are useful and one would be foolish not to take these internal similarities seriously. But Mayer would say the focus is too narrow for proper understanding. What he enables us to do, by contrast, is to see these forces as part of a family of counterrevolutionary phenomena whose practical results are, moreover, determined as much by the surrounding situation as by their intrinsic characteristics. After all, fascism in inter-war Europe, as Hobsbawm reminds us, was part of a larger threat to liberal democracy from the Right. It represented 'not merely a threat to constitutional and representative government, but an ideological threat to liberal civilization as such' in which 'by no means all the forces overthrowing liberal regimes were fascist'. Fascism 'inspired other antiliberal forces, supported them and lent the international Right a sense of historic confidence' (Hobsbawm 1994: 112).

Mayer (1971) saw counterrevolutionary groups as having a mass base and a leader. Though they could be part of the social base of mainstream right parties, they remained different and independent, 'a new but claimant political *counter-*

elite'. They could prove useful to established ruling groups, something which Brecht brought out so well in *The Resistible Rise of Arturo Ui*. Michal Kalecki saw the 'fascism of our times' in the 1960s in much the same terms, as 'a dog on a leash; it can be unleashed at any time to achieve definite aims and even when on the leash serves to intimidate the potential opposition' (Kalecki 1972: 104). Historically such counter-revolutionary groups have served to contain the left. In our times, however, the threat of challenge from the left and its prospect in the near future is minimal. Surely it is only the very volatility of right support, the meagreness of the economic concessions that are possible to enlarge and stabilise it, and the furious ambitions and greed of the propertied, which can explain the cultivation and toleration of these groups on the right. It is therefore the *hysterical* character of capital and capitalist ruling classes that is responsible for them. This is not even a case of what Mayer would call pre-emptive counterrevolution, nor anticipatory[5]. Rather it would be useful to add another category – hysterical counterrevolution. Herbert Kitschelt (Kitschelt and McGann 1997) has shown how the rise of extreme-right parties as distinct entities has occurred particularly in those countries where parties of the mainstream right have been less extreme, closer to the centre, though this situation, he observed in 1995, is fast disappearing. In other countries, these types of politics, and often the organisations themselves, are closely linked to the politics, of the mainstream right parties or are actively or tacitly tolerated and ideologically encouraged by them (Lee 2000). As the Christian Right gave a second term to George W. Bush in the US, as it had Ronald Reagan, the centrality of the extreme right to the politics of the right could hardly be underestimated.

If the foregoing strikes too dire a note, it may help to conclude with a consideration of the mutually destructive choreography of ideological *danse macabre* of neoliberalism and cultural nationalism. It makes the solidity of the New Right as a political formation more apparent than real. Cultural nationalism rests on a core of a 'national culture' which has its real, material, basis in the persistence of pre-capitalist and non-commodified (but in all class and patriarchal societies, always hierarchical and potentially authoritarian) social relationships. Its utility to the ruling classes lies precisely in the extent to which it culturally legitimises the ruling groups though establishing continuities, real and invented in differing degrees, with ruling groups in the past. But cultural nationalism today exhibits a new changeability and volatility. Not only has the intensification of capitalist penetration, extensive as well as intensive, undermined 'national cultures' based on pre-capitalist non-commodified social relations, they must now be generated, if they are to be renewed at all, in structures of cultural production, which are specifically capitalist and commodified. The forms they take are, to older eyes, inauthentic – TV shows, films, pop, rock and punk songs, videos, and other cultural *commodities* (rightly seen as the opposite of culture as hitherto understood). *Their* effect on the national cultures they claim to express can only be to mine and undermine them. And as commodities these cultural products are also subject to endemic ephemerality. In a situation where culture is commodified and the commodity (both its production and sale) is culturalised, culture is at once the basis of the domination of producers, the means through which 'material' commodities are marketed, and itself a commodity. The climate of late capitalism also, however, makes the life of a given cultural product short. Therefore cultural nationalism moves along on shifting bases and grounds, and appears very changeable precisely when its enduring character has become a resource of such importance in the stabilisation of inherently volatile political orders of the New Right. The *danse macabre* of neoliberalism and cultural nationalism may well exhaust its odious dancers: the very neoliberalism which requires cultural nationalism to legitimise it undermines the real basis of the culture from which cultural nationalism must draw its ideological power.

Notes

1 To my knowledge my M.A. thesis ('Second Hand Dealers in Ideas' Queens University, Kingston, Ontario, Canada, 1986) was the first major study of the British think tanks – the Institute of Economic Affairs, the Center of Policy Studies, the Adam Smith Institute, and the Institute of Directors – and by extension their international networks including the Mont Pèlerin Society. It was not published, however, until 1994 (Desai 1994a) and Richard Cockett's (1994) book appeared later in the same year.
2 In this book I discuss the nature of the attachment of the older generation of professionals to Labourism and the tensions within this relationship that led to the split in the Labour party in 1981, and subsequently to the creation of the Social Democratic Party.
3 That these assets are now worth $10,000 billion world-wide and that institutional investment in the US, for example, was 47 per cent of the total market capitalisation, give some indication of the relevance of this phenomenon (Blackburn 1999: 5–6).
4 Harold Perkin (1989) makes this distinction between the economic basis of the two main kinds of professionals and their political proclivities. Colin Leys and Leo Panitch (1998) discuss the social basis of the rise of New Labour.
5 Mayer (1971) considers the following types: pre-emptive, posterior, accessory, disguised, anticipatory, externally licensed and externally imposed.

13 The World Wide Web of anti-neoliberalism

Emerging forms of post-Fordist protest and the impossibility of global Keynesianism[1]

Ulrich Brand

The 'brave new world' of neoliberalism has been battered by the crises of South East Asia and other countries, and by the protests in Seattle, Genoa and elsewhere, even in the public opinion of Western countries. Hardly a politician or corporate executive can mount a public podium without speaking of the problems and dangers of capitalist globalization, although as a rule they append the corollary that nevertheless 'there is no alternative'. This much is clear, however: while the critique of neoliberal globalization in general, and of certain actors in particular, is enjoying increasing attention in the media, and networks like Attac use it quite cleverly, there are few changes to the general structural transformations in train or in neoliberal power relations. It would, of course, be nonsensical to lay this at the feet of a new, and still developing movement. It is nevertheless necessary to register the dangers and dead-ends which may lie ahead.

One of the chief dangers facing anti-neoliberal movements is surely that they may share the fate of the non-governmental organizations (NGOs) which were so celebrated in the 1990s. They launched themselves into the political fray with enormous effort and became 'cosmopolitan ghosts' (Drainville 2001: 15), focusing on a consensus with dominant forces. In doing this, however, they increasingly became an alternative resource for neoliberals in government as well as in international politics to be selectively resorted to as actors with experience and profound knowledge of complicated political and socio-economic processes. Moreover, as 'civil society' actors they provided legitimacy for the prevailing developments particularly as, at least on the 'soft issues' of environment, development, human rights and women's politics, 'civil society' sat at the table. The handling of 'hard' military or economic matters would, on the other hand, continue to be shielded from possibly critical eyes.[2] The relative failure of NGO involvement lay crucially in the lack of far-reaching critical understanding of the upheavals of neoliberal globalization among activists. This was to be especially clear in the debates and politics with regard to 'sustainable development' which were conducted more or less in isolation from the neoliberal transformation of society (Brand and Görg 2005). In the medium term it became possible that the new protest movements (or parts thereof) would become a sort of institutionalized bad conscience, with whom the powerful would meet amid high publicity, and which would always remind them to be conscious of the losers and losses of globalization and to take (usually merely symbolic) action on these now and again.

The fundamental argument of this chapter is that in order not to fall into these traps of irrelevance of the 1990s critical and emancipatory actors will have to attain clarity about the historical situation in which they operate. The configuration of post-war capitalism, usually termed Fordism, has since been transformed into 'post-Fordism.' It is still in the process of formation and does not, and probably never will, constitute a 'stable mode of development' corresponding to Fordism. Unevenness and crises are part of this new phase of capitalist development. Nevertheless, the contours of post-Fordism are identifiable and they constitute the conditions of (political) action (see Albritton *et al.* 2001; Brand and Raza 2003). This is especially the case in the capitalist centers. But since world-wide economic, political and cultural relations are dominated by these societies, features of post-Fordism do also exist in the capitalist (semi)periphery.

Herein lies the contribution of critical theory. It involves, first, working out the actual developments in bourgeois-capitalist social processes, their fractures and contradictions. This will make it clear that one of the most popular demands of the global social movements is beset with systemic problems. I am referring to the existing bias, particularly in the northern parts of the movements, in favor of a re-regulation of capitalism to deal with its rising dysfunctions; a form of (now necessarily global) Keynesianism. Proceeding from this I intend to show, second, that a critical theory of capitalist-neoliberal globalization, and an adequate concept of state and politics, can contribute substantively to detecting spaces for political action.[3] Third, however, I will also argue that theory does not furnish the 'correct politics' and nor does it develop specific strategies; developing strategies is a far more complex process. Theory can nevertheless do more to prepare the frames of reflection and thereby contribute to the further development of emancipatory movements.[4] And if this task is performed well, I argue fourth, it will no longer be necessary to take oneself onto the discursive and institutional terrain of the opponents, to accept their terms of discourse, in order to contest their claims and actions (Chesnais *et al.* 2001).

This must not be taken to mean that in order to 'have theoretical clarity' all activists will now have to read and understand Marx, Gramsci or postcolonial theory. Social movements are, thankfully, broader and very diffuse, and the motivations for protest very multi-faceted. Moreover, movements themselves develop ways of seeing and understanding the world they wish to change out of their many-sided practices: the circumstances, the opponents, the necessary strategic demands, etc. These condense themselves into concepts and overall orientations and are themselves variable. For a few years, the central focuses were concepts of 'globalization' and 'neoliberalism'. Since summer 2001 and the protests in Genoa and especially since 11 September 2001 and the following wars, the concepts of 'empire' (Hardt and Negri 2000) and 'imperialism' (Harvey 2003; Panitch and Leys 2003) became more important, the latter in order to identify the growing violence of global politics which is that of 'globalization'. Today we can state, that the movements have doubtless been successful in connecting neoliberalism to globalization. Recently, the debate about what could be unifying concepts and orientations has intensified, as Walden Bello's (2003) concept of 'de-globalization' shows.

I will begin by outlining some of the characteristics of the anti-globalization movement, and then consider one of its prominent actors, the network Attac. I will then go on to sketch some crucial ambiguities of the global social movements.

In a nutshell I call the incredibly diverse protests 'post-Fordist' not only in order to refer to the context in which they operate. The concept also makes sense because in a significant way, the ideal of Fordist society serves as a (highly problematic) reference point for parts of the actual movements. To that effect, I also narrow my focus to that part of the political spectrum with however critical-emancipatory demands. Right-wing movements and protests, which are actually stronger in many countries, fall outside the focus of this chapter, even though research and analysis of these is very important.

Aspects of global social movements[5]

Appraisals of the new protests are very different. For a long time, there was much discussion about exactly what these movements signified. Are they the 'first social movement of postmodernity' (*Der Spiegel*), a 'network guerilla' (*Financial Times*)? Are they movements for reform, or do they constitute a more fundamental opposition to neoliberal globalization? In any case, can we speak of a single movement, or are they more accurately movements? And what do they think they are about? *For* a globalization with a human face, global justice, control of (financial) markets, a re-regulation of the world economy, the democratization of international organizations, 'smash capitalism,' global socialism or communism? *Against* neoliberal globalization, the commodification of ever greater parts of the world we live in ('The world is not for sale!'), the negative consequences of privatization, the increasing gap between North and South, institutions such as the IMF/World Bank/WTO, brand-fetishism ('No Logo') and the rule of corporations? The list can go on, and is necessarily heterogeneous because the various parts of the movement are. The different interpretations do cohere, however, because to a significant extent these movements only create their effect, that is, find a certain resonance, through their reception in the media and in the prevailing political contexts.[6]

The Canadian political scientist Stephen Gill identifies a 'postmodern Prince' (a reference to the famous work of Machiavelli) in the emerging plural protests involving 'tendencies that have begun to challenge some of the myths and the disciplines of modernist practices, and specifically resisting those that seek to consolidate the project of globalization under the rule of capital' (Gill 2000: 137–8).

A central problem of political theory today is to understand and theorize these new forms of political identity and political action. The latter is, without doubt, crucial. The problem with Gill's concept of the 'postmodern Prince' is the analogy to Machiavelli and Gramsci. Machiavelli saw in the Prince the legitimate power which would solve the most important problem (which, for him, was the establishment of a unified state) and restore order. For Gramsci, the 'modern

Prince', the party, articulated particular interests into a collective will. The question then arises, what would correspond, today, to the two fundamental conditions of the 'modern Prince' – the formulation of a 'national-popular collective will' and intellectual, moral and economic reform programs (Gramsci 1975: 951–3). The actual protesters think of themselves rather differently; in particular they do not view themselves as future rulers.

Antonio Negri and Michael Hardt were styled theoretical heads of the movement in the summer of 2001 after the protests in Genoa as much by the bourgeois media as by parts of the movement itself. They see the emergence of a global 'multitude' which, as part of the global capitalism termed 'Empire', contributes to its overthrow. Capital will become superfluous and people will throw off its fetters. The attractiveness of this scheme lies not least in its (putative) coherence, consistency and positive tenor with respect to neoliberal globalization. However, the vertiginous, sometimes exhilarating, largely speculative theses of *Empire* (Hardt and Negri 2000; for a critique see Brand 2002) are mostly 'wishful thinking' and contain many weaknesses concerning a precise analysis of the contemporary situation which might help to clarify the general and specific conditions for actions for parts of the movements.

Even if one takes a closer look at particular parts of the movements, the evaluations do not become less ambiguous. Let's take the example of Attac, the most prominent part of the movement in Germany as well as in other European countries. The vice president of Attac-France, Susan George (2002), spoke of a 'zero hour'. This suggestion of great ruptures and departures served more to build a sense of identity, however, than as a realistic evaluation. At other places Susan George (2001) makes historical allusions to the fact that the counter-events at 'G-7 Summits' began as early as 1985 (as did the protests against the World Economic Forum in Davos). What was new about Seattle was that since then the protests began to be taken seriously by the media establishment. With the 'watershed' of Seattle, the diverse protests are no longer on the defensive.

Other interpretations do not hide their reservations. The new protests, according to Wolfgang Kraushaar (2002: 20–1), lack 'proofs of the practicability' of alternatives to economic liberalization and remain guilty of repeating obsolete anti-capitalist rhetoric which only attracts 'diverse left-radical groups'. Along the same lines, the German Foreign Minister Joschka Fischer saw only 'stale left-radical anti-capitalism' in the protests in Genoa (*Süddeutsche Zeitung*, 28 July 2001). This produces above all one effect: the views advocated by the protestors are denounced by mass media and politicians as unrealistic and therefore illegitimate. The one thing which the actual movements are good for lies in the demand that international organizations be democratized and thus helped to get over their legitimacy deficit (Kraushaar 2002: 11). Kraushaar is right in so far as no one can place him or herself outside the ruling system; but at the same time he portrays the process of globalization as immutable and without alternatives. It is this sort of analysis which most clearly demonstrates the need for a critical theoretical understanding of hegemony needed to overcome mainstream and schematic analyses of existing social relations.

While the *multi-faceted* character of the movements thus is usually seen as strength, many authors do point out that plurality should not become incoherence. In fact, the organizations and individuals come from different sectors of society with their experiences and focus on a wide variety of issues: (under)-development or environmental issues, peace and civil rights, labor and trade unionism, gender, feminism and anarchism, with members of progressive and radical left parties, church groups, and nationally/regionally defined groups. Moreover, the forms of action are different; some argue for information, publicity and peaceful protest, for others civil disobedience and non-violent action are important, and for others again, it is all about direct confrontation with 'the state'. A more precise typology is difficult because the phenomenon of the global social movements is hard to pin down. It does not exhaust itself in international demonstrations, but has complex and unpredictable consequences in everyday practices, and encourages and strengthens critical forces in institutions such as unions, parties, universities and elsewhere. The *label* 'anti-globalization' or 'critical of globalization', respectively, also encompasses theoretical and publicity-related activities that are not necessarily conceived of as parts of social movements. Calling the protests 'anti-globalization movement(s)' then is as much a matter of a unifying attribution by others such as the media and other interested forces, as it is of self-identification by particular actors in order to furnish themselves with an identity.

What is new? One can speak of an *international* protest movement since the confrontations over the Multilateral Agreement on Investment (MAI) in 1998 which led to a broad campaign of massive critique and, finally, to the failure of the agreement. To be sure, the critique of the MAI could be politicized because there were also contradictions within the groups of Western countries (between the USA and the EU). But since Seattle, protests against innumerable formal and informal meetings of neoliberal forces have been organized.[7]

International demonstrations are *points of crystallization* of the heterogeneous and multi-faceted movement. The spectacle of the international public events must not obscure one thing, however: the international protest movement has built itself up to a significant degree from local and national confrontations. Thus, traditional organizations such as trade unions identify themselves more and more as part of these global social movements (Moody 1997; Panitch 2000). Movements create, then, complex formative, or better, *fermenting processes*, even though their effects are not easily discernible. This perspective corrects the view of the bourgeois media which represents them as appearing from nowhere.[8] Such a 'zero hour' metaphor fails to recognize the importance of struggles that have taken place earlier and struggles that are not (or do not wish to be) counted among those usually categorized under labels such as 'global protest movements' or 'anti-globalization movements'.

The internationalization of protest and movement, which was already apparent before Seattle, has many prerequisites. Jackie Smith uses the concept of 'transnational social movement organizations', which form the backbone of the international protests, in her well-informed analysis of the Seattle protests. They emerged in the 1990s in response to international neoliberal economic policies. Smith's research supports the argument 'that social movements have developed more formalized, integrated, and sustained organizational mechanisms for transnational cooperation around global change goals' (Smith 2001: 12). Braithwaithe and Drahos (2000: 497) argue similarly, stressing particularly the role of transnational advocacy networks. The difference between more and less formalized groups is clarified to a certain extent by a division of labor between the two. The *International Forum on Globalization* (founded in 1994) or the *Third World Network* (founded in 1984) are referred to as 'cadre organizations' or 'paradigm warriors', whose public events are concerned with the critique of the neoliberal paradigm and with fundamental alternatives. The roles of alternative expertise, organizational experience and identity-formation are important for the collective learning processes, and they would be better provided by more formalized movement connections: 'formal social movement organizations play important roles in framing movement agendas, cultivating collective identities, and mobilizing collective actions' (Smith 2001: 6). Herein also lays, in my opinion, the significance of critical NGOs.[9] At the same time, as Smith argues, *groups external to the movement*, such as church organizations or trade unions, are important. Though they may, as a rule, have more limited goals, they create broader participation and legitimacy.[10] In conclusion, Smith argues:

> globalization processes have affected the ways that social movements mobilize and organize. They reveal substantial transnational ties among some of the key organizations behind the protests. While the masses of protesters were largely from cities around the United States and Canada, there was substantial representation from other parts of the world, particularly among the speakers at protest rallies and teach-ins.
>
> (Smith 2001: 11)

It was the same with the protests against the G-7 Meeting in Genoa. The broad mobilization came from Italy, in particular from trade unions and the *Rifondazione Comunista*. In Prague the mobilization was, conversely, less strong because just such local-national mobilizing actors were lacking.

A constitutional condition for the international protest movements is the possibility of faster and cheaper communication. In the shortest of times, a dense network of alternative communication has emerged through which not only factual information is exchanged but analytical perspectives and theory as well as organizational relationships are developed. Nevertheless, many of the effects unfold mostly within the bourgeois public sphere; here the social legitimacy of the causes and forms of action is struggled over just as hegemony is placed in question. Dieter Rucht (2002) is right that the protests have been strongly sustained on by their public credibility; he speaks of a 'perception revolution.' At the same time ongoing political struggle features strategies for the division of the opponents of globalization into 'good and legitimate' and 'bad and illegitimate,' generate attempts of co-option and repression (on further strategies see Smith 2002).

An unintended consequence of these strategies is to strengthen parts of the movement in that they involve providing positions for recognized spokespeople.

What do the recent events stand for in terms of their political content, not in the sense of a 'common denominator' but rather in terms of the political effects which they create? One of the most interesting aspects, certainly, lies in the fact that the movements have had success in inaugurating a new round of interpretation of the nature of social relations of our time. Meanings are always struggled over, but one central strength of neoliberalism lies, without doubt, in the fact that it has become perceived as 'everyday common sense.' In the new critiques of globalization this neoliberal everyday common sense has been put into question for the first time. The politicization of hitherto 'natural' developments follows from the critical discourses of the global social movements; their critique of neoliberal globalization may well be regarded as the smallest common denominator.

At the most general level the movement politicizes the *contradictions* of global capitalism. This is not insignificant, after years of neoliberal promises of well-being in the Western countries and its presumed inevitability in the peripheries. For instead of yielding freedom, autonomy and wealth, the practice of neoliberalism creates the opposite for many. In the center stands the deregulation and the related destruction of social rights, and further the re-commodification of social relationships, for example through the privatization of public enterprises, the destruction of social welfare institutions and the commodification of the social and natural worlds. In particular, the regulatory and systematic weaknesses of the global financial systems become ever more obvious. One central demand, namely the introduction of a tax on international capital transfers (the so-called Tobin Tax), could be politicized because it could be connected to 'insider' critiques (e.g. Soros 1998; Stiglitz 2002). The movements challenge dominant developments in categories of justice, a democratization of society (though it is unclear whether a fundamental transformation or thorough abolition of international political institutions is called for; Smith 2002), diversity (against monoculture) among others. Thus the limits of parliamentary democracy, which are evident not only in relation to the internationalization of social processes, can be held responsible for the undemocratic implementation of the neoliberal project. There is a broad consensus that non-violent direct action and civil disobedience are legitimate.

A more thoroughly conflict oriented understanding of politics was strengthened again with the new protests. Slogans such as 'Against Neoliberalism' or 'Against the Rule of Financial Markets' may be simplifying – however, they identify what every movement needs, an opponent (Bond 2003). In view of the paralysis of the Left in recent years, this is probably an advantage, a uniting general, opaque and yet undifferentiated formulae of the different segments helping to gear them for action. It will however be important in the future to analyze more precisely where social contradictions and fault-lines run today.

Finally, it is obvious that particularly at the beginning critique was expressed which was not yet backed up by any 'constructive proposals'. After many years of discredit, 'mere' protests have experienced a public rehabilitation – in particular in the form of mass protests. This appears to be related in particular to the crises of party-systems, which increasingly distinguish themselves by their refusal to cross the bounds of *Realpolitik*. Compared to this, the movements seem to offer a polyvalent space for alternative thought and action. However, over the years this point seemed to transform into a weakness, an issue to be further discussed later.

The movements in any case aim at intervening in a politically effective manner in the processes of the emerging forms of post-Fordist politics and their legitimation. This is particularly important because at the present moment different alternatives to neoliberal globalization are surfacing due to increasingly crisis-driven developments. Progressive solutions are presented in the discussion on *Global Governance* (Commission on Global Governance 1995; cf. Brand 2005). Right-wing approaches with their 'problem solution' of militarizing the globe and locking off the rich areas gain in significance at the same time (see Desai in this volume). Since the terrorist attacks on 11 September 2001 and the violent answer of the US and its allies with the 'war on terrorism' the question of war and open violence gained importance in the discussions of the movements.

While no comprehensive picture of the global social movements can be drawn in this chapter, the dominant segments of the movement in Germany and France can at least be sketched to subsequently address some important questions of problem diagnosis and strategy. The Attac network is paradigmatic for both the potential of the new social movements and for unresolved tensions as to where the movements are headed.

A 'face' of the global social movements: the Attac network[11]

In December 1998 the Chief Editor of *Le Monde Diplomatique*, Ignacio Ramonet, published an article titled 'Disarming Financial Markets'. At the end he proposed the establishment of the 'Association for a Taxation of Financial Transactions for the Aid of Citizens' (French *Association pour un Taxation des Transactions Financiers pour l'Aide aux Citoyens*) releasing a powerful dynamic. Bernhard Cassen, co-editor of *Le Monde Diplomatique*, became the President of the movement in France. The rise of Attac, at least in France, can only be understood in the context of the politicization which has taken place since the mid-1990s and the strike movement of the time. Its dynamic is also related to the currency crises in South East Asia which plunged so many societies into deep crisis in 1997–8. This brought the 'neoliberal globalization's subtle loss of acceptance' (Unmüßig 2002: 18) to a head. The enormous attraction of the Tobin Tax demand, which meanwhile has also been made by many governments, parties and even liberal economists, is easier to understand against this background.

In Germany, Attac was founded in January 2000 on the initiative of some Left NGOs. Here too the demands for a Tobin Tax and the democratic regulation of financial markets were of central importance. However, Attac-Germany initially did not have the same dynamism as its south-western neighbor. The organization became important only with the events of Genoa on the occasion of the G-7 summit which received such wide publicity and media attention. The media sought a 'face' of the movement and found it in Attac (Grefe *et al.* 2002: 156; Rucht 2002: 54).

In 2004, the network had a presence in about 40 countries and 80,000 members, half of these in France, 16,000 in Germany (www.attac.de). Loose coordination meetings take place throughout Europe every two months. The annual World Social Forum (Porto Alegre 2001, 2002, 2003 and 2005; 2004 in India) plays an important role for the international Attac movement as do the European Social Fora (Florence 2002, Paris 2003, London 2004, Athens 2006).

Attac-Germany sees itself as an 'innovative project' with a plurality of worldviews that attempts to build on the strengths of different types of organizations – NGOs, social movements, networks – and at the same time seeks to avoid their drawbacks (Attac-Koordinationskreis 2001). In fact, it is difficult to classify Attac as a particular type of organization: the initiative for its establishment came from NGOs which to this day decisively stamp its image. At the same time Attac does not behave very much like an NGO and successfully mobilizes on a broad basis. This is surely one reason for its attractiveness.

There are also no substantive 'general lines.' However, the identification of an overall orientation is possible (Attac-France 2002; Attac-Koordinationskreis 2002; George 2002). Attac concentrates on the economic dimension of globalization. According to it, the crisis dynamic of contemporary capitalism can be traced to its unleashing indicated by the dominance of financial over industrial capital. The market, it is assumed, has hastened the demise of the state and political regulation in the wake of globalization. Economic processes globalize while the political sphere remains captive of a national or, at best European framework. It may well be that it was governments which freed markets from their fetters. However, the role which the state plays in relation to unfettered markets remains shadowy. The theoretical source is usually the economic historian Karl Polanyi (1944; explicitly in George 2001: 6f.), who put forward the thesis that with the development of capitalism in the nineteenth century, the economy had 'disembedded' itself and has been socially and politically 're-embedded' through social struggles. It follows that through pressure from below, global capitalism must be re-regulated.

Neoliberal globalization as a phenomenon, meanwhile, is no longer equated with the internationalization and the instability of financial markets by Attac but is seen, rather, as a far-reaching process of social transformation which is productive of (new) power. To understand the developments taking place within the framework of globalization as an encompassing process of transformation in a critical fashion is itself a process of clarification and politicization that in turn made it possible to launch campaigns against privatization of pensions or health care. Privatization efforts in turn increasingly appear as special interest-driven processes that discriminate against many people and not as ideologically neutral processes expressive of an alleged public interest.

A few Attac intellectuals have explicitly formulated the project of a global Keynesianism. Susan George brought the concept of a 'planetary contract' into the discussion after 11 September 2001. According to this vision, environmental destruction, social division, the crisis of democracy and economic recession are increasing and must be fought worldwide. The main problem, in view of the discredited World Bank and IMF, is an 'institutional vacuum' to be filled (George 2001: 7). The political momentum appears to be towards functioning in the form of *checks and balances* in the sense of a countervailing control of power which would hold back the neoliberals and make a 'new modernized and globalized Keynesian strategy' possible. It would appear that for George it's all about a better regulation of global capitalism and a global Keynesianism (2001: 9–10).

Another important contribution was the Manifesto put forward in January 2002 by Attac-France, 'Re-conquer the Future with Attac' which was well received. It contains a remarkable text which indicates the breadth of the areas of conflict, and the range of possible alternatives. Certainly it seems to state clearly that the citizens' movement should prioritize work in the public sphere and the strengthening of national parliaments and their control, thus transforming state policies. Public education and awareness-raising about how corporations and neoliberal governments pursue their interests and commodify ever greater parts of human life is seen as crucial. It's a matter of formulating clear statements, identifying opponents and manifesting the indignation to be used in political engagement. However, the incomparably more complex process of dismantling political, economic and social relationships of domination in so many different areas of life is left out of sight. There are the good (us) and the bad (them); ambiguities and one's own entanglements remain outside this paradigm. Perhaps this must be so in a Manifesto aiming for broad public effect. But a number of questions must be raised. Will the post-Fordist social movements eventually generate a critical mass capable of convincing political elites to launch global re-regulation reminiscent of national welfare state politics? Or must their impact necessarily lie elsewhere due to the lack of important conditions for such a project owing to the intertwined transformations of the national and international political economies that effectively foreclose a strategy of 'super sizing' welfare politics akin to the 'embedded liberalism' of the Fordist era?

Some consequences: ambiguities of the global social movements

While other important conflicts need to be discussed such as the question of militancy (see BUKO 2001; Albert 2003) and the association with the bourgeois public sphere (see Rucht 2002), I want to confine the analysis in this section to the political-strategic orientation of a part of the global social movements with regard to global Keynesianism in order to clearly recognize and further elaborate on various, partly irresolvable *ambiguities*. After years of networking, construction and public debate it is quite obvious that there are some important strategic deficiencies notwithstanding notable success. And, even more important, the neoliberal/neo-imperial offensive of capital expressed in the transformation of the state, neoliberal international politics, the reconfiguration of power relations, the commodification of societal relations and growing violence have not been halted let alone reversed. From a general perspective there seems to be little space for emancipatory politics.

My argument here is that it could be helpful to think of the actual world order as the framework for strategies with the concept of hegemony in the sense Antonio Gramsci developed it. It combines aspects of 'political leadership' and 'consensus.' Hegemony is to be understood as the ability of the ruling groups and classes to pursue their interests in such a way that they are regarded as common or general interests by ruled groups and classes, and that there are broadly shared ideas about social relations and their development.[12] To this extent hegemony is the 'active consent of the ruled'. This does not mean only an apparent consensus around particular relationships and practices but rather an encompassing material praxis, 'that is to say, the daily initiatives of many individuals and social groups, in which they convey their acceptance of the regime in the form of an active consent to the commonly shared habits of the greater collective' (Demirovic 1997: 257). Consensus is neither a passive affair nor a harmonious balance of interests. The concept makes much better sense against the background of social struggles and the interests which are articulated in (and form themselves through) the political process. The relative pacification or institutionalization of struggles is achieved through (asymmetrical) social compromises, in which the relevant and articulated interests are accommodated. The social 'space' for struggles over hegemony is, according to Gramsci, civil society. The connection between the state in its narrow sense with its various apparatus and the *società civile*, the privately organized apparatus of hegemony, Gramsci conceptualizes as the integral state. Hegemony is, then, manufactured not only through the state but in a more completely social process. Social struggles focus not only on the apparatus of the state but on the balance or relationship of forces in what Gramsci understands as an expanded state, and on the terrain of private capitalist production. Neo-Gramscian approaches to 'International Political Economy' have worked out these concepts at the international level (Cox 1983; Bieling and Deppe 1996).

First, the new social movements clearly recognize that strengthening the power of capital (through the political deregulation of capital controls and subsequently increasing capital mobility in particular) was a key policy developed in order to overcome the unfolding crisis of Fordism since the mid-1970s. Different parts of the movement have successfully politicized the political architecture of 'casino capitalism' (Strange 1997). Differences are visible, however, with regard to the question of whether the growing power of capital is that of capital as a whole or above all that of finance capital, the one element of neoliberal globalization that is recognized to propel the actual crisis dynamic (Attac-Deutschland 2002). Global re-regulation perspectives focus primarily on the need to 're-embed' financial capital thus without addressing capitalist exploitation in a more systematic way.

Second, movement positions with regard to the state are even more ambiguous. The increasing adoption of neoliberal governance forms and ever-stronger neoliberal political practices have been criticized by the movements. Thus, the state has certainly been understood as a domination-creating institution by a great part of the movements. But nevertheless the state is also supposed to be a potential source of the representation of general societal interests. Here a view of the state, which can organize a relatively crisis-free functioning of capitalism through its intervention, is predominant. As for international politics, not only in the mainstream of political science, but also in parts of the actual protest movements, the assumption dominates that politics must embed the economic process of globalization. While considerable politicization processes have been successful, they have been connected with a very traditional element of 'everyday common sense,' namely the idea that the state must pursue public and general interests rather than those of special interests. Certainly this interpretation fails to solve theoretical contradictions with regard to an adequate understanding of the state and thus runs the danger of preserving a common economist misinterpretation of neoliberalism as a result of global capitalism, while implemented by governments (TINA!) ultimately 'against the state'.

The crucial question with regard to the role of state-centered politics in recent social transformations clearly needs to be answered in order to clarify the social movement perspective. Since political forces have propelled neoliberal processes actively empowered by changing power relations of social forces, politics at the local, national and international levels do not stand against the 'economy' and the neoliberal orientation of society as a whole; the transformation of the political system is characterized by processes of de-institutionalization of welfare state and corporatist class compromises and an institutionalization of neoliberal governance practices, institutionally and ideologically stabilizing and legitimizing neoliberal interests and trajectories so far. Given the contemporary situation, therefore, to expect anti-neoliberal politics from state actors appears to merely articulate wishful thinking. In large parts of the 'northern' anti-globalization movement the neoliberal perspective – 'market versus state' – is reproduced. The capitalist character of the state with its fundamental (but also contested) functions, its actual transformation from a social liberal welfare into a neoliberal competition state, and the dominant new constitutionalism of 'disciplinary neoliberalism' (Gill 1993) are hardly discussed. The current politicization and mobilization of people was certainly achieved with a common understanding of the state as a more or less 'neutral' element which normally pursues general interests and has actually become too close to dominant interests. The image of a rollback of the state in favor of the market as postulated by the neoliberals is uncritically accepted and countered with a reverse state–market-dichotomy to strengthen the state. With respect to international politics a similar pattern can be observed. Globalization is understood as an economic process which must now be politically re-regulated.

The paradox of the actual social transformation lies in the fact that contrary to the illusion of a complete emancipatory transfiguration of social relationships through the state we are anew confronted with the limits of state-centered politics. This should not occasion any self-satisfaction for Left positions, since it involves the dismantling of the fundamental rights of subjected social groups. A skeptical analysis of economics *and* politics in any case has to be more strongly 'linked ... to the idea of the self-defense of society against the disintegrating and atomizing thrust of globalizing economic forces' (Gill 1993: 17). A critical understanding of the state opens room for a more radical critique of relationships of power and domination, which have to be more fundamentally challenged in a truly emancipatory perspective. Sklair (1998), for example, emphasizes the disruption of consumerism at local levels as the possibly crucial aspect of the variegated fight against neoliberal globalization. There should be no illusion in any case that the bourgeois capitalist state is a central actor and terrain for the maintenance of power and domination and thus cannot be easily understood as a bulwark against neoliberalism. To take this up and to take it forward is one of the *essentials* of emancipatory politics. It also becomes clear just here that a resurrected Fordism must not serve as a background for actual critique. All the same, and this represents a further ambiguity, the defense of Fordist social welfarist attainments is an important and long-cherished aspect.

The contemporary movements definitely have, in my view, the potential to radicalize and internationalize the practical critique of state and politics in order to account for actual changes. A critical focus on the ruling political concepts can be relativized and at the same time radicalized with the actual (international, European or elsewhere articulated) protests. They can be *relativized* if state-centered politics is understood as one part of the broader transformations. The transformative power of alternative everyday practices can come into view leaving it no longer a matter (only) of 'the question of power' but of attempting an encompassing politicization and transformation of society in complicated 'wars of position' (Gramsci). The *radicalization* would consist in resolving the problematic narrowing-down of state and politics. In fact, the movements have been partly successful in this.[13]

To sum up, the global social movements and Attac in particular are a project full of necessary and widely accepted tensions which started with strong Neo-Kenynesian perspectives and is partly radicalizing due to an experience of governments and corporations not sufficiently responding to criticism and widespread protest. Discussions and learning processes are broadening the perspectives beyond a Neo-Keynesian project. The practical and theoretical critique of the state has to be internationalized to go beyond mainstream conceptions of 'global governance' as an alternative to global neoliberalism. International institutions such as the WTO, IMF and World Bank have experienced transformations analogous to the nation-states, expressive of the wider neoliberal social transformation which implies, in particular, the subordination of social action to the imperatives of international competitiveness and the uncritical acceptance of capitalist property and productive relationships (easily observable in the 'Washington Consensus' and the World Bank's 'new visions of growth'). While global institutions and international organizations are neither simply instruments of the ruling countries nor the lackey of capital, they do condense at the international level bourgeois-capitalist and imperialist relations of forces and the results of social struggles. Though foreign policies continue to be conducted with reference to alleged 'national interests', they also continue to be expressions of antagonistic power relations and social struggles still mostly contained in nation-state configurations.

Conclusion

A theoretical understanding of hegemony which does not depend on social dichotomies such as 'above/below' or 'evil/good' or state/market can be fruitfully connected with the concept of hegemony in the Gramscian tradition. For the future of the new social movements, this has at four implications.

The implementation of neoliberal globalization as a social project instead implies, first, that alternatives cannot focus solely on state-centered politics. It is a matter of transforming social relations of force. One rather narrowly formulated reform perspective urges – strategically or out of conviction – the belief that, with corresponding 'pressure from below,' enlightened elites can be convinced of the need to make political change.

A critical theoretical understanding of hegemony in relation to civil society implies, second, that alternative strategies or even counter-hegemonic projects definitely emerge from within civil society, but never from civil society as a whole. Civil society is itself riven with divisions; the dominant classes and forces establish themselves and operate precisely *in* civil society. In addition, the field of private production and therefore the significance of labor remains a fundamental terrain of social struggles (Sklair 1998; Panitch 2000). Neoliberal governmentality must then also be questioned because the actual situation clearly has a great plausibility for many. This questioning takes place in very different ways with many-sided approaches, which go beyond the attention-grabbing symbolic confrontations with the state, international institutions or capital.

One can speak of hegemony, third, if the ruling forces can successfully define the discursive and institutional terrain of struggles and compromise-building. (Chesnais *et al.* 2001). At the discursive level the movements can list a few successes, in particular – even though one should not entertain illusions about the broad social effects – the increasing questioning of neoliberalism as 'everyday common sense'. Here the question is how far certain 'discourse settings' should be accepted where accepted relationships of recognition and subordination are reproduced, for example in the form of lobbyism. This would hardly place such hegemonic forms of politics any more in question. On the institutional level it looks more difficult. As the debates around the MAI, the WTO, the IMF/World Bank, Group of 7 or the World Economic Forum show, the emerging forms of hegemonic politics are increasingly in question, and indeed not only by the international protest movement but also from some governments. The quarrel between the US and the EU about the MAI as also the growing critique of the developing countries – for example around the TRIPS agreement – make clear that the fundamental direction is by no means clear. This does not negate the domination of the international institutions and the overriding significance of a 'global economic constitutionalism', but does show the fragility generated not least by US unilateral reservations against a more coherent introduction of the 'global rule of law'.

The question of international hegemony leads to the fourth aspect, which prompts Joachim Hirsch (2002) to speak of a 'non-hegemonic situation'. If hegemony means – among other things (Alnasseri *et al.* 2001; Brand and Raza 2003) – that the ruling forces can exercise leadership and are able and willing to make material compromises with ruled social forces, then deregulation and privatization in the wake of neoliberal globalization have led to a situation where the dominant states can exercise hegemony less and less because – not to put too fine a point on it – they lack the means to do so. The alternative project of a global Keynesianism here becomes visibly fragile. Beyond this, a general limit on any Fordist–Keynesian style politics of global redistribution lies in the fact that the international capitalist state system is marked not only by corporate but quite decisively by economic and political competition. This constellation also leads us to see the assumptions of a global Keynesianism critically, and hope for further and genuinely innovative contributions from the new social movements.

Notes

1 Thanks to Christoph Görg, Joachim Hirsch, Albert Scharrenberg and the editors for their valuable comments and Radhika Desai for her excellent translation.
2 This is no NGO-bashing; naturally, there are, among them, very different actors. All the same, in the definition of the new protest movement, the outlines of an ideal-typical actor can be worked out.
3 This point is in no way exhaustive: analyses concerning subjectivities and identities, in light of a critical media theory, research about the internationalization of the economic in the narrow sense, that is, of markets and its actors, etc., are necessary.
4 The manner in which theoretical insights play a role in specific parts of movements is a more complex process which deserves to be researched in its own right.
5 In Germany the dominant concept is 'movement critical to neoliberal globalization' (in singular) or 'Movement against Neoliberal Globalisation' (Wahl 2003), in the Anglo-Saxon world it is referred to more often as the 'anti-globalization movement(s)', 'movement(s) against corporate globalization' or as 'global justice movement(s)'. Bond (2003) speaks, for example, of 'anti-capitalist movements', Callinicos (2003) of an 'anti-capitalist movement'. In recent years the concept of 'movement of movements' became more important. In recent time, the concept of (anti)imperialism was re-introduced and got some attraction. To me, the concept of global social movements appears most adequate.
6 In this section, I refer mostly to the German debate which I know best.
7 The more important among these have been the protests against the informal World Economic Forums and 'G-7' summits, against formal meetings of the IMF and the World Bank, against EU conferences and Free Trade Zone for the Americas planning meetings. The World Social Forum in Porto Alegre, which has been regionalized since 2002, would be seen as a qualitative leap (Köhler and Brand 2002).
8 Another early point of departure for parts of the movements has been the uprising of the Zapatistas in 1994 (Holloway and Peláez 1998; Ceceña, Seoane, Zibechi, Brand and Hirsch in the Antipode Intervention Symposium 36(3), June 2004) and the 'First Meeting against Neoliberalism and for a Human Society' held in Chiapas in the

summer of 1996. Many of the slogans being shouted across the world today – 'ya basta' (it's enough!) or 'Another World is Possible!' – came from the Zapatistas.
9 In the research on social movements this circumstance has already been pointed out. 'Movement organizations are voluntary associations (associations, clubs, civil associations, church institutions etc.) which to some extent constitute the chassis of a social movement ... Social movements *need* movement organizations as structural backbones, they *are* however no organizations, but rather dynamic public events beyond these organizations' (Janett 1997: 146). The concept of *movement infrastructure* is a further development from this insight, that is to say, 'the totality of the groups, organizations, networks which can be assigned to a movement or a family of movements' (ibid., Janett 1997: 52).
10 However, since the line between being part of the movements or not is not fixed groups in churches or unions understand themselves as parts of the global social movements.
11 Parts of this section have been taken from Brand and Wissen (2002) in which we look at Attac in greater detail.
12 Historically specific societal forms are not differentiated by class interests only. Rather there are also different interests that go beyond them: democratic, gender-specific, 'ethnic', on peace issues, or social-ecological interests. Many-faceted and contradictory strategies, also encompassing social practices, meet in the most different encounters and condense via social compromises into a generalised consensus. Social hegemony encompasses not only classes, but also other political forces; correspondingly struggles over hegemony always take place in coalitions.
13 To give an example: since Attac understands itself as an actor and space of *éducation populaire* it is interesting to see, taking the annual summer schools of Attac-Germany with 600 to 1,000 participants as an indicator, that there is an enormous will to understand the complex reality and to formulate feasible and at the same time radical proposals in order to change the world.

References

Adorno, Theodor W[iesengrund] (1963 [1955]) 'Aldous Huxley und die Utopie', in Theodor W. Adorno, *Prismen. Kulturkritik und Gesellschaft*, Munich: DTV.
AFX News Unlimited (2000) 'Summers Says IMF, World Bank Reform Proposal Would "Straightjacket" Agencies', in *AFX News Unlimited*, AFX-Asia, 23 March.
Aidt, Toke and Zafiris Tzannatos (2002) *Unions and Collective Bargaining*, Washington, DC: World Bank.
Aikman, David (1986) *The Pacific Rim: Area of Change, Area of Opportunity*, Boston: Little, Brown.
Albert, Michael (2003) *The Trajectory of Change. Activist Strategies for Social Transformation*, Cambridge, MA: South End Press.
Albritton, Robert, Makoto Itoh, Richard Westra and Alan Zuege (eds) (2001) *Phases of Capitalist Development. Booms, Crises and Globalization*, London: Palgrave.
Alnasseri, Sabah, Ulrich Brand, Thomas Sablowski and Jens Winter (2001) 'Space, Regulation and the Periodisation of Capitalism', in Robert Albritton, Makoto Itoh, Richard Westra and Alan Zuege (eds) *Phases of Capitalist Development. Booms, Crises and Globalization*, London: Palgrave: 163–78.
Alvarez Galván, José Luis and Enrique Dussel Peters (2001) 'Causas y efectos de los Programas de Promoción Sectorial (PROSEC) en la Economía mexicana: ¿un segundo TLCAN para con terceros países?', *Comercio Exterior*, 51(5): 446–56.
American Enterprise Institute (AEI) (2002) 'About AEI', Washington, DC: AEI. Available HTTP: www.aei.org.
Amsden, Alice H. (1989) *Asia's Next Giant: South Korea and Late Industrialization*, New York: Oxford University Press.
—— (2001) *The Rise of 'The Rest': Challenges to the West from Late-Industrializing Economies*, Oxford: Oxford University Press.
Anderson, Perry (1996) 'A Sense of the Left', in *New Left Review*, I(231): 73–81.
—— (1997) 'Neoliberalismus. Bilanz und Perspektiven für die Linke', in *Sozialistischen Zeitung* (supplement), 30 October.
—— (1998) *The Origins of Postmodernity*, London: Verso.
—— (2001) 'Testing Formula Two', in *New Left Review*, II(8): 5–22.
Anderson, Poul (1956) 'Margin of Profit', in *Astounding Science Fiction*, 58(1), New York: Street & Smith: 43–62.
—— (1978 [1967]) *World Without Stars*, New York: Ace.
Anheier, Helmut K. (2003) 'Das Stiftungswesen in Deutschland: Eine Bestandsaufnahme in Zahlen', in Bertelsmann Stiftung (ed.) *Handbuch Stiftungen. Ziele – Projekte – Management – Rechtliche Gestaltung*, Gütersloh: Verlag Bertelsmann Stiftung: 43–85.

Anheimer, Helmut and Nuno Themudo (2002) 'Organizational Forms of Global Civil Society: Implications of Going Global', in Helmut Anheimer, Marlies Glasius and Mary Kaldor (eds) *Global Civil Society 2002*, Oxford: Oxford University Press: 191–216.

Apeldoorn, Bastiaan van (2000) 'Transnationale Klassen und europäisches Regieren: Der European Round Table of Industrialists', in Hans-Jürgen Bieling and Jochen Steinhilber (eds) *Dimensions of a Critical Theory of European Integration*, Münster: Westfälisches Dampfboot: 83–110.

Appadurai, Arjun (1996) *Modernity at Large: Cultural Dimensions of Globalization*, Minneapolis: University of Minnesota Press.

Arestis, Philip and Panicos Demetriades (1999) 'Financial Liberalization: The Experience of Developing Countries', *Eastern Economic Journal*, 25(4): 441–57.

Ariyoshi, Akira, Karl Habermeier, Bernard Laurens, Inci Otker-Robe, Jorge Iván Canales-Kriljenko and Andrei Kirilenko (2000) *Country Experiences with the Use and Liberalization of Capital Controls*, IMF Occasional Paper No. 190, Washington DC: IMF.

Aspe Armella, Pedro (1993) *El camino mexicano de la transformación económica*, México: Fondo de Cultura Económica.

Aspinall, Edward and Mark T. Berger (2001) 'The Breakup of Indonesia? Nationalisms After Decolonisation and the Limits of the Nation-State in Post-Cold War Southeast Asia', *Third World Quarterly: Journal of Emerging Areas*, 22(6): 1003–24.

Atlas Foundation (2002) 'Freedom Directory'. Available HTTP: www.atlasusa.org/directory (accessed 30 April 2003).

Attac-Deutschland (ed.) (2002) *Eine andere Welt ist möglich*, Hamburg: VSA-Verlag.

Attac-France (2002) 'Manifest 2002 – Mit Attac die Zukunft zurückerobern', in Attac-Deutschland (ed.) *Eine andere Welt ist möglich*, Hamburg: VSA-Verlag: 30–49.

Attac-Koordinationskreis (2002) 'Zwischen Netzwerk, NGO und Bewegung. 8 Thesen', in Attac-Deutschland (ed.) *Eine andere Welt ist möglich*, Hamburg: VSA-Verlag: 12–7.

Aust, Andreas (2001) 'The Party of European Socialists (PES) and European Employment Policies: From "Eurokeynesianism" to "Third Way Policies"?', paper presented at the ECPR Joint Sessions in Grenoble, 6–11 April.

Ayer, Alfred J. (1936) *Language, Truth and Logic*, London: Victor Gollancz.

Babb, Sarah (2001) *Managing Mexico. Economists from Nationalism to Neoliberalism*, Princeton and Oxford: Princeton University Press.

Baker, James T. (1987) *Ayn Rand*, Boston: Twayne.

Balanyá, Belen, Anne Doherty, Olivier Hoedeman and Erik Wesselius (2000) *Europe Inc: Regional and Global Restructuring and the Rise of Corporate Power*, London: Pluto Press.

Balassa, Bela (1981) *The Newly Industrializing Countries in the World Economy*, New York: Pergamon Press.

—— (1982) *Development Strategies in Semi-Industrial Economies*, Baltimore: Johns Hopkins University Press.

—— (1988) 'The Lessons of East Asian Development: An Overview', *Economic Development and Cultural Changes*, 36(3), supplement: 273–90.

—— (1989) *Comparative Advantage, Trade Policy and Economic Development*, New York University Press, New York.

Balassa, Bela and J. Williamson (1990) 'Adjusting to Success: Balance of Payments Policy in the East Asian NICs', *Policy Analysis in International Economics*, 17: 1–137.

Balcerowicz, Leszek (1995) *Socialism, Capitalism, Transformation*, Budapest, London and New York: Central University Press.

Balibar, Etienne (1991) 'Es gibt keinen Staat in Europa', in *New Left Review* I(186): 5–19.

Bamyeh, Mohammed A. (2000) *The Ends of Globalization*, Minneapolis: University of Minnesota Press.
BANXICO (Banco de México) (2003) *Resultados de las encuestas de evaluación coyuntural del mercado crediticio. Cuarto trimestre de 2002*, México: Banxico.
Barber, Benjamin (1995) *Jihad Versus McWorld*, New York: Times Books.
Barnet, Richard J. and John Cavanagh (1994) *Global Imperial Corporations and the New World Order Dreams*, New York: Simon and Schuster.
Bartz, Olaf (2002) 'Das Konzept der "nachlaufenden Studiengebühren"', in BdWi/fzs (ed.): *Bildungsfinanzierung*, Marburg: BdWi-Verlag: 12–15.
Bates, Robert H. (1981) *Markets and States in Tropical Africa: The Political Basis of Agricultural Policies*, Berkeley: University of California Press.
—— (1989) *Beyond the Miracle of the Market: The Political Economy of Agrarian Development in Kenya*, Cambridge: Cambridge University Press.
Bauer, Peter T. (1981) *Equality, the Third World, and Economic Delusion*, Cambridge: Harvard University Press.
—— (1984) *Reality and Rhetoric: Studies in the Economics of Development*, London: Weidenfeld and Nicolson.
Bellah, Robert, Richard Madsen, William M. Sullivan, Ann Swidler and Steven M. Tipton (1985) *Habits of the Heart. Individualism and Commitment in American Life*, Berkeley: University of California Press.
Bello, Walden (2003) *De-Globalization: Ideas for a New World Economy*, London: Zed Books.
Bennhold, Martin (2002) 'Die Bertelsmann Stiftung, das CHE und die Hochschulreform: Politik der "Reform" als Politik der Unterwerfung', in Ingrid Lohmann and Rainer Rilling (eds) *Die verkaufte Bildung. Kritik und Kontroversen zur Kommerzialisierung von Schule, Weiterbildung, Erziehung und Wissenschaft*, Opladen: Leske + Budrich: 279–99.
Berger, Mark T. (1997) 'The Triumph of the East? The East Asian Miracle and Post-Cold War Capitalism', in Mark T. Berger and Douglas A. Borer (eds) *The Rise of East Asia: Critical Visions of the Pacific Century*, London: Routledge.
—— (1999) 'Bringing History Back In: The Making and Unmaking of the East Asian Miracle', *Internationale Politik und Gesellschaft* (3): 237–52.
—— (2001a) 'The Rise and Demise of National Development and the Origins of Post-Cold War Capitalism', *Millennium: Journal of International Studies*, 30(2): 211–34.
—— (2001b) 'The Nation-State and the Challenge of Global Capitalism', *Third World Quarterly: Journal of Emerging Areas*, 22(6): 889–907.
—— (2002) 'Battering Down the Chinese Walls: The Antinomies of Anglo-American Liberalism and the History of East Asian Capitalism in the Shadow of the Cold War', in Christopher Justin Wee Wan-ling (ed.) *Capitalism, the State and Local Cultures and Identities in the 'New Asia'*, Singapore: Institute of Southeast Asian Studies: 77–106.
—— (2003) 'The New Asian Renaissance and Its Discontents: National Narratives, Pan-Asian Visions and the Changing Post-Cold War Order', *International Politics: A Journal of Transnational Issues and Global Problems*, 40(2): 195–221.
—— (2004a) *The Battle for Asia: From Decolonization to Globalization*, London: RoutledgeCurzon.
—— (2004b) 'After the Third World? History, Destiny and the Fate of Third Worldism', *Third World Quarterly*, 25(1): 9–39.
Berger, Mark T. and Mark Beeson (1998) 'Lineages of Liberalism and Miracles of Modernisation: The World Bank, the East Asian Trajectory and the International Development Debate', *Third World Quarterly: Journal of Emerging Areas*, 19(3): 487–504.
Bergsten, C. Fred, Richard Huber, Jerome I. Levinson and Esteban Edward Torres (2000) 'Dissenting Statement', International Financial Institution Advisory Commission.

Available HTTP: http://banking.senate.gov/00_03hrg/030900/bergsten.htm (accessed 21 January 2005).
Bernstein, Jay (ed.) (1994) *The Frankfurt School: Critical Assessments*, vol. 1, London: Routledge.
Bertelsmann-Stiftung (ed.) (1997) *Operative Stiftungsarbeit. Strategien – Instrumente – Perspektiven*, Gütersloh: Verlag Bertelsmann Stiftung.
Bester, Alfred (1953 [1951]) *The Demolished Man*, New York: Signet.
Beveridge, William Henry (1944) *Full Employment in a Free Society*, Woking: Unwin.
Bhagwati, Jagdish N. (1987) 'Protectionism: Old Wine in New Bottles', in Dominick Salvatore (ed.) *The New Protectionist Threat to World Welfare*, New York: North Holland: 31–44.
—— (1988), *Protectionism*, Cambridge: The MIT Press.
—— (1991) 'Is Free Trade Passé After All?', in Ad Koekkoek and L. B. M. Mennes (eds) *International Trade and Global Development*, London: Routledge: 10–42.
Bhagwati, Jagdish N. and Anne O. Krueger (1985) 'Exchange Control, Liberalization and Economic Development', in Jagdish N. Bhagwati and Gene Grossman (eds) *Essays in Development Economics, vol. 2: Dependence and Interdependence*, Cambridge: The MIT Press: 68–79.
Bieler, Andreas (2000) *Globalisation and Enlargement of the European Union. Austrian and Swedish Social Forces in the Struggle over Membership*, London: Routledge.
Bieler, Andreas and Adam David Morton (2001) 'Introduction: Neo-Gramscian Perspectives in International Political Economy and the Relevance to European Integration', in Andreas Bieler and Adam David Morton (eds) *Social Forces in the Making of the New Europe*, Houndsmills: Palgrave: 3–24.
Bieling, Hans-Jürgen (2000) *Dynamiken sozialer Spaltung und Ausgrenzung. Gesellschaftstheorien und Zeitdiagnosen*, Münster: Westfälisches Dampfboot.
—— (2003) 'European Employment Policy Between Neo-Liberal Rationalism and Communitarianism', in Henk Overbeek (ed.) *The Political Economy of European Employment*, London: Routledge: 51–73.
Bieling, Hans-Jürgen and Deppe, Frank (1996) 'Gramscianismus in der Internationalen Politischen Ökonomie. Eine Problemskizze', in *Das Argument* 217, S. 729–740.
Bieling, Hans-Jürgen and Jochen Steinhilber (2000) 'Hegemoniale Projekte im Prozeß der europäischen Integration', in Hans-Jürgen Bieling and Jochen Steinhilber (eds) *Die Konfiguration Europas. Dimensionen einer kritischen Integrationstheorie*, Münster: Westfälisches Dampfboot: 102–30.
Bildungskommission der Landes NRW (1995) *Zukunft der Bildung – Schule der Zukunft*, Neuwied: Ministerium des Landes NRW.
Bildungskommision der Heinrich-Böll-Stiftung (1. Empfehlung) (= Böll I) (2001) *Bildungsfinanzierung in der Wissensgesellschaft*, Berlin: Heinrich-Böll-Stiftung.
Birner, Jack and Rudy van Zijp (eds) (1994) *Hayek, Co-ordination and Evolution: His Legacy in Philosophy, Politics, Economics and the History of Ideas*, London: Routledge.
Bishop, Matthew (2002) 'Capitalism and Its Troubles: A Survey of International Finance', *The Economist*, 18 May.
Bislev, Sven, Dorte, Salskov-Iversen and Hans Krause Hansen (2002) 'The Global Diffusion of Managerialism: Transnational Discourse Communities at Work', *Global Society*, 16(2): 199–212.
Bjork, James (1995) 'The Uses of Conditionality: Poland and the IMF', *East European Quarterly*, 29(1): 89–123.
Blackburn, Robin (1999) 'The New Collectivism: Pension Reform, Grey Capitalism and Complex Socialism', *New Left Review* I(233): 3–65.
Blair, Tony (1997) *New Britain. My Vision of a Young Country*, Boulder: Westview Press.

Blecker, Robert A. (1999) *Taming Global Finance*, Washington, DC: Economic Policy Institute.
Blinkhorn, Martin (ed.) (1990) *Fascists and Conservatives: The Radical Right and the Establishment in the Twentieth Century*, London: Unwin Hyman.
Blumenthal, Sidney (1986) *The Rise of the Counter-Establishment: From Conservative Ideology to Political Power*, New York: Times Books.
Boardman, Robert B. (1991) *Savior of Fire*, Melbourne Beach, FL: Blue Note Books.
Bobbio, Norberto (1994) *Rechts und Links. Gründe und Bedeutungen einer politischen Unterscheidung*, Berlin: Rotbuch Verlag.
Bockman, Johanna and Gil Eyal (2002) 'Eastern Europe as a Laboratory for Economic Knowledge: The Transnational Roots of Neoliberalism', *American Journal of Sociology* 108(2): 310–52.
Bohle, Dorothee (2002) *Europas neue Peripherie. Polens Transformation und transnationale Integration*, Münster: Westfälisches Dampfboot.
Bond, Patrick (2003) 'Embryonic African Anti-Capitalism', in Rachel Neumann and Andy Hsiao (eds) *Anti-Capitalism: A Field Guide to the Global Justice Movement*, New York: New Press.
Borden, William S. (1984) *The Pacific Alliance: United States Foreign Economic Policy and Japanese Trade Recovery, 1947–1955*, Madison: University of Wisconsin Press.
Bourdieu, Pierre (1982) *Die feinen Unterschiede. Kritik der gesellschaftlichen Urteilskraft*, Frankfurt/M.: Suhrkamp.
—— (1992) *Homo academicus*, Frankfurt/M.: Suhrkamp.
—— (1993) 'Der Rassismus der Intelliganz', in Pierre Bourdieu, *Soziologische Fragen*, Frankfurt/M.: Suhrkamp: 252–6.
—— (1996) *The State Nobility. Elite Schools in the Field of Power*, Cambridge: Polity Press.
—— (1997) 'Die Abdankung des Staates', in Pierre Bourdieu et al. *Das Elend der Welt. Zeugnisse und Diagnosen alltäglichen Leidens an der Gesellschaft*, Konstanz: Universitätsverlag Konstanz: 207–15.
—— (1998a) *Gegenfeuer. Wortmeldungen im Dienste des Widerstands gegen die neoliberale Invasion*, Konstanz: Universitätsverlag Konstanz.
—— (1998b) *Praktische Vernunft. Zur Theorie des Handelns*, Frankfurt/M.: Suhrkamp.
—— (2001) *Das politische Feld. Zur Kritik der politischen Vernunft*, Konstanz: Universitätsverlag Konstanz.
Bourdieu, Pierre and Jean-Claude Passeron (1971) *Die Illusion der Chancengleichheit. Untersuchungen zur Soziologie des Bildungswesens am Beispiel Frankreich*, Stuttgart: Ernst Klett Verlag.
Bourdieu, Pierre, Luc Boltanski, Monique de Saint Martin and Pascale Maldidier (1981) *Titel und Stelle. über die Reproduktion sozialer Macht*, Frankfurt/M.: Suhrkamp.
Bradbury, Ray (1958 [1950]) *The Martian Chronicles*, Garden City, NY: Doubleday.
Braithwaite, John and Peter Drahos (eds) (2000) *Global Business Regulation*, Cambridge: Cambridge University Press.
Brand, Ulrich (2002) 'Die Revolution der globalisierungsfreundlichen Multitude. "Empire" als voluntaristisches Manifest', *Das Argument*, 44(245): 209–19.
—— (2005) 'Order and Regulation: Global Governance as a Hegemonic Discourse of International Politics?', *Review of International Political Economy*, 12(1), 155–176.
Brand, Ulrich and Christoph Görg (forthcoming) 'Sustainablity and Globalisation: A Theoretical Perspective', in K. Conca, M. Finger and J. Park (eds) *Sustainability, Globalization and Governance*.
Brand, Ulrich and Joachim Hirsch (2004) 'In Search for Emancipatory Politics. The Resonances of Zapatism in Western Europe', *Antipode*, 36(3): 371–82.
Brand, Ulrich and Werner Raza (eds) (2003) *Fit für den Postfordismus? Theoretisch-politische Perspektiven des Regulationsansatzes*, Münster: Westfälisches Dampfboot.

Brand, Ulrich and Markus Wissen (2002) 'Ambivalenzen praktischer Globalisierungskritik. Das Beispiel Attac', *Kurswechsel*, 3: 102–13.

—— (2005) 'Neoliberal Globalisation and the Internationalisation of Protest: A European Perspective', *Antipode*, 37(1): 9–17.

Brand, Ulrich, Achim Brunnengräber, Lutz Schrader, Christian Stock and Peter Wahl (2000) *Global Governance. Alternative zur neoliberalen Globalisierung?*, Münster: Westfälisches Dampfboot.

Brannan, Tessa (2003) 'From "Antipolitics" to "Anti-Politics": What became of East European "Civil Society"?', Working Paper No. 03-41, Development Studies Institute, London School of Economics and Political Science. Available HTTP: www.lse.ac.uk/Depts/destin/workpapers/tessabrannan.pdf (accessed 30 April 2003).

Braunmühl, Claudia von (2000) 'Mainstreaming Gender zwischem herschaftskritischem und bürokratischem Diskurs', *Jahrbuch Lateinamerika. Analysen und Berichte*, 24: 139–52.

Brenner, Robert (1998) 'Uneven Development and the Long Downturn: The Advanced Capitalist Economies from Boom to Stagnation, 1950–1998', *New Left Review*, I(229): 1–264.

Bresser Pereira, Luiz Carlos, José María Maravall and Adam Przeworski (1993) *Economic Reforms in New Democracies. A Social-Democratic Approach*, Cambridge: Cambridge University Press.

Brühl, Tanja, Tobias Debiel, Brigitte Hamm, Hartwig Hummel and Jens Martens (eds) (2001) *Die Privatisierung der Weltpolitik. Entstaatlichung und Kommerzialisierung im Globalisierungsprozess*, Bonn: Dietz Verlag.

Brus, Wlodzimierz (1972 [1961]) *The Market in a Socialist Economy*, London: Routledge & Kegan.

Buchanan, James M. (1979) *What Should Economists Do?*, Indianapolis: Liberty Press.

BUKO–Arbeitsschwerpunkt Weltwirtschaft (2001) 'Globalisierungskritik, Genua, Gewalt', *analyse & kritik*, 8–9 August.

Bulan, Klaus (1999) 'Was kostet uns die Bildung? Zum Sachverständigengutachten zur Bildungsfinanzierung', *Sozialismus*, (5): 20–3.

Bultmann, Torsten and Oliver Schöller (2003) 'Die Zukunft des Bildungssystems: Lernen auf Abruf – eigenverantwortlich und lebenslänglich!', *Prokla*, 33(131): 333–54.

Bundesverband Deutscher Stiftungen (ed.) (2002) *Verzeichnis deutscher Stiftungen*, Darmstadt: Hoppenstedt.

Burch, Philip H. (1997a) *Reagan, Bush, and Right-Wing Politics: Elites, Think Tanks, Power, and Policy. The American Right Wing at Court and in Action: Supreme Court Nominations and Major Policymaking*, Greenwich, Conn.–London: JAI/Elsevier Science.

—— (1997b) 'Introduction to Reagan, Bush, and Right-Wing Politics: Elites, Think Tanks, Power, and Policy', *Research in Political Economy*, 16: 91–128.

—— (1997c) 'Summary of Reagan, Bush, and Right-Wing Politics: Elites, Think Tanks, Power, and Policy', *Research in Political Economy*, 16: 129–174.

Cafruny, Alan W. (2003) 'Europe, the United States, and Neoliberal (Dis)Order: Is There a Coming Crisis of the Euro?' in Alan W. Cafruny and Magnus Ryner (eds) *A Ruined Fortress?: Neoliberal Hegemony and Transformation in Europe*, Lanham: Rowman & Littlefield: 285–306.

Cafruny, Alan W. and Magnus Ryner (eds) (2003) *A Ruined Fortress? Neoliberal Hegemony and Transformation in Europe*, Lanham: Rowman & Littlefield.

Callinicos, Alex (2003) 'The Anti-Capitalist Movement After Genoa and New York', in Stanley Aronowitz and Heather Gautney (eds) *Implicating Empire. Globalization & Resistance in the 21st Century World Order*, New York: Basic Books: 133–50.

Callon, Michel (1986) 'Some Elements of a Sociology of Translation: Domestication of the Scallops and the Fishermen of St. Brieuc Bay', in John Law (ed.) *Power, Action and Belief: A New Sociology of Knowledge*, Sociological Review Monograph 32, London: Routledge & Keegan Paul: 96–233.

Calomiris, Charles W. (1998) 'The IMF's Imprudent Role as Lender of Last Resort', *Cato Journal*, 17(3): 275–94.

Campbell, John L. (2001) 'Institutional Analysis and the Role of Ideas', in John L. Campbell, and Ove Pedersen (eds) *The Rise of Neoliberalism and Institutional Analysis*, Princeton: Princeton University Press: 159–89.

—— (2004) *Institutional Change and Globalization*, Princeton: Princeton University Press.

Campos, Jose Edgardo and Hilton L. Root (1996) *The Key to the Asian Miracle: Making Shared Growth Credible*, Washington, DC: Brookings Institute Press.

Candeias, Mario (2004) *Neoliberalimus – Hochtechnologie – Hegemonie. Grundrisse einer transnationalen kapitalistischen Produktions- und Lebensweise. Eine Kritik*, Hamburg: Argument Verlag.

Carl-Bertelsmann-Preis (1990a) *Symposium. Evolution im Hochschulbereich*, ed. by the Bertelsmann-Stiftung, Gütersloh: Verlag Bertelsmann Stiftung.

—— (1990b) *Festakt. Auslobung, Laudatio, Reden der Preisträger*, ed. by the Bertelsmann-Stiftung, Gütersloh: Verlag Bertelsmann Stiftung.

—— (1996a) *Innovative Schulsysteme im internationalen Vergleich, Bd. 1, Dokumentation zur internationalen Recherche*, ed. by the Bertelsmann-Stiftung, Gütersloh: Verlag Bertelsmann Stiftung.

—— (1996b) *Innovative Schulsysteme im internationalen Vergleich, Bd. 2, Dokumentation zu Symposium und Festakt*, ed. by the Bertelsmann-Stiftung, Gütersloh: Verlag Bertelsmann Stiftung.

Carroll, William K. and Colin Carson (2003) 'The Network of Global Corporations and Elite Policy Groups: A Structure for Transnational Capitalist Class Formation?', *Global Networks*, 3(1): 29–57.

Carroll, William K. and Meindert Fennema (2002) 'Is There a Transnational Business Community?', *International Sociology*, 17: 393–419.

Carroll, William K. and Murray Shaw (2001) 'Consolidating a Neoliberal Policy Bloc in Canada, 1976 to 1996', *Canadian Public Policy*, 27: 195–216.

Cash, John M. (1996) 'Guide to the Papers of Michael Polanyi', *Tradition and Discovery*, 23(1); also as a Mimeo from the Department of Special Collections, University of Chicago Library (pages not numbered).

Castañeda, Jorge G. (1993) *Utopia Unarmed: The Latin American Left After the Cold War*, 2nd edn, New York: Vintage.

—— (1994) 'Latin America and the End of the Cold War: An Essay in Frustration', in Abraham F. Lowenthal and Gregory F. Treverton (eds) *Latin America in a New World*, Boulder, CO: West View Press.

Castel, Robert (1994) '"Problematization" as a Mode of Reading History', in Jan Goldstein (ed.), *Foucault and the Writing of History*, Oxford: Blackwell: 237–52.

Cato Institute (2002) 'About Us', Washington, DC: Cato Institute. Available HTTP: www.cato.org.

Caufield, Catherine (1996) *Masters of Illusion: The World Bank and the Poverty of Nations*, New York: Henry Holt.

CEPAL (Economic Commission for Latin America and the Caribbean) (2002) *México: Evolución Económica durante 2001*, México: CEPAL.

The Chairman's Favorite Author (1974) *Time*, 30 September: 53–4.

Chang, Ha-Joon (1998) 'Korea: The Misunderstood Crisis', *World Development*, 26(8): 1555–61

Chavance, Bernard (1994) *The Transformation of Communist Systems. Economic Reform Since the 1950s*, Boulder, Oxford: Westview Press.
Chesnais, François, Claude Serfati and Charles-André Udry (2001) 'Die Zukunft der "Anti-Globalisierungsbewegung"'. Einige überlegungen mit dem Ziel, ihre theoretischen Grundlagen zu festigen', *Sozialistische Zeitung*, 29 March.
Clarens, Carlos (1968) *An Illustrated History of the Horror Film*, New York: Capricorn.
Cockett, Richard (1994) *Thinking the Unthinkable: Think-Tanks and the Economic Counter-Revolution 1931–1983*, London: HarperCollins.
—— (1995) *Thinking the Unthinkable. Think-Tanks and the Economic Counter Revolution, 1931–1983*, London: Harper Collins.
Cohen, Stephen P. and Sumit Ganguly (1999) 'India', in Robert Chase, Emily Hill and Paul Kennedy (eds) *The Pivotal States: A New Framework for US Policy in the Developing World*, New York: W. W. Norton.
Commission of the European Communities (1998) 'Progress Report from the Commission on the Follow-Up of the Communication: "Incorporating Equal Opportunities for Women and Men into All Community Policies and Activities"', COM(98)122 final.
Commission on Global Governance (1995) *Our Global Neighborhood*, Oxford: Oxford University Press.
Corricelli, Fabrizio (1998) *Macroeconomic Policies and the Development of Markets in Transition Economies*, Budapest: Central European University Press.
Cox, Robert W. (1983) 'Gramsci, Hegemony and International Relations: An Essay in Method', *Millenium* 12, S: 162–175.
—— (1987) *Production, Power and World Order: Social Forces in the Making of History*, New York: Columbia University Press.
—— (1993) 'Gramsci, Hegemony and International Relations: An Essay in Method', in Stephen Gill (ed.) *Gramsci, Historical Materialism and International Relations*, Cambridge: Cambridge University Press: 49–66.
—— (1996) 'Towards a Posthegemonic Conceptualisation of World Order: reflections on the relevancy of Ibh Khaldun' [1992], in Robert Cox with Timothy Sinclair, *Approaches to World Order*, Cambridge: Cambridge University Press: 144–173.
—— (1997) (ed.) *The New Realism: Perspectives on Multilateral and World Order*, Basingstoke: Macmillan.
Cox, Taylor H., jr. and Stacy Blake (1991) 'Managing Cultural Diversity: Implications for Organizational Competitiveness' *Academy of Management Executive*, 5(3): 45–56.
Crewe, Ivor (1989) 'Values: The Crusade that Failed', in Denis Kavanagh and Anthony Seldan (eds) *The Thatcher Effect*, Oxford: Oxford University Press: 239–50.
Cumings, Bruce (1984) 'The Legacy of Japanese Colonialism in Korea', in Ramon H. Myers and Mark R. Peattie (eds) *The Japanese Colonial Empire 1895–1945*, Princeton: Princeton University Press.
—— (1987) 'The Origins and Development of the Northeast Asian Political Economy: Industrial Sectors, Product Cycles and Political Consequences', in Frederic C. Deyo (ed.) *The Political Economy of the New Asian Industrialism*, Ithaca: Cornell University Press.
—— (1997) 'Japan and Northeast Asia into the Twenty-First Century', in Peter J. Katzenstein and Takashi Shiraishi (eds) *Network Power: Japan and Asia*, Ithaca: Cornell University Press.
—— (1998) 'The Korean Crisis and the End of "Late" Development', in *New Left Review*, I(231): 43–72.
Cutler, A. Claire, Virginia Haufler and Tony Porter (eds) (1999) *Private Authority and International Affairs*, Albany, NY: State University of New York Press.

Dahrendorf, Ralf (1983) *Die Chancen der Krise. über die Zukunft des Liberalismus*, Stuttgart: Deutsche Verlagsanstalt.

Dahrendorf, Ralf and Timothy Garton Ash (2003) 'Die Erneuerung Europas', in *Süddeutsche Zeitung*, July 5; trans. Denis Thouard (2003) 'The European and the American we want'. Available HTTP: http://watch.windsofchange.net/themes_62.htm (accessed 2 December, 2004).

Dalós, György (1990) 'The Fidelity of Equals: Ilona Duczynska and Karl Polanyi', in Kari Polanyi-Levitt (ed.) *The Life and Work of Karl Polanyi: A Celebration*, Montreal: Black Rose Books: 38–42.

Demirovic, Alex (1997) *Demokratie und Herrschaft. Aspekte kritischer Gesellschaftstheorie*, Münster: Westfälisches Dampfboot.

Denord, François (2001) 'Aux origines du néo-libéralisme en France. Louis Rougier et le Colloque Walter Lippmann de 1938', *Le Mouvement Social*, (195): 9–34.

—— (2003) 'Genèse et institutionnalisation du néo-libéralisme en France (années 1930–années 1950)', unpublished PhD thesis, Paris: Ecole des Hautes Etudes en Sciences Sociales.

Desai, Meghnad (1994) 'Equilibrium, Expectations and Knowledge?', in Jack Birner and Rudy van Zijp (eds) *Hayek, Co-ordination and Evolution: His Legacy in Philosophy, Politics, Economics and the History of Ideas*. London: Routledge: 25–50.

Desai, Radhika (1994a) 'Second-Hand Dealers in Ideas: Think-Tanks and Thatcherite Hegemony', in *New Left Review*, I(203): 27–64.

—— (1994b) *Intellectuals and Socialism: Social Democrats and the Labour Party*, London: Lawrence and Wishart.

—— (2004) *Slouching Towards Ayodhya: From Congress to Hindutva in Indian Politics*, 2nd rev. edn, New Delhi: Three Essays Press.

—— (2005) 'The 2004 Indian Electoral Verdict: Consummation or Crucible?', *New Left Review*, II(30): 49–67.

Deutscher Bundestag (1997) 'Bericht für die Europäische Kommission zur Umsetzung des ESF in der Bundesrepublik Deutschland (Zeitraum 1994–1996)', Verwirklichung der Chancengleichheit von Männern und Frauen, 28 August (BT-DRs 13 / 8600-1997).

Dezalay, Yves and Bryant G. Garth (2002) *The Internationalization of Palace Wars. Lawyers, Economists, and the Contest to Transform Latin American States*, Chicago: The University of Chicago Press.

Diamond, Sara (1995) *Roads to Dominion. Right Wing Movements and Political Power in the United States*, New York and London: The Guilford Press.

Dick, Philip K. (1991 [1965]) *The Three Stigmata of Palmer Eldritch*, New York: Vintage.

Dixon, Keith (2000a) *Die Evangelisten des Marktes. Die britischen Intellektuellen und der Thatcherismus*, Konstanz: Universitätsverlag Konstanz.

—— (2000b) *Ein würdiger Erbe. Anthony Blair und der Thatcherismus*, Konstanz: Universitätsverlag Konstanz.

Domhoff, G. William (1998) *Who Rules America?*, 3rd edn, Mountain View, CA: Mayfield Publishing Company.

Drainville, André (2001) 'Québéc City 2001 and the Making of Transnational Subjects', in Leo Panitch and Colin Leys (eds) *Socialist Register 2002: A World of Contradictions*, London: Merlin Press: 15–42.

Dussel Peters, Enrique (2000a) *Polarizing Mexico. The Impact of Liberalization Strategy*, Boulder and London: Lynne Rienner Publishers.

—— (2000b) 'El Tratado de Libre Comercio de Norteamérica y el desempeño de la economía en México', Mexico: CEPAL. Available HTTP: www.cepal.org.mx.

—— (2003) 'Características de las actividades generadoras de empleo en la economía mexicana (1988–2000)', *Investigación Económica*, 63(243): 123–54.

Dussel Peters, Enrique, Luis Miguel Galindo and Eduardo Loría Díaz (2003) *Condiciones y efectos de la inversión extranjera directa y del proceso de integración regional en México durante los noventa. Una perspectiva macro, meso y micro*, Mexico: UNAM, BID, Plaza y Valdés Editores.

Dussel Peters, Enrique and Jorge Katz (2001) 'Diferentes estrategias en el Nuevo Modelo Económico Latinoamericano: Importaciones temporales para su reexportación y transformación de materias primas', paper presented at the Conferencia Internacional 'Producción de Exportación, Desarrollo Económico y el Futuro de la Industria Maquiladora en México', Center for US–Mexican Studies, UAM, Mexico, 14–15 July: 1–37.

Easterbrook, Gregg (2003) 'American Power Moves Beyond the Mere Super', *New York Times*, 27 April: 1 and 5.

The Economist (2002a) 'Takeovers in South Korea: One Step Forward, One Step Back', *The Economist*, 4 May.

—— (2002b) 'Trade Policy: Anatomy of Rotten Deal', *The Economist*, 18 May.

Edgard Campos, Jose and Hilton L. Root (1996) *The Key to the Asian Miracle: Making Shared Growth Credible*, Washington, DC: Brookings Institution Press.

Egan, Greg (1998 [1997]) *Distress*, New York: HarperPrism.

Ekiert, Grzegorz and Jan Kubik (1998) 'Contentious Politics in New Democracies: East Germany, Hungary, Poland, and Slovakia, 1989–93', *World Politics*, 4: 547–82.

Etzioni, Amitai (1993) *The Spirit of Community: Rights, Responsibilities and the Communitarian Agenda*, New York: Crown Books.

—— (1996) *The New Golden Rule. Community and Morality in a Democratic Society*, New York: Basic Books.

Europäisches Parlament (1997) 'Bericht über die Mitteilung der Kommission – Einbindung der Chancengleichheit in sämtliche politischen Konzepte und Maßnahmen der Gemeinschaft – "Mainstreaming", Ausschuss für die Rechte der Frau: Berichterstatterin Angela Kokkola, Anhänge: Stellungnahmen des institutionellen Ausschusses und des sozialen Ausschusses des EP, Reihe Sitzungsdokumente des EP vom 18. Juli 1997' (Doc DE/DE/RR 332/332385 – PE 222.553).

Evans, Peter (1995) *Embedded Autonomy: States and Industrial Transformation*, Princeton: Princeton University Press.

Expertenkommission Finanzierung Lebenslangen Lernens (ed.) (2004) *Finanzierung Lebenslangen Lernens – der Weg in die Zukunft*, Bielefeld: Bertelsmann.

FAZ (= Frankfurter Allgemeine Zeitung) (1993) 'Neues EG-Konzept für öffentlichkeitsarbeit', 1 July: 5.

Feldstein, Martin (1998) 'Refocusing the IMF', in *Foreign Affairs*, 77(2): 20–33. Available HTTP: www.imfsite.org/reform/feldstein.html (accessed 18 January 2005).

—— (1999) 'A Self-Help Guide for Emerging Markets', *Foreign Affairs*, 78(2): 93–109. Available HTTP: www.nber.org/feldstein/fa0399.html (accessed 18 January 2005).

—— (2002) 'Argentina Doesn't Need the IMF', *Wall Street Journal*, 28 May.

Fennema, Meindert (1982) *International Networks of Banks and Industry*, The Hague: Martinus Nijhoff Publishers.

Feulner, Edwin J. (1998) 'The IMF Needs Real Reform, Not More Money', *Heritage Foundation Backgrounder*, no. 1175.

—— (1999) *Intellectual Pilgrims. The Fiftieth Anniversary of the Mont Pèlerin Society*, Washington, DC: Heritage Foundation.

—— (2000) 'The Heritage Foundation' in James G. McGann and R. Kent Weaver, (eds) *Think Tanks & Civil Society. Catalysts for Ideas and Action*, New Brunswick: Transaction Publishers: 67–85.

Fischer, Frank (1996) 'Die Agenda der Elite. Amerikanische Think Tanks und die Strategien der Politikberatung', *Prokla*, 26(104): 463–81.

Flynn, Padraig (1998) '"Mainstreaming" – eine grundlegend neue Angehensweise der Chancengleichheit im Rahmen der künftigen Strukturfonds', *Frauen Europas Info*, (78): 1.

Forsberg, Aaron (2000) *America and the Japanese Miracle: The Cold War Context of Japan's Postwar Economic Revival, 1950–1960*, Chapel Hill: University of North Carolina Press.

Foxley, Alejandro (1988) *Experimentos neoliberales en América latina*, México: Fondo de Cultura Económica.

Frank, Thomas (1997) *The Conquest of Cool. Business Culture, Counterculture, and the Rise of Hip Consumerism*, Chicago, IL: University of Chicago Press.

Franklin, Bruce H. (1982) 'America as Science Fiction: 1939', *Science Fiction Studies*, 9(1), Terre Haute, IN: Indiana State University: 38–50.

—— (1983) 'Future Imperfect?, *American Film. Magazine of the Film and Television Arts*, 8, New York: BPI Communications: 46–9 and 75–6.

—— (1990) 'Visions of the Future in Science Fiction Film from 1970 to 1982', in Annette Kuhn (ed.) *Alien Zone. Cultural Theory and Contemporary Science Fiction Cinema*, New York: Verso: 18–31.

Franklin, John (1959) *The John Franklin Letters*, New York: Bookmailer.

Fraser, Nancy (2003) 'Social Justice in the Age of Identity Politics: Redistribution, Recognition, and Participation', in Nancy Fraser and Axel Honneth (2003) *Redistribution or Recognition? A Political-Philosophical Exchange*, London: Verso: 7–109.

Freedom House (1999) *Think Tanks in Central and Eastern Europe. A Comprehensive Directory*, Washington and Budapest: Freedom House.

Frieden, Jeff (1980) 'The Trilateral Commission: Economics and Politics in the 1970s', in Holly Sklar (ed.) *The Trilateral Commission and Elite Planning for World Management*, Boston: South End Press: 61–75.

Friedman, David (1989) *The Machinery of Freedom. Guide to a Radical Capitalism*, La Salle, IL: Open Court.

Friedman, Milton (1962) *Capitalism and Freedom*, Chicago: The University of Chicago Press.

—— (1975) *There's No Such Thing as a Free Lunch*, LaSalle, IL: Open Court.

Friedman, Milton and Rose Friedman (1980 [1979]) *Free to Choose*, New York: Harcourt Brace Jovanovic.

Gamble, Andrew (1985) *Britain in Decline*, London: Macmillan.

—— (1988) *Free Economy and the Strong State: The Politics of Thatcherism*, Basingstoke: Macmillan.

Gamble, Andrew and Anthony Payne (eds) (1996) *Regionalism & World Order*, New York: St Martin's Press.

Gamble, Andrew, Mancur Olson, Norman Barry, Arthur Seldon, Max Hartwell and Andrew Melnyk (1986) *Ideas, Interests, and Consequences*, London: Institute of Economic Affairs.

Garten, Jeffrey E. (2002) 'From New Economy to Siege Economy: Globalization, Foreign Policy and the CEO Agenda', *Business and Strategy*, 26(1): 44–53.

Gellner, Winand (1995) *Ideenagenturen für Politik und öffentlichkeit. Think Tanks in den USA und in Deutschland*, Opladen: Westdeutscher Verlag.

George, Susan (1997) 'How to Win the War of Ideas. Lessons from the Gramscian Right', *Dissent* (Summer): 47–53.

—— (2001) 'The Global Citizens Movement: A New Actor For a New Politics', paper presented at the Conference on Reshaping Globalisation, sponsored by the Central European University, October 2001.

—— (2002) 'Wir sind nicht mehr in der Defensive', in Attac-Deutschland (ed.) *Eine andere Welt ist möglich*, Hamburg: VSA-Verlag: 142–50.

Gerber, David J. (1994) 'Constitutionalizing the Economy: German Neo-Liberalism, Competition Law and the New Europe', *American Journal of Comparative Law*, 42(1): 25–84.

Germain, Randall D. (ed.) (2000) *Globalization and its Critics. Perspectives from Political Economy*, New York: St Martin's Press.

Germain, Randall D. and Michael Kenny (1998) 'Engaging Gramsci: International Relations Theory and the New Gramscians', *Review of International Studies*, 24: 3–21.

Giddens, Anthony (1994) *Beyond Left and Right. The Future of Radical Politics*, Cambridge: Polity Press.

—— (1998) *The Third Way: The Renewal of Social Democracy*, Cambridge: Polity Press.

Giegel, Hans-Joachim (1989) 'Distinktionsstrategie oder Verstrickung in die Paradoxien gesellschaftlicher Umstrukturierung? Die Stellung der neuen sozialen Bewegungen im Raum der Klassenbeziehungen', in Klaus Eder (ed.) *Klassenlage, Lebensstil und kulturelle Praxis. Theoretische und empirische Beiträge zur Auseinandersetzung mit Pierre Bourdieus Klassentheorie*, Frankfurt/M.: Suhrkamp: 143–87.

Giersch, Herbert (1985) 'Eurosclerosis', *IfW Discussion Paper* no. 112, Kiel: Institute for World Economics.

Gill, Stephen (1990) *American Hegemony and the Trilateral Commission*, Cambridge: Cambridge University Press.

—— (1992) 'Economic Globalization and the Internationalization of Authority: Limits and Contradictions', *Geoforum*, 23(3): 269–83.

—— (1993): 'Gramsci and Global Politics: Towards a Post-Hegemonic Research Agenda', in Stephen Gill (ed.) *Gramsci, Historical Materialism and International Relations*, Cambridge: Cambridge University Press: 1–18.

—— (1995) 'Globalisation, Market Civilization and Disciplinary Neoliberalism', *Millennium: Journal of International Studies*, 24(3): 399–423.

—— (1998): 'European Governance and New Constitutionalism: Economic and Monetary Union and Alternatives to Disciplinary Neoliberalism in Europe', *New Political Economy*, 3(1): 5–26.

—— (2000) 'Toward a Postmodern Prince? The Battle of Seattle as a Moment in the New Politics of Globalisation', *Millennium: Journal of International Studies*, 29(1): 131–41.

Gilpin, Robert (1987) *The Political Economy of International Relations*, Princeton, NJ: Princeton University Press.

Girvin, Brian (1994) *The Right in the Twentieth Century*, London: Pinter.

Glyn, Andrew, Alan Hughes, Alain Lipietz and Ajit Singh (1989) 'The Rise and Fall of the Golden Age', in Stephen A. Marglin and Juliet B. Schor (eds) *The Golden Age of Capitalism. Reinterpreting the Postwar Experience*, Oxford: Clarendon Press: 39–125.

Goffart, Daniel (1999) 'Die Finanzkrise ist teilweise hausgemacht', *Das Parlament*, 15–22 January: 13.

Gómez, Ricardo J. (1995) *Neoliberalismo y seudociencia*, Buenos Aires: Lugar Editorial.

Goodson, Larry P. (2001) *Afghanistan's Endless War: State Failure, Regional Politics, and the Rise of the Taliban*, Seattle: University of Washington Press.

Goss, Jasper and David Burch (2001) 'From Agricultural Modernisation to Agri-Food Globalisation: The Waning of National Development in Thailand', *Third World Quarterly: Journal of Emerging Areas*, 22(6): 969–86.

Gouldner, Alvin W. (1957) 'Cosmopolitans and Locals: Toward an Analysis of Latent Social Roles, I', *Administrative Science Quarterly*, 2: 281–306.
Gowan, Peter (1999) *The Global Gamble: Washington's Faustian Bid for World Dominance*, London: Verso.
Graaf, Vera (1971) *Homo Futurus. Eine Analyse der modernen Science-fiction*, Hamburg: Claassen.
Gramsci, Antonio (1971) *Selections from the Prison Notebooks*, New York: International Publishers.
—— (1975) *Quaderni del carcere*, 4 vols, critical edn by Valentino Gerratana, Turin: Giulio Einaudi editore.
Gray, John (1996) *After Social Democracy: Politics, Capitalism and the Common Life*, London: Demos.
—— (1998) *False Dawn. The Delusion of Global Capitalism*, London: Granta Books.
Green, Ken, Richard Hull, Andrew McMeekin and Vivien Walsh (1999) 'The Construction of the Techno-Economic: Networks vs. Paradigms', *Research Policy*, 28: 777–92.
Greenwood, Justin (2000) 'Organised Business and the European Union', in Justin Greenwood and Henry Jacek (eds) *Organised Business and the New Global Order*, London: Macmillan: 77–98.
Greenwood, Justin and Henry Jacek (eds) (2000) *Organised Business and the New Global Order*, London: Macmillan.
Grefe, Christiane, Mathias Greffrath and Harald Schumann (2002) *Attac. Was wollen die Globalisierungskritiker?*, Berlin: Rowohlt.
Greskovits, Béla (1998) *The Political Economy of Protest and Patience. East European and Latin American Transformations Compared*, Budapest: Central European University Press.
The Group of Lisbon (1995) *Limits to Competition*, Cambridge: MIT Press.
Gurría Treviño, José Angel (1993) *La política de la deuda externa*, México: Fondo de Cultura Económica.
Gutiérrez R., Germán (1998) *Etica y economía en Adam Smith y Friedrich Hayek*, Mexico, DF: Universidad Iberoamericana; also available as (1998) *Etica y economía en Adam Smith y Friedrich Hayek*, San José, Costa Rica: Departamento Ecuménico de Investigaciones.
Guzzini, Stefano (2000) 'A Reconstruction of Constructivism in International Relations', *European Journal of International Relations*, 6(2): 147–82.
Haas, Peter M. (1992) 'Introduction: Epistemic Communities and International Policy Coordination', *International Organization*, 46(1): 1–36.
Habermas, Jürgen and Jacques Derrida (2003) 'Nach dem Krieg: Die Wiedergeburt Europas', *Frankfurter Allgemeine Zeitung*, May 31; trans. Christian Bouchindhomme (2003) 'Europe: plea for a common foreign policy'. Available HTTP: http://watch.windsof change.net/themes_63.htm (accessed December 2, 2004).
Haggard, Stephan (1990) *Pathways from the Periphery: The Politics of Growth in the Newly Industrializing Countries*, Ithaca: Cornell University Press.
Hall, Peter (ed.) (1989) *The Political Power of Economic Ideas. Keynesianism across Nations*, Princeton, NJ: Princeton University Press.
Hall, Stuart (1983 [1978]) 'The Great Moving Right Show', in Stuart Hall and Martin Jacques (eds) *The Politics of Thatcherism*, London: Lawrence and Wishart: 19–39.
—— (1988) 'Learning from Thatcherism', in Stuart Hall, *The Hard Road to Renewal: Thatcherism and the Crisis of the Left*, London: Verso: 271–83.
Halliday, Fred (1986) *The Making of the Second Cold War*, London: Verso.
Hardt, Michael and Antonio Negri (2000) *Empire*, Cambridge, MA: Harvard University Press.
Harris, Nigel (1986) *The End of the Third World: Newly Industrializing Countries and the Decline of an Ideology*, London: I. B. Tauris.

Harris, Ralph and Arthur Seldon (1977) *Not From Benevolence: Twenty Years of Economic Dissent*, London: Institute of Economic Affairs.
—— (1981) *The Emerging Consensus*, London: Institute of Economic Affairs.
Harrison, Nathaniel (2000) 'Administration, Democrats Blast Congressional Failure on Debt Relief', *Agence France Presse*, 12 July.
Hart-Landsberg, Martin (1993) *The Rush to Development: Economic Change and Political Struggle in South Korea*, New York: Monthly Review Press.
—— (1998) *Korea: Division, Reunification and US Foreign Policy*, New York: Monthly Review Press.
Hartwell, Ronald Max (1995) *A History of the Mont Pèlerin Society*, Indianapolis: Liberty Fund.
Harvey, David (2003) *The New Imperialism*, Oxford: Oxford University Press.
Haug, Christoph (2002) 'Gesellschaftliche Integration durch Schweigen? über die Konsequenzen eines sozialpsychologischen Begriffs von öffentlicher Meinung', unpublished paper.
Hay, Colin (2000) 'Contradictions of Capitalism–Contemporary Capitalism, Globalization, Regionalization and the Persistence of National Variation', *Review of International Studies*, 4(26): 509–32.
—— (2001) 'The "Crisis" of Keynesianism and the Rise of Neoliberalism in Britain: An Ideational Institutionalist Approach', in John L. Campbell and Ove Pedersen (eds) *The Rise of Neoliberalism and Institutional Analysis*, Princeton: Princeton University Press: 193–218.
Hayek, Friedrich August von (ed.) (1935a) *Collectivist Economic Planning: Critical Studies on the Possibilities of Socialism*, London: Routledge.
—— (1935b) 'The Present State of the Debate', in Friedrich August von Hayek (ed.) *Collectivist Economic Planning: Critical Studies on the Possibilities of Socialism*, London: Routledge: 201–43.
—— (1937) 'Economics and Knowledge', in Friedrich August von Hayek, *Individualism and Economic Order*, London: Routledge & Kegan Paul: 33–56.
—— (1945) 'The Use of Knowledge in Society', in Friedrich August von Hayek, *Individualism and Economic Order*, London: Routledge & Kegan Paul: 77–106.
—— (1949a) *Individualism and Economic Order*, London: Routledge & Kegan Paul.
—— (1949b) 'The Intellectuals and Socialism', in Friedrich August von Hayek *The Collected Works of F. A. Hayek, vol. X: Socialism and War. Essays, Documents, Reviews*, (ed.) Bruce Caldwell, London: Chicago University Press: 221–37.
—— (1975a) 'Die Anmaßung von Wissen', *Ordo*, 26: 12–21.
—— (1975b) 'Der Wettbewerb als Entdeckungsverfahren', *Kieler Vorträge*, no. 56.
—— (1981) *Recht, Gesetzgebung und Freiheit*, vols I–III, Landsberg am Lech: Verlag Moderne Industrie.
—— (1990 [1960]) *The Constitution of Liberty*, London: Routledge.
—— (1991 [1944]) *The Road To Serfdom*, London: Routledge.
Heinlein, Robert A[nson] (1950) *Red Planet. A Colonial Boy On Mars*, New York: Scribner.
—— (1951 [1948]) 'Gentlemen, Be Seated', in *The Green Hills of Earth*, New York: Signet: 53–61.
—— (1951 [1949]) 'Delilah and the Space-Rigger', in Robert A. Heinlein, *The Green Hills of Earth*, New York: Signet: 13–23.
—— (1966 [1996]) *The Moon is a Harsh Mistress*, New York: Tor.
—— (1967 [1950]) *Farmer in the Sky*, London: Pan.
—— (1968 [1961]) *Stranger in a Strange Land*, New York: Putnam.
—— (1971 [1950]) *The Man Who Sold the Moon*, London: New English Library.

—— (1973) *Time Enough for Love. The Lives of Lazarus Long*, New York: Putnam.
—— (1980) *Expanded Universe*, New York: Ace.
—— (1980) *The Number of the Beast*, New York: Fawcett Columbine.
—— (1985) *The Cat Who Walks Through Walls. A Comedy of Manners*, New York: Putnam.
—— (1999 [1939]) 'If This Goes On -', in *Revolt in 2100 & Methusalah's Children*, Riverdale, NY: Baen: 7–174; differs from older versions of the story.
—— (1999 [1940]) 'Coventry', in *Revolt in 2100 & Methusalah's Children*, Riverdale, NY: Baen: 175–233.
Helleiner, Eric (1994) *States and the Reemergence of Global Finance. From Bretton Woods to the 1990s*, Ithaca: Cornell University Press.
Henessey, Peter (1989) *Whitehall*, London: Secker and Warburg.
Heritage Foundation (2002) 'About Us?', Washington, DC: Heritage Foundation. Available HTTP: www.heritage.org.
Hermann, Wolfgang A. (2002) 'Selber denken, nicht denken lassen' (Redeauszug des Präsidenten der Technischen Universität München zum Dies Academicus, 5 December), Available HTTP: www.tu-muenchen.de/ExcellenTum (accessed 11 December 2002).
Higgott, Richard (2000) 'Contested Globalization: The Changing Context and Normative Challenges', *Review of International Studies*, 26: 131–53.
Higgott, Richard A., Geoffrey Underhill and Andreas Bieler (eds) (2000) *Non-State Actors and Authority in the Global System*, London and New York: Routledge.
Hilley, John (2001) *Malaysia: Mahathirism, Hegemony and the New Opposition*, London: Zed Press.
Hinkelammert, Franz J. (1984) *Crítica a la razón utópica*, San José, Costa Rica: Departamento Ecuménico de Investigaciones.
Hirsch, Joachim (2001) 'Die Internationalisierung des Staates. Anmerkungen zu einigen aktuellen Fragen der Staatstheorie', in Joachim Hirsch, Bob Jessop and Nicos Poulantzas, *Die Zukunft des Staates. Denationalisierung, Internationalisierung, Renationalisierung*, Hamburg: VSA-Verlag: 101–38.
—— (2002) *Herrschaft, Hegemonie und politische Alternativen*, Hamburg: VSA-Verlag.
Hirschman, Albert O. (1991) *The Rhetoric of Reaction: Perversity, Futility, Jeopardy*, Cambridge, MA: The Belknap Press of Harvard University Press.
Hobsbawm, Eric (1994) *Age of Extremes*, New York: Pantheon Books.
Hochschulrektorenkonferenz (HRK) (1996) *Zur Finanzierung der Hochschulen*, Bonn, 9 July.
Hodgson, Geoffrey M. (1998) 'Socialism Against Markets? A Critique of Two Recent Proposals', *Economy and Society*, 27(4): 407–33.
—— (1999) *Economics & Utopia: Why the Learning Economy is not the End of History*, London: Routledge.
Hogan, James P. (1999 [1992]) *The Multiplex Man*, Riverdale, NY: Baen.
Hogan, Michael J. ([1987] 1989) *The Marshall Plan: America, Britain, and the Reconstruction of Western Europe, 1947–1952*, 2nd edn, Cambridge: Cambridge University Press.
Holloway, John and Eloina Peláez (1998) *Zapatista! Reinventing Revolution in Mexico*, Sterling/VA: Stylus.
Holzer, Jerzy (1984) '*Solidarität*'. *Die Geschichte einer freien Gewerkschaft in Polen*, München: C. H. Beck.
Honderich, Ted (1991) *Conservatism*, Boulder: Westview Press.
Hoover Institution on War, Revolution and Peace (2002) 'Mission and Philosophy', Stanford, CA: Hoover Institution. Available HTTP: www.hoover.org.
Hoskins, W. Lee and James W. Coons (1995) 'Mexico: Policy Failure, Moral Hazard, and Market Solutions', *Cato Policy Analysis*, no. 243.

Huben, Mike (2004) 'A Non-Libertarian FAQ, Version 1.5'. Available HTTP: http://world.std.com/~mhuben/faq.html (accessed 5 October, 2004).
Huber, Peter W. (1994) *Orwell's Revenge. The 1984 Palimpsest*, New York: Free Press.
Hufbauer, Gary and Jeffrey Schott (1993) *NAFTA. An Assessment*, Washington, DC: Institute for International Economics.
Hull, Richard (2000a) 'Knowledge and the Economy: Some Critical Comments' (essay review of *Economics and Utopia*, by Geoffrey Hodgson, 1999), *Economy & Society*, 29(2): 316–31.
—— (2000b) 'Knowledge Management and the Conduct of Expert Labour', in Craig Prichard, Richard Hull, Mike Chumer and Hugh Willmott (eds) *Managing Knowledge: Critical Investigations of Work and Learning*, London: Macmillan: 49–68.
—— (2001a) 'ICTs and the Knowledge Economy: An Historical and Ethnographic Study', unpublished PhD thesis, Manchester School of Management, UMIST.
—— (2001b) 'ICTs, the Knowledge Economy and Neo-Liberalism', *Bridges: An Interdisciplinary Journal of Theology, Philosophy, History & Science*, 8(3/4): 223–41.
Hurrell, Andrew and Ngaire Woods (1995) 'Globalisation and Inequality', *Millenium*, 24(3): 447–70.
Huxley, Aldous (1958 [1932]) *Brave New World*, New York: Bantam.
Hymer, Stephen (1979) *The Multinational Corporation: A Radical Approach*, Cambridge, England: Cambridge University Press.
INEGRI (Instituto Nacional de Estadística, Geografía e Informática) (2001) *Banco de Información Estadística*, Mexico: INEGRI.
Initiativkreis Bildung der Bertelsmann-Stiftung (1999) *Zukunft gewinnen – Bildung erneuern*, Gütersloh: Verlag Bertelsmann Stiftung.
International Monetary Fund (IMF) (2002) *World Economic Outlook* (September). Washington, DC: IMF.
Jacek, Henry (2000) 'The Role of Organized Business in the Formulation and Implementation of Regional Trade Agreements in North America', in Justin Greenwood and Henry Jacek (eds) *Organised Business and the New Global Order*, London: Macmillan: 39–58.
Jacobitz, Robin (1991) *Der Niedergang institutionalisierter Kooperation. Die Auswirkungen von Machtveränderungen zwischen den USA, Japan und Deutschland auf das GATT- und das IWF-Regime*, Marburg: Forschungsgruppe Europäische Gemeinschaften.
Jameson, Fredric (1982) 'Progress versus Utopia. Or: Can We Imagine the Future', *Science Fiction Studies* 9(2), Terre Haute, IN: Indiana State University: 147–58.
—— (1998) 'Notes on Globalization as a Philosophical Issue', in Fredric Jameson and Masao Miyoshi (eds) *The Cultures of Globalization*, Durham and London: Duke University Press: 54–77.
Janelli, Roger L. and Dawnhee Yim (1993) *Making Capitalism: The Social and Cultural Construction of a South Korean Conglomerate*, Stanford: Stanford University Press.
Jannett, Daniel (1997) 'Vielfalt als Strategievorteil', in Elmar Altvater, Achim Brunnengräber, Markus Haake and Heike Walk *Vernetzt und verstrict. Nicht-Regierungs-Organisationen als gesellschaftliche Productivkraft*, Munster, 146–173.
Jay, Martin (1994 [1974]) 'The Frankfurt School's Critique of Karl Manheim and the Sociology of Knowledge', *Telos*, (20): 72–89; reprinted, with some revisions in Jay Bernstein (ed.) (1994) *The Frankfurt School: Critical Assessments*, vol. 1, London: Routledge: 175–90.
Jessop, Bob (1999) 'Narrating the Future of the National Economy and the National State: Remarks on Remapping Regulation and Reinventing Governance', in George Steinmetz (ed.) *State/Culture: State-Formation after the Cultural Turn*, Ithaca: Cornell University Press.

—— (2000) 'Good Governance and the Urban Question: On Managing the Contradictions of Neo-Liberalism', comment on Urban21, published in German in Mieter-Echo, June 2000. Access HTTP: www.comp.lancs.ac.uk/sociology/papers/jessop-good-governance-and-the-urban-question.pdf (accessed 18 January 2005).

—— (2001a) 'Globalisierung und Nationalstaat. Imperialismus und Staat bei Nicos Poulantzas – 25 Jahre später', in Joachim Hirsch, Bob Jessop and Nicos Poulantzas *Die Zukunft des Staates. Denationalisierung, Internationalisierung, Renationalisierung*, Hamburg: VSA-Verlag: 71–100.

—— (2001b) 'Die Globalisierung des Kapitals und die Zukunft des Nationalstaates. Ein Beitrag zur Kritik der globalen politischen ökonomie', in Joachim Hirsch, Bob Jessop and Nicos Poulantzas *Die Zukunft des Staates. Denationalisierung, Internationalisierung, Renationalisierung*, Hamburg: VSA-Verlag: 139–70.

Job, Sebastian (2001) 'Globalising Russia? The Neo-Liberal/Nationalist Two-Step and the Russification of the West', *Third World Quarterly: Journal of Emerging Areas*, 22(6): 931–49.

Johnson, Bryan T. and Brett D. Schaefer (1997a) 'No New Funding for the IMF', *Heritage Foundation Backgrounder Update*, no. 287, Washington, DC: Heritage Foundation.

—— (1997b) 'The International Monetary Fund: Outdated, Ineffective, and Unnecessary', *Heritage Foundation Backgrounder*, no. 1113, Washington, DC: Heritage Foundation.

—— (1998) 'Congress Should Give No More Funds to the IMF', *Heritage Foundation Backgrounder*, no. 1157, Washington, DC: Heritage Foundation.

Johnson, Chalmers (1982) *MITI and the Japanese Miracle: The Growth of Industrial Policy 1925–1975*, Stanford: Stanford University Press.

—— (1999) 'The Developmental State: Odyssey of a Concept', in Meredith Woo-Cumings (ed.) *The Developmental State*, Ithaca: Cornell University Press.

Johnson, Simon and Marzena Kowalska (1994) 'Poland: The Political Economy of Shock Therapy', in Stephan Haggard and Steven B. Webb (eds) *Voting for Reform. Democracy, Political Liberalization and Economic Adjustment*, New York and Oxford: Oxford University Press: 185–241.

Josselin, Daphne and William Wallace (eds) (2001) *Non-State Actors in World Politics*, New York: Palgrave.

Kagan, Robert (2003) *Of Paradise and Power: America and Europe in the New World Order*, New York: Alfred A. Knopf.

Kalecki, Michal (1972) 'The Fascism of Our Times', in Michal Kalecki, *The Last Phase in the Transformation of Capitalism*, New York: Monthly Review Press: 99–106.

Kaminsky, Graciela L. and Carmen M. Reinhart (1999) 'The Twin Crises: The Causes of Banking and Balance-of-Payments Problems', *American Economic Review*, 89(3): 473–500.

Kang, C. S. Eliot (2000) 'Segyehwa Reform of the South Korean Developmental State', in Samuel S. Kim (ed.) *Korea's Globalization*, Cambridge: Cambridge University Press.

Kapur, Devesh, John Lewis and Richard Webb (1997) *The World Bank: Its First Half-Century, vol. 1: History*, Washington: Brookings Institution.

Keck, Margaret E. and Kathryn Sikkink (eds) (1998) *Activists Beyond Borders: Advocacy Networks in International Politics*, Ithaca, NY: Cornell University Press.

Keizer, Willem (1994) 'Hayek's Critique of Socialism', in Jack Birner and Rudy van Zijp (eds) *Hayek, Co-ordination and Evolution: His Legacy in Philosophy, Politics, Economics and the History of Ideas*, London: Routledge: 207–31.

Keller, Carsten and Oliver Schöller (2002) 'Autoritäre Bildung. Bildungsreform im Zeichen von Standortwettbewerb und neuen Eliten', in Uwe H. Bittlingmayer, Rolf Eickelpasch, Jens Kastner and Claudia Rademacher (eds) *Theorie als Kampf? Zur politischen Soziologie Pierre Bourdieus*, Opladen: Leske + Budrich.

Kellner, Douglas (1994 [1973]) 'The Frankfurt School Revisited: A Critique of Martin Jay's *The Dialectical Imagination*', *New German Critique*, (4): 131–52; reprinted, with some revisions, in Jay Bernstein (ed.) (1994) *The Frankfurt School: Critical Assessments*, vol. 1, London: Routledge: 41–62.
Kennedy, Paul (1987) *The Rise and Fall of Great Powers. Economic Change and Military Conflict from 1500 to 2000*, New York: Random House.
Keynes, John Maynard (1973 [1936]) *The General Writings, vol. VII: The General Theory of Employment, Interest and Money*, London and Basingstoke: Macmillan and St Martin's Press.
Kiely, Ray (1998) 'Neoliberalism Revised? A Critical Account of World Bank Concepts of Good Governance and Market Friendly Intervention', *Capital and Class*, 64: 63–88.
Kim, Kwang Suk and Michael Roemer (1979) *Growth and Structural Transformation (Studies in the Modernization of the Republic of Korea: 1945–1975)*, Cambridge: Harvard University Press.
Kim, Samuel S. (2000) 'Korea and Globalization (Segyehwa): A Framework for Analysis', in Samuel S. Kim (ed.) *Korea's Globalization*, Cambridge: Cambridge University Press.
Kirkpatrick, Jeanne (1979) 'Dictatorship and Double Standards', *Commentary*, 68(5): 34–45.
Kirzner, Israel M. (1984) 'Economic Planning and the Knowledge Problem', *Cato Journal*, 4(2): 407–18.
Kitschelt, Herbert with Anthony McGann (1997) *The Radical Right in Western Europe: A Comparative Analysis*, Ann Arbor: University of Michigan Press.
Kjær, Peter and Ove Pedersen (2001) 'Translating Liberalization. Neoliberalism in the Danish Negotiated Economy', in John L. Campbell and Ove K. Pedersen (eds) *The Rise of Neoliberalism and Institutional Analysis*, Princeton: Princeton University Press: 219–48.
Klausenitzer, Jürgen (2002) 'Altes und Neues. Anmerkungen zur Diskussion über die gegenwärtige Restrukturierung des deutschen Bildungssystems', *Widersprüche*, (43): 53–68.
Klein, Naomi (2001) 'Reclaiming the Commons', *New Left Review*, II(9): 81–9.
—— (2002) 'Farewell to "The End of History": Organization and Vision in Anti-Corporate Movements', in Leo Panitch and Colin Leys (eds) *Socialist Register 2002*, London: Merlin Press: 1–14.
Kleinfeld, Ralf (1996) *Kommunalpolitik. Eine Problemorientierte Einführung*, Opladen: Leske + Budrich.
Köhler, Bettina and Ulrich Brand (2002) 'Porto Alegre: Aufbruch und Kristallisation statt "Trap Watching"'. Available HTTP: www.links-netz.de.
Koman, Victor (1998 [1997]) 'Demokratus', in Brad Linaweaver and Edward E. Kramer (eds) *Free Space*, New York: Tor: 197–220.
Kommission der Europäischen Gemeinschaften (1996) 'Mitteilung der Kommission "Einbindung der Chancengleichheit in sämtliche politischen Konzepte und Maßnahmen der Gemeinschaft"', Luxemburg: KOM (1996/67).
—— (1998) 'Fortschrittsbericht der Kommission über Folgemaßnahmen zu der Mitteilung "Einbindung der Chancengleichheit in sämtliche politischen Konzepte und Maßnahmen der Gemeinschaft"', Luxemburg: KOM (1996/122), 4 March.
Konrád, György (1985) *Antipolitik: Mitteleuropäische Meditationen*, Frankfurt/M.: Suhrkamp.
Koo, Hagen and Eun Mee Kim (1992) 'The Developmental State and Capital Accumulation in South Korea', in Richard P. Appelbaum and Jeffrey Henderson (eds) *States and Development in the Asian Pacific Rim*, Newbury Park: Sage Publications: 121–49.
Kopytoff, Igor (1999) 'The Internal African Frontier. Cultural Conservatism and Ethnic Innovation', in Tobias Wendl and Michael Rösler (eds) *Frontiers and Borderlands. Anthropological Perspectives*, Frankfurt/M.: Peter Lang.

Kornai, János (2000) 'Ten Years After "The Road to a Free Economy." The Author's Self-Evaluation', contribution to 'Annual Bank Conference on Development Economics', 18–20 April, Washington, DC: The World Bank.

Kovács, János Mátyás (1991) 'From Reformation to Transformation: Limits to Liberalism in Hungarian Economic Thought', *East European Politics and Society*, 5(1): 41–72.

Kowalik, Tadeusz (1994) 'A Reply to Maurice Glasman', *New Left Review*, I(206): 133–44.

—— (2001) 'The Ugly Face of Polish Success', in G. Blazyca and R. Rapacki (eds) *Poland into the New Millennium*, Cheltenham: Edward Elgar: 33–53.

—— (2002) 'Poland', in Max Kaase, Vera Sparschuh and Agnieszka Wenninger (eds) *Three Social Science Disciplines in Central and Eastern Europe. Handbook on Economics, Political Science and Sociology (1989–2001)*, Bonn and Berlin: Social Science Information Centre (IZ), Collegium Budapest: 135–51.

Kraushaar, Wolfgang (2002) 'Die Grenzen der Anti-Globalisierungsbewegung', *Mittelweg*, 10(36): 4–23.

Krell, Gertraude (1997) 'Mono- oder multikulturelle Organisationen? Managing Diversity auf dem Prüfstand', in Ulf Kadritzke (ed.) *Unternehmenskulturen unter Druck. Neue Managementkonzepte zwischen Anspruch und Wirklichkeit*, Berlin: Fachhochschule für Wirtschaft. fhw-Forschung, no. 30–31: 47–66.

—— (2000) 'Managing Diversity – Chancen für Frauen', in Kobra (ed.) *Managing Diversity – Ansätze zur Schaffung transkultureller Organisationen. Kobra-Werkstattpapier zur Frauenförderung*, no. 14, Berlin: Kobra: 27–35.

Krueger, Anne O. (1978) *Liberalization Attempts and Consequences*, Cambridge: Ballinger Publishing Company.

—— (1983) *Trade and Employment in Developing Countries*, vol. 3, Chicago: University of Chicago Press.

—— (1992) *Economic Policy Reform in Developing Countries*, Oxford: Blackwell.

—— (1997) 'Trade Policy and Economic Development: How we Learn', *The American Economic Review*, 87(1): 1–22.

Krugman, Paul (2001) 'For Richer. How the Permissive Capitalism of the Boom Destroyed American Equality', in *New York Times Magazine*, 20 October: 61–7, 76–7 and 141.

Kupchan, Charles A. (2002) *The End of the American Era: US Foreign Policy and the Geopolitics of the Twenty-first Century*, New York: Alfred A. Knopf.

Kuttner, Robert (1992) *The End of Laissez-Faire. National Purpose and the Global Economy After the Cold War*, Philadelphia: University of Pennsylvania Press.

Lal, Deepak K. (1985) *The Poverty of Development Economics*, 2nd edn, Cambridge: Harvard University Press.

—— (1998) *Unintended Consequences: The Impact of Factor Endowments, Culture and Politics in Long-Run Economic Performance*, Cambridge: MIT Press.

Lall, Sanjaya (1996) *Learning from the Asian Tigers: Studies in Technology and Industrial Policy*, London: Macmillan

Lange, Oskar and Frederick M. Taylor (1938 [1937]) *On the Economic Theory of Socialism*, Minneapolis: University of Minnesota Press.

Larkins, John (2001) 'Return of the Behemoths', *Far Eastern Economic Review*, 11 October.

Lebaron, Frédéric (2002) 'Le "Nobel" d'économie. Une politique', *Actes de la recherche en sciences sociales*, (141–142): 62–6.

Lee, Martin (2000) *The Beast Reawakens*, London: Routledge.

Leftwich, Adrian (2000) *States of Development: On the Primacy of Politics in Development*, Cambridge: Polity Press.

Lehning, Thomas (2004) *Das Medienhaus. Geschichte und Gegenwart des Bertelsmann-Konzerns*, München: Fink Verlag.
León Pacheco, Alejandra and Enrique Dussel Peters (2001) 'El comercio intraindustria en México (1990–1999)', *Comercio Exterior*, 51(7): 652–664.
Leonhardt, David (2002) 'Scholarly Mentor to Bush's Team', *The New York Times*, 1 December.
Levin, Ira (1970) *This Perfect Day*, London: Michael Joseph.
Levinson, Jerome I. (1999) 'Certifying International Worker Rights', *EPI Briefing Paper*, Washington, DC: Economic Policy Institute.
—— (2000) 'Separate Dissenting Statement', unpublished manuscript, Washington, DC: American University.
Levitas, Ruth (1986) *The Ideology of the New Right*, Cambridge: Cambridge University Press.
Leys, Colin (1980) 'Neo-Conservativism and the Organic Crisis in Britain', *Studies in Political Economy* (4): 41–63.
—— (1996) *The Rise and Fall of Development Theory*, Bloomington: Indiana University Press.
Leys, Colin and Leo Panitch (1998) *The End of Parliamentary Socialism*, London: Verso.
Lichtheim, George (1970) *Lukács*, London: Fontana.
Liedtke, Rüdiger (2002) *Wem gehört die Republik? Die Konzerne und ihre Verflechtungen*, Frankfurt/M.: Eichborn Verlag.
Linaweaver, Brad (1998 [1997]) 'No Market for Justice', in Brad Linaweaver and Edward E. Kramer (eds) *Free Space*, New York: Tor: 61–8.
Lindgren, C., G. Garcia and M. Saal (1996) *Bank Soundness and Economic Policy*, Washington, DC: IMF.
Litván, György (1990) 'Karl Polanyi in Hungarian Politics', in Kari Polanyi-Levitt (ed.) *The Life and Work of Karl Polanyi: A Celebration*, Montreal: Black Rose Books: 30–7.
Lobdell, Jared (1998 [1997]) 'The Last Holosong of Christopher Lightning', in Brad Linaweaver and Edward E. Kramer (eds) *Free Space*, New York: Tor: 327–36.
Lobe, Jim (2000) 'US: Summers Proposes Reforms for World Bank, Other MDBs', *Inter Press Service*, 21 March.
López-Córdova, Ernesto (2001) 'NAFTA and the Mexican Economy: Analytical Issues and Lessons for the FTAA', *Occasional Paper* 9, Inter-American Development Bank, Washington, DC: 1–48.
McElroy, Wendy (2000) 'Gender Issues in the EU Charter of Fundamental Rights', a talk delivered at *Europe: The Ultimate Leviathan*, a conference in Milan, Italy, 8 December, www.zetetics.com/mac/talks/eu.html
McGann, J. G. and R. K. Weaver (eds) (2000) *Think Tanks and Civil Societies: Catalysts for Ideas and Action*, New Brunswick and London: Transaction Press.
McGlothlen, Ronald L. (1993) *Controlling the Waves: Dean Acheson and US Foreign Policy in Asia*, New York: W. W. Norton.
McMichael, Philip (1995) *Development and Social Change: A Global Perspective*, 2nd edn, Thousand Oaks, CA: Pine Forge Press.
McRobbie, Angela (1992) 'How to Cope When Class and Nation Aren't Everything', review of course material for new Open University course 'Understanding Modern Societies', *Guardian*, 22 August: 25.
McRobbie, Kenneth (1994) 'From the Class Struggle to the Clean Spring', in Kenneth McRobbie (ed) *Humanity, Society and Commitment: On Karl Polyani*, Montreal: Black Rose Books.
Magee, Bryan (1973). *Popper*, London: Fontana.

Marglin, Stephen A. and Juliet B. Schor (eds) (1991) *The Golden Age of Capitalism. Reinterpreting the Postwar Experience*, Oxford: Claredon Press.

Marsh, David and R. A. W. Rhodes (1992) *Implementing Thatcherism: Audit of an Era*, Buckingham: Open University Press.

Martino, Antonio (2001) 'Stupor mundi: the IEA and Its Impact', in Ralph Harris and Arthur Seldon (eds) *A Conversation with Ralph Harris and Arthur Seldon*, with Stephen Erickson, London: Institute of Economic Affairs: 81–4.

Matthews, Duncan and John F. Pickering (2000) 'Business Strategy and Devolving Rules in the Single European Market', in Richard A. Higgott, Geoffrey Underhill and Andreas Bieler (eds) *Non-State Actors and Authority in the Global System*, London and New York: Routledge: 107–20.

Mayer, Arno (1971) *The Dynamics of Counterrevolution in Europe: 1870–1956: An Analytic Framework*, New York: Harper and Row.

—— (1981) *The Persistence of the Old Regime: Europe to the Great War*, New York: Pantheon Books.

Media Transparency (2002) '$9.4 Million to the National Bureau of Economic Research', Minneapolis, MN: Media Transparency. Available HTTP: www.mediatransparency.org.

Meltzer, Allan H. (1998) 'What's Wrong with the IMF? What Would Be Better?', paper prepared for the Federal Reserve Bank of Chicago conference 'Asia: An Analysis of a Financial Crisis', Chicago, IL: Federal Reserve Bank of Chicago.

—— (2000) *Report of the International Financial Institutions Advisory Commission*, Washington, DC: US Congress.

Mendell, Marguerite (1990) 'Karl Polanyi and Feasible Socialism', in Kari Polanyi-Levitt (ed.) *The Life and Work of Karl Polanyi: A Celebration*, Montreal: Black Rose Books: 66–77.

Mestrovic, Stjepan G. (1994) *The Balkanization of the West: The Confluence of Postmodernism and Postcommunism*, London: Routledge.

Mills, C. Wright (1956) *The Power Elite*, London: Oxford University Press.

Ministerium für Arbeit, Soziales, Gesundheit und Frauen Brandenburg: Machbarkeitsstudie Gender Mainstreaming in der Strukturfondsförderung des Landes (2001), Brandenburg, Potsdam.

Mises, Ludwig von (1935 [1920]) 'Economic Calculation in the Socialist Commonwealth', in Friedrich August von Hayek (ed.) *Collectivist Economic Planning: Critical Studies on the Possibilities of Socialism*, London: Routledge: 87–130.

—— (1966 [1949]) *Human Action. A Treatise On Economics*, 4th revised edn, San Francisco: Fox & Wilkes.

Mittelman, James H. (2000) *The Globalization Syndrome: Transformation and Resistance*, Princeton: Princeton University Press.

Modzelewski, Karol (1993) *Dokad od kommunizmu*, Warszawa: Polska Oficyna Wydawn, BGW.

Mohn, Reinhard (1986) *Erfolg durch Partnerschaft. Eine Unternehmensstrategie für den Menschen*, Gütersloh: Verlag Bertelsmann Stiftung.

Mont Pèlerin Society (MPS) (2002) 'Short History and Statement of Aims'. Available HTTP: www.montpelerin.org/aboutmps.html (accessed 21 January 2005).

Moody, Kim (1997) *Workers in a Lean World. Unions in the International Economy*, London and New York.

Morton, Adam David (2001a) 'Historicizing Gramsci: Situating Ideas in and Beyond Their Context', *Review of International Political Economy*, 10(1): 118–46.

—— (2001b) 'The Sociology of Theorising and Neo-Gramscian Perspectives: The Problems of "School" Formation in IPE', in Andreas Bieler and Adam David Morton (eds) *Social Forces in the Making of the New Europe*, Houndsmills: Palgrave: 25–43.
Mosley, Paul, Jane Harrigan and John Toye (1991) *Aid and Power: The World Bank and Policy-based Lending*, vol. 1, London: Routledge.
Mückenberger, Ulrich, Gertrude Krell and Karin Tondorf (2000) 'Gender Mainstreaming', in Niedersächsischen Ministeriums für Frauen, Arbeit und Soziales, *Gender Mainstreaming. Informationen und Impulse*, Hannover: 1–22.
Múcsi, Ferenc (1990) 'The Start of Karl Polanyi's Career', in Kari Polanyi-Levitt (ed.) *The Life and Work of Karl Polanyi: A Celebration*, Montreal: Black Rose Books: 26–9.
Müller, Katharina (1998) 'Transformation als Lateinamerikanisierung? Die neue rentenpolitische Orthodoxie in Ungarn und Polen', *Prokla*, 28(112): 459–86.
Müller-Böling, Detlef (2000) *Die entfesselte Hochschule*, Gütersloh: Verlag Bertelsmann Stiftung.
Murphy, Craig N. (1994) *International Organization and Industrial Change*, Cambridge: Polity Press.
Murrell, Peter (1983) 'Did the Theory of Market Socialism Answer the Challenge of Ludwig von Mises? A Reinterpretation of the Socialist Controversy?', *History of Political Economy*, 15(1): 92–105.
—— (1994) 'Playing Political Economy: Goals and Outcomes of Russia's Economic Reforms of 1992', *International Journal of Political Economy*, 24(1): 34–51.
—— (1996) 'How Far Has the Transition Progressed?', *Journal of Economic Perspectives*, 10(2): 25–44.
Myhre, Øyvind (1990) 'Bull Running's War', in *New Libertarian*, 187, Fountain Valley, CA: New Libertarian Company of Free Traders: 12–14 and 55–9.
Nagy, Endre J. (1994) 'After Brotherhood's Golden Age: Karl and Michael Polanyi', in Kenneth McRobbie (ed.) *Humanity, Society and Commitment: On Karl Polanyi*, Montreal: Black Rose Books: 81–114.
Netzwerk Europäische Lernprozesse (NELP) (2002) 'Manifest "Bildung für die Arbeits- und Wissensgesellschaft"', Hannover. Available HTTP: www.nelp.de/beitraege/05_bildung/nelp2_manifest.doc (accessed 18 January 2005).
NIRA (2002) 'NIRA's World Directory on Think Tanks', web version, compiled and published by the Center for Policy Research Information, National Institute for Research Advancement, Tokyo. Available HTTP: www.nira.go.jp/ice/nwdtt/index.html#1 (accessed 5 June 2003).
Niven, Larry and Jerry Pournelle (1993 [1981]) *Oath of Fealty*, New York: Pocket Books.
Nohr, Barbara and Silke Veth (eds) (2002) *Gender Mainstreaming – Kritische Reflexionen einer neuen Strategie*, Berlin: Karl Dietz Verlag.
Nolan, Peter (2001) *China and the Global Economy*, Basingstoke: Palgrave.
Noland, Marcus (2000) *Avoiding the Apocalypse: The Future of the Two Koreas*, Washington: The Institute for International Economics.
Norberg, Johan (2001) *In Defense of Global Capitalism*, Stockholm: Timbro.
North, Douglass C. (1981) *Structure and Change in Economic History*, New York: W. W. Norton.
—— (1990) *Institutional Change and Economic Performance*, Cambridge: Cambridge University Press.
Norton, Robert E. (1994) 'Jeff Sachs – Doctor Debt', in P. W. Drake (ed.) *Money Doctors, Foreign Debts, and Economic Reforms in Latin America from the 1890s to the Present*, Wilmington: Scholarly Resources Inc.: 231–5.
Nozick, Robert (1974) *Anarchy, State, and Utopia*, Oxford: Blackwell.

Nullmeier, Frank (2000) '"Mehr Wettbewerb!" Zur Marktkonstitution in der Hochschulpolitik', in Roland Czada and Susanne Lütz (eds) *Die politische Konstitution von Märkten*, Opladen: Westdeutscher Verlag: 209–27.

Nye, Joseph S., jr (2002) *The Paradox of American Power: Why the World's only Superpower Can't Go it Alone*, Oxford and New York: Oxford University Press.

Orth, Michael (1990) 'Reefs on the Right. Fascist Politics in Contemporary American Libertarian Utopias', *Extrapolation*, 31(4), Wooster, OH: Kent State University: 293–316.

Orwell, George (1983 [1949]) *1984*, New York: Signet.

Ost, David (1990) *Solidarity and the Politics of Anti-Politics. Opposition and Reform in Poland since 1968*, Philadelphia: Temple University Press.

—— (1993) 'The Politics of Interest in Post-Communist East Europe', *Theory and Society*, (22): 453–86.

Ost, David and Marc Weinstein (1999) 'Unionists Against Unions: Towards Hierarchical Management in Post-Communist Poland', *East European Politics and Society*, 13(1): 1–33.

Overbeek, Henk (ed.) (1993) *Restructuring Hegemony in the Global Political Economy: The Rise of Transnational Neo-Liberalism in the 1980s*, London: Routledge.

—— (2000) 'Transnational Historical Materialism: Theories of Transnational Class Formation and World Order', in Ronen Palan (ed.) *Global Political Economy: Contemporary Theories*, London: Routledge: 168–83.

Overbeek, Henk and Kees van der Pijl (1993) 'Restructuring Capital and Restructuring Hegemony: Neo-Liberalism and the Unmaking of the Post-War Order', in Henk Overbeek (ed.) *Restructuring Hegemony in the Global Political Economy: The Rise of Transnational Neo-liberalism in the 1980s*, London: Routledge:1–27.

Pack, Howard (1988) 'Industrialization and Trade', in Hollis Chenery and T. N. Srinivasan (eds), *Handbook of Development Economics*, vol 1, Amsterdam: North Holland: 334–80.

Packenham, Robert A. (1973) *Liberal America and the Third World: Political Development Ideas in Foreign Aid and Social Science*, Princeton: Princeton University Press.

Panitch, Leo (1998) 'The State in a Changing World: Social Democratizing Global Capitalism', *Monthly Review*: 50, 5.

—— (1999) 'The Impoverishment of State Theory', *Socialism and Democracy*, 13(2): 19–35.

—— (2000a) 'Reflections on Strategy for Labour', in Leo Panitch and Colin Leys (eds) *Socialist Register 2001: Working Classes, Global Realities*, London: Merlin Press, 367–92.

—— (2000b) 'The New Imperial State', *New Left Review*, (II) 2, 5–20.

Panitch, Leo and Sam Gindin (2003) 'American Imperialism and Eurocapitalism: The Making of Neoliberal Globalization', *Studies in Political Economy*, 71/72: 7–37.

Panitch, Leo and Colin Leys (eds) (2003) *The New Imperial Challenge. Socialist Register 2004*, London: Merlin Press.

Pasche, Cécile and Suzanne Peters (1997) 'Les premiers pas de la Société du Mont-Pèlerin ou les dessous chics du néolibéralisme', *Les Annuelles*, 8(8): 191–230.

Paul, James A. (2001) 'Der Weg zum Global Compact. Zur Annäherung von UNO und multinationalen Unternehmen', in Tanja Brühl, Tobias Debiel, Brigitte Hamm, Hartwig Hummel and Jens Martens (eds) *Die Privatisierung der Weltpolitik. Entstaatlichung und Kommerzialisierung im Globalisierungsprozess*, Bonn: Dietz Verlag: 104–29.

PEF (Poder Ejecutivo Federal) (2002) *Segundo Informe de gobierno*, Anexo, Mexico: PEF.

Pelizzari, Alessandro (2001) *Die ökonomisierung des Politischen*, Konstanz: Universitätsverlag Konstanz.

Pender, John (2001) 'From "Structural Adjustment" to "Comprehensive Development Framework": Conditionality Transformed?', *Third World Quarterly: Journal of Emerging Areas*, 22(3): 397–411.

References 275

People for the American Way (PFAW) (2002) 'Buying a Movement: Right-Wing Foundations and American Politics', Washington, DC: People for the American Way. Available HTTP: www.pfaw.org/pfaw/dfiles/file_33.pdf.
Perkin, Harold (1989) *The Rise of Professional Society*, London: Routledge.
Perrow, Charles (1986) *Complex Organizations. A Critical Essay*, New York: McGraw-Hill.
Peschek, Joseph G. (1987) *Policy-Planning Organizations: Elite Agenda and America's Rightward Turn*, Philadelphia, PA: Temple University Press.
Petersen, Hans (1996) *Der Terminus frontier im Amerikanischen. Ursprung, Wandlung und Wirkung einer Sprach- und Denkform*, Kassel: Gesamthochschul-Bibliothek.
Piper, H. Beam and John J. McGuire (1958) *A Planet for Texans*, New York: Ace.
Plehwe, Dieter (2000) *Deregulierung und transnationale Integration der Transportwirtschaft in Nordamerika*, Münster: Westfaelisches Dampfboot.
—— (2002) 'Neoliberale Ideen aus der nationalen Peripherie ins Zentrum gerückt: Der Fall Mexiko', *Journal für Entwicklungspolitik*, 29(2): 249–64.
Plehwe, Dieter with Stefano Vescovi (2003) 'Beyond National Coherence: the Political Re-Grouping of European Companies', in Marie Laure Djelic and Sigrid Quack (eds) *Globalisation and Institutions – Redefining the Rules of the Economic Game*, Cheltenham and Northampton, MA: Edward Elgar: 193–219.
Plehwe, Dieter and Bernhard Walpen (1998) 'Ein "Art von internationaler fünfter Kolonne des Liberalismus". Die Bedeutung der Mont-Pèlerin-Society für den marktradikalen Neoliberalismus', in Regina Stötzel (ed.) *Ungleichheit als Projekt. Globalisierung – Standort – Neoliberalismus*, Marburg: BDWI Verlag: 367–80.
—— (1999) 'Wissenschaftliche und wissenschaftspolitische Produktionsweisen im Neoliberalismus. Beiträge der Mont Pèlerin Society and marktradikaler Think Tanks zur Hegemoniegewinnung und-erhaltung', *Prokla* 29(115): 203–35.
—— (2004) 'Buena Vista Neoliberal? Eine klassentheoretische und organisationszentrierte Einführung in die transnationale Welt neoliberaler Ideen', in Klaus-Gerd Giesen (ed.) *Ideologien in der Weltpolitik*, Wiesbaden: VS Verlag für Sozialwissenschaften: 49–88.
Polanyi, Karl (1944) *The Great Transformation*, New York: Rinehart & Co.
Polanyi, Michael (1946) *Science, Faith and Society*, Chicago: University of Chicago Press.
Polanyi, Michael (1951a) *The Logic of Liberty*, Chicago: University of Chicago Press.
Polanyi, Michael (1951b) 'Planning for Freedom', review of *Freedom, Power and Democratic Planning* by Karl Mannheim, *Manchester Guardian*, 3 July: 4.
Polanyi, Michael (1952) 'Mannheim's Historicism', review of *Essays on the Sociology of Knowledge* by Karl Mannheim, *Manchester Guardian*, 9 December: 4.
—— (1953) 'Scientism', review of *The Counter Revolution in Science* by F. A. Hayek, *Manchester Guardian*, 2 January: 3.
—— (1955) 'Preface', in *Science and Freedom: Proceedings of a Conference Convened by the Congress for Cultural Freedom, Hamburg, 1953*, London: Secker and Warburg.
—— (1958) *Personal Knowledge: Towards a Post-Critical Philosophy*, London: Routledge and Kegan Paul.
—— (1967) *The Tacit Dimension*, New York: Doubleday.
Polanyi-Levitt, Kari (ed.) (1990) *The Life and Work of Karl Polanyi: A Celebration*, Montreal: Black Rose Books.
Poulantzas, Nicos (1978) *Staatstheorie. Politischer überbau, Ideologie, Sozialistische Demokratie*, Hamburg: VSA-Verlag.
—— (2001 [1974]) 'Die Internationalisierung der kapitalistischen Verhältnisse und der Nationalstaat', in Joachim Hirsch, Bob Jessop and Nicos Poulantzas (2001) *Die Zukunft des Staates. Denationalisierung, Internationalisierung, Renationalisierung*, Hamburg: VSA-Verlag: 19–69.

Preston, Peter W. (1987) *Rethinking Development: Essays on Development in Southeast Asia*, London: Routledge and Kegan Paul.
Prosch, Harry (1986) *Michael Polanyi: A Critical Exposition*, Albany, NY: SUNY Press.
Prystay, Cris (2002) 'Malaysia: The Retail-Shopping War', *Far Eastern Economic Review*, 25 April.
Rand, Ayn (1943) *The Fountainhead*, Indianapolis: Bobbs Merrill.
—— (1989 [1946]) *Anthem*, New York: Penguin.
—— (1992 [1957]) *Atlas Shrugged*, New York: Signet.
Rawls, John (1972) *Theory of Justice*, Oxford: Clarendon Press.
Rees, Teresa (1998) 'Equal Opportunities and Mainstreaming in Leonardo Da Vinci', *femina politica*, 7(2): 56–60.
Regenhard, Ulla (1997) 'Dezentralisierung als Schritt zum Abbau der Geschlechterdifferenz?', *WSI-Mitteilungen*, 50(1): 38–50.
Reich, Robert (1991) *The Work of Nations. Preparing Ourselves for 21st Century Capitalism*, New York: Alfred A. Knopf.
Ricci, David M. (1993) *The Transformation of American Politics: The New Washington and the Rise of Think Tanks*, New Haven: Yale University Press.
Riedl, James (1991) 'Strategy Wars: The State of Debate on Trade and Industrialization in Developing Countries', in, Ad Koekkoek and L. B. M. Mennes (eds) *International Trade and Global Development*, London: Routledge: 62–82.
Ritch, William Alan (1998) 'If Pigs Had Wings', in Brad Linaweaver and Edward E. Kramer (eds) *Free Space*, New York: Tor: 247–62.
Robbins, Lionel (1971) *Autobiography of an Economist*, London: Macmillan.
Robinson, William I. (2004) *A Theory of Global Capitalism. Production, Class, and State in a Transnational World*, Baltimore: Johns Hopkins University Press.
Robinson, William I. and Jerry Harris (2000) 'Towards a Global Ruling Class? Globalization and the Transnational Capitalist Class', *Science & Society*, 64(1): 11–54.
Roelofs, Joan (2003) *Foundations and Public Policy: The Mask of Pluralism*, New York: SUNY Press.
Ronit, Karsten (2001) 'Institutions of Private Authority in Global Governance: Linking Territorial Forms of Self-Regulation', *Administration & Society*, 33(5): 555–78.
Ros, Jaime (1991) *Mexico's Trade and Industrialization Experience Since 1960: A Reconsideration of Past Policies and Assessment of Current Reforms*, Prepared for ONU/WIDER.
Rose, Gillian (1992) *The Broken Middle: Out of our Ancient Society*, Oxford: Blackwell.
Rose, Nikolas (1999) *Powers of Freedom: Reframing Political Thought*, Cambridge: Cambridge University Press.
Rosner, Peter (1990) 'Karl Polanyi on Socialist Accounting', in Kari Polanyi-Levitt (ed.) *The Life and Work of Karl Polanyi: A Celebration*, Montreal: Black Rose Books: 55–65.
Rubery, Gill and Colette Fagan (1998) 'Equal Opportunities and Employment in the European Union', publication of the Federal Ministry of Labour, Health and Social Affairs, Vienna, Austria.
Rubin, Barnett R. (2002) *The Fragmentation of Afghanistan: State Formation and Collapse in the International System*, 2nd edn, New Haven: Yale University Press.
Rucht, Dieter (2002) 'Von Seattle nach Genua – Event hopping oder neue soziale Bewegung?', in Attac-Deutschland (ed.) *Eine andere Welt ist möglich*, Hamburg: VSA-Verlag: 50–56.
—— (2003) 'Zivilgesellschaftliche Akteure und transnationale Politik', in Arnd Bauerkämper with Manuel Borutta (eds) *Die Praxis der Zivilgesellschaft – Akteure, Handeln und Strukturen im internationalen Vergleich*, Frankfurt/Main: Campus Verlag: 371–89.

Ruggie, John Gerard (1982) 'International Regimes, Transactions and Change: Embedded Liberalism in the Postwar Economic Order', *International Organization*, 36(2): 379–416.

—— (1983) 'International Regimes, Transactions and Change: Embedded Liberalism in the Postwar Economic Order', in Stephen D. Krasner (ed.) *International Regimes*, Ithaca: Cornell University Press: 195–232.

Rupnik, Jacques (1993) *L'autre Europe. Crise et fin du communisme*, Paris: Editions Odile Jacob.

Russell, Eric Frank (1993 [1962]) *The Great Explosion*, New York: Carroll & Graf.

Ryder, Jay (2000) '[LIBFUT] Libfic Scenario #1', LIBFUT mailing list, online posting. Available HTTP: www.uio.no/thomas/lists/libfut.html (accessed 8 June 2000).

Ryner, Magnus (2002) *Capitalist Restructuring, Globalisation and the Third Way*, London: Routledge.

Sachs, Jeffrey (1990) 'What Is to Be Done?', *The Economist*, 13 January.

—— (1993) *Poland's Jump to the Market Economy*, Cambridge, MA: MIT.

Sachverständigenrat Bildung bei der Hans-Böckler-Stiftung (1998) *Für ein verändertes System der Bildungsfinanzierung* (discussion paper no. 1), Düsseldorf: Hans-Böckler-Stiftung.

Salinas de Gortari, Carlos (2000) *México. Un paso difícil a la modernidad*, Mexico: Plaza & Janés Editores.

Salinas de Gortari, Carlos and Roberto Mangabeira Unger (1999) 'Hacia un mercado sin neoliberalismo', *Reforma*, 20 and 21 January: 8A and 18A.

Sandel, Michael J. (1982) *Liberalism and the Limits of Justice*, Cambridge: Cambridge University Press.

Sassoon, Donald (1997) *One Hundred Years of Socialism. The West European Left in the Twentieth Century*, New York: New Press.

Schaefer, Brett D. (1998) 'How Congress Should Reform the International Monetary Fund', *Heritage Foundation Backgrounder*, no. 1167, Washington, DC: Heritage Foundation.

Schelsky, Helmut (1975) *Die Arbeit tun die anderen. Klassenkampf und Priesterherrschaft der Intellektuellen*, Opladen: Westdeutscher Verlag.

Scherrer, Christoph (1999) *Globalisierung wider Willen? Die Durchsetzung liberaler Außenwirtschaftspolitik in den USA*, Berlin: Sigma.

Schmitz, Gerald J. (1995) 'Democratization and Demystification: Deconstructing "Governance" as Development Paradigm', in David B. Moore and Gerald J. Schmitz (eds) *Debating Development Discourse: Institutional and Popular Perspectives*, New York: St Martin's Press.

Schöller, Oliver (2001) '"Geistige Orientierung" der Bertelsmann-Stiftung. Beiträge einer deutschen Denkfabrik zur gesellschaftlichen Konstruktion der Wirklichkeit', *Prokla*, 31(122): 123–43.

—— (2003) 'Bertelsmann geht voran. Zur gesellschaftspolitischen Bedeutung eines deutschen Think Tanks', *Utopie kreativ*, (155): 803–11.

Schöller, Oliver, Ulrich Brinkmann, Dietmar Borchert, Anne Buchmann, Aziz Aygün, Sven Eisenmann, Nikolaus Steffen, Andreas Bülow, Thomas Prass and Birgit-Wagner Hilliger (2000) 'Der neue Lernbürger – oder: Bildung als Wettbewerbsfaktor. Zu den Vorschlägen des Sachverständigenrat Bildung bei der Hans-Böckler-Stiftung', *Sozialismus*, (4): 39–45.

Schonberger, Howard B. (1989) *Aftermath of War: Americans and the Remaking of Japan 1945–1952*, Kent: Kent State University Press.

Schulman, Neil J[oseph] (1996 [1983]) *The Rainbow Cadenza*, Long Beach, CA: Pulpless.

Schulman, J[oseph] Neil (1998) 'Day of Atonement', in Brad Linaweaver and Edward E. Kramer (eds) *Free Space*, New York: Tor: 49–60.

Schumpeter, Joseph (1942) *Capitalism, Socialism and Democracy*, New York: Harper and Brothers.

Schunter-Kleemann, Susanne (1993) 'Geschlechterdifferenz in der politischen Debatte zur Europäischen Union', *Prokla*, 23(92): 451–72.
—— (1999) 'Mainstreaming as an Innovative Approach of the EU Policy of Equal Opportunities?', Hochschule Bremen, University of Applied Sciences, Scientific Unit for Women's Studies and Women's Research, Discussion papers 3: 1–30.
—— (2000) 'Gender Mainstreaming as a Strategy for Modernising Gender Relations?', in Sylvia Trnk (ed.) *Family Issues Between Gender and Generations. Seminar Report*, Luxembourg: European Commission, Directorate-General for Employment and Social Affairs and European Observatory on Family Matters: 79–85.
—— (2002) 'Gender Mainstreaming, Work Fare und Dritte Wege des Neoliberalismus', in Barbara Nohr and Silke Veth (eds) *Gender Mainstreaming. Kritische Reflexionen einer neuen Strategie*, Berlin: Karl Dietz Verlag: 125–40.
Schwartz, Nancy (1974) 'THX 1138 vs. Metropolis: The New Politics of Science Fiction Film', in Ralph J. Amelio (ed.) *Hal In The Classroom: Science Fiction Films*, Dayton, OH: Pflaum: 60–71.
Scott, David (1999) *Refashioning Futures: Criticism After Postcoloniality*, Princeton: Princeton University Press.
Scott-Smith, Giles (2002) *The Politics of Apolitical Culture. The Congress for Cultural Freedom, the CIA and Post-War American Hegemony*, London and New York: Routledge.
Seldon, Arthur (ed.) (1985) *The New Right Enlightenment*, Seven Oaks: E & L Books.
Sell, Susan K. (1999) 'Multinational Corporations as Agents of Change: The Globalization of Intellectual Property Rights', in A. Claire Cutler, Virginia Haufler and Tony Porter (eds) (1999) *Private Authority and International Affairs*, Albany, NY: State University of New York Press: 169–98.
Sell, Susan K. (2000) 'Structures, Agents and Institutions: Private Corporate Power and the Globalisation of Intellectual Property Rights', in Richard A. Higgott, Geoffrey Underhill and Andreas Bieler (eds) (2000) *Non-State Actors and Authority in the Global System*, London and New York: Routledge: 91–106.
Seltzer, Mark (1992) *Bodies and Machines*, New York: Routledge.
Shaw, Martin (2000) *Theory of the Global State: Globality as an Unfinished Revolution*, Cambridge: Cambridge University Press.
Shields, Stuart (2001) 'Transnational Social Forces and the Configuration of Polish Transition: Neo-Liberalism Revisited', *Irish Studies in International Affairs*, 12(1): 21–37.
—— (2003) 'The Charge of the "Right Brigade": Transnational Forces and the Neoliberal Configuration of Poland's Transition', *New Political Economy*, 8(2): 225–44.
Sinclair, Timothy J. (1999) 'Bond-Rating Agencies and Coordination in the Global Political Economy', in A. Claire Cutler, Virginia Haufler and Tony Porter (eds) *Private Authority and International Affairs*, Albany, NY: State University of New York Press: 153–68.
Skidelsky, Robert (1997) *The Road from Serfdom. The Economic and Political Consequences of the End of Communism*, New York and London: Penguin Books.
Sklair, Leslie (1998) 'Social Movements and Global Capitalism', in Fredric Jameson and Masao Miyoshi (eds) *The Cultures of Globalization*, Durham: Duke University Press: 291–311.
—— (2001) *The Transnational Capitalist Class*, Oxford: Blackwell Publishers.
Skocpol, Theda (1985) 'Bringing the State Back In: Strategies of Analysis in Current Research', in Peter B. Evans, Dietrich Rueshemeyer and Theda Skocpol (eds) *Bringing the State Back In*, New York: Cambridge University Press.
Smith, Jackie (2001) 'Globalizing Resistance: The Battle of Seattle and the Future of Social Movements', *Mobilization: An International Journal*, 6(1): 1–20.

—— (2002) 'Bridging Global Divides? Strategic Framing and Solidarity in Transnational Social Movement Organizations', *International Sociology*, 17(4): 505–28.
Smith, James A. (1991) *The Idea Brokers. Think Tanks and the Rise of the New Policy Elite*, New York: The Free Press.
Smith, Joan (1997) 'The Ideology of "Family and Community": New Labour Abandons the Welfare State', in Leo Panitch (ed.) *Ruthless Criticism of all that Exists. Socialist Register*, London: Merlin Press: 176–96.
Smith, L. Neil (1996 [1980]) *The Probability Broach*, New York: Tor.
Smith, Martin (1999) *Burma: Insurgency and the Politics of Ethnicity*, 2nd edn, London: Zed Press.
Smith, Philip E. (1978) 'The Evolution of Politics and the Politics of Evolution. Social Darwinism in Heinlein's Fiction', in Joseph D. Olander and Martin Harry Greenberg (eds) *Robert A. Heinlein*, Edinburgh: Harris: 137–71.
Smith, W. Rand (1998) *The Left's Dirty Job. The Politics of Industrial Restructuring in France and Spain*, Pittsburgh: University of Pittsburgh Press.
Smolar, Aleksander (1991) 'The Polish Opposition', in Ferenc Féher and Andrew Arato (eds) *Crisis and Reform in Eastern Europe*, New Brunswick and London: Transaction: 175–252.
Soros, George (1998) *The Crisis of Global Capitalism: Open Society Endangered*, New York: Public Affairs.
Spindler, Manuela (2002) 'New Regionalism and the Construction of Global Order', CSGR Working Paper no. 93/02. Available HTTP: www2.warwick.ac.uk/fac/soc/csgr/research/workingpapers/2002/wp9302.pdf (accessed 21 January 2005).
Srinivasan, T. N. (1985) 'Trade Policy and Development', in Jagdish N. Bhagwati and Gene Grossman (eds) *Essays in Development Economics, vol. 2: Dependence and Interdependence*, Cambridge: The MIT Press: 88–122.
Staniszkis, Jadwiga (1984) *Poland's Self-Limiting Revolution*, Princeton: Princeton University Press.
Stark, David and Laszlo Bruszt (1998) *Postsocialist Pathways: Transforming Politics and Property in East Central Europe*, Cambridge: Cambridge University Press.
Stephenson, Neal (1993 [1992]) *Snow Crash*, New York: Bantam.
Steven, Rob (1994) 'New World Order: A New Imperialism', *Journal of Contemporary Asia*, 24: 271–96.
Stiegler, Barbara (1999) *Frauen im Mainstreaming. Politische Strategien und Theorien zur Geschlechterfrage*, Bonn: Friedrich-Ebert-Stiftung.
Stifterverband für die Deutsche Wissenschaft/Zentrum für Hochschulentwicklung (1998) 'Modell für einen Beitrag der Studierenden zur Finanzierung der Hochschulen (Studienbeitragsmodell)', Essen and Gütersloh. Available HTTP: www.che.de/downloads/Stgebmod.pdf (accessed 18 January 2005).
Stiglitz, Joseph E. (1998) 'More Instruments and Broader Goals: Moving toward the Post-Washington Consensus', The 1998 WIDER Annual Lecture, World Bank, 7 January, Helsinki.
—— (2000) 'Democratic Development as the Fruits of Labor', keynote address presented at the Industrial Relations Research Association, Boston, MA, January. Available HTTP: www.worldbank.org/knowledge/chiefecon/articles/boston.pdf (accessed 18 January 2005).
—— (2002) *Globalization and Its Discontents*, New York: W. W. Norton.
Stone, Diane (1996) *Capturing the Political Imagination. Think Tanks and the Policy Process*, London-Portland: Frank Cass.

—— (ed.) (2000a) *Banking on Knowledge. The Genesis of the Global Development Network*, London: Routledge.

—— (2000b) 'Private Authority, Scholarly Legitimacy and Political Credibility: Think Tanks and Informal Diplomacy', in Richard A. Higgott, Geoffrey Underhill and Andreas Bieler (eds) *Non-State Actors and Authority in the Global System*, London and New York: Routledge: 211–25.

Stone, Diane, Andrew Denham and Mark Garnett (eds) (1998) *Think Tanks Across Nations. A Comparative Approach*, Manchester and New York: Manchester University Press.

Stover, Leon (1987) *Robert A. Heinlein*, Boston: Twayne.

Strange, Susan (1988) *States and Markets. An Introduction to International Political Economy*, London: Pinter Publishers.

—— (1994 [1988]) *States and Markets*, 2nd edn, London–New York: Pinter.

—— (1996) *The Retreat of the State: The Diffusion of Power in the World Economy*, Cambridge: Cambridge University Press (Cambridge Studies in International Relations).

—— (1997) *Casino Capitalism*, New York: St Martin's Press.

Streeck, Wolfgang and Philip C. Schmitter (eds) (1985) *Private Interest Government. Beyond Market and State*, London: Sage.

Stubbs, Richard (1994) 'The Political Economy of the Asia-Pacific Region', in Richard Stubbs and Geoffrey R. D. Underhill (eds) *Political Economy and the Changing Global Order*, London: Macmillan.

—— (1999) 'War and Economic Development: Export-Oriented Industrialization in East and Southeast Asia', *Comparative Politics*, 31(3): 337–55.

Szacki, Jerzy (1995) *Liberalism After Communism*, Budapest, London and New York: Central University Press.

Taylor, Charles (1992) *Negative Freiheit? Zur Kritik des neuzeitlichen Individualismus*, Frankfurt a.M.: Suhrkamp.

Toffler, Alvin (1964) 'Ayn Rand. A Candid Interview with the Fountainhead of "Objectivism"', *Playboy*, March: 35–43 and 64.

Tondof, Karin (2001) 'Gender Mainstreaming – verbindliches Leitprinzip für Politik und Verwaltung', *WSI-Mitteilungen*, 54(4): 271–7.

Treanor, Paul (1996) 'Liberalism. Interacting to Conserve', *Politics*, 16(2): 121–6.

Turner, Frederic Jackson (1894) 'The Significance of the Frontier in American History', in *Annual Report of the American Historical Association for the Year 1893*, Washington, DC.: US Government Printing Office: 199–207.

Tusk, Donald (1987) 'Droga I wybor', *Przeglad Polityczny* 9 (written under the pseudonym of Tadeusz Donecki). Available HTTP: http://tusk.aompdt.com/publikacje.drogaiw.html (accessed 14 May 2001).

—— (1989) 'Prawo do polityki', *Przeglad Polityczny* 12. Available HTTP: http://tusk.aompdt.com/publickacje.prawodop.html (accessed 14 May 2001).

Unmüßig, Barbara (2002) 'Attac – Zwischenbilanz, Herausforderungen, Perspektiven', in Attac-Deutschland (ed.) *Eine andere Welt ist möglich*, Hamburg: VSA-Verlag: 18–24.

Useem, Michael (1984) *The Inner Circle*, New York: Oxford University Press.

Valdés, Juan Gabriel (1995) *Pinochet's Economists. The Chicago School in Chile*, Cambridge–New York–Melbourne: Cambridge University Press.

van der Pijl, Kees (1994) *The Making of an Atlantic Ruling Class*, London: Verso.

—— (1995) 'The Second Glorious Revolution: Globalizing Elites and Historical Change', in Björn Hettne (ed.) *International Political Economy. Understanding Global Disorder*, London and New Jersey: Zed Books: 100–28.

—— (1998) *Transnational Classes and International Relations*, London: Routledge.

Vester, Michael, Peter von Oertzen, Heiko Geiling, Thomas Hermann and Dagmar Müller (2001) *Soziale Milieus im gesellschaftlichen Strukturwandel. Zwischen Integration und Ausgrenzung*, 2nd expanded edn, Köln: Bund Verlag.
Vinge, Joan D. and Vernor Vinge (1987 [1975]) 'The Peddler's Apprentice', in Vernor Vinge, *True Names ... and Other Dangers*, New York: Simon & Schuster: 146–97.
Vinge, Vernor (1987 [1985]) 'The Ungoverned', in Vernor Vinge, *True Names ... and Other Dangers*, New York: Simon & Schuster: 200–54.
—— (2000 [1999]) *A Deepness in the Sky*, New York: Tor.
Wade, Robert (1990) *Governing the Market: Economic Theory and the Role of Government in East Asian Industrialisation*, Princeton: Princeton University Press.
—— (1996) 'Japan, the World Bank, and the Art of Paradigm Maintenance: The East Asian Miracle in Political Perspective', *New Left Review*, I(217): 124–37.
Wahl, Peter (2003) 'Is Diversity Really our Strength? Some Reflections on Diversity, Hegemony and Power inside the Movement against Neoliberal Globalization', presented at the Conference 'Hegemony and Counter-Hegemony in Global Capitalism', Porto Alegre, 21 and 22 January.
Wainwright, Hilary (1992) *The Politics of Knowledge: The Challenge of Neo-Liberalism to the European Left*, Manchester Sociology Occasional Papers no. 36, Manchester: Manchester University Department of Sociology; a slightly revised version appeared as Chs 2–4 of Hilary Wainwright (1994) *Arguments for a New Left: Answering the Free-Market Right*, Oxford: Blackwell.
—— (1994) *Arguments for a New Left: Answering the Free-Market Right*, Oxford: Blackwell.
Walby, Silvia (1998) 'The Implications of the Regulatory Powers of the European Union for Equal Opportunities Policies', paper presented to the Kvinfo Conference in Faaborg, Denmark, 14 and 15 May.
Walicki, Andrzej (1988) 'Liberalism in Poland', *Critical Review*, 2(1): 8–38.
—— (1991) 'Notes on Jaruzelski's Poland', in Ferenc Féher and Andrew Arato (eds) *Crisis and Reform in Eastern Europe*, New Brunswick and London: Transaction: 335–93.
Wallerstein, Immanuel (1999) 'The Rise of East Asia, or the World-System in the Twenty-First Century', in Immanuel Wallerstein, *The End of the World As We Know It: Social Science for the Twenty-First Century*, Minneapolis: University of Minnesota Press.
Walpen, Bernhard (2000) 'Von Hasen und Igeln oder: Ein Blick auf den Neoliberalismus', *Utopie kreativ*, (121/122): 1066–79.
—— (2002) 'Neoliberale Wissensproduktion in Taiwan. Eine erste Problemskizze', *Journal für Entwicklungspolitik*, 29(2): 209–24.
—— (2004) *Die offenen Feinde und ihre Gesellschaft. Eine hegemonietheoretische Studie zur Mont Pèlerin Society*, Hamburg: VSA-Verlag.
Walpen, Bernhard and Dieter Plehwe (2001) 'Wahrheitsgetreue Berichte über Chile: Die Mont Pèlerin Society und die Diktatur Pinochet', *1999. Zeitschrift für Sozialgeschichte des 20. und 21. Jahrhunderts*, 16(2): 42–70.
Watanabe, Takeshi, Jacques Lesourne and Robert S. McNamara (1983) 'Facilitating Development in a Changing Third World: Trade, Finance, Aid', Task Force Report #27, The Trilateral Commission.
Wee Wan-ling, Christopher Justin (2001) 'The End of Disciplinary Modernisation? The Asian Economic Crisis and the Ongoing Re-Invention of Singapore', *Third World Quarterly: Journal of Emerging Areas*, 22(6): 987–1002.
Weingart, Peter (1982) 'The Scientific Power Elite – a Chimera: The De-institutionalization and Politicization of Science', in Norbert Elias, Herminio Martins and Richard Whitley (eds) *Scientific Establishments and Hierarchies. Sociology of the Sciences: a Yearbook*, Dordrecht-Boston: D. Reidel Pub. Co.: 71–89.

Weinstein, Marc (2000) 'Solidarity's Abandonment of Worker Councils: Redefining Employee Stakeholder Rights in Post-socialist Poland', *British Journal of Industrial Relations*, 38(1): 49–73.
Weiss, Linda (1998) *The Myth of the Powerless State: Governing the Economy in a Global Era*, Cambridge: Polity Press.
—— (1999) 'Managed Openness: Beyond Neoliberal Globalism', *New Left Review*, I(238): 126–40.
Weller, Christian E. (2000a) 'Financial Liberalisation, Multinational Banks and Credit Supply', *International Review of Applied Economics*, 14(2): 193–211.
—— (2000b) 'Multinational Banks in Developing and Transition Economies', *EPI Technical Paper*, no. 241, Washington, DC: Economic Policy Institute.
—— (2000c) 'Meltzer Report Misses the Mark: Commission's Recommendations for World Bank, IMF Need Further Consideration', *EPI Issue Brief*, no. 141, Washington, DC: Economic Policy Institute.
—— (2001) 'Financial Crises After Financial Liberalization: Exceptional Circumstances or Structural Weakness?', *Journal of Development Studies*, 38(1): 98–127.
—— (2002) 'Austerity or Bust? Argentina's Options for Economic Revival', *Challenge*, 45(3): 44–57.
Westad, Odd Arne (2000) 'The New International History of the Cold War: Three (Possible) Paradigms', *Diplomatic History*, 24(4): 551–65.
White House (2002) 'The Millennium Challenge Account', Washington, DC: The White House. Available HTTP: www.whitehouse.gov/infocus/developingnations/millennium.html.
Whyte, William H. (1956) *The Organization Man*, New York: Simon & Schuster.
Wiegersma, Nan and Joseph E. Medley (2000) *US Economic Development Policies Towards the Pacific Rim: Successes and Failures of US Aid*, London: Macmillan.
Wilczyński, Waclaw (1999) *Wrogie państwo opiekuńcze*, Warszawa: PWN.
Williamson, John (1990) 'What Washington Means by Policy Reform', in John Williamson, (ed.) *Latin American Adjustment: How Much Has Happened?*, Washington: Institute for International Economics.
—— (1992) 'Democratization and the "Washington Consensus"', paper prepared for the conference on 'Economic Liberalization and Democratic Consolidation', University of Bologna, Italy, 2–4 April.
Wilson, F[rancis] Paul (1980 [1978]) *Wheels Within Wheels*, London: Sidgwick & Jackson.
Wilson, F[rancis] Paul (1980) *An Enemy of the State*, Garden City, NY: Doubleday.
Wissenschaftsrat (1985) 'Empfehlungen zum Wettbewerb im deutschen Hochschulsystem', Köln: Wissenscaftsrat Available HTTP: www.hopo-www.de/konzepte/wr-wettbewerb.html (accessed 18 January 2005).
Wittgenstein, Ludwig (1953) *Philosophical Investigations* (trans G. E. M. Anscombe), New York: The Macmillan Company.
Wolf, Charles (1998) 'Blame Government for the Asian Meltdown', in *Asian Wall Street Journal*, 5 February.
Wolfe, Alan (1980) 'Capitalism Shows Its Face: Giving Up on Democracy', in Holly Sklar (ed.) *The Trilateral Commission and Elite Planning for World Management*, Boston: South End Press: 295–307.
Woo, Jung-En (1991) *Race to the Swift: State and Finance in Korean Industrialization*, New York: Columbia University Press.
Woo-Cumings, Meredith (1997) 'The Political Economy of Growth in East Asia: A Perspective on the State, Market, and Ideology', in Masahiko Aoki, Hyung-Ki Kim and

Masahiro Okuno-Fujiwara (eds) *The Role of Government in East Asian Economic Development: Comparative Institutional Analysis*, New York: Oxford University Press.
—— (1998) 'National Security and the Rise of the Developmental State in South Korea and Taiwan', in Henry S. Rowen (ed.) *Behind East Asian Growth: The Political and Social Foundations of Prosperity*, London: Routledge.
Woodall, Pam (1998) 'Frozen Miracle: A Survey of East Asian Economies', *The Economist*, 7 March.
Woodcock, George (1956) 'Utopias in Negative', *Sewanee Review*, 64(1), Sewanee, TN: University of the South: 81–97.
Wooster, Martin Morse (1998) 'Libertarians in Space', Review of Brad Linaweaver and Edward E. Kramer (eds) *Free Space*, New York: Tor. Available HTTP: www.libertysoft.com/liberty/reviews/64wooster.html (accessed 27 October 2000).
World Bank (1987) *World Development Report*, New York: Oxford University Press.
—— (1990) *World Development Report 1990: Poverty*, Washington, DC: World Bank.
—— (1991) *World Development Report 1991*, New York: Oxford University Press.
—— (1993) *The East Asian Miracle*, Oxford: Oxford University Press.
—— (1995a) *Bureaucrats in Business*, Washington, DC: World Bank.
—— (1995b) *Labor and Economic Reforms in Latin America and the Caribbean*, Washington, DC: World Bank.
—— (1995c) *World Development Report*, Washington, DC: World Bank.
—— (1995d) *Priorities and Strategies for Education: A World Bank Review*, Washington, DC: World Bank.
—— (1997) *World Development Report 1997: The State in a Changing World*, Oxford University Press.
World Business Council for Sustainable Development (1997) *Annual Review*, Conches-Geneva: World Economic Forum.
World Economic Forum (WEF) (1995/96) *Annual Report*, Conches-Geneva: World Economic Forum.
Young, Brigitte (2001) 'Geschlechterdemokratie für Wertschöpfungsstarke', *Forum Wissenschaft*, 18(2): 38–41.
Young, Robert J. C. (2001) *Postcolonialism: An Historical Introduction*, Oxford: Blackwell.
Zamjatin, Evgenij (1970 [1924]) *We*, London: Cape.
Zedillo, Ernesto (1994) 'La propuesta económica de Ernesto Zedillo. Palabras de Ernesto Zedillo Ponce de León, candidato del Partido Revolucionario Institucional a la Presidencia de la República', in the forum 'Crecimiento económico para el bienestar familiar', in Mexico City, 6 June.
Ziegler, Astrid (2001) 'Europäische Beschäftigungsstrategie und Gender Mainstreaming. Neue Impulse für die Frauenförderung in Sicht?', in *WSI-Mitteilungen*, 54(5): 337–43.
Zmirak, John (2001) *Wilhelm Röpke. Swiss Localist, Global Economist*, Wilmington: ISI Books.
Zubek, Voytek (1994) 'The Reassertion of the Left in Post-Communist Poland', *Europe-Asia Studies*, 46(5): 801–37.

Index

1984 164
3E Network 44

ABB 61, 62, 63
Adam Smith Institute 41, 235
Adam Smith Research Center (CAS) 102
Adorno, Theodor 165
advocacy networks 11, 12, 241
advocacy think tanks 33, 40–4, 48–50
AEI *see* American Enterprise Institute
affirmative action 191–3, 195–7, 199, 201–2
Afghanistan 118, 223
Agenda 2010 1
Aidt, Toke 75, 78, 80
Allaire, Paul 61
America *see* United States
American Enterprise Institute (AEI) 71, 72, 73, 83
Amsden, Alice 111
Anderson, Perry 222
Anderson, Poul 157, 160
'Anthem' 166
anti-globalization movement 22, 41, 238, 240, 247
anti-neoliberalism: ambiguities of global social movements 245–9; aspects of global social movements 238–43; Attac network 243–5; overview 236–8, 249–50
Armacost, Michael H. 57
Aron, Raymond 23, 30
Asian financial crisis 105–8, 110, 114, 115, 243
Astounding 164
Atlas Foundation 29, 44
Atlas Shrugged 157, 160
Attac network 236, 238, 239, 243–5, 248
authoritarianism 106, 110–12, 114, 118, 122–3
Ayer, Alfred 148

Baker, J. R. 152
Balassa, Bela 109, 126
Balcerowicz Plan 89, 90, 98–101, 104
Balcerowicz, Leszek 96, 98, 99, 101
Balibar, Etienne 232, 233
Balkan Network 44
Bandung era 107–8
Barber, Benjamin 214
Barnevik, Percy 61
Bartók, Béla 143
Bates, Robert H. 119
Bauer, Peter T. 19, 20, 108, 119, 146, 147
Becker, Gary 71
Bell, Daniel 142, 149
Bello, Walden 238
Berlusconi, Silvio 39
Bertelsmann Foundation: competitive corporatism 184–5; financing education 181–4; new market of education 180–1; overview 21, 171, 177–8, 186; transnational discourse communities 178–80
Bester, Alfred 166
Bielecki, Jan Krzysztof 95, 96
Bilderberg Conferences: capitalist class formation 9, 53, 56, 57, 59; global corporate-policy network 28, 61, 62, 68; Mont Pèlerin Society 37
Black, Conrad M. 61
Blackburn, Robin 228
Blair, Tony 41, 54, 217
Boardman, Robert B. 164
Bobrowski, Czesław 92
Böhm-Bawerk, Eugen von 146
Bolkestein, Frits 39
Boskin, Michael 72, 83
Bourdieu, Pierre 171–7, 186
Bradbury, Ray 162
Bradley Foundation 73
Brambilla, Marco 165, 167
Brave New World 164, 166

Brecht, Bertolt 234
Bretton Woods 113, 116, 209
Brus, Włodzimierz 92
Bryan, John H. 61
Brzeski, Wladyslaw 100
Buchanan, James 71, 212
Bugaj, Ryszard 98
bureaucracy 168–9, 213
bureaucratic-authoritarian industrializing regime (BAIR) 111
Bush, George W.: cultural nationalism 223, 234; Meltzer Commission 18, 81, 83, 85; Millennium Challenge Account 18, 81, 85; protectionism 27, 117; think tank networks 40, 45, 72
Business Consultative Group 58–9

Calomoris, Charles 83
Campbell, Tom 84
Campos, Jose Edgardo 110
capital controls 74, 76–8, 80, 82, 211
capitalism: anti-neoliberalism 237, 242, 244, 247; class formation 51–3; communitarianism 207–10, 219; cultural nationalism 227, 228; hegemony 4, 5; Mexico 122–3; neoliberal knowledge 30
Carl-Bertelsmann-Preis 180–1, 187
casino capitalism 246
Cassen, Bernhard 243
The Cat Who Walks Through Walls 169
Cato Institute 71, 72, 73, 84
CCF *see* Congress for Cultural Freedom
Center for Budget and Policy Priorities 73
Center for Policy Alternatives 40, 73
Center for Political Thought (OMP) 102
Center for Social and Economic Research (CASE) 96, 102
Centre for a New Europe (CNE) 47
Centre for Regional Strategies (CRS) 59
Centre for the Development of Higher Education (CHE) 182, 183, 184
Centre International d'études pour la Rénovation du Libéralisme 31, 40
Center of Policy Studies 235
Cheney, Lynne 83
Chiapas 27, 223
Chicago School 2, 121
Chile 20, 97, 107
China 97, 105–7, 112, 118
Christian Democrats 232
Christian Left 152, 153
Christian Right 223, 234
Christianity 145
Chun Doo Hwan 114

churches 11, 12, 240, 241
civil disobedience 240, 242
civil service 225
civil society: anti-neoliberalism 236, 246, 249; hegemony 4; private authority 11, 12, 14; state power relations 7; transnational civil society 15
Civitas 47
Clarens, Carlo 166
Clarida, Richard 72
class: cultural nationalism 228; education 173, 175, 176–7; neoliberal knowledge 28; transnational capitalist class analysis 8–10, 28, 51–3, 67
Clausen, Tom 109
Clinton, Bill 54, 80, 217, 229
Coase, Ronald 212
Cold War 105–7, 108, 111–15, 168
Cole, G. D. H. 147
collective bargaining 78, 80, 198
Collomb, Bertrand 60, 61
Colossus: The Forbin Project 164
Committee on Science and Freedom 152
communism: markets, freedom and knowledge 143, 150; Poland 19, 91–7, 101, 103; science fiction 164; South Korea 107, 109
communitarianism: context 207–8; education 178; gender mainstreaming 202; and neoliberalism 2, 21–2, 211–14, 218–21; societal configuration 208–10; third way politics 214–18
competition: communitarianism 210, 212; education 175, 176, 181, 183; Mexico 122; national sovereignty 78, 79; socialist calculation 148; South Korea 106, 116
Congress for Cultural Freedom (CCF) 3, 23, 152
consent 7, 8, 14, 90, 246
Conservatism 222, 227, 228
constructive rationalism 122
consumerism 9, 28, 52, 67, 248
corporate-policy network: elite policy groups 63–5; as inter-organizational field 62–3; overview 60–2, 65–8
counter-revolutionary groups 233, 234
'Coventry' 166
Cox, Robert 16
Cracow School of Liberalism 95
Crane, Edward 84
Crewe, Ivor 224
critical rationalism 122
critical theory 144, 237
Cuba 107
cultural capital 172

cultural evolution 122
cultural nationalism: and neoliberalism 22, 230–5; New Right 227–30; overview 222–6
culture 28, 67, 234, 235
Cumings, Bruce 111

Dąbrowski, Marek 96, 98
Dahrendorf, Ralf 210
Davignon, Etienne 61
'Day of Atonement' 169
debt: communitarianism 209; gender mainstreaming 198; Meltzer Commission 74, 75–6, 81; Mexico 124, 127, 128; South Korea 108
A Deepness in the Sky 160
'Delilah and the Space Rigger' 161
Democratic Party 223, 229
'Demokratus' 159
The Demolished Man 166–7
Demolition Man 165–6, 167
Demos 214, 223
deregulation: anti-neoliberalism 242, 250; capitalist class formation 54; communitarianism 211, 214; gender mainstreaming 198; South Korea 109; think tanks 40, 75
Desimone, Livio D. 61
developing nations 19, 78, 82, 124, 249
development policies 78–81, 109, 236
developmental state theory 111, 112, 118, 119
Dick, Philip K. 170
dictatorship 106, 111, 169
Dilthey, Wilhelm 143
discourse communities 2, 5, 15, 178–80
discrimination 160–1, 190–2, 194, 199–201, 244
Distress 170
Duczynska, Ilona 145
dystopias, in science fiction 157–8, 163–7, 169
Dziekania 95, 104
Dzielski, Mirosław 95

East Asia: Bandung era 107–8; challenging neoliberalism 111–12; East Asian Miracle 105, 106, 109, 119; export-oriented industrialization 125; overview 118–19; post-Cold War order 112–18; rise of neoliberalism 108–10
Eastern Europe 13, 89
Economic and Monetary Union (EMU) 191, 198, 210, 220

Economic Freedom Network 44
Economic Policy Institute 73
economics 27, 30, 150–2, 175
education: Bertelsmann Foundation 21, 177–85; capital controls 77; class struggles 176–7; competitive corporatism 184–5; financing 181–4; gender mainstreaming 197; intellectuals and power 171–7; national sovereignty 80; New Bourgeoisie 175–6; new market 180–1; overview 171–2, 185–6; reform and revolt 173–5; transnational discourse communities 178–80
Egan, Greg 170
Einaudi, Luigi 39
Ejército Zapatista de Liberación Nacional (EZLN) 120
elites 159, 172, 175, 178, 215, 249
embedded liberalism 9, 209
Emerson, Ralph Waldo 165
empire 237, 239
employment 134–6, 137, 193, 197, 198
EMU *see* Economic and Monetary Union
An Enemy of the State 161, 163
Engels, Friedrich 143, 147
Enron 27
entrepreneurs 101, 154, 159–60
environment: anti-neoliberalism 236, 240, 245; global corporate-policy network 59, 68; think tanks 78, 82, 83; transnational capitalist class analysis 9
EOI *see* export-oriented industrialization
epistemic communities 3, 179, 208, 214, 219
equal opportunities 189, 190–3, 195, 197–9, 202, 216
Erhard, Ludwig 39
Escape from New York 164
ethnic diversity 118, 160, 189, 194
Etzioni, Amitai 214
Europe: anti-neoliberalism 28, 244; gender mainstreaming 189–97; integration 1, 191, 217; monetary union 191, 198, 210, 220; private authority 12; state power relations 7; third way politics 217; transnational capitalist class analysis 10
exchange rates: communitarianism 211; Meltzer Commission 75, 77; Mexico 126, 129, 131; South Korea 116
expert knowledge 171, 173, 179
export-oriented industrialization (EOI) 121, 124–7, 132, 137

Fabian Society 46, 214
Fabianism 143

Farmer in the Sky 162
fascism 32, 123, 233, 234
Feldstein, Martin 72
feminism 21, 202, 240
Feulner, Edwin 5, 46, 71, 84
films 161, 164, 165, 167, 168–9
Fischer, Joschka 239
Fisher, Anthony 40
Fisher, George M. 61
Fordism 5, 7, 9, 42, 208, 209, 219, 237, 246, 248
foreign direct investment (FDI) 9, 78, 130, 131
Foundation for Economic Education 31
The Fountainhead 160
Fox, Vicent 126, 127
France 76, 210, 239, 244, 245
Frankfurt Institute 41, 144
Franklin, Bruce 164
Fraser Institute 36, 41
free market 101, 103, 201, 211
free-market conservatism 54, 56, 59, 66
Free to Choose 163
free trade 12, 125, 129, 130, 160
Free Trade Area of the Americas (FTAA) 1
freedom: markets and knowledge 141, 142, 149; Mexico 122, 123; science fiction 158, 159, 160
freemasonry 23
Freedom of the World Report 41, 44
Friedman, David 157
Friedman, Milton: capitalist class formation 54; Mexico 121, 122, 123; Mont Pèlerin Society 36; neoliberal knowledge 31; science fiction 21, 157, 160, 163; think tanks 71
frontiers, in science fiction 20, 158–9, 161–5, 169
FTAA *see* Free Trade Area of the Americas

G7 summits 54, 239, 241, 243–4, 249
Gallatin, Albert 162
Gallilei Circle 143, 145
Garton Ash, Timothy 57
GATT (General Agreement on Tariffs and Trade) 7
Gdánsk Institute for Market Economics 96
gender equality 195, 197, 200–2, 240
gender mainstreaming: adopting for Europe 190–4; equal opportunities and affirmative action 191–4; implementation 197–200; lack of redistribution 200–1; origin and context 189–90; overview 21, 188–9, 201–2; pitfalls 194–7
Genoa protests 236, 237, 239, 241, 243

'Gentlemen, Be Seated' 159
George, Susan 239, 244, 245
Germany: anti-neoliberalism 239, 243; communitarianism 217, 232; education 21; fascism 32; gender mainstreaming 199; *see also* Bertelsmann Foundation
Giddens, Anthony 54, 214
Giersch, Herbert 47
Gill, Stephen 54, 238
Gingrich, Newt 83
Global Climate Coalition 10
global corporate-policy network: elite policy groups 63–5; as inter-organizational field 62–3; overview 60–2, 65–8
global governance 58, 243, 248
Global Leaders of Tomorrow 59
global social movements 245–9
globalization: anti-globalization movement 22, 41, 238, 240, 247; anti-neoliberalism 236–8, 249–50; communitarianism 210, 215, 217; global corporate-policy network 68; global social movements 27, 54, 239–44, 247, 248; private authority 12; South Korea 105, 106, 112, 114–19
government, in science fiction 156–9, 164, 166–9
Gramsci, Antonio 90–91, 238–239, 246; class formation 23, 67, 177; communitarianism 207; cultural nationalism 231; hegemony 3, 4; intellectuals 24; state power relations 7
Gray, John 47, 214
The Great Explosion 162
The Great Transformation 148
Greenspan, Alan 160
grey wealth 228, 229

Haas, Peter 3
Hall, Stuart 222, 223, 224
Hamilton, Alexander 162
Hans-Böckler Foundation 183, 184
Hardt, Michael 239
Harriman, Edward Henry 159
Harris, Jerry 51, 52, 54, 58
Hawthorne, Nathaniel 165
Hayek, Friedrich August von 121–3, 211–2, 223; Mont Pèlerin Society 20, 23, 28, 154; neoliberal knowledge 30–3, 141–2, 144, 146–51; think tank networks 40
health care 77, 80, 244
Hegel, Georg 143, 218
hegemonic constellations 3, 5, 6, 15
hegemony 3, 90, 223, 239, 246, 249–50
Heidelberg school 143, 145

Heinlein, Robert 157–60, 162, 163, 166, 169
Heinrich-Böll Foundation 183
Heritage Foundation 5, 41–2, 46, 71, 73, 84
higher education 21, 174
highly indebted poor countries (HIPCs) 74, 75, 81
high-performing Asian economies (HPAEs) 110
hillbilly culture 162
Hirsch, Joachim 250
Hobsbawm, Eric 233
Hogan, James P. 158, 168
Holman, Otto 8
Hood, Robin 161, 162
Hoover Institution on War, Revolution and Peace 71, 72, 73
Hoskins, John 225
Hoskins, W. Lee 84
'hot money' 76
Hubbard, R. Glen 72, 83
Huben, Mike 156
Huber, Peter W. 166
human rights 11, 12, 201, 236
Hungary 92, 93, 142
Hunold, Albert 31, 34
Huxley, Aldous 164, 166

ICC *see* International Chamber of Commerce
ideas 1–5, 16, 18, 20–3, 29, 31–2, 46, 70, 72, 83–5, 91–2, 95, 97, 100, 108–9, 141, 148, 154–5, 157, 165, 189, 194, 198, 207–8, 211, 214–5, 217–9, 220–1, 224; battle of 90; materiality of 5; role of 23; second-hand dealers in ideas (Hayek) 28, 40, 220
ideology 142, 144, 149, 226
Ideology and Utopia 144, 145, 153
IEA *see* Institute of Economic Affairs
'If Pigs Had Wings' 169
'If This Goes On' 166
IFIs *see* international financial institutions
ILO (International Labor Organization) 82, 86
IMF *see* International Monetary Fund
imperialism 6, 237
import-substituting industrialization (ISI) 124–5, 127–9
India 107, 118, 222, 225, 232
individualism 54, 156, 160, 166–8, 213
Indonesia 77, 107, 114, 118
inflation 209; Mexico 128, 129, 130; Poland 99; science fiction 164

Institute for Market Economics (IbnGR) 102
Institute for Policy Studies 73
Institute for Public Policy Research 214
Institute of Directors 235
Institute of Economic Affairs (IEA) 40, 41, 47, 223, 235
intellectuals: communitarianism 219, 220; cultural nationalism 224, 225; education 171–7; global neoliberal projects 17, 19; hegemony 4, 5; neoliberal knowledge 20–2, 31–3, 144–5; organic intellectuals (Gramsci) 4–5; Poland 19, 94; think tanks 28, 29
InterAcademy Council 58
International Chamber of Commerce (ICC): global corporate-policy network 60–2, 66, 67; international policy groups 55–7, 59; Mont Pèlerin Society 37
international financial institutions (IFIs) 70, 73, 80, 82, 85, 86
International Forum on Globalization 241
International Labor Organization (ILO) 82, 86
International Monetary Fund (IMF) 222, 238, 245, 248, 249; capitalist class formation 51, 54; global corporate-policy network 68; Meltzer Commission 73–4, 76–9, 83–4; Mont Pèlerin Society 36; overview 18, 70–1, 85; Poland 99; policy influence 72; reform agenda 81, 82; South Korea 105, 108, 109, 114, 115
investment 9, 77–8, 130–1, 240
Iraq 7, 223
Ishikawa, Rokuro 61
ISI *see* import-substituting industrialization

Jameson, Frederic 164
Japan 65, 66, 78, 105–7, 109, 111–13, 118, 222
Jaruzelski, Wojciech 93
Jászi, Oszkár 145
Jefferson, Thomas 165
Johnson, Chalmers 111

Kalecki, Michał 92, 234
Kant, Immanuel 143, 218
Keough, Donald R. 61
Keynes, John Maynard 33, 209
Keynesianism 121, 124, 177, 237, 244–5, 250
Kim Dae Jung 114, 115
Kim Young Sam 114
Kirkpatrick, Jeane 83, 123
Kisielewski, Stefan 95

Kissinger, Henry 61
Kitschelt, Herbert 226, 230, 234
Klaus, Vaclav 39, 99, 104
Klemm, Klaus 183
knowledge: communitarianism 212; and economics 150–2; education 171, 172, 185; Mont Pèlerin Society 20, 154; overview 141–2; private authority 13; and science 148–50, 152–4; socialist calculation debate 146–8; state, society and economy 142–6; transnational civil society 15, 16, 17
knowledge society 141, 185
Kohl, Helmut 108
Koman, Victor 159
Korea 76, 77, 112; *see also* South Korea
Korwin-Mikke, Janusz 95, 97
Kraushaar, Wolfgang 239
Kuhn, Thomas 153
Kurón, Jacek 97
Kyoto protocol 8, 10

labour market: communitarianism 214, 216; cultural nationalism 232; gender mainstreaming 189, 192–3, 196–7, 199–200; Mexico 135; South Korea 114; think tanks 75, 78, 82
Labour Party 214, 216, 223, 224
Łagowski, Bronisław 95
Lal, Deepak 109
Lange, Oskar 92, 148
Laski, Harold 33
'The Last Holosong of Christopher Lightning' 160
left-wing politics 231, 234, 240, 242, 247
Leninism 121, 147
Levin, Ira 165, 166
Levinson, Jerome 75, 86
Lewandowski, Janusz 95
Lewis, William W. 57
liberalism 30, 150
liberalization 83, 109, 114, 126–30, 137
libertarian ideology in science fiction: adventure capitalism and merchant heroes 160–3; bureaucracy to state conspiracy 168–9; entrepreneurs 159–60; the frontier 158–9, 165; government prohibitions 169; individual in peril 166–8; overview 156–7, 169–70; role of science fiction 157–8; utopias and dystopias 163–6
Linaweaver, Brad 158
Lindsay, Lawrence 72, 83
Lipiński, Edward 92

Lippman, Walter 30, 31
Lipton, David 100
Lobdell, Jared 160
Locke, John 218
Logan's Run 165
Logical Positivism 146, 148, 149
London School of Economics (LSE) 31, 149–50
Lucas, George 167
Luhnow, Harold 31
Lukàcs, George 20, 143–6
Lundberg, Eric 39
Lüthje, Jürgen 183

Maastricht Treaty 191, 198
Machaivelli, Niccolo 238
Machlup, Fritz 147, 149
MAI *see* Multilateral Agreement on Investment
Malaysia 77, 109, 118
The Man Who Sold The Moon 159
managing diversity 189, 190, 200
Mannheim, Karl 20, 142–6, 149–50, 153
manufacturing 124–6, 129, 131–3, 135–6
market: anti-neoliberalism 244, 247; communitarianism 210, 212, 218; definition of neoliberalism 2; and knowledge 29, 141–2, 144, 154; Mexico 123; Mont Pèlerin Society 34; science fiction 160, 161; think tank networks 45; transnational civil society 15
market socialism 89–93, 97, 99, 100, 148
Marshall Plan 112
martial law 91, 93–4, 97
The Martian Chronicles 162
Martino, Antonio 39
Marx, Karl 23
Marxism 121, 123, 141, 143, 146, 149
materialism 143
Maucher, Helmut O. 61
Mayer, Arno 227, 230, 233, 234
Mazowiecki, Tadeusz 98
McGuire, John J. 163
McNamara, Robert 109
media: anti-neoliberalism 239, 240, 244; cultural nationalism 224, 231; Mont Pèlerin Society 40; neoliberal knowledge 32; think tanks 72
Meltzer Commission: capital controls 76–8; debt forgiveness 75–6; development policies 78; framework 74–5; national sovereignty 78–80; overview 18, 70, 73–4, 85; political infrastructure 82–4; scope 80–1

Meltzer, Allan 70, 74, 79, 83, 85
Melville, Herman 165
Mexico: cultural nationalism 222; debt crisis 108; employment 134–6; export-oriented industrialization 124–7; liberalization strategy 127–30; macroeconomic performance 130–1; manufacturing performance 131–3; Meltzer Commission 76, 84; neoliberalism in 121–3; overview 20, 120, 137; policy groups 54; private authority 11; US protectionism 45
military power 6–8, 106, 111, 161
Millennium Challenge Account (MCA) 18, 81, 85
Mises, Ludwig von 20, 30–1, 92, 146–8, 151, 164
Mohamed, Mahathir 109
Mohn, Reinhard 178, 182
monetarism 36, 54, 177
Monks, John 57
Mont Pèlerin Society (MPS) 223; global neoliberal projects 17, 18; history and membership 33–40; markets, freedom and knowledge 142, 148, 152, 154; Mexico 127; neoliberal knowledge 20, 28–9, 31, 33; think tank networks 41, 45, 71, 72, 83, 235
The Moon is a Harsh Mistress 157, 162, 163, 169
The Moot 145, 153
Morita, Kosuka 61
movies 161, 164, 165, 167, 168–9
MPS *see* Mont Pèlerin Society
Müller-Böling, Detlef 182
Multilateral Agreement on Investment (MAI) 54, 240, 249
multinational corporations 11, 80
The Multiplex Man 158, 168
Municipal Socialism 146
Murofushi, Minoru 60, 61
Myhre, Øyvind 161

NAFTA *see* North American Free Trade Agreement
National Bureau of Economic Research (NBER) 72
national sovereignty 75, 78–80, 116
nationalism 230, 231
nation-state 107, 112, 116–17, 231, 248–9
Nazism 233
NBER *see* National Bureau of Economic Research
Negri, Antonio 239
neo-classical economics 108, 109

neoliberal regulationists 55, 56, 59, 60, 66
neoliberal structuralists 54, 56, 60, 66
neoliberalism, definition 2
Nestlé corporation 11
Network European Learning Processes (NELP) 184
Neurath, Otto 146, 147
New Bourgeoisie 175–6
New Deal 168
New Democrats 41, 216
New Labour 214, 216
New Opportunities for Women (NOW) 192
New Public Management (NPM) 179, 180
New Right: historical perspective 227–30; neoliberalism and cultural nationalism 231, 233, 234; overview 22, 222–6
new state nobility 172, 177–85, 186
'New Utopia' 157
newly industrializing countries (NICs) 105, 106, 108, 113
Nexus 214
NGOs *see* non-governmental organizations
NICs *see* newly industrializing countries
Nivens, Larry 167
Nixon, Richard 116
No Blade of Grass 164
'No Market for Justice' 158
Nobel Prizes 27, 39
non-governmental organizations (NGOs): anti-neoliberalism 22, 236, 241, 244; global corporate-policy network 68; IFIs 82; private authority 11
North American Free Trade Agreement (NAFTA): Mexican employment 136; Mexican liberalization strategy 127–30; Mexican manufacturing performance 131–3; overview 20, 120, 137; private authority 11, 12; transnational capitalist class analysis 10
North Korea 106, 115
Nozick, Robert 212
nuclear safety 8, 164
Nullmeier, Frank 185
The Number of the Beast 163
Nye, Joseph 7

O'Neill, Paul 72
Oath of Fealty 167
objectivity 149, 152, 153
OECD *see* Organisation for Economic Co-operation and Development
Oldham, J. H. 153
Olin Foundation 73

Organisation for Economic Co-operation and Development (OECD) 116, 179
Orwell, George 164
Orwell's Revenge 166
Overbeek, Henk 8, 51
Owen, Robert 147

Paint Your Wagon 161
Park Chung Hee 114
passive revolution 91, 101, 210
'The Peddler's Apprentice' 160
People for the American Way 72–3
Philadelphia Society 36
philosophy 142, 153
Pinochet, Augusto 20, 123, 127
Piper, H. Beam 163
A Planet for Texans 163
Plehwe, Dieter 126, 177
Poe, Edgar Allen 165
Poland: Balcerowicz Plan 98–101; informal neoliberal networks 95–6; market socialism 91–3; neoliberal ideology 96–8; new anti-politicians 94–5; overview 19, 89–91, 101–3; reforms and martial law 93–4
Polanyi, Karl 143, 145–6, 147, 148, 244
Polanyi, Michael: Congress for Cultural Freedom 23; on knowledge 30, 141–3, 145–6, 149–50, 152–4; Mont Pèlerin Society 20, 154
Popper, Karl 20, 121, 142, 146, 149, 153–4
positive discrimination 191, 192; *see also* affirmative action
positivism 20, 142, 149, 150, 153
post-Fordism 208, 237, 238, 243
Pournelles, Jerry 167
poverty 82, 109, 110, 162
power: anti-neoliberalism 248, 249; gender mainstreaming 200, 201; intellectuals 171–7
Prescott, J. B. 61
private authority 10–14, 15, 16
privatization: anti-neoliberalism 242, 244, 250; cultural nationalism 229; education 184; gender mainstreaming 198; Mexico 129; Poland 94, 96; South Korea 114; think tank networks 40, 80, 83
The Probability Broach 161, 162
problem of the division of knowledge (Hayek) 141, 151, 154
Progressive Policy Institute 41
property 227, 228, 230, 231, 232
prostitution 193, 202
protectionism 27, 45, 117, 125

protest movements: anti-neoliberalism 236–41, 243, 247, 249; education 173–5, 177
public sector employment 198, 199
public-private partnership (PPP) 179, 180

racial discrimination 160, 194, 228
The Rainbow Cadenza 167
Rambo: First Blood Part II 169
Ramonet, Ignacio 243
Rand, Ayn 20, 157, 159, 160, 166
rational choice theory 110, 212
Rawls, John 213
Reagan, Ronald 7, 40, 53, 83, 108, 234
recession 108, 209, 220, 245
Red Planet 161
reform: education 173–5, 177, 179, 182, 185; Poland 89–90, 92–4, 98–9, 101, 103; think tanks 70–1, 81–2
Reich, Robert 214
relevant knowledge 150, 151
religion 9, 118
rent-seeking behaviour 125, 212
right-wing politics 223, 231, 233, 234, 243; *see also* New Right
Ritch, William Alan 169
Robinson, William 51, 52, 54, 58
Rockefeller Foundation 152
Rockefeller, David 57
Root, Hilton L. 110
Röpke, Wilhelm 30, 34
Rose, Nikolas 154
Rotary Club 23
Rougier, Louis 30
Rucht, Dieter 241
Ruggie, John 7, 9
ruling class 171–5, 177, 231, 234
Russell, Bertrand 144
Russell, Eric Frank 162
Russia 77, 141; *see also* Soviet Union

Sachs, Jeffrey 100, 104
Salinas de Gortari, Carlos 126, 128
Sandel, Michael 212
Savior of Fire 164
Scaife Foundation 73
Schelsky, Helmut 175
schools 175–6, 180, 182, 184
Schröder, Gerhard 41, 196
Schulman, J. Neil 167, 168, 169
Schumpeter, Joseph 146, 151
Schwab, Klaus 58
science 121–2, 142, 144–5, 150, 152–4
science fiction: adventure capitalism and merchant heroes 160–3; bureaucracy to

state conspiracy 168–9; entrepreneurs 159–60; the frontier 158–9, 165; government prohibitions 169; individual in peril 166–8; overview 20, 156–7, 169–70; role of 157–8; utopias and dystopias 163–6
scientific Marxism 146, 149, 153
scientism 149, 150, 153
Seattle protests 68, 236, 239, 240
Second Internationale 143, 144
Seltzer, Mark 158
Sen, Amartya 27
September 11 attacks 27, 105, 117–18, 237, 243, 245
sexual norms 161, 167–8
Simon, Nikolaus 184
Singapore 113, 118
single market 191, 210, 220
Sklair, Leslie 8–9, 28, 51–2, 67, 248
Smith Foundation 73
Smith, Adam 121
Smith, Jackie 240, 241
Smith, L. Neil 161, 162
Snow Crash 166
social Darwinism 122, 172
social democracy 216–18, 220, 222, 227, 229
social movements: ambiguities of 245–9; anti-neoliberalism 27, 237, 249, 250; aspects of 238–43; Attac network 243–5; communitarianism 217; private authority 11, 12
social sciences 121, 122, 142
social security 209, 217
socialism: communitarianism 219; gender mainstreaming 200; Mont Pèlerin Society 37; neoliberal knowledge 31, 33, 151; Poland 19, 89–93, 95, 100, 101
socialist calculation debate 92, 142, 146–8
Society for Freedom in Science 152
sociology of knowledge 20, 141, 144, 145, 149, 151
Solidarity 19, 91, 93–4, 96–9, 103
Sorel, George 142, 143
South Korea: Bandung era 107–8; challenging neoliberalism 111–12; overview 19, 105–7, 118–19; post-Cold War order 112–18; rise of neoliberalism 108–10
sovereignty 75, 78–80, 116
Soviet Union 7, 107, 112, 145
Soylent Green 164, 165
spontaneous order 144, 151
The Sprites (Szellemkek) 143, 144
Stalinism 121

state: anti-neoliberalism 244, 246, 247, 248; communitarianism 213, 217, 218; Mexico 123, 125; Mont Pèlerin Society 33; neoliberal knowledge 2, 30, 150, 154; power relations 6–8; science fiction 159, 162, 168–9; South Korea 109, 110, 111, 117, 118; think tank networks 45; transnational civil society 14, 15
Stephenson, Neal 166
Stern, Cornelia 183
Stiglitz, Joseph E. 27, 55, 78, 80
Stockholm Network 44, 47
Stockholm Progressive Summit 41
Stone, Diane 13
Strange, Susan 16, 46
Stranger in a Strange Land 161
student movement 173, 209
subsidies 117, 129, 183
Summers, Lawrence 80, 81
superpowers 6, 8, 16
sustainable development 9–10, 59, 77–8, 236
Sutherland, Peter 61
Sweden 39, 100
Syndicalism 142, 143
Szabó, Ervin 142, 143
Szomburg, Jan 95

tacit knowledge (Polanyi) 141, 152, 153
Taiwan 105, 106, 113
tariffs 7, 117, 125, 129–30, 133
Tashlin, Frank 167
taxes 156, 157, 159, 161–3, 215
Taylor, Charles 212
Taylor, Frederick 92
TC *see* Trilateral Commission
technocracy 171, 172
terrorism 8, 230, 243
Thailand 77, 114, 118
Thatcher, Margaret 1, 53, 108, 225
Thatcherism 7, 222–4
Them 168
think tanks: communitarianism 207, 219; cultural nationalism 223–6; education 21, 171, 172, 178; global neoliberal projects 17–19; hegemony 4; Mont Pèlerin Society 28–9, 33, 36, 40, 48–50; networks 40–4; Poland 19, 102, 103; private authority 11, 12, 13; World Bank and IMF 70–3, 83–5
third way: communitarianism 22, 214–18; cultural nationalism 222, 229; education 177; gender mainstreaming 202; Poland 89, 99–101, 103; policy groups 54

Third World Network 241
This Perfect Day 165, 166
Thoreau, Henry David 165
Three Stigmata of Palmer Eldrich 170
THX 1138 167
TINA (There Is No Alternative) 1, 222, 247
Tobin Tax 27, 242, 243
totalitarianism 31–2, 71, 141–2, 149, 168–9
trade unions: anti-neoliberalism 240, 241; communitarianism 209, 211, 212, 214, 220; education 177, 184; gender mainstreaming 198, 199; Meltzer Commission 78, 80, 82; Mexico 129; Mont Pèlerin Society 154; Poland 19, 93, 101; private authority 11, 12; South Korea 114
transnational advocacy networks 11, 12, 241
transnational capitalist class (TCC) analysis 8–10, 28, 51–3, 67
transnational civil society 14–17
transnational discourse communities 3, 15, 178–80
transnational high-tech capitalism 210, 211, 219
Treaty of Amsterdam (TEC) 193
Treaty of Rome 192
Trilateral Commission (TC): global corporate-policy network 60–2, 66, 68; international policy groups 3, 9, 28, 53, 56–9; Mont Pèlerin Society 37
TRIPS (Trade-Related Intellectual Property Rights) 249
Tusk, Donald 95, 100
Tzannatos, Zafiris 75, 78, 80

UNCED (UN Conference on Environment and Development) 59
UNCTAD (UN Conference on Trade and Development) 55, 59
unemployment: capital controls 75, 76; communitarianism 209, 215, 220; education 172; gender mainstreaming 199; Mexico 126, 134–6; science fiction 162
UNEP (UN Environmental Programme) 59
The Ungoverned 157, 162–3
unions *see* trade unions
United Nations 41, 55, 59, 179, 191
United States: cultural nationalism 223; intellectuals 24; Kyoto protocol 10; science fiction 156, 158, 162–3, 165, 168–9; and South Korea 105–7, 112–13, 115–19; state power relations 6–8; think tank networks 40, 44; US hegemony 115–17

universities 36, 73, 175, 180–2, 184–5, 225
utopias in science fiction 157–8, 160, 162–6, 169

van der Pijl, Kees 8–9, 23, 28–9, 51, 66
Veblen, Thorstein 142, 148
vigilante justice 163, 166
Vinge, Joan 160
Vinge, Vernor 157, 160, 162
Volker Fund 31, 152
Volkholz, Sybille 183

wages 135–8, 193, 198–9
Wall Street Journal 72
Walpen, Bernhard 126, 177
Walras, Léon 92
Walters, Alan 36, 225
war on terrorism 8, 230, 243
Warsaw School of Planning and Statistics 96
Washington Consensus 45, 53–5, 124, 248
Washington, George 162
WBCSD *see* World Business Council for Sustainable Development
We 164
WEF *see* World Economic Forum
Weingart, Peter 46
welfare state: communitarianism 209, 212, 215, 217, 220; cultural nationalism 228, 230; education 177, 178; gender mainstreaming 198, 201, 202; global social movements 247; Mexico 122, 123, 124; neoliberal philosophy 2; science fiction 166, 168; think tank networks 42
Wheels Within Wheels 160
Will Success Spoil Rock Hunter 167
Williamson, John 53, 126
Wilson, Francis Paul 160, 161, 163
Wilson, Roert N. 61
WISSENTransfer 41
Wittgenstein, Ludwig 145, 149, 153
Wollstonecraft, Mary 192
women's rights 188, 194–7, 199, 201–2, 236
Wooster, Martin Morse 157
World Bank: anti-neoliberalism 54, 68, 238, 245, 248, 249; gender mainstreaming 189; Meltzer Commission 18, 74–5, 77–8, 80, 83–4; Mexico 126; Mont Pèlerin Society 36; overview 70–1, 85; policy influence 72; reform agenda 81; South Korea 108–11; think tank networks 45; transnational discourse communities 179

World Business Council for Sustainable Development (WBCSD) 10, 53, 56, 59–62, 66, 68
World Chambers Federation (WCF) 55
World Economic Forum (WEF): anti-neoliberalism 239, 249; global corporate-policy network 61, 62, 68; international policy groups 3, 51, 53, 56–60; Mont Pèlerin Society 37
World Link 57
World Social Forum 244
World Trade Organization (WTO): anti-neoliberalism 238, 248, 249; international policy groups 51, 54, 55, 68; scope 1; state power relations 7; US hegemony 117

World Without Stars 158
Wright-Mills, C. 24
WTO *see* World Trade Organization
Wunder, Dieter 183

X-Files 169

Young Men's Christian Association (YMCA) 23
Yugoslavia 92, 93

Z.P.G. 165
Zamjatin, Evgenij 164
Zedillo, Ernesto 126, 127, 128